Roger W. Haskell, M.D.

THE
RUSSIAN
SYNDROME

Also by
Hélène Carrère d'Encausse

*The Great Challenge: Nationalities and the Bolshevik
State, 1917–1930*

Big Brother: The Soviet Union and Soviet Europe

THE RUSSIAN SYNDROME

One Thousand Years of Political Murder

Hélène Carrère d'Encausse

Translated by Caroline Higgitt

**FOREWORD BY
ADAM B. ULAM**

HM

Holmes & Meier
New York / London

Published in the United States of America 1992 by
Holmes & Meier Publishers, Inc.
30 Irving Place
New York, NY 10003

Originally published in French under the title
Le malheur russe: Essai sur le meurtre politique,
copyright © 1988, Librairie Arthème Fayard, Paris.

Book design by Adrienne Weiss

This book has been printed on acid-free paper.

Library of Congress Cataloging-in-Publication Data

Carrère d'Encausse, Hélène.
    [Malheur russe.   English]
    The Russian syndrome : one thousand years of political murder
(political murder in Russian history) / Hélène Carrère d'Encausse :
translated by Caroline Higgitt.
    p. cm.
    Translation of: Le malheur russe.
    Includes bibliographical references and index.
    ISBN 0-8419-1293-9 (acid-free paper)
    1. Soviet Union—History. 2. Assassination—Soviet Union—
History.   3. Political crimes and offenses—Soviet Union—History.
I. Title.
DK43.C3613 1992
947—dc20

                              91-3752
                              CIP

Manufactured in the United States of America

To Nathalie and Marina

Contents

13

Thou Shalt Not Kill 361

The Survivors' Pact • The Murderer Murdered • Memory Regained • Killing without Death • The Second Thaw • The Quest for Truth • Glasnost • Reforms to Save the System

Conclusion 393

Foreword

Adam B. Ulam

The Bolshevik *coup d'état* in October and the Civil War that followed it transformed what had been the Russian Empire into the Union of Soviet Socialist Republics. As its name signified, the USSR was to be a supranational state, where, in contrast to policy under the Empire, there was to be absolute equality of all of its numerous nationalities. As such, the Soviet state would be both the model and vanguard of a future worldwide federation of socialist countries.

Yet, even at the beginning of the Communist experiment and in its most messianic phase, there were signs that Russian nationalism, though officially repudiated, still exerted powerful influence on the minds of the new rulers. It was Lenin who had already observed that if you scratched the ideological varnish off some Communists, you would find beneath it Russian chauvinism. In its centralization of power and suppression of all dissent, the Communist state soon and far surpassed its Imperial predecessor. And with Stalin, "Soviet patriotism" became but a thin veneer for Russian nationalism, which in all but name was installed as the official ideology of the tyrant's regime. Imperial Russia's conquests of other nations, once condemned by the Bolsheviks, were now hailed as progressive acts. While overt russification was not forced upon the numerous other nationalities, as was the practice under the tsars, the Soviet regime attempted to impose upon them a kind of politico-cultural homogenization that was to induce in the Ukrainians, Uzbeks, Georgians and others the conviction that their fate was indissolubly linked with that of the "great Russian nation."

Expressive of this policy was the adoption in 1943 of a new national anthem of the USSR. The *Internationale,* with its evocation of supranational class and revolutionary solidarity, was replaced by a new anthem that began, "An unbreakable union of free republics was forged forever by Great *Rus'* [the historical Russian state]. Long live the great and mighty Soviet Union created by the will of the peoples." The same theme was taken up by Stalin in his victory speech of May 1945 when he hailed the "great Russian nation" as the leading nation of the Soviet Union, and the major contributor to the victory over fascism.

Now, this self-identification of the Soviet state with Russian nationalism has naturally stirred up a debate as to whether there was something specifically Russian about Communism. Or, to put it differently, was the October Revolution a decisive break in the country's history, or did Communism, after a brief internationalist interlude, revert to and intensify those allegedly characteristic traits of Russian political life: absolute domination of the state over the individual, rejection of political pluralism, intolerance of any ideology except the one officially endorsed by the absolutist state?

Typical of the views of those who reject such an identification of Communism with the Russian national tradition is the position taken by Alexander Solzhenitsyn. For this great writer, Communism is something quite different from and alien to Russia. Although admittedly the country has been for most of its history under authoritarian rule, its culture has been expressive of the people's longing for freedom. Prerevolutionary Russia was evolving away from authoritarianism, and developing parliamentary and independent judicial institutions; it was only the seizure of power by people who had repudiated their national heritage which derailed that development toward democracy and brought about those seventy years of political and spiritual slavery.

A superficial reading of Mme Carrère d'Encausse's book might lead some to believe that she belongs to those who think that there is a great deal of continuity between the spirit of prerevolutionary Russia and Communism. But her message is quite different: unique historical circumstances—not something inherent in the Russian national character—are responsible for the prevalence of the state's arbitrary power throughout one thousand years of the Russian statehood. The French title of this book, *Le Malheur russe,* could also have been translated as *"Russia's Misfortune,"* though stylistically *"The Russian Syndrome"* is more attractive. If postrevolutionary Soviet Russia's misfortune was to be seized by fanatical sectarians, who soon evolved into cynical bureaucrats, then what fatally changed the character of old Russia and delayed its development into a modern state was another historical catastrophe—the Mongol yoke. For two hundred years a society that until the thirteenth century had been developing not very differently from those in the West was subjugated by oriental despotism. National survival required that Muscovy, the predecessor of imperial Russia, would develop along the oriental model, rather than that of England or France.

It is violence that, according to the theme of this book, has been "Russia's misfortune." Each decisive turn in the country's history was precipitated or accompanied by internal violence. It was the forcible conversion of Kievan Russia to Christianity that laid the foundations of the state. Western rulers, too, resorted to violence to destroy feudalism in their states, but hardly on a scale and with the cruelty exhibited during the reigns of Ivan III and Ivan IV. And it was a series of fiats by Peter the Great rather than a lengthy period of social developments or parliamentary acts that thrust Russia into the mainstream of European politics and made it a great power. Thereafter the very weight of the Empire's power acted as a barrier to constitutionalism and the civil rights of its subjects. A vast, nationally heterogeneous state could seemingly be kept together only by an authoritarian regime. Plans for reform faltered repeatedly on the realization by the would-be reformers that political freedom might spell the disintegration of the Empire into its national components, an issue very relevant to the current problems of the Soviet Union.

Still, the tsarist era witnessed, especially in the 1860s and after 1905, periods of progressive and far-reaching reform. That these reforms did not find their consummation in a constitutional system was due to fears about the survival of the empire, but also to "Russia's misfortune," the tendency for the political arena to generate violence. Unable to stir up the masses, the would-be, radical reformers turned to assassination to coerce the government to grant freedom. Attempts at political murder were a frequent occurrence following the era of the Great Reforms of the 1860s. One such attempt, the assassination of Alexander II on March 1, 1881, which was crowned with success, enabled the forces of reaction to check any further progress, and thus to set the stage for the eruption of a much more widespread and elemental burst of violence—the Revolution of 1905.

The legacy of individual terror of the nineteenth and early twentieth centuries had a fateful influence on the Soviet regime. From the beginning, the Communist leaders were determined that, unlike the empire of the tsars, theirs must not be shaken by the activities of a handful of conspirators. That very largely was the rationale behind the mass terror which, first employed by the Bolsheviks during the Civil War, remained a feature of Communist rule in peacetime, and assumed surrealistic character and dimensions under Stalin.

Incongruously, until very recent years, the Soviet Union itself was ruled in a conspiratorial way. Under the nineteenth-century Empire, the lack of nationwide representative institutions had already made rule by the tsars and top bureaucrats more closely resemble a conspiracy than a government in the European sense of the term. The mass of the people were left in ignorance concerning how, why, and by whom decisions were made that regulated their everyday lives. As with almost every negative feature of old Russia, this conspiratorial manner of governing was not only duplicated but greatly magnified in the Soviet Union. Representative institutions, including those within the Communist party, atrophied or more precisely, were never allowed to function properly. Power was concentrated in the hands of the leader and his henchmen and, after Stalin's death, in an oligarchy of some fifteen to twenty members of the Politburo circle recruited through co-optation, and in fact responsible to no one. Mass terror was discarded by Stalin's heirs; the Soviet Union became a "normal" police state with the difference that the measures of repression employed by the ruling oligarchs against every form of dissent remained more refined and extensive than those in most dictatorial regimes.

For all the measures of repression employed by the state, dissent grew in the post-Stalin Soviet Union, just as the absolutist government of the tsars proved incapable of destroying revolutionary activities and movements in Russia prior to 1917. But there was a basic difference between dissidents in the USSR and their predecessors during the imperial era: those fighting for freedom against the

Communist regime renounced violence as a weapon in their struggle. The thirty-year period between Khrushchev's 1956 "secret" speech, which for the first time officially acknowledged the crimes of the Stalin era, and 1986, when perestroika was launched, did not witness a single political assassination. This absence of violence cannot be credited solely or even mainly to the efficiency of the KGB. As one of the most notable representatives of dissidence, General Pyotr Grigorenko, once said in the presence of this writer, Russian history has taught the dissidents only too well that violence begets violence that leads to tyranny. Individual terror, as practiced before the Revolution by the militant populists as well as (despite their disclaimers) by the Bolsheviks, undermined not only the old regime but also the moral foundations of Russian society. It imparted the belief that the bomb and revolver were legitimate weapons in the struggle for freedom. There then remained but a short step to the argument that the firing squad was a legitimate means of defense of the "workers' and peasants' state" against the counter-revolutionaries. The bloody purges of 1936–1939—the high point of terror—had as their rationalization fictitious plots, including attempts at assassination, allegedly directed against the Communist leaders. At the time this rationale, fantastic as it seems to us today, was found convincing not only by the masses in the Soviet Union but by many, not necessarily of the Left, in the West.

The motto of a number of revolutionaries in the nineteenth century was "the worse it is the better." This meant that anything undermining the existing order—defeat by a foreign enemy, famine, cruelty of the authorities—was beneficial to the cause of the revolution. Such logic clashed with that of democracy, since it implied indifference to the welfare of one's own nation, and it extolled revolution or, more properly, seizure of power by the revolutionaries as a goal in itself. Compare it to the stance of Solzhenitsyn and Andrei Sakharov, the most eminent critics of the politics of the pre-1985 Soviet state, whose attitudes embodied the utmost solicitude for the spiritual and material welfare of their fellow citizens. They struggled against the oppressors not with the gun, but with appeals to the nation's moral sense. A striking attribute of all fighters against Communism during the Khrushchev and Brezhnev eras was precisely their eschewing any call for violent action against the government. The government spared no chicanery to suppress their activities, from exile to the forcible internment of some perfectly sane dissidents in mental institutions, the latter again taking a leaf from nineteenth-century methods of dealing with the critics of tsardom. Modern critics of the Soviet Union scorned conspiratorial methods. They defied the Kremlin openly. Their goal was not seizure of power, but a moral rebirth of the nation.

If some derided the dissidents' activities in the pre-1985 Soviet Union as actions of an isolated group of individuals, incapable of affecting the course of history, then such judgments seem most nearsighted from today's perspective. What has been called the third Russian revolution has, at least until now, taken place peacefully largely due to the example and the preaching of those brave men and women who raised their voices against the regime when it was still confident and ruthless toward its critics. One might have expected that once the regime acknowledged its bankruptcy, that avowal would be followed by an eruption of violence, triggered by long-repressed passions and calls for retribution. Yet that has not happened. The country had been awed by the revelations of the inhumanities and inanities of the pre-1985 Soviet regime, but they have not been followed by a bloodbath. True, ethnic violence has not been absent in areas such as the Caucasus and Central Asia, and the government has not entirely refrained from the use of brute force, as shown last January in the Baltic region. But given the scale of the political, social, and economic turbulence accompanying perestroika, such incidents fall considerably short of what might have been expected.

Has the "Russian syndrome" finally been exorcised from Soviet politics, or would such a conclusion be premature? Whatever the answer, the future historian will profit from the beguiling narrative against which Mme Carrère d'Encausse poses this question.

It has always been the strength of Mme Carrère d'Encausse's writings on the Soviet Union that she has viewed its current problems from a broad historical perspective. She has stressed what we have become acutely aware of only recently: that the fundamental problem of the Soviet empire lies not in ideology, but in its multinational character. And this rich panorama of Russian history illuminates not only its violent past, but also fundamental questions about the Soviet state's future.

August 1991

Preface

This book is not a chronicle of political murder through the ages: a hundred books would not suffice for that. If Russia, Russian culture, and the Russian people provide the basic material for illustrating its development and analysis, this book does not claim, even remotely, to be a history of, first, Russia and, later, the Soviet Union.

This country, in its unparalleled misfortune, remains an enigma for students of its history. In trying to shed light on the underlying causes of this age-old tragedy, a specific—and always damaging—link has emerged between the seizing or maintaining of power and the practice of political murder, be it individual or mass, real or symbolic.

This was the starting point of this essay, a new way of reading a history told by others, a history that a few have made or believed they made and for which many have died.

H. C. E.

Introduction

◆

Murder is an art; but not all murders are works of art and not all murderers are artists. Thomas de Quincey, the author of this strong statement, was not thinking only of ordinary murder—the first, and for him rather uninspired, example of which was that committed by Cain, the "father of the art"—but also of "a branch of the art that has flourished by intermittent fits"— political assassination. Through the centuries there have been countless works of art of this type, giving nourishment simultaneously to history, art, and philosophy. There is Romulus who in killing his brother Remus gives political murder its full meaning: the ousting of the rival, Rome's inviolability assured, the ever-present threat of civil war, the sacrifices to the gods to ward off this threat, to calm their fury and their curse. And there are Macbeth and the "glorious pleiad of murders" that in a short space of time removed William the Silent and three French Henrys (Henry, Duke of Guise, Henry III, and Henry IV). "In these assassinations of princes and statesmen," writes De Quincey, "there is nothing to excite our wonder; important changes often depend on their deaths; and from the eminence on which they stand they are peculiarly exposed to the aim of every artist who happens to be possessed by the craving for scenical effect."

It is hard not to go along with such a reasonable view, and the remarkable link made between power and murder. We can also agree with De Quincey's analysis of the aberrations which were to emerge over the centuries in this unbreakable relationship. Men have become accustomed to the idea that, in order to seize power, one can, like Macbeth, kill the person who holds it, or that, like Sulla, when in power one can kill anyone who sets himself up as a rival. Similarly, one can kill the man who uses power to become a tyrant, the fate that met Caesar. Despite these assumptions, we cling to certain illusions that are constantly contradicted by the long history of human civilizations. Many philosophers have tried to give a rational explanation for political murder. Some hoped that the progress of the human mind, of knowledge, and of political order would tame this wild beast, moderating its relations with its fellow men, attempting by laws agreed on in common to determine power and limit its authority in the common interest. Others have believed in a utopia where, once violence had died out and men were all equal—making relationships of power meaningless—murder would, in turn, disappear. Finally, those who saw history as continual progress believed that when the cause of human conflict—the class struggle—was overcome, power would be replaced by harmony and murder by fraternal solidarity.

This dream of a Golden Age—a projection into the future of a lost Eden—when power would not favor murder has been cruelly shattered by history. Quite the reverse is true: to the simple killings of early times have been added complex murders where the theater so dear to Thomas de Quincey has been enriched by new themes and unexpected actors, and where the number of dead becomes the measure of the skill of the murderer. The artist comes to be interested not so much in the subtlety of the design, the perfection of the work of art, as in spectacular effect. Murder loses in quality but often gains in effectiveness.

Murder justified and made legitimate by duty, which could be called ideological murder—killing the oppressor—was quickly followed by functional murder, which used terror to subject the world. The artist who invented this genre in the Middle Ages merits a mention. This was the Old Man of the Mountain, the founder of a strange sect, the *Hashashin,* from which we derive, rightly or wrongly, the word *assassin.* A product of the Islamic world, this sect, which terrorized not only the Christian crusaders but also the Muslims, developed on fertile ground. Islam, when it moves into the political arena, gives a privileged place to murder. Of the first four caliphs who succeeded the Prophet and preserved his heritage, three were assassinated, and early in its history, Islam questioned the duty of the faithful toward leaders who had departed from the straight and narrow path. Perhaps this explains why terrorism, the planned and systematic use of mass murder for political ends, was born in the Islamic world. The Old Man of the Mountain created it, just as Cain had invented murder itself. Mass murder that seeks to destroy the existing order, not just the tyrant himself—a perfect organization, secret and with its hierarchies and rules, which supports a long-term political plan, an ideology that legitimizes terror—all this took shape long ago in the East.

To all these types of assassination—individual murder for personal reasons, tyrannicide carried out by an individual or a handful of conspirators, the terrorism that first flourished in the Middle Ages—the modern world has added only two variations. One descends from the genealogical tree of original murder, while the other belongs to the exuberant imagination of Thomas de Quincey. The mass destruction of groups of people, as practiced by Hitler and Stalin, and imitators like Mao Zedong and the Khmer Rouge, who used terror to oppress every individual indiscriminately to the point of paralyzing their reflexes and personality, is at odds with the various known types of political murder. Terror may pursue precise aims—the destruction of the Sunnites for the "Assassins," the creation of a homeland for the Palestinians, a solution to the Irish problem. Here the terrorist action is on a scale proportionate to the realization of the plan and is in some sense an expression of the despair of the deprived. The two greatest murderers of the twentieth century replaced this type of terrorism with the terrorism of power. It was for them a political instrument that had only one object, the limitless expansion of their power. The underlying plan of these two masters of murder was an insane dream of a humanity forced by terror to conform to their personal conception of the Golden Age. There is a considerable gulf between a terrorism that seeks to benefit the outcast—though that is no kind of justification—and a terrorism whose aim it is to subject man to a utopia. A whole civilization nearly perished in such an attempt.

But there is another, and until now exceptional, variant of political murder that points to a disquieting future. There have been other assassinations of American presidents, from Lincoln to Kennedy, but until now the man who aimed a gun at the president had some political reason for his action. The most recent of these attempts, which in 1981 almost cost Ronald Reagan his life, is indicative of the development and changes in the political order.

The would-be assassin made an amazing and, for any observer of political life, most disconcerting, statement. To the question "Why did you want to kill the president?" he answered unambiguously that it was "to impress a woman by doing something extraordinary." And what more impressive action could there be than the murder of an all-powerful president, the center of world attention, whose death would have mobilized all the world's communication systems? Was it the action of a madman? On the contrary: here was the plan of an accomplished artist who, wishing to present his love with an unparalleled masterpiece, chose the one that, in the modern world, would be the most exceptional, the most successful, with the greatest repercussions. The unsuccessful attempt on the life of President Reagan marks the end of a period of the evolution of political murder that began with the killing of Remus. Then man killed to gain power. Today, power attracts murder not for the power that will, in turn, be conferred on the murderer but simply because, in a world where the media reign supreme, no one is more newsworthy than he who holds power and who thus becomes the ideal victim of murder as spectacle. By committing murder, a man can attract attention to himself, raising himself for an instant to the height of those who owe their powers chiefly to the mass media. This kind of murder is not only gratuitous in terms of political change but also indicative of the diminishing importance of politics and the increasing power of the media. The idea that power can be merely a pretext for the glory of others raises interesting implications.

Political murder has also developed along another path. For a long time it aimed only at power in the heart of cities. Between cities, from one country to another, there were wars, global clashes that defined relations according to strength. Here too a line should be drawn in time between the assassination of leaders, which rarely took the place of wars, and terrorism which, with the exception of the Old Man of the Mountain, is a relatively modern phenomenon. It is true that World War I began with the murder of an Austrian archduke. But it is doubtful whether this murder had in itself the ability to unleash a war for which all the conditions were ripe, any more than it could have led to the final collapse of the Austro-Hungarian Empire. Gavrilo Princip and his fellow conspirators, who killed the Archduke Francis Ferdinand, were inspired by nationalist aspirations within the Hapsburg empire and not by a desire to change the international order. In this respect, contemporary terrorism, which often seeks to put pressure on the international policies of different countries—as in the case of the American and French hostages in Lebanon—is distantly related to the activities of the Assassins who wanted both to destroy Islamic orthodoxy wherever it had taken root and to escape the temporal power of the Seljuk Empire. "Individual" variations of political murder occurred in the interwar years, and particularly in 1934, which saw in France the murders of the king of Yugoslavia and of Louis Barthou and in Austria that of Chancellor Dollfuss. Beyond the differences that separate these tragedies we can glimpse one unifying factor at this decisive moment when Europe hesitated between democracy and totalitarianism: those who guided the hands of the assassins believed they were striking a blow against the old Europe and opening the way for the "New Order."

An attempt to plot political murders in time and space leads to three conclusions. No society has been entirely immune from political murder in its broadest sense. But there have been certain periods where it has been particularly prevalent: in Europe in the sixteenth century, for example; and again in the twentieth century when, in the form of mass terror and terrorism, it has reached into every part of the globe. There have also been moments when political murder receded and appeared only exceptionally as a method of resolving power struggles. Thomas de Quincey was right, in his "artistic" vision, to stress the interruptions and intermittent occurrence of political murder. In general, the political progress of society tends to lead to the resolution of conflict by other methods. There is, however, one exception to this view that puts all nations at one time or another on the same level and makes political murder the key to the tragic episodes in their history. This exception—not perhaps the only one, but the most striking since it is a large European country—is Russia.

This country, Tocqueville predicted, would be called "by a secret design of Providence one day to hold in its hands half the world," equal only to the United States, of which he says that the world "will discover at one and the same time its birth and its greatness." And the history of Russia is first and foremost a *continu-*

ous history of political murder. From the time that Russia was founded and began to be converted to Christianity in the ninth century to the height of its power as predicted by Tocqueville, there has hardly been a generation that has not been a terrified witness to the eternal link between murder and politics. The only moments of respite have been in time of war and invasion—alternative forms of violence and death, but ones that, coming from outside, have the effect of temporarily uniting sovereign and society against a common murderous enemy. If the Romans, haunted by the original murder that cost Remus his life, were never at peace with their gods, their successors in the city founded on this crime have long since forgotten it. It is preserved only in legend. The Russians might well ask what curse still hangs over them, what exceptional crime they have committed so that murder and political life go forever hand in hand.

This long tradition of murder has doubtless created a collective consciousness that has little hope for a pacified political world, while violence or the fear of violence remains deeply rooted. What is the cause and what the effect of this tragedy so deeply felt through the ages and which has been called superficially the "Russian soul"? Is it the long history of political murder that has produced an unhappy and submissive social consciousness, one that is therefore incapable of imposing, as in other countries, another direction on politics? Or is it that this unhappy, frightened consciousness calls down upon itself, if not the the anger of the gods, then at least the fury of the murderers?

I

The Age of Fratricide

◆

The Choosing of a God

In the year 882, a legendary prince, from no one knows where, arrived on the banks of the Dnieper and founded a kingdom. At first sight it was a well-chosen spot. Kiev—the name of both the state and the town that was its center—lay between two powerful poles: northern Europe and Byzantium. The Dnieper, the source of life, was consequently also a source of wealth. But when everything was taken into account it was a very dangerous site. The envious eyes of empires and tribes from the surrounding steppes coveted this strategic spot.

For its protection, Kiev had many gods. To the most greatly revered of all—Perun, god of thunder and fire—altars were raised on the cliffs overlooking the Dnieper around the city. Here prisoners were sacrificed on return from battle. Later a woman, Olga, was to reign over Kiev. She succeeded her husband Igor who was hacked to pieces by his enemies. Olga was a determined woman, obsessed with the desire to avenge her husband's death. She was not lacking in inventiveness, burying some enemies alive, burning others in her bathhouse, and setting fire to an entire town. Perun's fire featured strongly in her revenge. But once her fury had been assuaged, this pagan princess was suddenly to turn her back on Perun and embrace Christianity. It was probably a conversion of convenience, sealing the end of the wars that had until then set her against the Byzantine Empire. Earlier, in wars against the Rome of the East, Olga's soldiers had delivered up to the flames of Perun all the churches they encountered while hammering nails into the heads of any priests found inside. This habit, which did not prevent Olga's conversion, did little to encourage that of her subjects. It was too soon to force them to accept a single God.

It fell to her grandson, Vladimir, to lead a whole people to Christ. However, like his grandmother, he was not known, before his conversion, for his gentleness. It is true that the only way he could succeed to power in Kiev was by crushing anyone who stood in the way. The prevailing law of succession was simple; it was that of the clan. The eldest succeeded his father; the others received, in decreasing order of age, conquered territories to administer. This was their "privilege." If a brother died, all the survivors went up one rung. Since they all aspired to rule over Kiev instead of being vassals of the reigning prince, they had no alternative but to kill one another. Ties of kinship were no protection in this murderous rivalry and neither affection nor respect had any influence on the relationships within the clan. In this fratricidal struggle for supreme power, Vladimir dealt with his two elder brothers with exceptional savagery. He killed only one of them, since his victim had previously done away with the other in order to seize his possessions. But besides his eldest brother, Vladimir had also to get rid of the former's father- and brother-in-law. He massacred them all and added to his hundreds of concubines the beautiful Greek nun captured earlier in the Byzantine Empire, beloved of the brother whom he had just killed and carrying his child. Debauched and criminal, Vladimir was nevertheless zealous in his devotion to the gods of Kiev. And yet it was this same Vladimir who suddenly devoted himself to the service of a single God, the God of the Christians, to whom he offered in addition the entire population of Kiev.

The Soldier of God

By the end of the first millennium, most leading nations worshipped a single God. Finally rid of his brothers and becoming increasingly powerful, Vladimir decided to do the same. But which God should he choose? On the banks of the Dnieper this was not such an easy thing to do; although the surrounding empires may have worshipped only one God, this God varied from place to place.

The chroniclers tell how Vladimir in his dilemma decided to make an informed choice, sending embassies to the faithful of the neighboring states to inquire of the different religions. His envoys to the Bulgar Muslims returned disappointed. Circumcision and the prohibition of alcohol, so contrary to Russian customs, had greatly displeased them. The visit to the Khazar Jews was equally unsuccessful. It was unthinkable that Vladimir, the conqueror and empire-builder, should embrace the religion of a defeated, landless people who wandered over the four corners of the earth. There remained the Christians. Vladimir's envoys had not been impressed by the simplicity and austerity of the Latin rite which they had found in Germany. The splendor and richness of the Byzantine Church, on the other hand, dazzled them. They had little difficulty in convincing Vladimir that this religion, in this triumphant form, was worthy of a great prince's devotion.

Vladimir's baptism, the result of a rational and politic choice, can be narrated in two ways. The first, highly colored account is that of the chroniclers, probably more legend than fact, but a superb legend nevertheless. Vladimir the conqueror viewed his baptism as one more conquest. That is why he conquered the Byzantine citadel of Kherson in the Crimea and then, fortified by this success designed to impress the Byzantine emperor, informed him that he intended to take at one and the same time baptism and the hand of Anna, the emperor's sister. On his return, now a Christian, to Kiev, accompanied by Anna and a train of priests and church ornaments like so much booty, he devoted himself at once to the conversion of his subjects.

The second version of events, more rigorous and certainly true, is found in Vladimir Vodoff's *La Naissance de la Chrétienté russe (The Birth of Christianity in Russia)*. The Byzantine emperor, Basil II, threatened from outside, appears to have sought the aid of his powerful enemy Vladimir and, in order to persuade him, offered him his sister's hand in marriage. This was a useful alliance for the emperor, but how much more prestigious for the prince of Kiev! If he was baptized, it was because a Byzantine princess could not marry a pagan prince.

Whether we accept the legend or the historical version, the conclusion is the same. Back in Kiev, Vladimir the conqueror devoted all his violence to the service of God. He unleashed it on the multiple gods revered only yesterday: all the idols were smashed and the huge statue of Perun publicly whipped before being thrown into the Dnieper. The same violence was used to baptize his people. Vladimir forced all his subjects into the river while he stood on the bank, surrounded by priests, reciting the baptismal prayers. Entering Christianity as a soldier, Vladimir was to become the soldier of God. Unlike Clovis who was not deterred by baptism from later wiping out the Frankish kings, his kinsmen, Vladimir changed totally in behavior after his baptism. Repudiating his concubines in favor of Anna alone, the Byzantine princess who had arrived with his conversion, the debauched and violent man of yesterday turned into a model of virtue and gentleness. He became concerned for the happiness of his subjects and adopted for his first rule, which he never infringed, never to kill a fellow man. Thus it was that in the course of time the image of the fierce young prince gave way to that of the saint who baptized a whole people: Vladimir "the Great," Vladimir "the Bright Sun."

This conversion, political in origin, also had some long-lasting political consequences. The sacrament of a people willed by the man who dominated the state, this baptism was thereafter to unite state and church while recognizing a certain primacy for the head of state.

Christianity in Parentheses

Although he had chosen to follow the religion of the Byzantine Empire, Vladimir did not at the same time adopt its political system. The method of succession in the empire, where power was handed down from father to son without the dispersal of any possessions, preserved the throne from disputes over succession and the state from disintegration. For having failed to understand this and for continuing to obey the rules of the clan, Vladimir, who had at such cost unified his lands, bears the responsibility for their breakup and for the return to the bloody conflicts between rival brothers. Christianity in Kiev was still very precarious.

Vladimir shared among his many sons the immense number of possessions that he had accumulated. Eight heirs, seven sons and a nephew, were, after his death in 1015, to give themselves up to a pitiless, bloody struggle, as if the word of Christ, which Vladimir had tried to incorporate into the morals of his lands, had never been heard. The society of the clans, knowing no other norm than force, but formerly kept under control by the powerful Vladimir, regained all its rights and reappeared to annul all the achievements of the "Bright Sun."

Vladimir himself had the chance to observe this precariousness before his death. One of his sons, Yaroslav, to whom he had given Novgorod as "appanage," or princely share, suddenly rose up against him, refusing to pay him tribute as a vassal should. Worse, this delinquent son called on external support against his father from the Varangians (the Norsemen). There were no other ways to resolve a conflict between father and son than by weapons and betrayal. Vladimir the Christian, who had never ceased since his conversion to ask, "Who am I to decide on the fate of a man's life?", was now obliged to take up arms against his son. Death, which overtook him on the road to war after forty-five years of rule, spared him a confrontation, but the evidence was there: he had once ordered the murder of his brother; now at the end of his life, he had almost spilled the blood of his son.

He was spared, but his sons were not. His death unleashed personal ambitions and intrigues. Of all his sons the most threatening was the eldest, his adopted son whose real father had been Yaropolk who had assassinated his own brother and whom Vladimir had killed in turn and in terrible circumstances. The violent instincts of this son, Svyatopolk, known in history as the Accursed, were revealed at once. Although Vladimir had given him the principality of Turov in the land of Minsk, it was Kiev, whose splendor rivaled that of Constantinople, that fascinated him. Kiev was supposed to come to Vladimir's favorite son, Boris, prince of Rostov, who had accompanied him on his last campaign and in whose arms he had died. Svyatopolk saw only one way to get rid of this rival—murder, which always clears the way to power. By deceit and force Svyatopolk took over the command of Kiev and sent assassins to liberate it from Boris. This murder revealed the Accursed's boundless cruelty. The victorious Svyatopolk, sitting on the coveted throne, learned that his hired killers had been unable to finish off their victim who, though grievously wounded, was still breathing. The killers who had struck the murderous blows, suddenly overcome by pity, had been unable to finish the job. Svyatopolk, unable to understand this compassion, sent for new killers; he would not rest until he was sure that the man who throughout his adolescence had been a true brother to him had been finally removed.

Obeying the logic of a system that necessitated either sharing power with one's kin or eliminating them all without exception, Svyatopolk set about getting rid of all Vladimir's successors, one after the other, so as to be able in his turn to reunite those lands that had for a while been split up. Having finally had Boris killed, he set a trap for Gleb, prince of Murom and another of Vladimir's sons, calling him to the side of his supposedly dying father—who was in fact already dead. When Gleb learned simultaneously of the death of his father and of the assassination of his brother Boris, he wanted to turn back, but too late. His servants, who had understood the power of the Accursed, betrayed him, giving their loyalty to the conqueror. It was to be Gleb's own cook who undertook to cut his throat. Next it was the turn of Svyatoslav who had received the principality of the Drevlyanians. Learning in time of Svyatopolk's murderous intentions, he tried to flee, seeking refuge with the Poles. It was to be in vain: the assassins dispatched after him overtook him and slew him.

Thus in a short time, Svyatopolk, firmly entrenched in Kiev, was able to assassinate three of Vladimir's sons. There remained Yaroslav, prince of Novgorod, who had rebelled against his father. His situation, with the news of the disappearance of his brothers, was far from secure. It was true that he had Novgorod, whose inhabitants, alarmed by the rumors of Svyatopolk's murderous exploits, had no desire to fall into the hands of so cruel a prince. On the other hand, Yaroslav had not shown himself to be any more magnanimous toward his subjects. The Varangians, whom he had shortly before summoned to his aid against his father, had made him pay dearly for this assistance by raiding his lands. Murder, rape, and pillage were the daily lot of the people of

Novgorod, made all the more intolerable by the fact that the town was not at war and that the demands of the Varangians, the price of the prince's weakness, seemed never-ending. Thus it was that, pushed to the limit, the people of Novgorod decided in this time of general upheaval in Russia to take their fate into their own hands, rebelling against both their prince and the Varangians.

Yaroslav's revenge was horrible. With the help of those troops who had remained faithful, he massacred his subjects. No sooner had this bloody settling of accounts taken place than the prince learned of the threat from Svyatopolk. To save himself he was forced to turn to his only possible support—those same people of Novgorod on whom he had just inflicted such carnage. Despite the recent massacre, they came to his aid: Yaroslav had humbled himself sufficiently and agreed to act in future with justice and moderation. To the people of Novgorod, the murderous fury of Svyatopolk seemed even more threatening than that of their own prince.

The last stage in this series of deaths was the bloody confrontation between the two survivors and their armies. Syvatopolk obtained the help of the king of Poland, Boleslav the Brave, his father-in-law, who saw, as he was supposed to, an opportunity to acquire some land in Russia. But the victor was to be Yaroslav. Svyatopolk the Accursed, dazzled by his previous successes over his rivals and his brain dulled by excessive drinking, was also a coward. When things came to a head he took to his heels, seeking shelter with his protector Boleslav. He died miserably, a half-mad exile, after committing a few more massacres and betraying his father-in-law in order to get out of difficulties. The legend circulating in Poland about this appalling and cowardly prince tells how the earth, disgusted by his innumerable crimes, opened up at his feet one day and swallowed him forever.

Yaroslav's hour had come at last. Kiev was his. He was to reign over Vladimir's lands from 1019 to 1054, under the name of Yaroslav the Wise, a clear indication that, like his father, he was able to change from ambitious war leader, with little respect for the rights of his kin and his subjects, to just and revered sovereign, a new Charlemagne of Russia.

The long period of murders that came to an end in this way prompts a question. In these fratricidal struggles, what had happened to the religion adopted by Olga and Vladimir? Had it left no trace at all in the depths of the consciences of their heirs? Of course, history abounds with examples of followers of the faith of Christ who have forgotten His teachings, whose only thought is of the extermination of their rivals. But in the present case, it was the model itself of the soldier of God that seemed to vanish, reverting to the murderous world preceding Vladimir's conversion.

And yet the work of transformation in men's consciences was less superficial than it might appear. While the princes saw their struggles over the succession in the light of the old tradition of murder, the people of Kiev, as described in the chronicles, were already seeing the actors in this long family tragedy with a partly Christian eye. In newly baptized Rus, the pagan world, its idols, and its beliefs constantly reemerged from beneath the surface of Christianity. Nevertheless, it divided the saints from the cursed in Christian terms. Even before they were canonized by the church in 1072, Boris and Gleb, two of Syvatopolk's victims, were saints in the eyes of the common man. Their youth and their innocence aroused pity, which was not the case with Svyatoslav, the third victim of this series of murders. The first saints recognized as such by Russia, long before Olga and Vladimir were thus popularly chosen—probably in the thirteenth century—were Boris and Gleb. The legend was to depict them not so much as exceptionally virtuous but rather as expiatory victims necessary for the redemption of their people, of the land of Russia, who had accepted martyrdom as Christ himself had accepted it. Their humility, their submission to the will of fate, and their compassion explained the popular demand for the sanctification of the two princes and were to be traits that the Christian culture of the Russian people was to promote in the future. If Boris and Gleb were venerated from this time, it is because a popular concept of the relationship between power and the people was emerging amid the tragedies in the struggle for power and the emptiness of the political system. The saints would intercede on behalf of the people with the holders of power, a power that could rule without any constraints since it was conquered in violence and blood. In the absence of a political order, the intercession of the saints represented the first step in the establishment of a system of power that could be predicted and controlled.

The Triumph of Kiev: Power Pacified

Yaroslav the Wise only once resorted to the murderous madness that dominated the road to power in Rus, when he rebelled against his father. Vladimir's sudden death spared him from committing parricide. Once in power in Kiev, he was to become the incarnation of peaceful authority. His reign was not without its wars—quite the reverse—but Kiev had always been surrounded by enemies: the Asian hordes continued to pour onto the steppes; the Poles were using the support they had given to Svyatopolk as an excuse to seize lands to the southwest of Kiev; the Byzantine Empire, coveted as ever, remained for that very reason a disturbing presence. To the enemies from without could be added the never-ending civil war. Once again it was to be a brother who rose up against Yaroslav, the master of Kiev, to seize power.

Mstislav the Brave, prince of Tmutorokan, a principality in the Kuban area, had distinguished himself in the wars against the Khazars and was not a rival to be ignored. But it is precisely here that we can measure the difference between Yaroslav and the many other princes crowding this troubled history. Instead of resorting to assassination to resolve his dispute with Mstislav, he imposed a solution worthy of Solomon. In 1026 he agreed with his brother on a division of the kingdom, whereby he kept Kiev and the lands west of the Dnieper, while Mstislav reigned over Chernigov and the territories stretching east of the river. This division lasted until the death of Mstislav in 1036, at which time Yaroslav became the prince of all Rus.

Although unable to enjoy total peace—local revolts alternating with rebellions among tribes still clinging to outlawed pagan beliefs—Yaroslav never, during all his long reign, spilled the blood of fellow members of the clan. With his power confirmed by negotiation and not murder—war being another, and inevitable, matter—he used his power to raise Kiev to a glory without precedent. Like Charlemagne, he saw himself as the founder of a state dominated by law and enlightenment, and his ambition was to make Kiev even more brilliant than the eastern Rome. The capital was able to boast not only of the cathedral of St. Sophia, with its dazzling mosaics worthy of those of Constantinople, which he built, but also of its Golden Gate, its monasteries, palaces, and ramparts. The town on the Dnieper was rapidly invaded by merchants traveling from many parts, whether by the royal road, the river, or by land. Hundreds of churches proudly proclaimed the might of Christianity in this city that rivaled the capital on the Bosphorus and to which Greek artists came to decorate the churches and public buildings. The Monastery of the Caves drew huge crowds of pilgrims and miracle-workers, while some walled themselves up alive there, their cells becoming their tombs. This was a far cry from the hesitant Christianity of Vladimir's time. Yaroslav's religious zeal caused him to go so far as to disinter his uncles Yaropolk and Oleg, who had died pagans, in order to baptize their remains and thereby ensure, he believed, their eternal salvation.

Like Charlemagne, Yaroslav built schools, notably that of Novgorod which could accommodate three hundred adolescents. He had a mint set up, producing coins symbolic of his dual role as prince of Kiev and Christian: on the obverse his Slav name—Yaroslav—written in Slavonic; on the reverse his Christian name—Georgios—written in Greek. Similarly, Greek was used for all the inscriptions in St. Sophia and the churches.

This Christian prince, still barbaric in the passionate manifestations of his faith, was also a legislator. Kiev already had some laws, of course, but in 1017 Yaroslav endowed it with a proper code, the *Russkaia pravda* (Russian Justice) which attempted to organize society in Kiev and define its rights and duties. Notable is the organization of punishment and revenge. Yaroslav included in his code the supreme punishment—the death penalty—for crimes of blood. His sons were to decide later to spare their subjects from punishment by death, and they removed it from the code. Very precise, even minute, regulations surrounded the right to take revenge on others. In the case of murder, only the son, the father, the brother, and the nephew of the victim had the right to exercise the *lex talionis*. When the right to take the life of another—whether it belonged to the state or to the authors of the vengeance—was removed, the "blood price" was replaced by a monetary compensation, the amount of which was carefully fixed according to the status of the victim. This hierarchy of social class as indicated by the amount of compensation set for different individuals is one of the peculiarities of the code. At the top of the ladder stood the chief dignitaries of the state, while at the bottom were the slaves. But a female slave was worth more than a male one; workers were more esteemed than farm laborers; people who looked after children (nurses or tutors), even if slaves, had a high compensation price. Legitimate defense was allowed, but though it was permissible to kill those who threatened or stole at night, if it happened in the daytime the matter had to be referred to the prince's tribunal. The judicial duel and ordeal by hot iron or boiling water were legal, but if the accuser was unable to substantiate his allegations then he would be made to undergo the same ordeals. This desire to protect life after so much abuse made Kiev, once the country of fratricide, a place where the legal system came very close to that of eleventh-century western Europe.

This "enlightened" and humane policy accounts for the eminent position that Yaroslav held among the ranks of sovereigns. While an alliance with the Byzantine Empire had been sought after in the time of Vladimir, now, in the reign of Yaroslav the Wise, an alliance with Kiev had great prestige. Yaroslav's daughters married into important families: Maria married King Casimir of Poland; Anna became queen of France by marriage to Henry I; another, Elizabeth, married Harold the Brave, king of Norway; the last, Anastasia, married Andrew I, king of Hungary. It was not the first time that the princes of Kiev had allied themselves with foreign families, but under Yaroslav these more frequent alliances attest to the fact that Kiev was very much part of the world of the great principalities. Rus was now a great Christian state of Europe. Yaroslav the Wise, Yaroslav the Lame as the soldiers had called him, mocking his limping gait, more than completed the work started by his newly converted ancestors, Olga and Vladimir.

The world of strife-ridden clans gave way to a powerful state that seemed to be on the way to becoming a state guided by law. There still remained, however, serious weaknesses. Two systems were juxtaposed. The old clan rule still survived, with the warrior leader, the leader of the group who had triumphed over his rivals, surrounded by his *druzhina* (followers), demanding tribute from his vassals. But the political system of the Byzantine Empire, brought to Kiev with the Greek priests, was beginning to be adopted, with the idea of the *basileus*, God's representative on earth, to whom the people had delegated sovereignty. He was not the leader of a clan, but the master of an empire that could not be claimed by others and that he could not divide up among his heirs. The empire had to be passed on intact to a successor. In the eleventh century this idea of the indivisible empire, single and enduring, imposed on the people, and supported by cohorts of officials and by the army, was only beginning to be glimpsed by the sovereign and the high-ranking men of Kiev. But the Byzantine clergy and, later, the Russian clergy were beginning to promote this idea, even if the old Rus of the clans, temporarily weakened and overshadowed by the brilliance of Yaroslav's reign, was still there. This coexistence of the two incompatible systems of power foreshadowed the day when the clan tradition would give way to a single political vision.

The Awakening of the Clans

Although bestowing on Kiev a period of exceptional glory, Yaroslav's strong personality was not enough to lead to a permanent and perceptible change in the state. Once again it was to be the problem of succession that destroyed the work of the wise sovereign, rturning Kiev to the old internal strife, hastening its decline, and contributing to the final collapse. Like his grandfather Svyatoslav and his father Vladimir, Yaroslav made the mistake of dividing his lands between his five sons. Byzantine law, whereby the entire inheritance went from father to eldest son, had not yet become sufficiently deep-rooted to prevent the old Slav practice reasserting itself as in the past. This practice was very complex. On one hand, it asserted the primacy of the eldest, the prince of Kiev, over his brothers, who were to a certain extent his vassals. On the other, it always involved succession between brothers: if a prince died, it was the next brother in line, and not the son, who inherited. Thus, in the distribution of privileges, each time a brother died the younger brothers climbed up one rung, while at the same time disinheriting the sons of the deceased. At his death, Yaroslav hoped, like his predecessors, that the period of stability which he had brought to his country would have encouraged both the acceptance of the authority of the eldest son, the prince of Kiev, and peace between brothers. None of these wishes were respected; his death opened a new period of fratricide and merciless civil war that resulted in the ultimate catastrophe, the end of the glory of Kiev.

The discussion of the succession had, in fact, started auspiciously. On the death of their father, the five sons had met to decide together on the fate of one of their uncles, kept in prison by Yaroslav for twenty-four years. (The peace-loving sovereign did not hesitate to get rid of his rivals in this less murderous, but equally cruel, manner.) The nephews agreed to grant their uncle a privilege. However, so long a period in chains appears to have made the prisoner either scorn or fear the goods of this world, and, preferring the cloister, he retired there for the rest of his life. Behind this pleasant episode it is possible to detect the recognition by eternal rivals that a coming together—a collegiality, as we might say today—could have beneficial and protective aspects. But this dialogue did not last long and the old demons made short work of its destruction. As usual, the division of the inheritance by the father had created nothing but discontent; what other way to remedy this than by killing one's rivals?

The first victim of this return to tradition was Yaroslav's eldest son, Izyaslav, grand prince of Kiev, to whom his juniors owed respect as one owes respect—the wise Yaroslav had insisted—"to a father." Having briefly supported the normal order of succession, Yaroslav's second son decided to cut in and oust his elder brother from power. In 1073—after a long period of peace between the brothers resulting from the external wars necessary to defend their states against the ambitions of foreign tribes—Svyatoslav, prince of Chernigov, embarked on a campaign against his brother and, sword in hand, conquered Kiev. That he failed to kill Izyaslav was due more to chance than to fraternal clemency. But the fortunate survivor was to last for some time. The dethroned prince fled to the court of the Holy Roman emperor, Henry IV, though the latter could scarcely help him regain his throne. From 1073 to 1113, a long period of struggles between brothers and nephews ravaged the inheritance of Yaroslav the Great. But something new was happening: every now and again, the rival brothers, thinking of the price of these internal wars, revived the idea of discussing their disputes together. Then they would meet in small peace conferences, in an attempt to find a solution and survive these rivalries that could only lead to their annihilation. They grasped confusedly that no one would emerge unharmed from the continuous slaughter unless they could come up with some new system based on common agreement—in other words, an accepted sharing of power.

Unfortunately this realization—and the periodic meetings show that no one was satisfied any longer with the barbaric system still in existence—was short-lived. No sooner had a meeting finished than the first brother to set a trap would get rid of his immediate rival, or the one who barred his way to the more important principalities. When the last of Yaroslav's sons had been exterminated in these internal wars, it was the turn of his nephews, whose behavior was scarcely more pacific. In 1097, Yaroslav's heirs held another meeting, at Lubich in Volhynia, for the purpose of taking an oath to live in peace and to avoid resorting to bloodshed to settle a dispute. Scarcely had the oath been taken when one of the parties to it, Prince David, decided to get rid of one of his cousins, a grandson of Yaroslav the Wise called Vasilko, and replace him with the grand prince reigning at that time in Kiev, Svyatopolk II, son of Izyaslav. David told the latter that Vasilko intended to seize Kiev by treachery. The boyars and priests begged the grand prince to act with clemency. Remembering his recent oath and reluctant to revive the incessant bloodshed, he refused to intervene. Nevertheless, he allowed David to act, even though the results were predictable. The crime that was committed revealed how flimsy was the reconciliation between the members of this second House of Atreus. David seized his cousin, using unusual violence, and had him dragged to a deserted house where four stout fellows held him down by sitting on a board on his chest while one tore out his eyes and half-killed him.

The story goes that David then had this unfortunate prince brought to his territories, blind and dying, so that he could finish him off at leisure. The prince, coming round from the unconsciousness caused by pain and loss of blood, realized that his butchers had, as well as everything else, torn off his bloody shirt. Before dying he is supposed to have said, "I would have wished to have appeared before eternal God in that shirt of suffering."

Shocked by this crime, the other princes decided to deprive the murderer of the fruits of his victory by uniting against him. The latter, however, followed the usual practice of calling on the help of outsiders, first the Poles and then the Hungarians. Another twist was added to the infernal spiral of fratricide and war, whether civil or external, increasing with each turn the weakness of Kiev. The princes felt this decline deeply, even if they themselves hastened it by their rivalries. Thus it was that, while still undecided between hostility and the desire for agreement, they met once again in 1100, on the left bank of the Dnieper, to attempt to find a peaceful settlement to their accumulated disputes. From this meeting was to emerge the remarkable figure of the last "wise" ruler of Kiev, Vladimir Monomakh.

The Last Flowering of a Power in Decline

Vladimir, called Monomakh, ascended the throne of Kiev in unusual circumstances. To start with, the throne should not have come to him. His father, Svyatopolk, had held it until 1113 and, although he had linked Vladimir with his reign, according to the rules of succession the throne ought to have reverted to the sons of his uncles, older than his own father. Respectful of the national law, Vladimir made way for his cousins; and it took all the persuasion of the people of Kiev, much attached to this prince whose virtues they knew at first hand, to make him agree finally to infringe the rules of succession. This popular pressure in support of a prince was evidence of a change in society. From time to time, of course, the people had become involved in the power struggles but, generally, it was after a period of terrible killing, when each of the rivals was looking for support from sections of society. The inhabitants of Kiev would then try to ensure the victory of the prince who seemed to them to be most attentive to the troubles of the people. In 1113, things were different: the princes were not at war with one another and it was within Kiev itself that problems unrelated to rivalries over succession forced a rapid solution.

The town was in the throes of a social crisis. Certain members of the propertied class were deeply in debt, and they turned their wrath on the Jews, the traditional moneylenders whose commercial and fiscal role had greatly increased and who were determined to recover their debts. Symbols of the new distribution of wealth, the Jews were ideal targets for the people's anger. Subjected to massacre and pillage, after Vladimir's accession they were, in addition, hunted out of the country, not to return for many centuries. By removing them from his lands, Vladimir believed, in fact, that he was showing great magnanimity: he sought to preserve their lives while at the same time curbing their economic power.

Spared family conflicts—his reign was peaceful in that respect—Vladimir Monomakh was not, on the other hand, immune from wars and threats from outside. He had to fight the Poles, the Hungarians and, above all, the nomadic Polovtsi who, like the Pechenegs before them, made repeated raids into his territory. Despite these wars, however, in twelve years of rule Vladimir Monomakh was able to restore to some extent the lost grandeur of Kiev. Imposing his authority on the princes endowed with privileges, he was for them the "father" that his predecessors had failed to be. Thanks to the wars, he was able to extend greatly the influence of the city. Finally, he continued the legislative work begun by the great Yaroslav, concerning himself particularly with matters of commerce and its financing, and laying down rules about the proper condition of slaves. To his sons he dedicated a remarkable testament, where he preached clemency and charitable deeds as the keys to eternal life: "Do not have either an innocent or a guilty man put to death, for nothing is more sacred than the life and the soul of a Christian." He advised his sons to be fathers to orphans and protectors to widows, and to respect knowledge. He also recommended the pursuit of learning: "Without ever having left his palace, my father could speak five languages: it is this that makes us admired by foreigners." Thus ran Vladimir's testament, and such was the grand prince of Kiev, and the ideal that he put before his children at the dawn of the twelfth century. Despite the crimes that punctuated its history, Rus had no reason to envy the France of Louis VI, who was waging war in an attempt to impose his authority on the barons of the Ile-de-France, or any other European state.

But this happy reign, when the greatness of Kiev seemed for a time to have been restored, was in fact to be its last chapter. In 1124, a tragic event occurred that was to symbolize the dark days to follow. An immense fire ravaged Kiev, destroying nearly six hundred churches and most of its buildings. The effect of this fire on the imagination of the ordinary people, quite apart from the damage it caused, can easily be imagined. Fire was the creation of the god Perun, outlawed from Kiev by Vladimir, but never wholly forgotten. Was it not a sign of the god's anger against those who had permanently infringed his laws? Was it not a warning of worse things to come, the price of all the murders committed in order to conquer power in Kiev? The confused anxiety of the people of Kiev was justified. The following year, Vladimir Monomakh died, and with his death came a new period of internal wars that were to lead to the destruction of Kiev.

Everything had, however, pointed to a peaceful settlement of the succession. Vladimir Monomakh did not have any brothers, so the throne naturally reverted to his eldest son. It seemed for once as if the division, and the inevitable disputes and betrayals that followed, could be avoided. But he had several sons and, in a short time, the brothers and nephews of his successor reverted to the old habits and called on neighboring countries to help them. The peaceful principles preached to his descendants by Vladimir Monomakh were quickly forgotten. The people of Kiev were once again offered the spectacle of burning towns, blindings, and torn-out tongues, as a result of the constantly renewed rivalries between all those who claimed to rule the city of Kiev, whose importance was in any case rapidly diminishing.

In the mid-twelfth century, one of Vladimir's grandsons, Yury Dolgoruky (George "Long-arm"), then prince of Suzdal, challenged his uncle then reigning in Kiev; since he came from the senior branch of the family, he declared that the succession should revert to him. Behind the clash of these two views of the succession—from brother to brother or from father to son—another clash was looming, between the forests of the northeast, from which had poured the Finnish tribes, and the southern steppes. Yury certainly aspired to the title of grand prince of Kiev, but he sought it for what it symbolized—the glorious past of the "mother of Russian cities"—and not to dominate it. In this last struggle for the conquest of a state in decline, each of the rivals turned to those tribes of mercenaries that had, since time immemorial, attacked Kiev and who were now only too glad to assist. Yury turned to the Polovtsi, against the Pechenegs and Turkic nomads who were allied with the grand prince of Kiev of the moment. Yury suffered a humiliating defeat and Kiev then saw a whole series of grand princes who passed the power around as if they could not wait to be rid of it.

Finally, in 1155, after yet more fighting, Yury obtained the longed-for title. It was to be a bitter victory. He was sixty-three years old, and he was as much exhausted by excesses of the flesh and of good living as by war. His battles to achieve power had caused rivers of blood to be shed, ruined his lands, and entrenched his enemies, the Polovtsi, more firmly than ever in the territory of Kiev. In the capital, once so prosperous, where everything suddenly pointed to its decline, the adventurers who had accompanied him on his march to power now had no hesitation in pillaging and terrorizing the inhabitants, carrying off their wives and daughters, and seizing their goods. Hated by his subjects, who had deposed him three times, Yury died in 1157 at the moment when public exasperation had reached a peak. He had scarcely breathed his last when the people of Kiev began to sack his palace and public buildings and to massacre his relations and supporters. For all that, Yury Dolgoruky was not a prince who deserves to be forgotten. He was a builder, raising towns that were to survive long after his day, and it was he, above all, who laid the foundations of the city of Moscow.

After him, Kiev was to know a confusing succession of ephemeral princes. Ousted one minute and then, in a nightmarish rhythm, returning to the throne from which they had recently been removed, all were incapable of pursuing a policy that would restore to Kiev any of its former glory. The coup de grâce was struck in 1169 by Andrei, prince of Bogoliubovo (Andrei Bogoliubsky), the ruler of Suzdal—once again, it was a power from the northeast that was to decide the fate of Rus—and son of Yury Dolgoruky. Eager, like his father, to acquire the title of grand prince of Kiev—all that now remained of the city's old splendor—he established himself as head of a confederation of princes that he then launched into an attack on the town of St. Vladimir. The captured town was subjected to unbridled pillaging, sparing neither the palaces, churches, and libraries, nor the people who inhabited them.

The attack on Kiev and the brutalities that followed should not, for all that, blind us to Andrei's achievements in a Russia seeking stability and political progress. In many ways, the prince of Suzdal was a man before his time, with a very clear understanding of Russia's political needs. Early on, he realized that its future was moving away from the banks of the Dnieper and, although his military successes would have allowed him to reclaim power in Kiev, he had chosen to be a northern prince. In making this choice he was, moreover, embarking on a new concept of power. The inhabitants of Suzdal elected him as their prince, but he was unwilling to be dependent on their assemblies (*veche*). He aspired to create his own power base, thus allowing himself to design its form. This was the origin of the town of Vladimir and its temporal and spiritual powers, which at the same time deprived Kiev of its primacy. Most important, he opposed the system of privileges and refused any share to his brothers and nephews; ignoring his father's last words, he even expelled his brothers from his land: unity was triumphant. He also broke with the principle of the *druzhina;* his boyars were no longer companions, but subjects who owed him obedience. Finally, he allied himself with the clergy, depending on the church to legitimize the unifying, centralizing, and total authority that he sought to incarnate. The result hardly comes as a surprise. Andrei was too much in advance of his age to make a success of this concept of a centralized state. He was overtaken by his time: his angry boyars assassinated him in 1174 in his palace at Bogoliubovo. For them, Andrei was a tyrant: they did not recognize in him the statesman of times to come and so they hastened to overthrow him in order to restore the rule of shared power.

For Kiev, the period of Andrei's rule was a tragedy. This city, the cradle of Christianity in Russia, had known many enemy attacks. But now a glorious history was to end in defeat and destruction by Christian princes, descendants of Vladimir. It was also the triumph of the forest over the steppes, and of different routes of communication. The victorious princes preferred the north, Suzdal with its increasing importance and then Vladimir which had become the new capital on the devastated banks of the Dnieper. In the face of this decline, the nomadic hordes, which Kiev had hitherto managed to hold off, did not rest until they had got hold of all that remained of Kiev's former riches. The area around the Dnieper now appeared inhospitable and insecure, and all those with an eye to the future were now looking toward the Volga basin, a world of protecting forests. In 1240, when the Mongols descended on Kiev to finish it off and ravage the surrounding region, they did not find the onetime center of Russian Christianity or any trace of its glory. The city had not developed: three centuries of fratricidal wars, when assassination had been the surest route to gaining or retaining power, had defeated its glory.

Weakened by the constant warring of the princes and the opportunities this offered to neighboring tribes, Kiev did not escape religious crisis. In 1147, the election of a Russian metropolitan, the monk Clement, independent of the rules and authority of the Byzantine Church, provoked a schism that, after a few years of uncertainty, the wise holder of this contested title brought to an end—by voluntarily resigning and retiring to a monastery—in the interests of unity in the church. But it was symbolic of the decline of Kiev that the first schism in Russia should emerge here, in the very heart of Christian Russia.

The Fall of Kiev

In its time, Kiev had been a wonder of civilization. In those glorious centuries, the state of Kiev was in no way inferior to the states that were emerging at the same period in the West. In many respects it was more civilized than some of them. This flourishing state dominated a vast area, covered with prosperous towns, and controlled important communication routes. Unlike other European centers, however, Kiev practiced slavery, which played a considerable part in its exports. Commerce and agriculture were the twin pillars of its wealth, and explain how it was that this state was able to exercise its authority over such a large population, thought to number some seven or even eight million inhabitants. It had a strict social structure, headed by the prince and those who served him—his *druzhina*—dominating the nobility (the boyars), the burghers, a large peasantry, and, at the very bottom of the ladder, the slaves. Finally, well-established institutions, from the prince to the boyars' Duma and the *veche,* or town council, allowed a measure of democracy to temper the power of the prince. The development of this social and political organization had favored the remarkable cultural flowering of Kiev. Anna of Russia, when she arrived at the court of France, was astonished to find neither books nor scholars as were common in her country.

Thus established, Kiev seemed, until the twelfth century, set fair for a long period of glory. It was not to be. The final disaster had long been brewing—the result of two weaknesses that had dominated the state of Kiev throughout its history.

The first was the repeated incursions of the nomads from the steppes, a foretaste of the last and most fatal invasion, that of the Mongols (or Tartars, as some prefer to call them). Long before the Mongols reached the first Russian state, the peoples of the steppes had been a constant threat to its safety. The history of Kiev is first and foremost the history of the permanent battle to repel in turn the Khazars, the Pechenegs, and the Polovtsi, to mention only the largest groups. The princes of Kiev had to devote a considerable part of their energies to the fight against these successive waves of invaders. Though their courage was immense, it did nothing to further internal political progress or social cohesion. The external pressures were intolerable for this society, and as the centuries passed the temptation to take refuge in the north, among the less exposed forest lands, became increasingly strong.

The second of Kiev's weaknesses, it cannot be repeated too often, resided in the feudal system of clans, whereby the state had to be shared between brothers in the form of privileges, whose unequal value and status turned the brothers into merciless rivals. The preeminent status of Kiev and the theoretical lordship of the prince of Kiev were the indispensable sources of a national unity that overrode this division into privileges. But this symbol of unity was constantly being challenged by the division of principalities and weakened by the instability of power in the families that ruled over them. The system whereby the brothers were moved on at each change in the succession, a kind of game of musical chairs, meant that neither could they become attached to their principalities nor could the people become attached to a prince and a dynasty, which were constantly changing. Feelings of dependence and vassalage toward the eldest brother could never become established in the princes, when from one moment to the next they themselves could be substituted for him. The stability of the father-son relationship was always lacking in the old Russia, thus giving rise to the ambitions of the brothers.

It is remarkable that, out of this unstable and threatening world, some exceptional personalities emerged who, for a brief space, were able to push back the tradition of division and murder and establish a period of unity and peace. Vladimir after his conversion, Yaroslav the Great, Vladimir Monomakh, and, finally and in a different way, Andrei Bogoliubsky were figures who began to represent a national unity. With these rulers, a combination of the tradition of peace and humanity of Christianity and the strong national and unifying tradition of the Byzantine world appeared to relegate to a pre-Christian past the merciless world of the clans. They represented a definite political progress, but only a temporary one. If they failed to pass on their concept of power, it was because at the moment power was transmitted they always reverted to the old system of privileges, which annulled the newly gained national unity and was eventually to kill it altogether. These exceptional men, in this turbulent history, are an expression of the double tension that bore down on Kiev: the old tradition of a society where power is a family, or rather clan, affair; and the future tradition, the path demonstrated by the Byzantine Empire, where the state imposed itself on different interests and the holder of power symbolized the unity and interests of the whole nation. If the grand princes, from Vladimir to Andrei, incarnated this tension rather than allowing the transition from one tradition to the next, if they failed to complete the work they realized was necessary, they did at least show the way for those who were to follow. After the dark period of the Mongol domination, the princes of Moscow, taking up the torch from Kiev, were to find their inspiration in the lessons of their distant predecessors, finally bringing unity to triumph over division. But just as division had resulted in an entrenched pattern of political murder, so the march toward unity was to bring a similar use of murder in its train.

2
The Renaissance of Russia

♦

In 1480 the grand prince of Moscow, Ivan III, later called "the Great," declared the end of the Tartar domination. Exhausted by their incursions, the conquerors who had oppressed and laid waste to Russia since the middle of the thirteenth century were unable to oppose this desire for freedom. By the end of the fifteenth century, which marks the fall of the Golden Horde, the primacy of Moscow in the Russian world was clear to all. This was a political primacy, for it was Moscow that was providing the focus for the "gathering of the territories" of Russia. To reach this goal, the princes who ruled there had been able to take advantage of both the disastrous system of privileges and the presence of the Tartars. Because the division and redivision into privileges weakened the principalities, Moscow could progressively absorb the weakest of them. As long as the Tartars were powerful, Moscow had bowed to their authority to obtain, in exchange, the recognition of a de facto primacy over the other Russian principalities. When the Tartars faltered, Moscow was able to confirm its primacy by holding aloft the banner of revolt.

The Third Rome

But the church, too, occupied an important place in this change in political balance. From the beginning of the fourteenth century, Moscow had been the seat of a metropolitan; that is, it became the capital of Christian Russia, previously in Vladimir. For the Russian people, dominated by a foreign conqueror who was hostile to their religion, Christianity offered, in the times of oppression, an important symbol of identity. The monasteries that had grown up in the north of the country became places of refuge for a terrified population and the only guardians of a national culture. The Monastery of the Miracles in the Kremlin and the Monastery of the Holy Trinity, situated in the forest outside Moscow, both founded by Sergius of Radonezh, were to give the Russians a firm religious and national focus. It was no coincidence that during this same period the Russian peasant began to use a term, never to be abandoned, to identify himself—krestianin, practically the same as the word for Christian, *khristianin.*

These monasteries, which were increasing in number, not only provided a cultural focus and consolation for a desperate people, but they were also a rallying point. Sergius of Radonezh was not content just to pray for those fighting the Tartars, but he also put the resources of the monastery at the disposal of the soldiers. In addition, he sent two monks to enroll the troops who, under the leadership of Dmitri Donskoy, were to be victorious in the decisive battle against the Tartars at Kulikovo in 1380. The links between the church and a nation broken by the invader and seeking an identity were being indestructibly forged.

The problems of the Byzantine Empire in the fifteenth century were to confer an immeasurable prestige on this church, and Moscow also benefited. The failure of the union of churches, attempted in Florence in 1439, confirmed the existence and the importance, outside the Roman world, of the Eastern Church. The fall of the Byzantine Empire in 1453, to the armies of Mehmet II, resulted in the transference of all the authority of the "Second Rome" to Moscow, which now became the center of eastern Christianity. The Christian tsar was now no longer the Byzantine emperor; this role now fell to the ruler of Moscow, whose power was growing ever greater. Ivan III put the seal on this in 1472, shortly before challenging the Tartars, by marrying Sophia Palaeologa, niece of the last Byzantine emperor, Constantine Palaeologus. Through this marriage a subtle link was established between the "mother of the Eastern churches," which had for so long dazzled the Christian world, and Moscow, which was promoted by external circumstances as well as by the progress in its national church to the rank of "Third Rome." Everything confirmed the constant historical and cultural progress that made Moscow—despite the disasters resulting from the long period of subjugation to the Tartars—a state that was no stranger to the civilization of the rest of Europe. One has only to think, in the religious field, of the towering figure of Sergius of Radonezh, who was to become one of the most revered saints of Russia and who recalls, more than any other, St. Francis of Assisi.

But one obstacle still lay between Muscovy and political development: power. Although freed from the Tartar yoke, it had not yet attained a national dimension. The old disputes over the succession, the result of the feudal system and the distribution of privileges, acted for a long time as a curb on the authority of the grand princes of Moscow.

Ivan III is a case in point. His father had divided up his possessions among his five sons. Aware, however, of the destructiveness of this system, he had at the same time attempted to neutralize it by asserting the preeminence of the grand prince over the others and instituting the system of direct descent. In order to do this, during his lifetime he had shared his power with his eldest son, Ivan. Thus Ivan III represented two contradictory systems of authority and succession. In this ambiguous situation he both followed and rejected tradition. He removed his rivals but showed a desire to develop a system of lineal descent. On the death of his brother Yury, far from sharing his privilege, he seized it, ignoring the recriminations of his brothers. He then threw another brother into prison where ill-treatment rapidly led to his demise. Ivan once again added to his territory. A third brother met the same fate and eventually Ivan held all of his father's possessions in his own hands. As he advanced, he would make abject confession to the church of his cruel behavior, presenting himself in tears before the metropolitan and bishops begging to expiate his unbrotherly deeds. Having listened to their exhortations to charity, and finding peace of mind in absolution, he would hurry off to acquire more lands.

In fact, it was not only on his brothers that Ivan mercilessly inflicted his power over life and death. He enjoyed the sufferings of his enemies, and would command them to be brought before him for his diversion. Anyone, however important, who resisted his commands would immediately be tortured. Thus he had an archi-mandrite publicly flogged, his son's advisers mutilated, and two conspirators burned alive in a cage. The church, which supported him, did little to soften his behavior. But his political vision was clear: striking a balance between the concessions imposed on him by the attitudes of the time and the demands of future unity, he cleverly arranged his succession. He distributed privileges to his children, but privileges that had in fact lost their meaning. Revert-ing to his father's desires, he confirmed that the eldest son was the natural successor to the father, and his heirs after him. The endowed princes, to whom the rule of inheritance also applied with regard to their privileges, also had to submit to the grand prince and could command neither their own finances nor diplomacy. Their indepen-dence was at an end.

Ivan III in many ways resembled his French contemporary Louis XI, who, like him, had brought the fight against feudalism into the very heart of his family. Louis had put an end to the attacks of the English, as Ivan had done with the Tartar domination, and he had tried to adjust the laws to the new order, as Ivan had done in his code *(Ulozhenie)* of 1497. Similar in temperament and ambition, both men served the greatness of their countries by showing them-selves pitiless in the face of those who got in their way. But in Russia, the question of the succession was still not settled legally, despite the compromise solutions adopted. A new period of murder and intrigue was to be required to settle the matter. It was another Ivan, called "the Terrible," who in the sixteenth century was to complete the work of his predecessors in a wave of blood and terror.

The Renaissance: Russia and Europe

The sixteenth century in Europe was, above all, the century of the Renaissance, of humanism and a more secular world. The word "Renaissance" first evokes the cultural miracle of western Europe, the splendor of Italy, and the grandeur of the French kings. Never-theless, even in this privileged part of Europe that had not been deprived of its national history for almost three centuries by a conquering power, the Renaissance was anything but peaceful. The sixteenth century was as bloody as any, as soon as power was threatened. It is interesting to compare western Europe with the political situation of Russia, devastated at the moment of a revival of national life when its natural genius had begun to unfold.

In early sixteenth-century Italy, heartland of the Renaissance, the list of those who stained their hands with the blood of their relatives is endless, even if their exploits are more legendary than real. Cesare Borgia, Machiavelli's "Prince," can be taken as representative of an age when the art of assassination triumphed, assuring the reputation through the centuries of some of the most accomplished murderers in history. Whether a Borgia, Sforza, or Medici, the Italian princes did not only show an exceptional disregard for the life of others, but certain of their crimes, provoked by passion, were committed in places of worship, even though the medieval church had made strenuous efforts to moderate men's behavior and exercise some control over political violence. In fact, a church was the most convenient place, at that period, to commit a criminal act. There, the victim was confined and unarmed, open to murder. The age of humanism was also the age of murderers.

Outside Italy the religious wars had consequences that were every bit as bloody as the personal rivalries between the Italian princes. Curiously, the record for political murder was held then by England and France, followed by Spanish Flanders, while the German-speaking world seems to have been preserved from this homicidal fury; it would not be many centuries, however, before the balance was redressed. In these troubled times, murder was a matter, first and foremost, for the state and for the ruler of the state who affirmed his absolute right to suppress any hostile behavior, generally called treason.

Henry VIII and Elizabeth I carried out many executions—often little more than murders—of those whom they accused of betraying them, from Sir Thomas More, beheaded in 1535, to Mary Stuart who met the same fate in 1587. In France the kings were more inclined to have their enemies killed on a charge, or pretext, of heresy (for example, Etienne Dolet in 1546, Admiral Coligny in 1572), but also for treason (the Duke and Cardinal de Guise in 1588 at Blois). Fate took its revenge and sometimes they themselves were assassinated by fanatics, as in the case of Henry III, who was murdered in 1589 by the monk Clement, a deed that anticipated the murder of Henry IV at the beginning of the following century.

An important characteristic of this period of murders is that not only were the holders of power not spared, but the right to kill a sovereign was not the privilege of other sovereigns only or the result of rival claims to the succession. It came about often as a result of a decision of the people about the inviolability of God's elect. Until then, the church had guaranteed the legitimacy of royal power and, consequently, its security. In the sixteenth century, it was in the name of faith itself that believers debated their right to depose a sovereign if they saw him as a traitor to the true church. The idea of treason, which justified the murder of an enemy by the sovereign, justified in turn the murder of the sovereign himself. In the first instance, the victim, having set himself against royal power, is accused of opposing the divine nature of this power. In the second, the sovereign is seen as a traitor to his own divine nature who, thereby losing all legitimacy, may be removed. The sixteenth century was a time when power and religion continued to be merged, but where religion no longer provided power with an absolute protection. The right of criticism, emerging in the Reformation, had a revolutionary effect on the very idea of power.

Thus it is not surprising that the sixteenth century was marked by a debate on the difficult matter of tyrannicide. Should the tyrant be shielded from the fury of the just? The French Protestants devoted much attention to this theme, which gave rise to a whole school of thought, that of the *Monarchomaques*. For them, a prince who betrayed the divine law had been abandoned by God and therefore could be handed over to man's laws. In *Vindiciae contra tyrannos,* published in France in 1579 under the pseudonym of Junius Brutus, the author, without going so far as to justify violence against the tyrant, gives such a vivid picture of power that the conclusion is clear: the best part of society—officers and leaders in the provinces and municipalities—have the right to rebel. In England, George Buchanan raised the same question in a book so scandalous that Parliament had it burned: *De jure regni apud Scotos*. For his part, the Jesuit Juan de Marina, whose teaching was famous all over Europe, went so far as to wonder about the proper use of poison in such circumstances. If no one actually stated clearly that it is a duty, or a right at least, to kill a tyrant, they all raised the two questions: can society judge a tyrant? and what is the difference between a legitimate tyrant and an impostor? They concluded that the latter should be systematically and by whatever means removed.

This "desanctification" of the person of the sovereign, now forced to submit to the critical eye of his subjects, is characteristic of European development in the sixteenth century. It coincided with a certain weakening of the power of the church. Divided in itself by the great debates resulting from the ideas of Calvin and Luther and too closely involved or used in political struggles, the church was no longer the absolute guarantor of the nature of royalty that it had once represented. And the kings no longer always left it to the church to guarantee their right.

This evolution diverged widely from the development of the idea of monarchy then prevailing in Russia during the period between the defeat of the Mongols and the reign of Ivan IV, where power continued to be closely linked with the church.

Power and the Third Rome

At the end of the fifteenth century, the church, which had played such an active role in the period of oppression and the struggle for freedom, was to undergo a profound change that would leave a permanent mark on the national culture of Russia.

The Russia of this period appears at first sight to be characterized by ever-increasing spirituality. The monasteries, whose importance in the previous century we have seen, continued to multiply. They had great prestige; at the time of the political division resulting from the quarrels over inheritance and the Mongol occupation, they were the places where national feeling could find reasons and symbols for survival. This national function encouraged the princes early on to go beyond the limited horizons of their privileges and obtain endorsement from the monasteries. They made frequent pilgrimages, seeking the advice—and the blessing—of the most famous monks before making any important decision. The prince of Moscow, especially, saw the authority of the monastic world as a way of reinforcing his power. In his attempt to unite the divided world of the rival principalities, he embodied the desire for unity and nationhood that was expressed by the Russian monarchy. It was the church and especially the important monasteries that conferred this legitimacy, allowing the prince of Moscow to use any means to impose his authority on the other princes, for the church saw the reconciliation of the concepts of God and Caesar in the person of the sovereign.

The chief theoretician of princely legitimacy at the beginning of the sixteenth century was a monk, the founder and superior (*Igumen*) of the great monastery of Volokolamsk. Joseph of Volotsk played a central role in defining the relationship between the church and power, which was to enable the latter to depend on the support of the former. He spoke up with passion, against that other great monastic figure of the day, Nil Sorsky, for the monastic communities, on which he imposed a strict discipline, saying that they should exist alongside the state—not cut off from the world—in the service of all. Joseph had an acute understanding of the new political and social realities of his time, and saw the necessity for the church to retain its authority in the face of a growing state. He realized that to ensure its independence the church needed economic power. Central to his reasoning was the acceptance of the fact that the developing state would have only a partial need in future for the church, and that this need was decreasing. It had got rid of the Mongols, and its legitimacy was established. All this had been attained with the help of the church, but the stage when this support had been needed was now coming to an end. Joseph the visionary was obsessed with the need to preserve the church's function as a partner in the state with the sovereign. Thus he argued tirelessly for the necessity of wealth, against the idea of monastic poverty put forward by Nil Sorsky.

This debate between the supporters and adversaries of ecclesiastical wealth was not only a religious debate over two opposing views of the monastic life. It was a fundamentally political question, involving the balance of relations between church and state. Aware of the deep significance of this question, Ivan III was inclined to support the view of those who renounced worldly goods, which would allow him to take over the property thus abandoned and bring a dispossessed church under his control. But it was to be Joseph's ideas that triumphed, because they sprang from the popular confidence in a church that had for so long been identified with the nation, and because the two advocates of poverty, Ivan III and Nil Sorsky, died at almost the same time (1505 and 1508). Joseph's rigorous ideas and organization prevailed, leaving their mark not only on monastic life, but also on power and society as a whole.

Joseph preached an absolute rigor in life, even to its external aspects, with a constant discipline of the body and soul in order to achieve internal rigor, if not perfection. The central and administrative authority of the *Igumen* was imposed on all. Under his patronage the monasteries became the very models of political government. But the important thing is that this model was then applied to the state. Strengthened by their continued economic independence, Joseph, and then his successors after his death in 1515, exerted their influence on the idea of the state to which the monastic system of organization was to be extended. Muscovite Russia, in their opinion, was a religious community over which the prince ruled as *Igumen.* Thus invested with religious authority, the sovereign benefited in the eyes of the people from the authority of the monastic world whose mission and teaching he appeared to be continuing. The barriers between state and monastery, society and religious community, were becoming blurred; and the principles of discipline and central authority imposed in the name of a divine plan going beyond the temporal underlay the relations between society and the state. Obedience to the prince and acceptance of his authority was, in the last analysis, to obey God and accept His will. Sixteenth-century Russia had become a giant monastery. And, in return, the monasteries were used to shut up those who infringed the rules common to God and the sovereign, which Joseph's theory had allowed to be confused. It is scarcely surprising, in this transformation of power and of society, that the prince, relying on the monasteries, got into the habit of handing over to them all those—unsuitable wives, rebellious sons, rivals, declared enemies—of whom he wished to be rid, whether or not innocent of any crime.

At the same time that the influence of the doctrine of Joseph of Volotsk was thus showing itself, the inheritance of his adversary, Nil Sorsky, and beyond that the deeply rooted spiritual inheritance of Sergius of Radonezh, made themselves equally felt in the consciousness of society and in religious life.

This period was to see the development of two extreme forms of spirituality, the effect of which on Russian culture was to be far-reaching. The "holy fools" *(iurodivie)* are inseparable from the religious—and not only religious—history of Russia. Their logic was derived from St. Paul who, in the First Epistle to the Corinthians (4 : 10), proclaimed, "We are fools for Christ's sake." The holy fool rejected the reason of the world in the name of Christian truth and found refuge, in order to resolve the contradiction, behind a mask of madness. But he was not mad, and Russian Christianity took this strange species to be men of God *(Bozhie liudi)* and martyrs in the cause of righteousness. These holy fools offered themselves in sacrifice, fighting evil fearlessly and everywhere, with a desire to save the sinner by the gift of themselves to this hopeless cause. No one was exempt from their plans, whether bandit or revered sovereign. The popular veneration for these holy fools was confirmed by the church, which canonized a number of them over the centuries, while places of pilgrimage marked their eternal wanderings in the service of God. To this chapter in the spirituality of the time, which was to become part of the collective memory, there should be added the contemplative ascetics who practiced total immobility, such as Ilya Muromets, who is supposed to have sat praying on a pillar for thirty years without moving.

Thus there gradually developed, in a Russia already impregnated with religion, a collective consciousness that combined the authoritarian and organizing vision of the Josephite tradition, the individualistic ascetic teaching of Nil Sorsky, and finally, the sacrificial message of the holy fools and the contemplatives. For those princes of Moscow who lacked experience in the matter of political organization—they had inherited a firm tradition of the struggle to seize power, but had little to fall back on when it came to giving it a structure—the church was able to offer reassuring solutions, tried and tested by the monastic world and readily accepted by the people.

The popular consciousness was able to simplify the task of the political authorities, in that the habit of submission was already established, strengthened by experience and reinforced by the church. Its ideal models were the first national saints that the church had given it to revere: the two young princes who had been sacrificed long ago in the race for power—Boris and Gleb. These princes, it should be remembered, died without defending themselves, canonized because they symbolized expiatory victims, in the name of Christ and in imitation of His sacrifice. In Russian they were given the name *Strastoterptsi,* which means suffering the Passion. For had not Boris said as he died: "Lord Jesus Christ . . . , You accepted the Passion to wipe out our sins, help me to accept mine"? The cult of these two martyrs was the first to develop in Russia. For the popular faith, their example signified the sanctity of power and the necessity to submit to it as to God, but also the absolute value of sacrifice in imitation of Christ. M. Cherniavsky, author of an enthralling work on Russian myths, has stressed how the sanctification of Russian princes rapidly became a habit that had little to do with their personal merits, but gave an indisputable content to the developing national sentiment. Out of twelve princes of Moscow between the thirteenth and sixteenth centuries, seven were recognized as saints, adding to the list of those from Kiev that was already very long. As power moved toward Moscow, so saintliness took the same path. The church found its saints principally in the sphere of power and not among the people. Hence in the early sixteenth century, the holders of power looked constantly to the church, since it was the church that so strongly legitimized their authority by creating "saint-princes." Hence also the popular attitude to religion, full of humility, compassion, and submission to redeeming suffering, but submission also to an authority willed and guaranteed by God. Russian national consciousness was created at this period, around a collective memory whose traits constituted its essential elements.

This poses the question: did not the Tartars, dominating Russia for almost three centuries, leave any trace of themselves in this collective consciousness and in political attitudes? Pushkin gave a partial answer when he wrote: "The Tartars were very different from the Moors. They conquered Russia, but brought her neither algebra nor Aristotle." In other words, the cultural contribution of the Tartars was very small. Their raids contributed in all probability to the spread of the spirit of submission and the consoling idea of God. Christianity symbolized lost liberty, and a world less cruel than that of the invaders. The role played by the monasteries in the national renaissance and the cross that adorned the banners borne in the battles for the reconquest of Russia contributed to the development of the national consciousness around the idea of Christianity. If the Tartars did anything, it was to anchor Christianity firmly in the sentiment of national identity. Feelings of suspicion and insecurity toward anything coming from outside, brought in by foreigners, must also have figured in the legacy of those centuries of humiliation.

And what of the influence of the invaders on the political system? The Tartars had propagated the model of an authoritarian and centralizing state, a vehicle for a world ideology. Through their wars they sought to install an empire, extending their principles to all the conquered peoples: the supreme authority of the khan and a social order based on justice and equality. The Tartar state was not the first ideological state in history—Mohammed's empire had already opened the way. But though it may not have been the first to introduce a similar world view, it was certainly the most long-lasting. Without doubt it had an influence on the quarreling princes; for the "law of the khan" imposed on them the beginnings of unity. The khan pursued a policy of keeping a balance between rivals and appealing for cooperation—or even collaboration—from some of them. These the khan rewarded with promotion. As for the political model in its developed form, the later period was to reveal the influences of this time.

During the Renaissance there seemed to be little difference between a Russian and a French sovereign. At the beginning of the century, political struggles were resolved by bloodshed in all quarters of Europe. In time, though, as Russian power became stronger, it was to develop along its own lines. The Renaissance in Russia, the renaissance of an independent state, moved in a direction different from that of the rest of Europe. But if these different paths had anything in common, it was a scant respect, the moment power was threatened, for human life.

3
The Beginnings
of Tyranny

◆

The reign of Ivan IV, which lasted for half a century—1533 to 1584—was the longest and the most decisive in the entire history of Russia. It brought to fruition all the changes that his predecessors had attempted or encouraged, and gave Russian power a finished form and its own particular identity that are still detectable four centuries later.

Ivan's succession to the throne was revealing of the new political situation in Russia and its inherent tensions. The struggle of central power against the centrifugal forces of the endowed princes had changed in character. The principalities that had for so long opposed Moscow, like the republics of Novgorod, Pskov, and Vyatka in the north, had lost their independence. The ceaseless activities of the grand princes of Moscow were responsible for this development and by now all the neighboring states had come under Moscow's authority. While internal wars had almost ceased, it was now the turn of foreign wars, and the greater part of the sixteenth century was to be taken up with ridding Russia once and for all of threats from outside—the Lithuanians, Tartars, Swedes, and the Livonian Knights of the Sword. Now deprived of their independence, the princes who formerly had ruined any attempt at unity began to look inward, to the central power in Muscovy.

Although the grand princes' desire for unity rendered the petty princes impotent, they did not for all that disappear. The force of arms and of money had got the better of their power, but not of their existence. They were forced to come to the court of the grand prince, in the service of Moscow. Unification had been achieved by the integration of all the opposing princes, but they were not at all inclined to accept the new order of things. Clinging to their ambitions and rivalries, they merely transferred them to Moscow, where the court became a microcosm of the old world of hate and intrigue. The princes who had been so proud of their descent from Rurik—Belsky, Shuisky, Kurbsky—and those who no less proudly claimed a connection with the Lithuanian ruler Gediminas, or the Tartar princes who had become Christian and been integrated into Russia, were now reduced to the rank of mere boyars of the grand prince of Moscow, equal in rank to the old boyars. Their position was imposing, but scarcely enviable, for they were deprived of any political choice. When the lands of Russia were divided, they had been able to decide whom to serve, or what principality to support. By the beginning of the sixteenth century, the only states that existed were those of the grand prince of Moscow, leaving them little choice but to submit to him. The only alternative now lay outside Russia, with the foreign kings, traditional enemies of the Russian people. Changes in alliance or service, so common in the past when adversaries in internal struggle relied on help from neighboring states, were to take on a very different meaning in the face of a Russian state. Now, to serve another court meant to serve the foreigner, the enemy—in other words, to betray. The notion of treason, once so vague, when legitimate power changed hands so frequently, acquired a precise meaning. To move away from the grand prince or to oppose him was not only to betray him, but also to betray the Russian cause. This new definition of treason was to have considerable consequences for the behavior of the sovereign.

Once again, the evolution of the preceding centuries can be detected in the vocabulary. The verb *izmenit'*, which meant "to change," gave rise to the noun *izmenik*, which means nothing less than "traitor." Of all the neighboring states, only one was now open to those who refused to accept centralization: this was Lithuania which, embracing Polish provinces to the west and Russian provinces to the east, was difficult to disentangle from the Muscovite possessions. The eternal problem of nonexistent natural frontiers and unstable political boundaries explains why Lithuania was able to exercise a dangerous attraction on all those who rejected the growing authority of Moscow. The prince of Moscow, whose elite was being drawn away, was well aware of the threat to his states posed by Lithuania. A pitiless struggle between Russia and

Lithuania was inevitable, since the uncertain division of lands and peoples could not last and would have to be resolved by the total defeat of one or the other country.

The internal struggles at the court of the grand prince thus arose both from the bitterness and hate born of lost independence and from the desire of the princes to block the growth of the autocratic power of Moscow in favor of their own power as princes. Unable to escape from their new master, the princes tried to create a position of strength where they would be peers and companions of the grand prince, instead of merely his subjects. The stakes in this battle were high. Just as formerly at the court of the Capetian kings, Charles VII, Louis XI, and Charles VIII had had to impose their authority on the princes who had taken over and fortified their lands of Burgundy or Orleans, so the grand prince of Moscow had to take on the whole of his family—brothers, cousins, uncles, and nephews. The latter, at the court in Moscow as formerly in their principalities, fought tooth and nail to defend their position. These battles and coalitions, products of an already outdated political order, continued to threaten the still-fragile edifice of the unified Russian state.

A Bloody Regency

It was to the throne of this unstable and troubled court that Ivan IV, grandson of Ivan III, was to succeed at the age of three. That he took the title of "grand prince" was already a challenge, for it upset the established order of succession, whereby the line descended from father to eldest son. This system had gradually managed to oust the destructive feudal system. Ivan III had married twice, his first wife being a princess of Tver, the second Sophia Palaeologa. He should have been succeeded by his eldest son, also Ivan, from his first marriage, and then by the latter's descendants, ignoring the younger branch, Sophia's children. At first, faithful to his desire to strengthen the monarchy as far as possible, Ivan III had his grandson Dmitri crowned grand prince in 1497 during his lifetime.

Dmitri was the son of Ivan III's eldest son, Ivan, who had died prematurely a few years earlier. Ivan's choice, made while he was still reigning, of a boy of only fifteen shows his concern to impose a regular succession and to prevent any dispute. But this was to be only a temporary choice, upset by the old ambitions of the dispossessed princes. To prevent his interfering or intriguing against this choice, Ivan's second son, Vasily, had first been thrown in prison by his father when he had chosen his grandson as heir. But, invoking his maternal Byzantine ancestors, Vasily managed to trick his father into turning against his heir-designate. Once again, the order of succession was upset. Ivan III removed the unfortunate Dmitri, stripping him of his possessions and throwing him into prison on some feeble pretext, along with his mother. Imprisonment at that time was tantamount to a death sentence. Dmitri did indeed die, in 1509, leaving the way open to Vasily, father of the future Ivan the Terrible.

On the death of Vasily, these dynastic quarrels were no longer relevant, since the senior line had disappeared. Eldest son of the reigning grand prince, Ivan had only one brother, which would limit disputes on this side. Nevertheless, Ivan's reign did not look very promising. A three-year-old prince, on the throne in a Russia that was forever trying to establish a system of stable and centralized power, represented a great temptation for those at court who fed on rancor and ambition. Ivan was probably crowned straightaway, but however splendid, the ceremony did not at that time have great importance. It symbolized power only when the figure wearing the crown was already himself powerful. The political system had certainly developed all the symbols of power, but it had not yet managed to suppress all those who opposed it. Power still depended on the relationship between him who incarnated the process of centralization and those who wished to obstruct it in order to revive their old territories. The balance of strength, in the year 1533, was unclear. Although the rule of succession whereby the eldest son inherited from the father seemed firmly established, the fact that it favored such a young child could not fail to revive the demands of those who favored the old system. When he died, Grand Prince Vasily was survived by two younger brothers: Yury, prince of Dmitrov, and Andrei, prince of Staritsa, either one of whom might have aspired to the throne. Not content with keeping them from the throne, Vasily had also deprived them of their power, thus preventing them from attempting to alter his decision by forcefully deposing his young heir.

A three-year-old grand prince meant that a regency was inevitable. Vasily had entrusted this task to his wife and to a council of seven tutors, all related in various degrees to Ivan, headed by the uncle of the princess-regent, Mikhail Glinsky. Vasily's own brothers were excluded. It was immediately apparent that such a solution, intended to balance or prevent opposing ambitions, was full of anomalies.

The choice of a female regent was the first anomaly. Both the people and the princes of Russia were used to seeing the wife of a sovereign ill-treated. For as long as she was able to please her husband, she stayed by his side, but wielded no power, leading a secluded life in the oriental manner in a part of the palace reserved for women, the *terem*. The sixteenth century was not like the time of Olga, when a woman of sufficient character could exercise authority. The Byzantine Empire and then the rule of the Tartars had left a profound mark on Russia, placing woman under the authority of man, reducing her to the dual role of comforter of the warrior and mother of his children. Thus, when they ceased to please, the princesses were sent into convents where they were shut up for life, losing their worldly names and forced to take vows. They were dead to the world long before their deaths.

Elena Glinskaya was able for a time to break this tradition. This young and beautiful princess came from a Lithuanian family. She was remarkable not only for her looks, but also for her firm character, her receptive mind, and her level of education. More westernized than was usual for Russian women at the time—things had changed since Anne of France had contrasted the flourishing culture of Russia with the boorishness of her new home!—Elena intended to use her powers as regent. Vasily may well have anticipated the ambition shown by this remarkable woman in the performance of her task, but it came as a shock to the other members of the advisory council. For them, a woman should be silent and obey. They had assumed that her son would be no more than the pawn in their ambitions, and probably their victim.

The ruptures and clashes to come were immediately apparent in this premature accession. On one side was the princess-regent, determined to have her authority respected and to protect her son's rights. On the other were the guardians, united in their desire to remove the regent and each separately determined to further his own interests as much as possible, perhaps even aspiring to power. Set apart from the central group were Vasily's two brothers, who could not accept being thus excluded from the magic circle of power when it seemed likely to change hands. Finally, on the edge of things, stood the boyars, aware that the instability of the situation might allow them to regain some authority, anxiously trying to decide which camp to support in order to be on the winning side. In addition, further away were the foreign enemies, the kings of Poland and Lithuania, the Swedes, and even the Tartars who were still occupying the Crimea and Kazan and who anticipated that these disputes might favor their territorial ambitions or, in the case of the Tartars, their dreams of revenge.

Once again, in 1533, Russia had successfully overcome the hurdle of succession by direct line, but only rarely had the immediate succession of a deceased sovereign been so full of menace for the future. These threats were to stain the childhood of the young grand prince with violence and blood that may well have left an indelible mark on his character.

The first five years of Ivan's reign were dominated by Elena's regency. She quickly showed considerable authority, making it clear that she would not tolerate any trespassing on her prerogatives. Closer in many ways to the refined manners of the European Renaissance than to those of her compatriots, this woman nevertheless had no hesitation in resorting to the cruelest devices known in Russia to eliminate her enemies. The first to declare himself was of course her brother-in-law, Prince Yury of Dmitrov. His elder brother Vasily had sought, by condemning him to enforced celibacy, to eliminate any other branch of the family other than his own, without resorting to actual murder. In addition to this grievance, the accession of the three-year-old aroused both Prince Yury's rancor and his hopes. He set about substituting his own authority, for a time at least, for that of the powerless grand prince. He called together all the boyars to persuade them to acknowledge his right to the throne and support him in his attempt to seize it. But they, aware that he had no other support than his closest servants, ignored his call. The only person to pay any attention to this failed coup d'état was the regent. Without delay she sent soldiers to seize him and throw him into prison, where he died a lingering death within two years.

This plot was rapidly unmasked by Elena, her brother-in-law having overestimated his prestige and his strength. The next plot was to come from within her own family. Her uncle, Mikhail Glinsky, the most prominent in the council of governors, had thought that he could play the part of true regent, instead of a woman who, in his eyes, because of her sex, had no right to any power whatsoever. Elena, supported by one of the members of the council (who was in all probability also her lover) strongly challenged this assumption, instead affirming her authority ever more firmly. Conflict broke out between niece and uncle, encouraged by the boyars who hoped to recover some of their influence during this regency.

Accused of abuse of power and debauchery, Elena resorted to the habitual method of resolving disputes: she took the initiative. On her orders, Prince Glinsky's eyes were put out and he was thrown into a monastery where he died not long afterwards. At the same time, Helen removed most of the governing council, using the accusation of treason to get rid of those who stood between her and total power.

But she was constantly haunted by the knowledge that another of her husband's brothers, Prince Andrei, was still living in his lands in Staritsa, and that to make matters worse, he now had a son, Vladimir, who was thus in the same line of succession as her own children. To deal with him, she invited him to come to Moscow to discuss matters of state. This pretext did not impress the prince. He was aware that the growing unpopularity of his sister-in-law meant that the boyars, terrified by the rigorous methods used by Elena and her favorite, were beginning to look to him, as was a people made desperate by the increasing difficulties of everyday life and the spectacle of renewed bloodletting in high places. The idea of inheritance from one brother to another was still sufficiently embedded in the mind of the people for it to seem a possibility. It was further reinforced by the ferocious methods adopted by Elena in settling accounts. Although of a peaceful nature—even rather weak—Prince Andrei was forced to face up to the fact that he would have either to rebel or be disposed of like the others. The invitation to Moscow seemed too much like a trap for him to think of accepting it. But the very act of refusing placed him in the camp of the opposition. Interestingly, this device intended to liquidate an enemy was to be used again, centuries later, by another tyrant who dominated Russia. Stalin was to try by the same means to get rid of a rebel of quite another caliber—Tito.

Frightened, Prince Andrei fled to Novgorod, assembling around him all those boyars and nobles alarmed by the regent's ways and indignant at having to submit to the will of a three-year-old child. Thus aligned—with Andrei and those who had followed him on one side and Elena's favorite and her supporters on the other—the two factions nearly came to war. But curiously, the rebel prince suddenly faltered in his tracks. He may have had scruples about the legality of his actions, or feared plunging the country into a prolonged conflict, particularly when in the same year (1537) there were indications that the Tartars, who had retreated to Kazan, were in a vengeful mood. Whatever the reason for his change of mind, it was to cost him his life. He obtained a promise of clemency from his enemy, Elena's favorite, in exchange for laying down his arms; Elena refused to abide by it. Brought back to Moscow, Andrei was thrown into prison and, a few months later, taken to his death. His followers were horribly tortured and then executed.

Elena had gone too far. Despite the defeats inflicted by the military leaders loyal to her on the Tartars and then on the armies of the king of Lithuania which had come to the support of her opponents, none of the boyars was prepared to tolerate this cruel and arrogant princess for another moment. In 1538 she died suddenly, suffering agonizing pains. There is no doubt that poison had ensured her elimination more reliably than the traditional removal to the cloister. The fate of her lover was equally unpleasant: after prolonged torture, the executioner literally made mincemeat of him, while his sister—young Ivan's nurse and much loved by him—was thrown into a convent.

Thus ended a regency very different from that ruled by Olga long before in Kiev. The difference lay not only in the fact that in sixteenth-century Russia domination by a woman was very shocking, nor in the murderous nature of Elena's power. It came above all from the logic that underlay this power. Superficially, when she did away with those who surrounded her—uncle and brothers-in-law, not to mention their supporters—Elena seemed to be acting like all those others who, through the centuries, had been accustomed to decimating their kin. But, in 1533, power was handed down from father to son; a change in the line of descent was not a normal thing, and murder was no longer a useful way of speeding up a legal process. Now it was used to maintain the existing and legally inherited power. If Elena killed her brothers-in-law, it was not because of some clan logic that required the elimination of all the siblings, but purely and simply to avoid a return to this logic, at a time when the rules of hereditary succession were beginning to take hold.

The barbarity of the regency disguises a change in the practice of power. Hereditary succession ensured a stable relationship between the holder of power, his line, and society, and thus the identification of the nation with this line. National unity, now almost accomplished, could not accommodate a step backward to a revival of the clan system. As far as history is concerned, it is not significant that Elena's brief regency was marked by the rise of a favorite and intolerable abuses of authority. However deplorable these characteristics, they are found in all periods and in almost all types of power. They do not disguise the essential feature: the still-fragile political system, desired by so many sovereigns, had been maintained by the pitiless princess-regent. In the future, blood— once spilled to remove those who stood in the way of power—was to be shed in order to preserve power. The way in which this power was handed on, if not its exercise, already represented progress in Russian political life.

For the young Ivan, the end of the regency was a personal tragedy. Until then, in the shadow of the Kremlin dominated by his mother, he had passed his days playing games with a simple-minded brother. Suddenly his childhood, symbolized by his mother and his nurse, was over; he was not yet eight years old. Certainly, no one disputed his legitimacy. But the governorship of the boyars which now began, with two princely families, the Shuiskys and the

Belskys, fighting bitterly over the regency, was to represent a real challenge to his theoretical sovereignty. In the clash of the most incredible ambitions and intrigues, power passed from hand to hand, while a succession of executions, murders, imprisonments, and exiles took place. No one was safe in those troubled times, when the sense of state was buried beneath fierce rivalries, and even the church paid a tragic price in these bloody upheavals, the rival princes having no hesitation in deposing and arresting its leaders. Although he survived this period, Ivan saw it in all its horror and terror. Despised by those who were quarreling over power, he trailed around the Kremlin in a state of near-poverty, watching the dispersal of his property which was snatched shamelessly by those around him, a witness to the worst kind of excesses. Yet he was still required to retain, when necessary in the face of his enemies, the appearances of a power of which he was in fact stripped. Thus, when ambassadors came to Russia, the miserable child was placed on the throne, dressed in all his finery, to show them that order reigned and that the dignity of the sovereign was not eclipsed. No sooner was the audience over than he would be relegated again to the usual moral and material poverty.

It is scarcely surprising that the adolescent Ivan, isolated in this solitude, developed into a complex and contradictory personality, which his heredity could only reinforce. On the one hand, he had a taste for study and meditation, through which he could forget an unfriendly world. His reading was above all religious—the Bible, the lives of the saints—and historical—the old chronicles. From these studies he was to derive a confused religiosity and a sense of the greatness to which he was heir that were to last all his life. On the other hand, he displayed a spirit of revenge, allied to an instinctive cruelty, that time was only to confirm. From adolescence, deprived of all moral guidance that might have restrained such a complex and excessive personality, Ivan indulged all his whims, all the impulses to violence prompted by circumstances. Unable, in these difficult years, to attack people, he inflicted terrible cruelties on animals, revealing all the accumulated anger in his heart, which he could express in no other way.

Uncertain Beginnings

In 1543, however, when he was still only thirteen, he took a first step toward power and revenge. He unexpectedly called together the boyars to rebuke them with great vehemence for their misdeeds. And he announced without hesitation that by way of example he was going to punish, if not the most guilty of them, then at least the most highly placed. On his orders, his huntsmen seized Prince Andrei Shuisky, the real head of government, and handed him over to the hunting dogs which tore him to pieces in view of the people of Moscow. With this veritable coup d'état, which taught the boyars that the hour for a return had struck, Ivan was able to assert himself: suddenly he was the master. Four years later, in 1547, he decided to have himself crowned, taking the title of tsar. After a period of ten years of bloody interludes, fourteen years after the death of Vasily III, the throne of Moscow had found a proper occupant, even if this occupant was not yet eighteen years old.

These tragic beginnings, following on a tragic childhood, did not augur well for Ivan's reign. Nevertheless, the pomp of his coronation, not just as grand prince but as tsar, and his marriage to Anastasia, a young Russian noblewoman of the Romanov family which was to rule Russia from 1613 to 1917, seemed to point to a stable and peaceful reign. But scarcely had the celebrations come to an end when Ivan's Russia was struck by a drama that opened the way to a new period of bloodshed. Once again, the unrest started with flames. A huge fire ravaged Moscow, leaving in its wake only ashes and dead bodies. Fire was inevitable in a city built entirely of wood, and whether spontaneous or the work of invaders, it had been one of the scourges of the Russian people for many centuries. It seemed to follow times of joyful celebration, and it cast a shadow of fear on the people who still remembered that the great god Perun, cast down in the name of Christ, had been the creator of fire. Their old pagan beliefs, which had never completely disappeared and coexisted with a vigorous Christianity, would reemerge at such moments.

With the fire came rioting, the inevitable companion of the flames that destroyed everything in their way, heightening the tension along with the elements that had sparked the crisis, and then affecting the daily life of all. Life was hard for the ordinary man, and discontent had been smoldering for a long time. In the fire, the great bell of the Kremlin crashed to the ground. The people, who had risen up in one of those vast spontaneous movements that were henceforward to punctuate the history of Russia, saw in this event the indisputable sign of divine anger against the sins of those who ruled over them. As always at such moments, miracle-workers, "holy fools," ordinary monks, and a whole world of religious beliefs came to feed the mystical, superstitious anxieties that had taken hold of these people in the blazing streets, exhorting them to repent, announcing the end of the world and eternal hell-fire as well as many other punishments. The wildest rumors circulated among the people seeking out the guilty. Princess Anna Glinskaya, a close relative of Ivan, was accused of having started the fire with her witchcraft. To satisfy the people, expiatory victims were necessary, who could, as in the past, be sacrificed—not to the gods this time, but to the one God, revered in Russia since the baptism of Vladimir. Ivan had temporarily taken refuge from the threatening flames and crowds in his estate at the village of Vorobyevo (the Mountain of Sparrows, across the river from Moscow). The rioters in their fury had killed his uncle, Prince Glinsky. Although he had them dispersed and quelled by force, Ivan nevertheless opted for a conciliatory approach rather than trying to reestablish order by violence. He must certainly have thought of punishing the ringleaders, but quite apart from the fact that they had fled from Moscow when it looked as though order was to be reestablished, he saw that severity could be dangerous. He was moved to clemency by the extent of the destruction, the depth of discontent, the reality of the underlying poverty, together with the resurgence of the threat from the Tartars who saw in the Moscow fire a new chance to regain their power. More than that: he was prompted to examine his conscience.

He made an act of contrition on the square facing the Kremlin, in public, promising to mend his ways and govern for the good of his people. All those whose excesses had impoverished the state, and thus society, provoking the wrath of God, would also take second place to the people. This solemn confession, in the presence of a clergy that had lost so many members in the fire (the churches were in ashes), the promise to crush the arrogance and authority of the nobles, standing like vampires around the tsar, and the alms distributed to the poor—everything was going according to the wishes of the ordinary people. The nation suddenly coalesced around the young sovereign who had heard their anger and had taken on his shoulders and confessed to the sins of the past in order to show that a time of innocence and forgetfulness should begin.

These terrible days could be said to cut the history of Russia into two halves. The arrogant princes, still fighting for their interests, bleeding the state and driving the inhabitants into poverty and violent despair, were now in flight. Those who remained saw their former power condemned by the groups in the middle of society, merchants and artisans, who had made up their minds to be heard. Between the sovereign and this society that had suddenly regrouped around the old communal structures of the past—the powerful group of the boyars seeming to have lost all its authority—a direct line of contact was briefly established. The holder of power had overcome the crisis without undue loss of blood—the repression had been harsh, but without giving rise to revenge. For a while it seemed as if this power, handed down from father to son, in seeking God's forgiveness was going to take on a human face, as if the days of misfortune had gone forever.

Ivan the Reformer

Historians often divide Ivan IV's reign into two contrasting periods: the first, a happy one ruled by a reforming sovereign who was to make far-reaching changes in his country; the second, the tragic one that was to earn Ivan his name, "the Terrible."

The person and character of the Ivan of the first period are worth examining. The sovereign who emerged from the crisis of 1547 was still a young man. His appearance, as depicted in contemporary engravings and descriptions, reflected the drama of his childhood and a nature torn between two opposite poles. He is tall and thin, and one is struck immediately by his piercing, restless, anxious eyes. The curved nose and long face show a hardness that confirms the expression of the eyes. The length of his profile is exaggerated by the reddish-brown beard. The whole picture is one of power, of strong will, and of self-gratification. An early adolescence spent in drinking and depravity, hunting and running with the hounds, does not, however, give us the whole picture. The other side of the coin shows an adolescent and then a youthful sovereign avid for knowledge, immersing himself in books, reading everything with the same frenzy with which he threw himself into debauchery. This thirst for learning gave him an encyclopedic mind, though his accumulated knowledge was very much that of a self-taught man incapable of digesting acquired facts. But Ivan followed those great thinkers of the day for whom, according to Pico della Mirandola, knowledge cannot be divided. For them, everything that has been written, said, and accumulated by man in the course of time should be absorbed by anyone who wishes to understand the world.

But beyond Ivan's passion for learning, which led him to travel the length and breadth of his kingdom, lurked the constant fear of God and a religiosity that sometimes remained buried, sometimes bursting out in a frenzy of pilgrimages, prostrations, public repentance, and acts of thanksgiving. He felt the presence of God at his side constantly. God had made him tsar, it was God whom he challenged, God whom he believed he represented. He surrounded himself with clerics, but they were only there as extras. Conscious of his rank and of the divine element in his position as tsar, Ivan was answerable only to God. Even if, in the course of time, these contradictory characteristics were to become more and more marked, Ivan's complex personality already revealed all these traits in those early, happy years at the outset of his reign. The happiness he found with his new bride Anastasia—a happiness that seems to have filled and mellowed him, guiding his life—appeared at the time to be able to lead this contradictory soul away from its darker inclinations, raising it up toward higher and better things. We can only imagine the outstanding sovereign, a humanist in the century of humanism, that Ivan might have been if this pull toward the light had been maintained. The iconography of the time, idealizing his reign, shows what might have been. A miniature from the Chronicle of Kazan depicts Ivan defeating the Tartar dragon; his young and angelic face recalls the pure figures of the first two Russian saints, Boris and Gleb, now no longer oppressed but triumphant. Like them, he incarnates the first innocence of the Russian people, bringing salvation and redemption.

In these early days of his long reign, Ivan's achievements were astonishing. He surrounded himself with new counselors, spelling the end of the coteries and intrigues of the princes. The whole world of boyars and princes suddenly became a thing of the past. At the heart of Ivan's council composed of nobles and clerics, the dominant figure was that of the metropolitan Macarius, his spiritual guide, the head of the church, the priest Sylvester and, among the small number of representatives of the nobility, two brilliant young men in whom he placed his trust and whose fortunes he made. These were his chamberlain, Alexis Adashev, of relatively humble birth, and Prince Andrei Kurbsky, a man of outstanding intelligence who proudly claimed descent, like the tsar, from Rurik. The political achievements accomplished in a short time with the cooperation of this council were impressive. In 1549, Ivan called together what amounted to assembly of the estates of the realm— Zemskii sobor—an enlarged version of the Duma,[1] in order to lay before it his plans for juridical and administrative reform. This was the first time such an assembly had come together in Russia. The following year, he got the assembly to approve not merely the plans, but the reforms themselves. In the new code—the Sudebnik—he was continuing and coordinating the legislative work of his grandfather Ivan III of half a century earlier. Ivan did not seek to overturn that body of law, but rather to make it an instrument in the pursuit of national unity. The law should override the old customs where the privileges of local princes had created exceptions and differences, and should be applied in an identical way throughout the land. He introduced a strict judicial hierarchy dominated by the supreme court of Moscow, the election of judges by the population of the local communities, a precise definition of crimes and punishments

---

1. The Duma of Boyars was the sovereign's council, going back, in its organized form, to the state of Kiev. At the beginning of its development in Moscow, this council consisted chiefly of the grand prince's counselors, his relatives, men in his service, and representatives of the nobility. In the sixteenth century, when the power of the latter was weaker, although the Duma was still basically composed of members of the nobility, its numbers were made up by government officials and a sizable number of the clergy.

(from the knout to the death sentence) and the fixing of a price scale for legal procedures. All these measures were intended to bring justice under the control of the state, depriving the nobility, once so powerful, of their powers of jurisdiction acquired through their considerable authority over society. With this legal system, which expanded work already begun, Ivan had a triple goal in mind: to reinforce the authority of the state; to continue the task of weakening the old rivals for central power by encouraging, to their detriment, the rise of new social classes that moved upward in the service of the state; and lastly, to attempt to curb the corruption that poisoned social relations.

The administrative reforms were even more decisive for Russia's future. For Ivan, it was a matter of offsetting the authority of his representatives in the land (who had been building up fiefs and patronage networks) by the development of a real local power that would make possible the smooth running of a territory that had greatly expanded and that wars were to enlarge even further. He decided to set up an elective system that would allow the people to choose their representatives instead of the state imposing its own men. The responsibility of the elected authorities was both administrative and fiscal, the tax paid to the treasury forming the permanent link between the center and the regions or communities. Even when this elective system could not be applied in its entirety, the control of the local authorities was intended to be exercised over the representatives of Moscow.

To this measure was added a second and more radical one: Ivan decided to distribute the lands around Moscow to some thousand "children of boyars." These in reality were children of the petty nobility or even descendants of slaves. They were given the title, formerly restricted to boyars, of "*dvorianin* [nobles] of Moscow"; in exchange, they had to be ready to serve Ivan. Thus was created a new ruling class, separate from the traditional nobility and bound in obedience to the sovereign who, according to a long-established system, ensured its promotion. For the nobility that had for so long dominated Russia, it was a threat. It seemed that Russian society was rich enough in talent to allow Ivan to draw from it the forces necessary to change progressively the whole organization of society.

Next, the reorganization of the army was to provide Ivan

with the instrument of conquest that he needed. A form of military service, provided by the nobles, had already existed in Russia. The richest served at their own expense, while the rest received a small reward of money or land. When the country was threatened, all took up arms, and even the church supplied weapons and horses. This was not enough, however, for an ambitious state seeking to establish itself, which had to be able to call on a proper army, with soldiers supplied with similar types of weapons and possessing a modicum of knowledge of the military art. From 1545, even before embarking on this feverish period of reform, Ivan had realized the urgent need to equip himself with a reliable army. The result was the *streltsi* (sharpshooters), half militia, half regular regiments, one section acting as his personal guard and the greater part attached to the army. Thus, within the ranks of the more untrustworthy mercenaries, he established a stable and well-trained core. It is worth remembering that a country like France had already set up a similar nucleus of a regular army almost a century earlier. . . .

Finally, with the calling of a church synod in 1551, Ivan undertook both to lay down the relations between the church and the state and to persuade the former to become more organized. The "Code of a Hundred Chapters" that resulted from the synod pronounced strictly on all matters relating to the religious life, from the proper appearance of the beard to the painting of icons. The church began to compile a massive edition of the lives of the saints, complemented by large numbers of canonizations. Father Sylvester added his own contribution by overseeing the writing of the great *Domostroi,* the book on good house management that was for long to regulate, and restrict, the life of the Russian people. Moral rigor, uniformity, and restrictiveness were the chief elements of this product of the synod.

From a society of lax morals, already tempted by alcohol and used to corruption, Ivan had wished to forge a rigorous society, closely reflecting the monastic life. In this too, he was trying to perfect the work begun by Ivan III. For all that, he, too, was unsuccessful in his relations with the church over the same point as Ivan III. Wanting to limit the church's economic power by making it seek prior permission before acquiring land, he was never able to get this measure put into practice.

As well as a reformer, Ivan was also, at this time, a remarkable war leader, or at least the inspiration for wars that would free Russia from the presence of those who had for so long threatened her integrity and very existence.

The Tartar khans had never been prepared to admit defeat. From their states of Kazan and Astrakhan, they multiplied their raids on the north, pillaging, and bringing back slaves to be sold in all the markets of the East. Demoralizing for the threatened peoples, these raids were particularly humiliating for an established state like Russia. In 1551, Ivan decided to put a stop to them, launching an attack on Kazan. The fall of Kazan in 1552 was, for the Russian people, a wonderful revenge for centuries of oppression. In 1556, the khanate of Astrakhan was in turn conquered and annexed to Russia. The last of the khanates, the Crimea, which had been stepping up its attacks, was more difficult to conquer. With the end of the Golden Horde, the Crimea had passed into the authority of the Sublime Porte, and had adopted a particularly hostile attitude toward Russia. Ivan's relative moderation, as his soldiers repelled the Crimean Tartars' raids, advancing ever further into the steppes but yet not driving home their advantage, can be easily explained: behind the khanate of the Crimea stood the Ottoman sultan, then at the height of his power. In defying him and annexing a state that was vassal to the Ottoman Empire, Ivan would have run the risk of a dangerous reaction, at a time when, on the northwest frontier, the war being waged against the Livonians toward the Baltic, and then against the Polish-Lithuanian armies, was allowing him to advance unhindered toward the sea. The conquest of the Crimea, begun by Ivan, was not to be fully achieved until the end of the eighteenth century in the reign of Catherine II.

If we draw up a balance sheet of this period, the achievements are impressive. Ascending to the throne at the end of a period of upheaval and strife when authority over the state was being passed from hand to hand, being used for the benefit of a few individuals and, in its violence, taking Russia back to its darkest days, Ivan was able at a stroke to break free of these fatal chains. In the place of general disorder he substituted order through reform. In the space of a few years he made great strides in the realization of a political plan sketched out and many times abandoned by his predecessors.

His first concern was the state. He defined his authority. He belonged to no one faction or noble group. He was above society. So that state and society could agree, Ivan IV endowed the first with permanent structures, formerly the prerogatives of the princes, ensuring their success by providing them with men and material means: administration, army, the judiciary—nothing escaped his attention. To do this work he relied on those officials and soldiers whom he intended to make the permanent and capable instruments of the state. They were at his service, and not the potential masters of a weak state, or the privileged instruments of the conquest of power, as the nobility had formerly supposed. After his predecessors had weakened the privileges of the endowed princes, and then reduced them to mere subjects of Moscow, Ivan IV undertook to bring them within a social organization where they were still able to believe that they were at the top of the hierarchy, retaining something of their old power.

In 1560, Ivan was not more than thirty, his effective reign had lasted for only seventeen years—or only thirteen, if dated from his coronation—and yet so much had already been accomplished. The reformer could congratulate himself. His country now bore little resemblance to what it had been at the time when he took over the reins of power. State, society, and frontiers were all quite altered in aspect. He had completed the creation of the state; he had turned society upside down, raising up the petty nobility and almost entirely quelling the princes and breaking up their fiefs; he had pushed back the frontiers of the country. And he could congratulate himself on the fact that this immense task had been accomplished with very little bloodshed. Leaving aside the wars—though they were necessary for the security of Russia, and there is no argument about the price paid for this security—Ivan spared his countrymen. He had observed the promises he had made in his public expression of remorse in the smoking ruins of the Moscow fire amid the corpses of those who had been burned there or who had perished in the riots. Revealing himself as a humane prince, Ivan proved that it was possible to reform Russia without violence. The old curse that had for so long made Russia a breeding ground for murder, around the throne and for it, seemed at this time to have been lifted. If the course of history had been different, if Ivan had died at this moment of success, he would have handed on to his successor a state that was already centralized, with new attributes of authority, a large and secure territory, and a belief that progress could be achieved without murder.

4
Absolute Tyranny

◆

From this period of peaceful political order, Russia was to leap abruptly to a time of terror and absolute tyranny. From a power that had rejected murder as a tool of government, it passed to a power that saw murder as the only way to solve all those conflicts inherent in any normal society. The moment that marks the transition from the first to the contrasting second part of the reign of Ivan IV was the year 1560, when Anastasia, so long his companion and a calming influence, died.

The Age of Suspicion

In reality, the crisis that was to transform a wise sovereign into a murderous tyrant had been smoldering for several years. Some time before, in 1553, Ivan had been seriously ill and thought he was dying. Haunted, like his predecessors, by the problem of the succession, and also drawing on his own experience, he was anxious to secure the rights of his eldest son, Dmitri. But Dmitri was only a baby. Pressed by Ivan to swear loyalty to the legitimate heir to the throne—the rule of succession from father to eldest son now being accepted—his immediate entourage, consisting of the council and the high nobility, appeared reluctant and hesitated. To place a baby on the throne would be to relive the terrible experience of the regency and its factional infighting. Anastasia was already re-awakening memories of the ambitious Elena Glinskaya. Unpopular among the nobles, she could not boast of a glorious ancestry, while her influence on Ivan was regarded with suspicion. Instead of this infant in the cradle and a regency under Anastasia, the nobles favored another prince, or, in other words, a change of dynastic line. Everything seemed to point to Vladimir, Ivan's first cousin and son of his uncle Andrei of Staritsa, assassinated in prison on Elena's orders in 1533. Despite this murder committed a generation before, Vladimir, the son of the victim, had been the inseparable companion of the son of the woman who had ordered the murder. It seemed that this friendship between the two cousins—as if Ivan had in this way tried to wipe out his mother's crime—would result in the usual crossing of lines of inheritance, and a return to the clan law whereby the throne passed from brother to brother. Everything pointed to this solution: the age of the legitimate heir, the unpopularity of the probable regent, the popularity of Vladimir, and the intrigues of his mother who, for twenty years, had longed for revenge. Everyone spoke up for Vladimir, from Father Sylvester, Ivan's respected spiritual mentor, to his closest counselors like Alexis Adashev.

But contrary to expectations, Ivan recovered and they had to think again. Perhaps seeing the threats to his family—a princess and a legitimate heir once removed from power would have little chance of surviving—and to his work, Ivan had returned literally from the kingdom of the dead where he seemed already to have sunk. Terrified by this apparent manifestation of the supernatural, those who—including Vladimir and his followers—the night before had refused to comply now hastened to take the oath.

But the harmony between the cousins was broken forever. Ivan had seen what might happen: despite the established rules, as soon as a potential successor appeared, reviving the old system of transference of power, anything was possible. He had also discovered the frailty of the support of those whom he had raised up around him. "Trust no one" was the bitter lesson he learned from this crisis, even though he had crushed it so rapidly. He would hereafter trust no one, except Anastasia. When she died, the last link attaching him to any confidence in human relationships was broken, as was that which imposed on him any restraint in his private life. Deprived of his refuge with a woman both respected and loved, Ivan gave free rein to his nature and his excessive and changeable appetites. A stability of affections and senses gave way to unbridled debauchery. As well as making seven successive marriages, he surrounded himself with an unknown but impressive number of temporary or more permanent mistresses. In this area, Ivan's cynicism knew no limits. His legitimate wives followed one another in quick succession, carried off by illness (poisoned, Ivan was to assert), or repudiated and buried in a convent. One of them, suspected of adultery, was condemned to watch her lover being impaled before her eyes. Another was tied to a carriage pulled by horses. Whipped until they bled, the horses dragged her to a river that swallowed up the whole infernal device. Not content with that, with calm effrontery in 1567, when he already had a wife, Ivan asked for the hand of Elizabeth I of England. Had she accepted his suit, unless he were to commit bigamy, he would have had to get rid of an inconvenient wife by fair means or foul. . . .

The Avenger

This sudden collapse in Ivan's private life was mirrored by a total transformation of his personality, or perhaps revealed a return to the sadistic instincts of his childhood, which had apparently disappeared but in fact were lurking beneath the surface. At first it was Ivan's desire for revenge that emerged. Driven to despair by the death of Anastasia, Ivan believed she had been poisoned, though no one knew by whom. But he began to associate this accusation with the memory of the support refused him by his closest counselors at the moment of the crisis of succession.

Father Sylvester and Alexis Adashev were the first to pay for these accumulated resentments. Sylvester sought refuge from this rising tide of hate in a monastery, but Ivan forcibly removed him. Though the sovereign did not yet dare raise his hand against a man of God, he wanted to ensure that Sylvester found not refuge but a certain place of death. Ivan sent him to a monastery more like a prison, on the terrible and inhospitable island of Solovetsky in the White Sea, where life was a living hell. Centuries later, the same island was to serve as the tomb of those whom another power was to take for "enemies of the people." This island, originally the site of a monastery and a place of meditation and peace, has over the centuries acquired the reputation of a cursed place whose very name is enough to awake terror in those threatened with it.

Alexis Adashev, Ivan's old confidant, had like Sylvester to pay for the crime of having hestitated when it appeared that the problem of the succession was raised. Ivan had him imprisoned in Dorpat. Two years later, Adashev was found dead in his cell. Ivan claimed that the deaths around him were poisonings, but a large question mark hangs over the real causes of such a convenient demise. Though there was no proof against the sovereign, it is certain that from this date he intended to remove all those whom he could not trust, whether because they had once opposed him, or had failed to support him, or even because they might behave that way in the future. To faults committed he had added a new crime: faults that might be committed. From this time, the scope for repression had no boundaries and the steps he took to protect a power that he imagined to be under threat became murder pure and simple.

The first victims were to be the close relatives or collaborators of those whom he had already eliminated. They would be likely, Ivan thought, to wish to seek revenge: Adashev's brother, a hero of the wars of reconquest, and then of course, with an eye to the future, the son of this unfortunate man, then only twelve years old.

Adashev's relatives and friends, along with their children, were all to meet the same fate. Ivan's perverse mind had revived the old idea of the clan in order to exterminate ever wider circles of all those who had links, close or distant, with his first victim. The nobility panicked. The murderous fury of an unrecognizable Ivan seemed to know no limits. There was only one response in such a situation—flight. In this climate of insidious terror, of uncertainties over whose turn it might be on the morrow, no one thought of standing up to this newly emerged tyrant. The automatic reaction of his court was to flee and many set off on the road to Lithuania. Ivan had them caught and forced everyone, whether they had fled or not, to agree in writing not to leave Russian territory. Thus he armed himself with a new weapon; flight into an enemy country— Russia was at war with Poland and King Sigismund—was treason and, in addition, perjury. He now had legal pretexts for his ruthless actions.

Indictment of the Tyrant

But these measures were not enough to prevent some men from escaping, particularly the remarkable Prince Andrei Kurbsky, in whom Ivan still had confidence. A descendant of a grand prince of Kiev, Mstislav the Great, Andrei Kurbsky enjoyed the double prestige of his ancestry and his victories against the Tartars at the capture of Kazan. First at his sovereign's side, and then opposed to him, he always felt he had a right to treat Ivan as an equal. But a defeat in Livonia, just at the time when Ivan was turning tyrant and beginning to decimate his entourage, persuaded the prince to look toward a more lenient king. To the terror and arbitrary justice of Russia, Kurbsky was to prefer Poland and negotiations with the king of Poland. Sigismund saw that he could profit from Ivan's excesses by attracting Ivan's best men to his court. Kurbsky asked him for a command and land that would make him as powerful in Lithuania as he had been at the Russian court. In 1554, despite the prohibitions, the prince fled to Poland, leaving behind in Russia his wife and children, defenseless against the fury of the tsar. Until the day he died, Ivan was obsessed with having the exile assassinated. He was to send countless murderers after Kurbsky, with instructions to get rid of him forever, even later when Kurbsky was too old and infirm to defend himself. This obsessive pursuit of an isolated enemy, by now weak and hiding here and there to evade his murderers, was to be repeated by another tyrant, centuries later. The epilogue was to be enacted in the suburb of a Mexican town where a twentieth-century Kurbsky was to fall under the blows of the ice-pick of a certain Ramón Mercader. . . .

In acting as he did, Kurbsky made himself the spokesman of all those whom Ivan had already sacrificed, and the advocate of a mode of government that Ivan had abandoned in favor of pure violence. He had sent a message to the tsar that represents a true manifesto, and was to give rise to an exchange of letters—five in Kurbsky's hand and two written by the tsar—which provide a remarkable picture of the political system of Russia.

At the moment of his flight, Kurbsky produced an indictment in the names of those who had supported and accompanied the early part of Ivan's reign:

Tsar once glorified by God, who formerly shone like a torch of orthodoxy, but who today, because of our sins, reveals another aspect, with a stained and leprous conscience not found even among pagan barbarians. Persecuted by you, my heart is full of bitterness, yet I wish to address these words to you. O tsar, why did you cause the strong men of Israel to perish? Why did you torture to death the brave *voevodi* whom God had placed around you? Why did you spill their victorious blood on the profaned pavements of God's churches? . . . Was it not their daring that overthrew and placed before you the proud kingdoms of the Volga where our ancestors were slaves? Do you not owe the cities taken from the Germans to their zeal and intelligence? . . . You exterminate us in whole families. Do you think then that you are immortal, O tsar? Or, seduced by some heresy, do you believe that you can escape the incorruptible judge, Our Lord Jesus? No. He is judge of the whole universe, and all the more so of a proud persecutor. My blood, which once was shed for you like water, will cry out against you. . . . In your pride, you depend on your armies to reassure you and to continue, in this brief life, to invent new instruments of torture to inflict on human beings, in order to tear and disfigure the body of man that was made in the image of the angels. Can you depend on your servile flatterers, your companions in debauchery and orgies, and on your quarrelsome boyars who destroy your body and your soul, push you into the debaucheries of Venus, and make you sacrifices worthy of Satan?

Kurbsky's first letter is not just a true indictment of Ivan's increasing exactions, it also poses a fundamental problem that hitherto had not been explicitly addressed in Russia: the legitimacy of the tyrant. Although he speaks in the name of Ivan's victims, Kurbsky's text is not a vengeful one. He invokes, instead, the right to judge Ivan's evolution in the names of the very rules that established his legitimacy. Ivan, he writes, has betrayed the rules of God, of the God to whom he owes his power, the faithful servants whom God has placed at his side, the victories that these men have brought him. Debauchery, orgies, and murder are here all listed under a single heading: heresy, born of Ivan's revolt against God and his teaching.

Kurbsky was using the same arguments as those used thousands of miles and four centuries away in western Europe by John of Salisbury, the companion of Becket, assassinated by the king of England. Salisbury said that a king was a divinity, made in the image of God; but the tyrant is made in the image of the devil. This same view of the tyrant is also found in St. Thomas Aquinas in the thirteenth century, where he says that the duty of the just—not only the individual, but any elite within society, the *melior pars*—is to set up against the tyrant what could be called an "institutional rebellion." It is unlikely that the words of the Angelic Doctor reached sixteenth-century Russia, so distant from the Latin world, and it was not them, nor the work of John of Salisbury, that lay behind Kurbsky's letter. Nevertheless, the question—posed equally clearly by Cicero in his day—was the same, and it occupied the minds of those in Russia in the reign of Ivan and inspired Kurbsky: How to respond to the tyrant? The response was, in part, that which ran through most political thought of Europe: a realization of lost legitimacy, since royal power emanates from the law of God. Whoever betrays the law of God—as in the case of the tyrant—is a heretic, and thus loses his source of legitimacy. But Kurbsky stops here; if the tyrant is not legitimate, then the only action is to desert his service in favor of that of another sovereign. He does not pose the burning question of the right to overthrow the tyrant, perhaps because his respect for royal authority, still very recent, was too great. The time for tyrannicide in Russia had not yet come.

Nevertheless, from this point onward, Ivan's reign was to become more tyrannical and unrestrained than ever. It became impossible to halt a development that not even Prince Kurbsky could have imagined. It was a time of permanent, generalized murder, respecting neither the number not the rank of its victims. The story of Ivan's treatment of his old counselor, Shibanov, is well known. Bringing a message to the tsar, the unfortunate man was literally transfixed by the furious tsar who nailed Shibanov's foot to the ground with the spiked staff he habitually carried. Shibanov had to read out the long epistle in this appalling position. This episode is indicative of the kind of terror Ivan now inspired in all those who approached him. It was also symbolic: nailing one's enemies to the floor, or to a cross—was not this the very image of the Antichrist, whom Ivan seemed to resemble more and more, and who was implied in Prince Kurbsky's letters, giving him the right—even the duty—to leave the service of his tsar?

For a moment the tsar wavered, or appeared to waver. At the end of 1564, he suddenly left Moscow with his family and established himself fifty-six miles from the capital, in his *sloboda* at Alexandrov. From there, after four weeks of silence, he addressed a message to the Metropolitan Athanasius, announcing that he wished to renounce the throne. He denounced those who, he said, had always paralyzed the exercise of power—the nobles attached to their privileges and despising the common interest. To the people, he addressed a second message to explain why he was unable to fulfill the mission conferred on him by God.

Why did Ivan behave like this? Did he really intend to give up power, or was it rather that, with this unusual and dramatic gesture—leaving the capital deserted and with a long silence before the arrival of the messages explaining his departure—he wished to shock the people? Did he wish to demonstrate, through the reaction that would result, that for the people he was still the legitimate sovereign, giving the lie to Prince Kurbsky?

He was proved right by the popular reaction. His withdrawal from power, total power, was more frightening than reassuring. Even the nobility and the clergy, who knew well the threat represented by Ivan to their personal security, do not seem to have been tempted to take advantage of this sudden void to put another branch of the family on the throne. Fear was everywhere. The nobility and the clergy were terrified by the possible popular reaction that such a power-vacuum might engender, and by the idea of a return to the old confrontations. The ordinary people were afraid that there might be a return to the cruel and chaotic reign of the rival princes. It seemed that, all in all, the cruelty that was supposed to be an expression of the divine will was preferable to any other. The people were unanimous in their call to Ivan to return to govern them. Thus the legitimacy of Ivan's claim to the throne was enhanced—or replaced, if Kurbsky was right—by a popular legitimacy: that of a people unable to imagine the departure of Ivan, and that of a helpless nobility and clergy.

Whatever his true reasons, Ivan had taken a dangerous gamble, and had emerged the winner. He thereby established two new political realities: that the law of inheritance, in the handing down of power, was already firmly anchored in people's minds (no one, for example, in those troubled days, had thought of calling on Ivan's cousin Vladimir); and that an immense power, however threatening, has within itself such strength that its sudden disappearance is more frightening than comforting and does not necessarily imply the search for an alternative.

The Prince of Darkness

This knowledge, which should have reassured Ivan and encouraged him to adopt a gentler style of government, had the opposite effect. Sure now that he had entire power over—or rather, against—his subjects, he demanded as the price of his return to affairs that his right to do what he wanted should be recognized. Stating that his desire to abdicate was due to the fact that it was impossible to govern in the prevailing conditions, he imposed two innovations: a new style of government, very different from the familiar political institutions, and the absolute right of life and death over his subjects. To start with, he decreed that Russia should be divided into two parts. One would keep the existing institutions, essentially the Duma, which would be called the *zemshchina,* or government of the country, over which Ivan reserved a simple control and the right to deal severely in cases of treason. The other, the *oprichnina* (from the word meaning "apart"), was his own private domain, where his own law applied to the exclusion of any other. In this political kingdom, cut off from the rest of Russia, Ivan set up a body of administrators devoted entirely to him, and a special guard whose members, called the *oprichniki,* immediately started to spread fear and terror. Their physical appearance was enough for this: these men, dressed entirely in black, riding black horses with a dog's head and a broom dangling from their saddles, were eloquent symbols of the task given them by Ivan of biting the tsar's enemies and sweeping clean the land of Russia. This body of cutthroats, answerable to no law, consisted originally of a thousand members; eventually it had as many as six thousand—enough to terrorize totally the population of this extraordinary domain.

The creation of the *oprichnina* was not just the product of a diseased mind, obsessed by the suspicion of treason; it was also the instrument of a rigidly pursued political plan. By different methods, Ivan's predecessors had each attempted to break the remnants of the old territorial nobility, but neither they nor Ivan had been completely successful. Deprived of their bases in the principalities, the old ambitions and rivalries of the nobles had reemerged around the throne, within the state itself. The *oprichnina* was to be the decisive blow to these survivals of an earlier age.

Ivan removed from the sphere of common law all those areas where the authority of the state was still at odds with traditional authority or influence. He thus eradicated by force the last pockets of resistance from the nobility. In this way the *oprichnina* took over whole districts, or even streets of the capital, along with small towns and regions that the sovereign showed a desire to absorb. Here the *oprichniki* were able to establish their own law with complete immunity. They seized property, expelling the nobles. Very occasionally, if these nobles were not held to be rebels, they were compensated with property elsewhere.

Behind this institutional division lay a geographical and historical logic. The *oprichnina* chiefly operated in the central regions of the kingdom, while the area under common law lay principally on the edges, in the lands conquered during the previous century by Ivan III and Vasily, Ivan's two immediate predecessors. So the intention was clearly to put an end to the last vestiges of the feudal territories of the nobles, survivals of old Russia.

In addition to the crushing of the traditional nobility, this reform had another consequence. The peasants who lived in the lands confiscated from the boyars wanted to flee from their new masters whose cruelty was immediately manifest. The areas won from the Golden Horde needed to be colonized to defend them from a possible return of the Tartars, still powerful in the Crimea. The

runaways were attracted to these areas and were to establish themselves as the first population of these new Russian territories.
Beneficial in this respect, nevertheless the massive exodus to these
areas had serious consequences for the central state. With the
villages deserted and the land abandoned to the ever-encroaching
forest, agricultural production fell and sources of finance dried up,
since the fleeing peasants were also escaping from taxes. The state
was also losing its soldiers. As the nobility became poorer in land
and peasants, so their obligations to come to the defense of the state
correspondingly decreased. It was to be Ivan's successors, inheritors
of the strong state being created by Ivan's plans, who recovered the
resources that Ivan might have lost. But, at the price of these
economic difficulties, Ivan was able, through his unorthodox policies, to create the definitive notion of the state. When they took
their oath of loyalty to him, the *oprichniki* included in the formula
not only the obvious promise of total and blind fidelity to the
sovereign, but also—and this was the important innovation—to the
state.

Terror without Bounds

The era of the *oprichniki,* and indeed the rest of the period of Ivan's
reign, was called by contemporaries *t'ma* (darkness), a word borrowed from the Tartars—surely no coincidence.

The dark years of the Tartar domination had now been
followed by the domination of a tyrant whose cruelty was unprecedented in man's memory. The bloody exploits of Ivan IV and his
praetorian guard of murderers made victims of individual members
of the nobility and the clergy, but also of society as a whole. We have
seen how Ivan pursued with his vengeful arm all those who had
connections with Kurbsky, whether as relations or fellow boyars.
After his messenger Shibanov, whose foot he had pierced and who
died under torture, Ivan set about dealing with the prince's family.
He threw Kurbsky's wife into a convent and caused the disappearance of their son. From this point the list of his crimes is

endless. On the square facing the Kremlin, executions became a daily occurrence. From the moment the *oprichnina* was set up, the boyars were handed over to the executioner. Sometimes, father and son would face one another at the block, the son raising up the head of his father before himself dying under the axe. The heads of the boyars, important or not, rolled without end.

Assisted by his new favorites, the Basmanovs, father and son, and Malyuta-Skuratov, all sadistic, perverted men and his companions in debauchery and murder, Ivan perfected a terrible new system that contributed to the development of his policy of extermination. Any conspiracy, any threat of a conspiracy, or even the possibility of one had immediately to be denounced to the *oprichnina*. Failure to do so meant an accusation of intention to commit treason and execution along with friends and family. Infinitely extensible, this idea of conspiracy that included even the intention to conspire and even a hypothetical intention, associated with the implicit adoption of the principle of collective responsibility, elevated denunciation to a duty to the state while nondenunciation became treasonable. By virtue of the rights over life and death, which Ivan had assumed on his return to power, and thanks to this crime of treason for which the first comer could so easily be accused, Ivan was able to have anyone that he suspected, anyone pointed out to him by his henchmen, put to death at a moment's notice.

Among his most illustrious victims was his first cousin, Prince Vladimir, who he could not forget had almost replaced him at the time of his illness. Though he had concealed it for years, his hate remained. Unsure of the propriety of shedding the blood of his own family, after years of hesitation Ivan made up his mind in 1569. All those who had wavered in 1553 had already been exterminated. There remained only Vladimir, an object of hate because of the past and a possible rival in the future.

Ivan invented a supposed conspiracy in order to get rid of his cousin without bearing the visible responsibility. Vladimir was to be accused of having tried to poison the tsar, a crime of *lèse-majesté*, but also a crime against God, of whom the tsar was the representative on earth. The logic of the accusation is clear: if the tsar can pardon in his own name, he cannot pardon the injury to God. He enjoined Vladimir, summoned with his followers to the Kremlin, to drink the poison that he was supposed to have prepared for Ivan. Before the eyes of the impassive sovereign, his childhood companion Vladimir, together with his wife and daughter, swallowed the poison offered to them and died in atrocious agony. Ivan did not believe in half-measures, and he included in the massacre Vladimir's own servant who, bribed or terrified by the *oprichniki,* had denounced the supposed plot (the mechanism of denunciation was working to perfection), the princess's maids-in-waiting, and Vladimir's mother, Ivan's own aunt, whom he had already shut up in a convent and who was to be drowned. It was this wiping-out of whole families, this mass extermination that Prince Kurbsky had denounced four years before. Probably in order to prove Kurbsky wrong, Ivan decided to spare those of his cousin's children who were not present at the Kremlin that day. But it goes without saying that the property of all those who were executed—relatives or boyars with no family connections—was immediately confiscated. Thus the royal domain continued to grow.

Rupture with the Church

Nor did the church, which guaranteed Ivan's authority, escape his murderous hand. Not only did his killers have no hesitation in tracking down their victims who took refuge on holy ground, but in 1568 Ivan was to attack the most important of the Orthodox hierarchs. The Metropolitan Philip, an ascetic and highly cultured man of noble birth, had been summoned by Ivan to replace the Metropolitan Athanasius on his retirement to a monastery. From the start, Philip had attempted to restrain Ivan and persuade him to dissolve the *oprichnina* and unite the two parts of Russia under the reign of law.

The only response from Ivan was an insistence that Philip promise to abstain from intervening in affairs of state, observing the separation of the spiritual and temporal, and confining himself to the former. Philip agreed, hoping in exchange to put pressure on

Ivan in order to obtain certain measures of clemency, but toward Ivan's henchmen he adopted a severe, inflexible attitude, ceaselessly condemning their excesses, holding up the law of God in the face of the bloody lawlessness of Ivan's rule.

Once again, Ivan attempted to get rid of an opponent without appearing to bear the responsibility for his death. From a series of denunciations extracted from various disreputable characters, including some men of the cloth, he constructed an outrageous accusation, a mixture of vice and betrayal, that allowed him to bring the metropolitan to judgment and sentence him to life imprisonment in appalling conditions. The crowds of faithful that gathered before the walls of the monastery where the metropolitan was imprisoned forced Ivan to move him constantly from one prison to another. Realizing that the old man, though broken by suffering, remained unbending in his condemnation of his persecutors—the servants of the state—Ivan had no choice but to finish the job which he had begun with his challenge to the church: to rid his master of this inconvenient witness of God, Malyuta-Skuratov strangled the metropolitan with his own hands.

This unforgivable crime broke the continuity that united the state to the church, and particularly to the monastic world. In the eyes of a suffering people, the martyrdom of a man of God was the supreme outrage. Just as popular devotion centuries earlier had centered on the two princes, Boris and Gleb, associating the twin concepts of sainthood and princeliness, after 1568 Philip played a similar role. Before long the Solovetsky monastery that housed his remains became, despite its distance from Moscow, a center of pilgrimage to rival the monastery founded by Sergius of Radonezh at Zagorsk. Up until 1568, the saints of Russia had usually been princes, and this notion of the "holy prince" or "pious prince" conferred on the throne itself an aura of sanctity. All of them, in different ways, had contributed in the name of the throne to the defense or resurrection of the nation against the infidel. In 1568 it was from this same throne that the death-blow came that made Philip a martyr of the church. Holiness deserted the throne and asserted itself against it. The monasteries too, which had until then extended and sustained royal authority, suddenly found themselves separated from it, since the Solovetsky monastery was henceforth to derive its prestige from the fact that it housed the remains of the man who had cried out against the crimes of the sovereign and had died at his hands. Ivan had labored powerfully to impose the idea of the state, but it also needed the support of the church. With the murder of the Metropolitan Philip, he caused irreparable damage to this ambition. By suppressing him, he had attempted to prevent the church disputing his power. In doing this, not only had he not achieved his aim—the people revered Philip for the very deed that had brought about his martyrdom—but he had also lost a part of his legitimacy, that conferred on him by the church as representative of the divine will. From the time of this murder, the enemies of the tsar became, in the popular mind, the true defenders of Holy Russia, a task that had previously fallen to the sovereign.

From Genocide to Infanticide

But the crimes of Ivan and his band of murderers were not limited only to boyars and their families or to priests. Unchecked, the *oprichniki* terrorized the towns and villages, killing, raping, and abducting the people and pillaging everything they could carry off. Not content with this, Ivan coldly decimated whole towns, beginning with Novgorod in 1570. Believing—with or without reason, it made little difference—that the inhabitants of this city, brought under the crown a century earlier, were conspiring with the king of Poland, he decided to "punish" the whole city. Besieged by his troops, Novgorod was subjected to a terrible martyrdom that spared no one, neither old nor young, nor even clerics. For weeks whole families were methodically brought out onto the main square to be tortured before Ivan's approving eyes. The number of victims of this extermination varies according to the writer, but the essential point is Ivan's desire to annihilate, after horrific suffering, all those whose only crime was to be citizens of Novgorod. This can only be defined as genocide.

Other towns were, to a lesser degree, to undergo the same fate. Only Pskov, which Ivan descended upon scarcely had he left the smoking ruins of Novgorod, escaped the massacre, because a "holy fool" suddenly appeared at the gates of the town in the tsar's path. Ivan's superstition took strange forms: a man who had murdered a metropolitan and, like the infidels, had burned down the churches after shedding rivers of blood could yet be moved by an unarmed "holy fool." For once he turned back.

That same year, the infernal cycle of murder took a new turn. Ivan had decimated the ranks of his enemies, his people, and whole towns. His vengeance was now turned on his favorites, the executors of his base desires, for a murderer always fears his accomplices. The *oprichniki* and their leaders had become too powerful. After successfully carrying out the extermination of his subjects in Novgorod, Ivan returned in strength to Moscow, and so that everyone should know that he was back he presented himself as the leader of the *oprichniki,* dressed in their uniform. The weight of the *oprichnina* fell once again on Moscow. Ivan was busy fabricating another conspiracy as only he knew how, this time involving some of his most faithful servants, including the two Basmanovs. For once, the *oprichnina,* which had raised itself above the law in order to decimate society, was choosing victims from within its own ranks. The commander of this massacre of the murderers was the most terrifying of them all, Malyuta-Skuratov. Through this series of executions of his fellows, he was able to move further into the confidence of his sovereign who understood no other language than that of denunciation and execution. In his eyes all men were potential enemies, except those who continued to fuel the infernal cycle of violence with ever new denunciations.

In 1572, however, Ivan decided to abolish the *oprichnina.* He had both internal and external reasons for doing this. Internally, the power and arrogance of this band of assassins made him fear that, despite the number he had had executed, their strength might one day turn against him and serve a rival ambition. The accumulated wealth of the *oprichniki,* if confiscated, could also go to swell his coffers and pay for new loyalties, which would be more reliable because more recently acquired. But more important, a compelling external reason pushed Ivan into bringing an end to this reign of arbitrary justice. King Sigismund II of Poland had just died. A new occupant had to be chosen to fill the empty throne, and Ivan offered himself. The *oprichnina,* having fulfilled its role of liquidating what was left of the power of the boyars, now became an inconvenience, doing little for Ivan's reputation. With a stroke it was suppressed, even a mention of its name being forbidden on pain of death.

For all that, Ivan's behavior changed little. To his dying day he was to believe that murder was the surest way of consolidating his power. It was this belief that led him to the most tragic action of his life, the ultimate crime: the murder of his son. On November 19, 1581, in one of his habitual fits of anger, Ivan struck and killed his own son and heir, Ivan, son of the beloved Anastasia, with his iron-tipped staff. A slight disagreement had sparked the tragedy, but Ivan IV's uncontrollable violence made it almost inevitable. He had already shed enough of the blood of his family in killing his cousin Vladimir. The murder of his child outdid even the horror of that event. Although Ivan did not die for another two years, this last crime opened the gates to a hell that made his death a liberation.

Ivan well deserved the name given him by his subjects and preserved through history; *groznii,* which means bringer of thunderbolts, or more simply, "terrible." It is hardly necessary to recall again that the god Perun, to whom the ancestors of the Russian people had sacrificed so many victims, was the god of thunder. Ivan's nickname was not the product of chance, nor an accident of vocabulary. In 1584, Russia could see no end to the numbers of victims sacrificed to this "man of thunder."

There exists a very curious document that gives an idea, albeit only a hint, of the reality of this murderous frenzy, which was not entirely without its own logic. The synodal book of the monastery of St. Cyril lists a series of Ivan's victims for whom he wished prayers to be said. This list has the names of 3,470 victims, of whom 968 are referred to by their patronymic. Several names are followed by a particularly sinister addition "with his wife," "with his son," "with his children," extending to: "Kazarin Dubrovsky, with his two sons and ten men who came to their aid"; or again, "twenty men of the village of Kolomensko"; and we find more general references: "Remember, O Lord, the souls of your servants of Novgorod, in all 1,505 people." These prayers for the victims were ordered by Ivan himself, so far was he convinced of the rightness of killing them, in obedience to duty, that is, to God. His concept of power explains his concept of murder.

The Tsar: Divine Nature and Human Nature

When he died in 1584, dressed like his predecessors in a monk's habit and having made his peace with God, Ivan seemed to reconcile the two extremes of his nature, at once human and divine, the basis of the political theory of absolutism. The total power that he had exercised in such terrible ways was not just the product of his will. This power, much discussed since the beginning of the sixteenth century, even before Ivan had succeeded his father, was part of a coherent political idea that originated in the very heart of the monastic world. Before existing in practice, the tsar's absolute power had already been accepted in theory. The most developed theories on power in that period of progress toward national unity and absolutism can be found in the ideas of Joseph of Volotsk, founder of the monastery of Volokolamsk.

Defender of a church feeling its freedom to deal with the state, Joseph was equally concerned to define the authority of the state, and, first of all, that of its incarnation, the sovereign. He looked to the Byzantine Empire to find support for a concept of royal power, a concept he was always to defend. His principal source of inspiration was the writings of Agapetus, who, in the sixth century, had theorized about the nature of the sovereign. At the heart of Agapetus's ideas lies the duality of the royal nature: "An emperor, in his body, is like other men, but, in his power, he is like God." But this divine part of the nature of the sovereign was no longer inspired by the same concept of God that had dominated the prince-saints of past centuries. The suffering and redeeming Christ, full of charity, the model of Boris and Gleb, had by now been replaced by Christ Pantocrator, the omniscient judge. The sovereign's divine nature makes him all-powerful rather than compassionate. Even if, by reason of his divine nature, he should aim at perfection in his human behavior, his absolute authority does not depend on the virtues that he shows. The rigor of the rule imposed by Joseph on his monks was to be echoed in the rigor of the imperial rule imposed by Ivan on his subjects. To this fundamental element should be added other components elaborated during the reigns of Vasily III and Ivan himself: Moscow boasted of being the Third Rome and also the last Rome in human history. A monk of Pskov, Philotheus, assured Vasily in 1511: "In all the universe, you are the true tsar of the Christians. . . . Listen, pious tsar, all the Christian kingdoms are gathered in your kingdom. Two Romes have disappeared, the third is here, and there will never be another."

The unique and exemplary character of the tsar's kingdom, identified forever with the most perfect expression of Christianity, is found here. There is complete identification between the tsar willed by God and this Third Rome also willed by God. It was the source of immense responsibility and, hence, of an equally immense power.

This Third Rome was a synthesis of the two earlier Romes. The Russian clerics, and particularly the Metropolitan Macarius, one of Ivan's first counselors, devoted much energy to demonstrating that the tsar was descended from Emperor Augustus.[1] The Russian sovereigns, Christian princes ruling the third and last Rome, ensured the survival of the Orthodox Church, as was confirmed by the synod of 1561. Some authors even went so far as to add the idea of the responsibility of the tsars for the whole of Christendom. For all these reasons, the tsar was invested not only with temporal duties but also with a spiritual mission that was an integral part of his divine nature.

This ideology of total power, which naturally suited Ivan very well, was backed up by one of his counselors who, during Ivan's reign, was the chief apologist for a theory of absolutism which was already less religious than that of Father Joseph. For Ivan Peresvetov, naked power and its manifestations were the definitive elements of a successful regime: "A weak and humble tsar condemns himself to the weakening of his authority and his glory. A tsar who combines

---

1.   The *History of the Princes of Vladimir*, written at the beginning of the sixteenth century, advanced the idea that Rurik was the direct descendant of Prus, the father of Emperor Augustus, and was thereby a legitimate heir of the Roman emperors.

fear and sagacity *(grozen i mudr)* increases his authority. . . . . A tsar who exercised authority without fear would be like a rider on an unharnessed horse."

This absolutist view was not, however, unanimously accepted. If Ivan adopted it without reservations from 1560, it was against the recommendations and advice of a whole school of thought that believed that absolutism was not fixed for all time as the only path for political progress in Russia. The unadorned rigor of Father Joseph was answered by the luminous figure of Maximus the Greek, whose ideas bore the imprint of a humanism borrowed from the Italian Renaissance. After time spent in Italy and then under the discipline of Mount Athos, Maximus had come to Russia in 1518 where he was to spend the rest of his life. He answered Joseph's triumphant absolutism with a denunciation of a church enmeshed in the pursuit of material riches and hence incapable of following the true path taught by Jesus. He ceaselessly preached moderation to the young Ivan, inspired by a political viewpoint based on the idea of the limitation of power. "Nothing is more necessary on earth than justice," he told Ivan. This justice could not be practiced by the sovereign without the correct personal qualities, starting with moral rigor and humility. For Maximus, the human side of the prince's nature could not be ignored; on it depended the orientation of the power that he wielded. He disputed the sovereign's right to interfere in the life of the church and affirmed the contrary view—that it was the church's duty to moderate the prince. Relations between church and state were tipped by Ivan and his Josephite counselors at the synods of 1561 and 1584 in the direction of the supremacy of the latter over the former; according to Maximus, things should be the other way around. And he warned the prince that an excess of power exercised by "a tyrant unworthy of the title of tsar" invariably resulted in the decline of an empire. The question of the legitimacy of power, when he who holds it abuses it, was thus implicitly posed.

It was a question that was to be developed at length by Maximus's disciple, Prince Kurbsky, in his polemical correspondence with Ivan. Having listed Ivan's crimes, the prince was to go on to accuse him of having betrayed Holy Russia *(Sviataia Rus')* and thus of leading it to destruction. The implications of Kurbsky's violent attack were decisive for the future of Russia. By exalting Holy Russia and contrasting it with Ivan's crimes, he distinguishes between the nation and the master, shifting the divine will, the divine nature of the tsar toward the nation and reducing the sovereign to his temporal nature. The symbiosis of the two natures, an essential part of the political philosophy of the Josephites, is implicitly called into question by Kurbsky who is here following the reasoning of Maximus. The divine part of the tsar's nature only exists insofar as he incarnates Holy Russia and its commandments. It is the sanctity of Russia that is important; the tsar must integrate into it and conform with it.

This shift of ideology is only implied in Kurbsky, but taken with his systematic denunciation of the iniquity of the sovereign, showing that there is only evil in him, it is clear that the basis of what Ivan claimed to be his legitimacy is being challenged. Legitimacy came from the perfect identification of Holy Russia and Holy Tsar. If this identification disappeared then Holy Russia, permanent guardian of legitimacy, was obliged to ask questions about the tsar. It appears that Ivan devoted two letters to answering Kurbsky's attack with its serious implications for absolutism. It was no ordinary occurrence for an all-powerful sovereign to dispute with an exile threatened on all sides. But the stakes were high.

Like his correspondent, Ivan makes appeal to the Christian basis of autocracy. But he turns the argument around. The order willed by God requires all Christans to submit to it. By rebelling, Kurbsky has placed himself outside this order. As a traitor to Ivan, he is a traitor to God, and Ivan's sacred duty is to punish him. Furthermore, Ivan accuses Kurbsky of heresy for having denied the human element in his nature: "I am a man too. And no man is without sin. Only God is without sin." But this humanity that he openly claims is dominated and absorbed by the divine part. By criticizing the man in him, Kurbsky is again attacking God, laying himself open to damnation.

Ivan holds firmly to the Josephite theory, to the definition of a power that has no limitations and to which its subjects must bend. In practice, however, this disciple of total absolutism, who refers so often to intangible myths of origin—the Third Rome, the inheritance of Augustus, divine will, and the sanctity of the prince—

manifested from time to time an attitude that directly threatened this same ideological edifice. In 1566, when he was defending against Kurbsky his notion of total power, he called together the *Zemskii sobor* to place his problems before them, and principally that of the war with Livonia. Although it is not easy, from the existing documentation, to know the exact nature and extent of the powers of this assembly, yet it seems to contain within it the germ of the idea of national consultation. It should of course be remembered that, under Ivan, the members of this assembly were named not elected, and there is no indication that any of the meetings that he called—in 1545, 1566, and 1575—attempted to limit his powers. Their chief merit was to bring face to face the sovereign and the representatives of different classes of society: nobles, clergy, officials, townspeople, and later peasants. Together with the local self-administration set up by Ivan in his reforms of 1555, this assembly of the estates of the realm represented a slight relaxation in the system of absolute centralization that elsewhere he took to extremes.

Another exception to his ordinary behavior, and the most inexplicable, if not completely eccentric, was his decision in 1575 about the succession. In 1572, a revival of Tartar power threatened Moscow. An attack on the ill-prepared capital was followed up with the usual pillaging and fires. The disturbing and hated figure of the destructive Tartar had suddenly reappeared. It was in this context that three years later, Ivan, first crowned tsar of Russia, retired to his *sloboda* at Alexandrov to announce that he was abdicating and that as his successor he had chosen nothing less than a Tartar khan converted to the Orthodox religion! The farce was, no doubt, short-lived. Ivan was soon back in power as if nothing had happened. But he had delivered a fatal blow to his life's work. The order of inheritance from father to son, established with such difficulty, at the cost of so much bloodshed, was suddenly being challenged. The whole system of inheritance was once again in the melting pot. Ivan's decision suggested that the bloody battles over the succession were not yet over. It caused a profound shock to Holy Russia to find the myth, so patiently built up, of the half-human, half-divine king, heir to Christianity and the Roman Empire, called into question. It was unthinkable that this king could overnight renounce, of his own volition, and transfer to another—and a Tartar to boot!—what God had entrusted to him. The saintly prince, focus of all the loyalties of the nation, thus damaged his own authority, as was to become clear later. This erosion of the myth of the tsar was further increased when Ivan murdered his son, breaking with his own hands the chain of succession whose continuity he had so stoutly defended up until 1575.

Was this sovereign, the major part of whose reign was devoted to an interminable series of murders, mad? Certainly many aspects of his behavior suggest insanity: the enormity of the murders committed, the perpetual wavering between violence and religiosity which, after he had delighted in the spectacle of burnt flesh, torn-out eyes, children tortured in front of their parents, caused him to run, a grieving penitent, to the monasteries to accuse himself and order prayers for his victims. The apparently gratuitous nature of the murders raises the same question. Ivan's power was unchallenged and no one made an attempt on his life, even though he constantly suspected others of wishing to poison him or of having poisoned members of his family. Why then did he have to kill ceaselessly? Was he an insane murderer? Should he simply be categorized as one of those monsters who also featured in the history of that time, such as a certain prince of darkness who, not far away in the Carpathian mountains, was giving rise to so many legends—Dracula?

Even if Ivan's murders were not, as in earlier times, aimed at clearing the route to power, nor even at protecting this power—which in Ivan's case was never seriously under threat—it has to be said that they all followed a certain logic. They formed part of his concept of absolutism which necessitated the sacrifice of all those who, because of their rank, could threaten the order of succession (Vladimir); all those who could hold back the development toward absolutism in the name of their past privileges (the boyars); and those who opposed the logic of tsarist power and the state order, superior to any other, with another logic, that of the church and its rules (the Metropolitan Philip).

But for all that, was it necessary for these murders to lead to the mass killing of whole families and towns? The answer has to be yes. Absolute terror is the only kind that suppresses all other alternatives. The survivors of the victims would inevitably harbor a spirit of revenge, and hence a desire for a new order. By removing the wives and children of those whom he liquidated, Ivan removed a whole section of society. It was impossible for the ambitions of the boyars to revive when anyone even remotely connected with them had been wiped out. As for the massacre of whole towns like Novgorod, it was as with the boyars: by massacring all living beings in them, Ivan was suppressing the alternative represented by the past and the democratic traditions of these towns. In the name of the future of absolutism, Ivan eradicated—literally tearing out anything left living—all traces of the past and the traditions of an order that, in this period of transition, had not yet completely passed away. Ivan's murders had the effect, in essence, of making a *tabula rasa* of the society that had preceded him, in the name of a utopian dream of total power over all men and things. As with all tyrants, the basis for his vision was the destructive powers of a body of murderers of terrifying brutality. When they became a threat, Ivan was to destroy them also at a particular moment in his bloody progress. His history finally descended into madness when he raised his hand against his own flesh and blood. He was finally overtaken and brought down by his own logic.

The two very different parts of his long reign resemble the two aspects of his nature, the divine, concerned with the emancipation and construction of Russia, and the human, with all its brutality. In 1560, Ivan could congratulate himself on having repelled the Tartars, assembled a *sobor,* instituted important reforms, and centralized the state, overcoming all individual interests. At the moment of his death, the balance sheet looked far more gloomy: the country was ravaged by the massacres that he had ordered, while his own political certainties were beginning to waver. On the frontiers, the troops, exhausted by too many wars, were powerless in the face of attacks from the new king of Poland, Stephen Batory—Ivan's successful rival in the choice of a new sovereign—to save Russian strongholds. Nor were they any more successful in resisting the Swedish breakthrough. The Baltic, which Ivan had so passionately wished to gain, was to remain closed to him. The final disaster was that the succession was no longer assured. With the murder of his son Ivan, the tsar had no one to succeed him except an heir weak in mind and body and a very young boy. His absolute power, built on great mounds of dead bodies, seemed about to fall. The end of Ivan's reign was also to pose a question that was to be repeated again and again throughout the history of Russia: was it inevitable that the march of progress out of barbarism should itself pass through a barbaric period, or even lead to barbarism in excess?

5

True and False Tsars

♦

The death of Ivan was to begin the "Time of Troubles." Alain Besançon[1] has rightly stressed the importance of a proper understanding of this phrase, "which should be taken literally. The time of troubles (*smutnoe vremia*) means a time when one cannot see clearly, a time of chaos, sin, death, and misfortune for the land of Russia." He could have added that it was also a time of murder creating trouble and confusion, rather than murder pursuing an implacable logic in the organization of power, as were the first murders committed within the ruling dynasty or later those of Ivan.

A Dynasty in Decay

In fact, it was Ivan himself who started the disturbance and chaos in 1575 by upsetting the order of succession, breaking it with a fatal blow of his iron-tipped staff. Nevertheless, when he died it appeared that the succession could be observed. He was survived by two sons: the elder, Fyodor, son of Anastasia; the second, Dmitri, son of his last wife, Maria Nagaya. But both these sons were open to challenge, one by his unsuitability, and the other in law. Fyodor, a particularly pious young man, was more suited to be a monk than a tsar. To start with, his physical appearance was against him: small and squat, with short arms and no neck, his face wore a permanent smile described by witnesses, depending on their point of view, as one of either metaphysical ecstasy or simple-mindedness. No one

---

1. *Le Tsarévitch immolé*, p. 103.

87

ever praised his intelligence, and it was decided at once that he needed a solid council to make up for his manifest lack of political ability. As for his half-brother, Dmitri, who had been little more than a baby at the time of Ivan's death, his claim to the throne was very dubious. Ivan IV had married many times and discouraged the church—which in canon law only allowed three—from blessing the later unions. He had used many expedients in order to take a new wife, calling on a benediction from some prelate in his service, and the legality of some of these marriages was very debatable. In the eyes of the church, which had not sanctioned his marriage to Maria Nagaya, the last of Ivan's long series of wives, young Dmitri was simply an illegitimate child. It should be added also that Fyodor, although married, had no children, meaning that his line could come to an end at any moment.

The council around Tsar Fyodor, immersed in his prayers, and particularly the most powerful of its members, his brother-in-law Boris Godunov, had good reason to fear that young Dmitri might become the pawn in plots and intrigues to place him on the throne, despite his illegitimacy. There was no question of simply removing him. His brother was tsar, he was no threat to the throne, and the pious tsar owed it to himself to protect the half-brother who would one day be the only continuation—little matter if legitimate or not—of the line. But for his entourage, things were different. The Duma of boyars included many men illustrious in name and in deed: Prince Ivan Shuisky, descended from Rurik; two descendants of Gediminas, the princes Ivan Mstislavsky and Bogdan Belsky; and above all the heads of two boyar families who already had links with the throne: Nikita Romanov, the brother of Anastasia, Ivan's first wife and mother of Tsar Fyodor; and Boris Godunov, his brother-in-law. Given that their sovereign was so weak, they must all have been devoured with ambition. They hoped to take advantage of this weakness to increase their own powers and return to the old division of authority. But of them all, the most ambitious was Boris, who, a sorcerer had predicted, would one day be tsar and whose reign would last for seven years.

The fear of intrigues that might threaten the presence on the throne of such a passive tsar, and one without an heir, replacing him with the young tsarevich and a family far removed from the throne, led to Dmitri and his family being sent away to his estate of Uglich, while Boris managed in a short time to remove all his rivals from the council. Accused of plotting or of treason, these rivals were forced to enter monasteries or to take up residence far from Moscow where they could not influence the appointed sovereign.

It should be stressed that Boris managed this slow but sure progress to a privileged position at the foot of the throne without bloodshed. He removed from his path anyone who was in his way, cheerfully confusing his rivals with enemies of the tsar and ensuring the loyalty of those whom he protected thanks to the power that he acquired in what became a true regency. But Boris was also working for Russia. In 1586 the king of Poland, Stephen Batory, died. Boris supported Fyodor's claim to this throne. The failure of the plan was probably due not so much to Boris—though he had been rather sparing with the financial inducements to the voters—as to Polish reluctance to have a prince who was not a Catholic. But Boris's greatest achievements during the reign of Fyodor were internal. The changes in the status of the peasants and the installation of the patriarchate were to have a far-reaching influence on the social and political future of Russia.

The mobility of the peasantry had for a long time been a source of concern to the state. In an attempt to restrict it, a law of 1497 had decreed that no Russian peasant could leave the estate where he worked except during the two weeks around the feast of St. George (November 26 according to the Julian calendar). But the attraction of the "black lands" opened up to colonization after the conquest of the Tartar khanates of Kazan and the Crimea and fear of the *oprichniki* had encouraged the peasants, in the reign of Ivan IV, to flee regardless of dates. Confirmed by the censuses of 1581 and 1592, this flight from the rural areas forced those in power to take increasingly severe measures. In 1580, still in Ivan's lifetime, the right of all peasants to move on St. George's day was temporarily suspended. In 1603, this interdiction became permanent. In the meantime, the cadastral roll set up between 1581 and 1592 made it possible to keep track of every peasant. In 1597, the government decided that all runaways who had moved before 1592 would be free to stay where they were, but that those who had fled after this date would have to be returned to their masters. In 1649, the new code was to remove any temporal limit beyond which a peasant might keep his freedom of movement, attaching him permanently to his master. By this series of measures of 1550–1649, the system of serfdom was greatly developed during the reign of the weak Fyodor. It was to be one of the curiosities of the Russian state that once again social changes were occurring that followed a unique and radically different course from that developing in other parts of Europe. Serfdom in western Europe, which had come about as a result of the breaking up of state authority, disappeared between the thirteenth and fourteenth centuries when the restoration of a centralized power led to a collapse of the feudal system. A late phenomenon in Russia, serfdom was, by contrast, a product of the development of the state to the detriment of the old principalities and the monastic estates, and one of the elements in the tsar's power. Boris Godunov played a decisive role in this development both during the regency and in the short period of his reign.

The second major innovation was the installation of a patriarchate in Russia in 1589. Since Constantinople was in the hands of the Turks, the Russian church claimed that its dependence on a patriarchate on infidel soil was intolerable. Patriarch Jeremiah of Constantinople accepted the argument. Boris succeeded in having Metropolitan Job, whom he had already promoted to replace one Dionysius—a man little inclined to pursue his own ambition—as metropolitan of Moscow, appointed as patriarch of Russia. Thus, by 1590, Boris had surrounded himself with influential supporters: the patriarch of Russia, glorying in his new authority; and the small landowners who had been almost ruined by the flight of the peasantry and who now, with the new restrictions on movement, could feel secure again. A time of stability seemed to lie ahead.

But suddenly, in 1591, news came from Uglich of the death of the Tsarevich Dmitri. On the May 15, the child was found in the palace courtyard with his throat cut. With the alarm bell ringing wildly, people rushed to the scene, ignorant of the circumstances of the death. In the general confusion a massacre broke out, resulting in the deaths, among others, of the officers whose duty it was to protect the child. A committee of enquiry was sent to Uglich, presided over by Prince Vasily Shuisky. The enquiry was hasty and clumsy; the explanation, imprecise and full of contradictions, was that it had been an accident. The child was apparently epileptic; while playing with a knife, he was supposed to have fallen on the blade, thus cutting his own throat. . . . After this report, the Nagoy family, accused of having been overhasty in taking revenge on innocent men, was strongly reprimanded. This family's fall conveniently helped to clear the path leading Boris to power.

The death of the tsarevich was the decisive factor in what was to be the Time of Troubles, opening up the Russian political scene to all the malcontents, troublemakers, and dissidents whom Boris had been able hitherto to keep at bay.

The crisis burst with Fyodor's death in 1598. Russia was suddenly plunged into a totally new situation. More than seven centuries of dynastic continuity—maintained at the cost of so much bloodshed—had suddenly come to an end. With the tsar dead, the tsarevich gone, there was no one left. All the efforts of generations of sovereigns to unite the Russian nation around the inheritance of Rurik were canceled at a stroke.

Tsar Boris: The Dawn of a Dynasty?

Fyodor's widow, Irina Godunova, could have taken over in the interim—but in the place and name of what successor? She took the veil, despite the boyars' desire to swear loyalty to her, terrified by this break in the dynastic line. There remained only her brother, Boris, who had no links with the broken dynastic line, but who had the advantage of having run the regency, in other words held power, for years. He was closer to the throne than anyone else, through his policy, pursued to make up for his lack of rank, of rewarding powerful supporters cultivated over the years, particularly those in the church, which he had raised to independent status. There were plenty of others in Russia who claimed descent from Rurik, but they were not connected with any of the grand princes who had contributed to the building of the state. An arbitrary choice from among these branches unconnected with the throne would mean that any one of them could dispute this choice in order to advance their own cause. Such a hypothesis implied a return to the old conflicts and their train of murders.

If it were a question of changing dynasty, then who better to support than the man who was already nearest to the throne and whose ability to reign was not in doubt? Certainly, there was little to legitimate Boris's ascension to the throne. Against him were his Tartar origins, his title to the nobility, which was tenuous compared with those of his important rivals, and his role at the side of Ivan at the time of the *oprichnina*. But something had to be done, and soon, if a social crisis was to be avoided. Boris was the best placed, because he was already wielding the power, and he was able to give his claim the unexpected appearance of a popular plebiscite. Insisting on the support of the representatives of the nation, he was elected by the *Zemskii sobor* where those whom he had assisted—the petty nobility and the clergy—were in the majority. In a strange political reverse, the crown, whose direct inheritance so many sovereigns had passionately defended, was now disposed of by a hastily called assembly. Not only was the chain of inheritance broken, but also an implicit law. Until then, no one had dared challenge the successor to the throne, precisely because he was there by virtue of his inheritance and the mythology that surrounded it. The break of dynasty in 1598 and the form this break took were to end this tradition. Society had intervened in the choice of dynasty, exercising a right to be involved in the choice of a sovereign. From this moment the sacred nature of a dynasty was lost.

In the face of this sudden change, people were troubled. And there was trouble already in society, the peasants being the chief cause. The status imposed on them, leading inexorably to serfdom, was intolerable. Tied to the land, under pressure from the landowners who were in turn being forced to contribute more to the state, obliged to bring under cultivation land that had often been abandoned or was hard to work, the peasants had only one idea— flight. The runaways went to swell the colonies of Cossacks who, in the Russian borderlands, were consumed with hate for a state that they had abandoned. They vowed never to fall beneath its yoke and fought constantly against any attempt at integration. The peasants who failed to get away or were caught and returned to their masters were forced reluctantly to accept the servile condition to which they had been condemned. Rural life suffered, and its decline was to lead to a return of the great famines that always triggered social explosions in Russia.

Tsar or Usurper?

But men were troubled for other reasons. The phantom of the tsarevich who died in 1591 returned to haunt Russia. The rumors that had started to circulate at the time of his death suddenly became deafening: the tsarevich's death had not been accidental, and the sudden end of the dynasty proved it; he had been assassinated by the very man who had had himself placed on the throne, Boris. And there were other rumors: the tsarevich had not died at all; another child had had his throat cut in his place. In both variants, Boris was nothing more than a usurper, using murder to seize the throne.

This rumor, making Godunov the murderer of the tsarevich in a premeditated desire to seize the throne, was to be very persistent. There was no actual evidence, and the chronicles and, later, historical research show that it took shape when Boris was already tsar, when social problems were causing discontent that was only increased by Boris's policies. Everything about him went against the way of thinking of the Muscovites. Although uneducated, he was keen to learn from and imitate the West. He showed this enthusiasm in many ways: he encouraged his subjects to shave off their beards—an outrageous practice in the eyes of the faithful; he employed foreign talents, and he sent young Russians to western Europe. Worse still, he extended his protection to religious communities outside the Orthodox Church. When the terrible famine that was to last for three years broke out in 1601, the fury of the people reached a peak. Boris was accused of everything: not only the death of the tsarevich, but also that of Ivan the Terrible and his predecessor Fyodor, and even that of the latter's son, who had never existed! Boris was blamed for every death that had ever chanced to cross his path. How else could he have got to the throne, founding a new dynasty, except by murder? He was similarly credited with the fire that ravaged Moscow in 1591, which he had started, said his detractors, in order to divert attention from the murder at Uglich. Finally he was accused of the famine, and of the plague that spread in its wake.

In 1604 Boris had been reigning for six years. The sorcerers had predicted seven. In this feverish and unhappy climate, when no one doubted the words of soothsayers, it was hardly surprising that the supernatural entered into the political sphere in the form of the resurrected Tsarevich Dmitri. But there had already been signs of this as early as 1601. In that year a rumor—grafted onto the variant of the tsarevich miraculously saved at Uglich, thanks to the substitution of another child—had begun to spread around the country, coinciding with the beginning of the famine, that Dmitri had reappeared, the true heir to a throne that should never have left the reigning dynasty. This Dmitri, of whom very little is known, has come down to us as the monk Gregory Otrepyev. This mysterious person, returning from the kingdom of the spirits and claiming to be the real Dmitri, was both the first of the self-proclaimed sovereigns—*samozvanets*—of Russia, the first of a long line of impostors, and the first embodiment of troubled times and social disorder. Until that time the monarch had been the living symbol of order in the face of these frequently unchained social forces. But now this Dmitri, recognized by history as an impostor, was to ascend the throne that he claimed to be his.

Tsar or Impostor?

The sequel to these events smacks of the detective novel. The false Dmitri appeared like a will-o'-the-wisp in many places at once, arousing in his wake sudden loyalties born as much of men's frustration at the troubled times as from a real belief in the pretender. Dmitri went to Poland, seeking the aid of King Sigismund in his attempt to take the throne. Although the king's support was rather lukewarm, Dmitri aroused fanatical devotion in the king's subjects, who were fascinated by his adventure. He formed an army of these men, with Cossacks from the Don and Dnieper and bands of peasants who had rebelled against the laws that had deprived them of the right of mobility. With this army he invaded Russia to seize "his" throne by force. As long as Boris was alive, he was able to answer this attack. He mobilized above all the moral authorities, Patriarch Job, his protégé, and Vasily Shuisky, who had presided over the commission of enquiry in 1591. They both reaffirmed repeatedly that the child who died at Uglich was indeed Dmitri and that the man who claimed to be him was only a usurper, a defrocked monk and a tool of the Poles and the Jesuits. These statements had little effect on a Russia smoldering with anarchy. The north, beginning with Novgorod, opened the way to Dmitri's troops. The boyars, to whom Godunov's reign was a personal insult, began to murmur that the impostor was the man on the throne, not the one who stood outside the walls. The troops assembled by Boris against those of Dmitri wavered: what if they were setting out to attack the true tsar in the name of the false one? Confusion reigned, with no one able to distinguish any longer between true and false sovereign. The temptation to side with Dmitri was all the stronger because with him the dynastic line would be reestablished, while Boris's dynasty had no roots. Dynastic loyalty and growing anarchy combined increasingly to shake Godunov's fragile kingdom. After the north, the south—the steppes, land of the Cossacks and the outlaws—rebelled, rallying to Dmitri who increasingly appeared to represent the opposition to the impostor Godunov.

The predictions of the soothsayers came about, adding to the confused atmosphere of superstition of those years. Boris died in 1605. The fortune-tellers had foretold that he would reign, and that his reign would last for seven years. But they had never promised him that he would found a dynasty. This prediction of a short-lived reign contributed to the erosion of his legitimacy. His attempts to pass on his throne to his heirs were to be in vain, for the duration of a dynasty requires both strength and a certain degree of social acquiescence. By now almost powerless, Boris could do little more than entrust his son—the legitimate heir to the throne in his eyes— to the patriarch, the boyars, the people, and his faithful Fyodor

Basmanov, head of the army. All took the oath of allegiance, only to desert the cause of the new tsar soon after. Aware that society had already sided with the man who incarnated the miracle of the resurrection in a period when despair and death were everywhere, Basmanov immediately joined those boyars opposed to Godunov and thus prepared even to support Dmitri. Whether or not he was the real Dmitri mattered little to them. Their first priority was probably to liquidate the Godunovs. Without delay, Basmanov addressed the troops who were supposed to defend the true heir, the son of Boris, telling them that the real claimant was Dmitri. He then rushed to join Dmitri, who was marching on Moscow.

Once again, power changed hands in bloodshed. In the general confusion, the most important thing was to destroy the Godunov family. Boris's son and widow were killed on the spot. The Godunov dynasty had been able to establish itself because of the murder of Dmitri at Uglich; it was overthrown by the murder of Boris's successor. The seven years of glory of the founder of the dynasty, seven almost enchanted years, based on the strength of a prediction, were thus encompassed in a framework of murder, so often associated with the exercise of power in Russia.

The result was very strange: an entire population cried with joy as a complete stranger ascended the throne. They had only the word of a man vaguely identified as a defrocked monk that he was the child believed to have had his throat cut fourteen years earlier to go by. Amid the general and inexplicable rejoicing, Vasily Shuisky was the only one to continue to swear that he had seen with his own eyes the real Dmitri dying in a pool of blood, and that therefore the throne was in the hands of an impostor. But he was not believed, and the general fervor around the resurrected tsar was such that Dmitri, to show his clemency, had Shuisky brought down from the block when the executioner had already raised the axe that was to punish Shuisky for the crime of *lèse-majesté*. Thereafter, Shuisky kept silent. What else could he do, when Dmitri's own mother, Maria Nagaya, hastily brought back to Moscow, fell into the arms of the new tsar and cried out publicly that she recognized him as her own son? What choice had he when the patriarch—no longer Job, dismissed because of his faithfulness to the "impostor" Boris, but his successor, no less obedient to the new tsar, the Greek Ignatius—threw his weight, and with good reason, behind the man who had installed him on the patriarchal throne?

The reign of Tsar Dmitri, though brief, was very strange. He surrounded himself with "his" family, the Nagoy family, and the Romanov relations of Ivan's first wife, whom Boris had shut up in the cloister. The sovereign did not, however, much resemble "his" father. Neither the acts of clemency nor the behavior were those of Ivan. Naturally, he had hardly known him, and many years had passed. . . . This ill-favored, wretched figure, his face spoiled by a disproportionately large nose ornamented with a wart, behaved in a way that his people found incomprehensible. He ate veal, did not sleep after dinner, did not attend prayers, borrowed money from the monasteries, and made fun of the "barbaric" habits of the boyars. In fact, he was not without qualities. Very educated, with an extensive knowledge of many disciplines, he was enthusiastic about western Europe, resembling in this Boris, whom he had just replaced. Like him, he spoke of sending young Russians to be educated abroad, and he surrounded himself with Germans. No less distasteful to his subjects was the tolerance that he showed toward the Poles and to the Catholics whom his wife, the Polish Marina Mniszech, had brought in her suite. Despite his keen intelligence, a remarkable physical courage, and the aura of his supposed ancestry, after a few weeks Dmitri the miraculous became intolerable, if not to the majority of his subjects, then at least to those in Moscow, the town where legitimate authority was made and unmade.

The boyars who had sided with Dmitri, in order to bring him to power, or perhaps rather in order to get rid of Godunov, changed horses once again. Their candidate's personality was too strong and independent for them to be able to use him to reassert their authority, which had been gradually eroded by a succession of Russian sovereigns. Like Boris Godunov, Dmitri refused to be the hostage or the pawn of their personal ambitions. Scornfully turning his back on them, he reigned with his eyes turned to the states of western Europe where the hegemony of the great vassals was a thing of the past. Unlikely alliances of rival boyars began to form against him, ready to take on anyone who tried to restrain their ambitions.

On May 17, 1606, less than a year after his coronation, Dmitri fell beneath the blows of this coalition. The assassins invaded the Kremlin, seized him, threw him from a window, and then murdered him in the courtyard. It seemed as if Dmitri was being stabbed for a second time, and for a second time deprived of his throne. But the boyars had taken their precautions. For months they had carefully encouraged the rumor that the man that they had placed on the throne was in fact an impostor who had deceived them all. Once again, the evidence of the mother of the murdered tsarevich was required, but this time to produce a different version. Although a nun—forced into a convent at an earlier date—Maria Nagaya now denied her recent statements. Dmitri was not her son; he was clearly an impostor. As for her real son, she now swore that she had seen him die. Which of these two sworn statements was true? Which was the true Maria: the one who recognized Dmitri in order to unmask Godunov's deception and thus take her revenge for the fate to which he had condemned her (which would not perhaps have prevented her belief in the murder of her child)? Or was it the Maria who refused to recognize her child—lost, if only from sight—in Dmitri?

Henceforth it was believed that the real Dmitri died years earlier at Uglich. This second death of the young Dmitri with the rejection of Tsar Dmitri as an impostor was surrounded with symbolic ceremonies intended to show that, after a period of darkness, Russia had returned to a tangible reality where the dead did not suddenly come alive again and where usurpers could not triumph for long. In order to suppress all rumors, the murdered corpse of the "false" Dmitri, together with that of Basmanov, who had tried to defend him, were exhibited on the execution square, their faces covered with grotesque masks. Finally, the impostor's body was burned—a fate reserved usually for witches—since he had clearly used supernatural powers in order to deceive those around him so successfully. His ashes were scattered to the winds by being shot from the mouth of a cannon.

All traces of the now officially false Dmitri were thus removed. It now remained to relegate the murdered child to the next world, in order to avoid a repetition of the imposture. As soon as the impostor had been dealt with, the dead child received the due honors. In June 1606 the dead tsarevich was canonized and his remains transferred to the capital.

A Clash of Beliefs

There remained the problem of the throne. It had to be given to someone with an appearance of legitimacy, but to whom? And how should that person be chosen, when the Russian state knew only the law of inherited power?

The first to vouch for the murder at Uglich, a consistent opponent of Dmitri and chief author of the plot that ended his reign, Vasily Shuisky thought that the throne should come to him. He was, what was more, descended from Rurik, from Vladimir Monomakh and Alexander Nevsky, as were Ivan IV and the tsarevich of Uglich. Although, since the time of Alexander Nevsky, the line had come down through a different branch, now that this branch had died out, his early ancestry could justify the choice of Shuisky. Uncertain of the best course to follow, the boyars thought of inviting the *Zemskii sobor* to decide, as it had done before for Boris. It was preempted by Vasily, who literally pounced on the throne, having himself acclaimed by his supporters and a crowd of Muscovites. In an age when power was changing hands so frequently, this was not a very sound basis for legitimacy.

Vasily probably hoped to win over the boyars by promising to fulfill some of their expectations. Henceforth no boyar would be put to death without the sentence being confirmed by the Duma; the property of the condemned man would no longer be confiscated and his family would be exempt; calumny and denunciations would be severely punished. We see here the beginning of a remarkable change in the authority of the tsar. Russia, in the early seventeenth century, seemed to be following in the direction of Poland where royal power had become much less secure and the choice of a successor was no longer from father to son, but was beginning to be made by election. At each new stage the sovereign had to sacrifice another part of his authority to those who had elected him. The gradual building up of central authority that had taken place since the fourteenth century now seemed to be threatened by the troubled times.

But the real problem, which the arrangements at the top between the sovereign and his rival companions failed to address, was that of the need for popular support and restored confidence in the throne. However many precautions Vasily took to ensure that no pretenders challenged his rule, society was not convinced and continued to wonder about "true" and "false" pretenders. It was hardly possible, in the space of a few weeks, to denounce the reigning sovereign as a usurper, resuscitate a murdered tsarevich, confer on him the authority of a true tsar, then dismantle this edifice and turn truth upside down, without some damage. Even at the dawn of the seventeenth century, at a time when the ordinary man was not well-educated and the information issued from the throne scarce, such changeable versions, truths that overnight turned into lies, while lies were promoted to the rank of truths, could no longer convince society, even at the most humble level. On the contrary, the instability of official statements and the precariousness of truth and falsehood led to popular confidence being placed elsewhere. The more confused people were, the greater the effect of uncontrolled rumors, faith-healers, sorcerers, prophets, and a whole world of beliefs outside the officially constituted power and authorities. In a time of disorder, those who enjoyed the biggest audiences were those who incarnated it, those who rose up against order or were on the edges of it. The Muscovites had not forgotten that the corpse of Dmitri had been exhibited with a mask over the face. A new rumor was born: why the mask, if it was really the true Dmitri? Men claiming to be Dmitri came from the four corners of the land. If he had escaped one attempt on his life, why should the second attempt have been any more successful? Russian society was bewildered and discontented: the provinces, which had not been consulted over the installation of the false Dmitri, his fall, or the choice of a successor, were full of doubts; the peasants were as frustrated as always about their condition; the Cossacks and other groups saw the state of affairs as so many opportunities to affirm their independence. In short, Russian society was coming apart at the seams, moving ever closer to anarchy, grasping at any hope of salvation represented by the many "real" Dmitris. A pretender with an even more legitimate claim to the throne, being directly related to Fyodor, was invented: a supposed son who had been hidden and was now suddenly discovered. Thus the people were able to reconcile the myth of the reappearance of the legitimate tsar with respect for the martyrdom of the tsarevich at Uglich. Of all these fads and popular movements in favor of some supposed tsar, two were to take the country to the brink of collapse.

In 1606–7, in the south, a revolt led jointly by a Prince Shakhovskoy and a bizarre character, Ivan Bolotnikov, a one-time serf, roused the towns with the help of the tribal groups, proclaiming the need for a new political and social order. For these rebels, "Dmitri" was no more than a pretext, and in fact the leaders of the movement called up support not only for the prince of Uglich, to give substance to the mythical pretender, but also for "Tsarevich Peter," the recently invented son of Fyodor. Their troops reached the gates of Moscow, the mere mention of the name "Dmitri" opening the way to them, and it was of course in Moscow that the memory of the corpse with the hidden face was strongest.

A second serious impostor, who claimed to be both Dmitri the tsarevich and Dmitri the tsar, evidence of a double false death, suddenly appeared on the borders of Lithuania, then installed himself with his army in the village of Tushino, outside Moscow. He set up a veritable court, with an administration, challenging the "impostor tsar" in Moscow with the power of the "true tsar of Tushino." He was joined by Marina, wife of the false Dmitri, and recognized once again by the mother of the Uglich prince, Maria Nagaya. This "Tsar of Tushino," known to his enemies as the "Thief of Tushino," saw many of the supporters of Tsar Vasily come over to his side, a sign that Russia was uncertain of the outcome of this duel. All the while, in the background in the depths of the countryside, a considerable number of other Dmitris waited.

Russia Lost, Russia Saved

In the total anarchy of a disintegrating country, Vasily tried to dislodge the other "tsar" from his base in Tushino. At the same time, those who were hesitating between the false tsar and some other solution thought that they could put an end to the confusion by placing a fifteen-year-old Polish prince, Wladislaw, the son of King Sigismund III, on the throne. This is a clear indication of the degree of disintegration that had affected Russia. Ivan IV's strong state, not knowing which tsar to support and besieged on all sides, was on the point of handing itself over to the traditional enemies of Russia in order to reestablish a semblance of order.

Meanwhile, the "true" tsar was demonstrating his inability to influence events. Faced with the false Dmitri's horde of supporters, far from asserting his authority over them, Vasily lurched from one disaster to another. At the end of their patience, the Muscovites rose up again and sent a delegation to their insubstantial sovereign asking him to give up the throne. He obeyed and retired to a monastery, marking the end of yet another dynasty, so recently installed.

Abandoned to its own devices, Russia looked set to become a fief of the king of Poland, Sigismund III. Those who sensed which way the wind was blowing rallied periodically to the side of this powerful sovereign, rather than decide between the various false Dmitris (a third was to appear during this even more confused period). The reaction was to come from the Russian people themselves. The patriarch on one side and, on the other, a butcher from Nizhni Novgorod, Kuzma Minin, and Prince Pozharsky, a hero of many battles, called on the country to reestablish internal order and come to the defense of its threatened independence. The troops that answered the call were as varied as Russia itself. But the Russians— boyars, townspeople, peasants from the Don or the north—put all their wealth at the disposal of this new Russian crusade. This effort, full of patriotic emotion, enabled Moscow to be liberated after a siege during which the Poles were reduced to eating human flesh. The year 1612 came to be regarded in the collective memory as one of the decisive dates—after Kulikovo and the taking of Kazan—in the history of the nation. Exactly two centuries later, when faced with a new threat to the independence of Russia, and after a decisive rejection of the new occupier, the parallels with 1612 were underlined. It was at that time that the monument commemorating the two heroes of the uprising of 1612, the butcher Minin and Prince Pozharsky, was placed opposite the Kremlin.

It was essential to back up the reconquest of independence with a consolidation of power. The *Zemskii sobor* was called together to choose a new dynasty by the election of a sovereign.

It is remarkable that, after fifteen years of political chaos and a collapse of the state, with "miraculous" apparitions of the many false heirs, it was possible to reestablish the throne legally and with a procedure of irreproachable correctness. So much political sense after a time of such madness is astonishing. Furthermore, this decisive choice, which was to found a dynasty lasting for three centuries, was made in a time of civil peace, without threats, betrayals, and above all, without murder. The assembly, which in 1613 gathered together properly appointed delegates, consisted of important church dignitaries and representatives of the nobility, officials, townspeople, and even peasants. Its choice was Michael Romanov, a boy of fifteen whose family had been related by marriage to Ivan IV and whose father, forced by Boris Godunov to enter holy orders, had become the respected Metropolitan Filaret. The church, which had once again played a major role in the reconquest of independence, now had close links with the throne.

Not only did the tenuous relationship between Michael and Ivan IV seem to provide Russia with a link with the powerful state unified by the "terrible" sovereign, thus wiping out the memory of the intervening troubled times, but the choice of a Romanov also ensured that no blood stained this new house. Its occasional participation in the ruling power had not been marked by any murders. The Time of Troubles, which had begun with the murder of the tsarevich, closed with the peaceful election of a young boy tsar, the very embodiment of innocence. The period had opened with innocence profaned; now innocence triumphed. Russia, like the phoenix, had risen once again, showing astonishing maturity after a period of national enthusiasm. It seemed as if a page of history had finally been turned, leaving behind the times when violence and bloodshed had been the inevitable companions of power.

What Is a Tsar?

The Time of Troubles led those who were involved with power in
Russia to reflect anew about its nature and that of the sovereign.
Political thought in Russia developed at this time and provided the
reestablished state with a coherent ideology. Political certainties had
been seriously shaken by earlier events, as can be seen from the
popular reaction to the claims of the various Dmitris. But how
could it have been otherwise when, after almost four centuries of
efforts to maintain dynastic continuity, Russia had seen three dynasties in fifteen years—Godunov, Dmitri, and Vasily Shuisky—and
four sovereigns? A crowd of strange characters had appeared out of
the blue, each proclaiming to the four corners of the land that he
was the real heir to the throne, the boy who had died at Uglich, the
corpse at the Kremlin, the nonexistent grandchild of Ivan IV, or
some combination of these. Too much violence had been done to the
notions of true and false by those who maintained one thing one day
and the opposite the next: Vasily Shuisky, who swore that he had
seen the tsarevich dead at Uglich and then immediately said the
contrary; the tsarevich's mother who recognized one Dmitri, denied
him, and then recognized another. . . .

In the popular mind this rush of events and contradictory
assertions was disconcerting to say the least. But more tragic than
this was the problem of avoiding an error that was prejudicial to the
divine will. How should one know the true tsar, he of the divine
nature, and how could one avoid the false one? The problem was
aggravated by the fact that the Dmitris themselves probably did not
always know if they were or were not the boy of Uglich. If the
Dmitri of Tushino was from all the evidence a conscious and well-
organized impostor, if Bolotnikov's false Dmitris were his creation,
it does not follow that this was true for all of them, particularly the
first, who reigned and still today has his partisans who maintain
that he was the true Dmitri.

To complicate things further, usurping and legitimate tsars
could equally well be judged according to their virtues and their
crimes. In this respect, Ivan the Terrible, whose legitimacy was not
in question, had an impressive record of brutality. But the political
theory of his times would have made it impossible to question the

link between deeds and legitimacy. Boris Godunov had pursued more moderate policies, even if growing difficulties had caused him to become harsher; nevertheless, when Dmitri appeared on the scene, it was not Boris's actions that were condemned, but the simple fact that he was a usurper. When Dmitri was, in his turn, "unmasked"—not that this denunciation brought Boris any support—the latter did not for all that recover his lost legitimacy. The succession of false Dmitris was a sign of the deep malaise felt by the Russian people over the question of continuity.

The origins of this malaise and of the frantic search for a real Dmitri to return to his people were to be found in the murder of the tsarevich. Until then, murders had taken place within the family, without causing breaks in the dynasty. The murders carried out by Ivan, apart from the killing of his son, did not affect the continuity of the line of Rurik, while their logic, monstrous but implicitly accepted, was aimed at the strengthening of the state. In any case, Ivan was the legitimate tsar. The murder of the tsarevich at Uglich was another matter; it contravened the meaning of all the murders that had preceded it. According to the popular belief—and it matters little that this has almost certainly been proved incorrect by history—this murder, perpetrated by someone from outside the dynasty, who had no right to the throne, could only be intended to open the way to a usurper and to break the order guaranteed by God. Thus the tsarevich's death symbolized a double murder: that of the innocent redeemer, who in this way joined the two first prince martyrs, Boris and Gleb, in the people's pantheon; but also that of order in Russia, in a state that was one with its sovereign in a secular harmony. Having reemerged with difficulty from a traumatic and chaotic period of history, the nation found it hard to accept that the elements around which its unity had been built—Russia, its land and its state seen as one, and the tsar who was its embodiment on the throne—could be torn apart. The importance of the terms used to describe these two elements has rightly and frequently been commented on. Russia is the mother—*Matushka Rus'*; the sovereign is the father—*batiushka*. The murder of the child at Uglich, the last link in the chain of a dynasty, marked the end of this indestructible partnership forged by the Russian nation. This was the reason why, when all its certainties were shaken, Russia turned to symbolic or illusory representations of the unstable order: saints and impostors. No history is richer than that of Russia in saints who were first princes destined for power, or in impostors who arose in times of crisis to remind people that the order that they were supposed to incarnate could not be broken for long.

When this order was restored in the seventeenth century with the first Romanov, the political theorists reemerged. The most important was Ivan Timofeyev, chronicler of the early years of the new dynasty. It was his task, in this time of dynastic change, to define clearly the nature of power and that of the prince. The notion of the prince had taken some battering in a period when there had been nothing to allow men to distinguish definitely between true and false. It had seemed to imply that they were completely interchangeable. Since 1598, a more or less regular election had been used to choose the prince, showing both that a choice was possible and that nothing was inherent. It had become a matter of urgency to array the prince once more in all the metaphysical authority of which he had been stripped in the course of the previous fifteen years of uncertainty. Thus it was that Ivan Timofeyev's efforts were chiefly directed at the restoration, and even the extension, of the divine part of the nature of the prince, that part which removed him from the danger of judgment by his fellow men.

For Timofeyev, so long as the tsar was legitimate and thus identified with Russia—an impostor represented only himself and had nothing to do with Russia—his actions, whether good or bad, were nevertheless the actions of a tsar; they did not diminish his legitimacy in any way. Timofeyev takes the example of the short-lived tsar Vasily Shuisky, whose behavior and unfitness for office he harshly criticizes. For all that, in his eyes, Vasily was the tsar and neither his incompetence nor his faults gave his subjects the right to remove him from the throne. He applies the opposite reasoning to Boris Godunov in whom he recognizes many virtues, but who had no claim to legitimacy. Since Boris was only a usurper, it was not important that he did or did not rule well: he is condemned for the initial usurpation. But what made him a usurper and not Vasily Shuisky? Why was one legitimate and the other not? Here Timofeyev cannot use the argument of the break in the inherited line and the election, without destroying his justification of the legitimacy of Michael Romanov, who had also come to the throne as the result of an election and was the head of an new dynasty. He has thus to try to retain these principles and at the same time explain the troubles and break in the order. Paradoxically, it is only Boris Godunov who, despite political and human qualities far more evident than those of Shuisky, can be used as an illustration. If the murder of the tsarevich of Uglich is laid at his door—and for good measure Ivan Timofeyev adds that of Ivan the Terrible and his son Fyodor, which raises doubts about the figure of Dmitri—then it is clear where the illegitimacy lies. Boris was nothing more than a parvenu who assassinated the last members of a dynasty in order to substitute his own. Timofeyev had a specific ideological reason for the denunciation of the murder of the tsarevich: it allowed him to strike out Boris Godunov from the line of true tsars and to demonstrate clearly the demarcation line between the tsar who should be obeyed and the tsar who should be removed.

With such arguments, Ivan Timofeyev not only reinforced the authority of the tsar, but also helped to answer the crucial question of how to recognize a false tsar or an impostor. That the tsar is on the throne because he has assassinated another who should be there is only a partial answer. Ivan IV is not disqualified by the murder of his son because, being tsar, his crime, although enormous, is nevertheless the crime of a tsar, and thus does nothing to alter his nature. Boris was not tsar when he assassinated Dmitri, but did it in order to become tsar; achieved through murder, his position as tsar does not confer its nature on him. It is not possible to become tsar simply by virtue of sitting on the throne.

But what about Dmitri? How could he be recognized as a true tsar? Even supposing he had, as a child, escaped his murderers, that did not prove that the man who had reappeared after so many years was Dmitri. If the behavior of a tsar has no influence on the permanence of his nature as tsar, was it possible to infer from Dmitri's behavior on the throne whether or not he was the true tsar? Ivan Timofeyev's silence, or rather his confusion, on this point, essential to the future—when so many impostors were to continue through the centuries to appear from nowhere—speaks volumes. He is forced to admit that he does not know how one can recognize an impostor. On the other hand, he underlines the tragic history resulting from imposture. To obey the impostor is to sin against the order willed by God. From this sin flows terrible misfortune for Russia. The Time of Troubles was the price paid by the nation for the confusion into which it had sunk. The troubles had, however, begun at the time when Ivan IV had died and Boris Godunov had revealed his ambitions, which he carried as far as the ultimate crime, the murder of the tsarevich. But to whom should responsibility be attributed? Here Timofeyev adds to the duality of the nature of the tsar another dimension hitherto little mentioned: the idea of individual responsibility. A tsar who commits crimes himself creates disorder. Timofeyev attributes to the demands of the man Ivan IV a significant part of the responsibility for the misfortunes which followed. The murders committed by him did not detract from his legitimacy, but they did engender Russia's misfortunes.

From these thoughts that opened the reign of the Romanovs there emerged a more complete conception of the nature of the sovereign. The prince, who during the Time of Troubles had ceased to be identified with Russia and the state, if only because of the multiplicity of pretenders to the throne, now became one again with the idea of Russia. The divine and the human were perfectly reconciled in him: the one endowed him with legitimacy, raising him above the judgment of men; the other imposed on him behavior that could be ratified by their judgment in order that the man-tsar might rise to his function, identified with the divine part of his nature and guaranteeing it.

After such tumultuous times, a reappraisal was necessary in order to push back the anarchy that had crept in everywhere. For the tsar to be able to regain lost political ground, he would have to be more a tsar than ever before, approved by God and showing moral qualities that could no longer be ignored in a tsar. This new vision marks a considerable change from Joseph of Volotsk's view of an infinitely powerful tsar above morality.

6

The Limits of the "Civilized State"

◆

Despite chaos and tragedy, Russia was to develop along a coherent path until the eighteenth century. The geography of Russia, belonging clearly neither in Europe nor in Asia, had led it to incline now more to this side, now more to that. Nevertheless, ever since it had opted for the Orthodox Christianity of the Byzantine Empire, Russia had always thought of itself as a Western country, albeit from a distance. Twice this determined march toward the West seemed to have been interrupted. The first time was when the Mongols imposed their law and domination. In the long run, Russia was able to absorb this "Asianization" of the country, retaining only some forms of power and the vocabulary associated with them. The second "trial by fire" was the social and political chaos of the terrible Time of Troubles when Russia appeared so close to turning its back on all that had so patiently been accomplished. It seemed as if the country would break up into its diverse components and merge with the strong nations that surrounded it. Twice rescue came from the depths of the country. The entire nation, still so unsure of itself, had set in motion a veritable crusade to chase out first the invading Tartars in the fifteenth century, the foreign pretenders to the throne, and then the rebels in the seventeenth century.

The Early Romanovs: Revolt and Schism

United around a prince of the church identified more with Russia than with the state, the Russian nation became aware of its identity through these movements that snatched it from the abyss. During various intervals over a period of several centuries, the nation, the sovereign, and the state were perceived in a confused sentiment of unity, as a single entity. The nation discovered, affirmed, and consolidated itself around the idea of the state identified with the sovereign. Despite all the crises that Russia had known, this sense of unity had been felt to some degree throughout its history. It was at this time that Peter the Great came to the throne, breaking completely with the past.

Like all his predecessors, he wished to push the country toward Europe. Although perhaps going further and faster, his policy did not differ from those preceding it. However, he saw the process of westernization in terms of a radical break with the entire past history of his country. Peter the Great wielded a giant axe that cut Russia in two—both Russia as a historical development and Russia as a cultural phenomenon. Peter's axe made two Russias— the old and the new—and two social cultures—the vertical culture of the state with its elites, and the horizontal culture of the people. Such a radical break with the past could not come about without its tragedies. The woodcutter's axe will permanently wound a tree; Peter's axe, striking to left and right, could not fail to cause bloodshed, reviving the tragic cycle of murder.

The years separating the political solution that ended the great crisis of the Time of Troubles from the reign of Peter the Great were, however, relatively peaceful, favoring gradual evolution. The Romanovs came to the throne in 1613; almost seventy years passed before the accession of Peter the Great in 1682, more than a man's lifetime at that time. The state needed at least that amount of time for the stability of its institutions to be reestablished and the wounds of the Russian people to heal. Nevertheless, the first three Romanov tsars—Michael (1613–45), Alexis (1645–76), and Fyodor (1676–82)—did not have an easy task, each managing as best he could. But the progress made, both externally and internally, up to the end of this period was clear; the way to significant reform seemed to be opening up.

The first Romanov tsar, Michael, made it clear that the choice of a Romanov had been a good one and that the Romanov dynasty should be continued. Compared to the precariousness of the two preceding dynasties in the Time of Troubles, the three centuries of the Romanov dynasty that opened with Michael's reign were undoubtedly a success. With the emergence of a lasting dynasty and the achievement of external peace—although dearly bought— Michael Romanov was able to pass on the throne to his son without upsetting the fate of the new dynasty.

Alexis's reign was nevertheless to be full of difficulties. A contradictory character in a turbulent age, Alexis was seen both as a prince of exceptional human qualities and great gentleness—he was given the title of *Tikhaishi,* the "very gentle"—and as a tyrant deserving the reputation of Antichrist. He was indeed able to combine a peaceful gentleness with the violence of a despot. But it is this qualification of "gentle" that is significant in a time when those who had meditated on the nature of the tsar had declared that the human side of his nature was also important. A remarkable development had taken place between the time of the "Terrible," the fulminator whose ideologues were there to reinforce the belief that power *ought* to be terrible, to the present glorification of extreme gentleness. He was passionately interested in the West and its culture; nevertheless, it was this same gentle sovereign who, in the code of laws of 1649 (the *Ulozhenie,* which was to survive until the nineteenth century) established the definitive system of serfdom in Russia. He abolished any differences between peasants, imposing the principle that anyone who cultivated the land on a private estate was a serf, and that anyone who had been a serf would always be one. Flight became impossible. The code of 1649 also saw the final unification and universal application of the Russian legal system.

Peasant discontent and financial difficulties that had plagued the dynasty since 1613 gave rise to some dramatic revolts, the most famous of which was that of Stenka Razin in 1670–71. This was a revolt against the tsar's new order and against the growing problems for which this order was blamed, but not against the sovereign himself, who was still regarded as sacred. It is significant that this vast uprising, led by a man who seemed to have appeared from the world of the supernatural—it was said that he was part sorcerer and that when pierced by swords, bullets, and even cannonballs, he was unharmed—claimed to support the throne, that of the *true* tsar, against the disputed tsar. Stenka Razin's supporters, fighting against the order of Tsar Alexis but not infringing the divine order, proclaimed that the true tsar, the Tsarevich Alexis, was marching with them along the Volga on his way to take his due place on the throne. It mattered not at all that this tsarevich had died in 1670—his name and his shadow performed the same function as those of all the false Dmitris of the beginning of the century. They bore witness to the people's confusion, swinging between the ideal image of the tsar, re-created at every moment, and that of the real tsar. This was a compromise that avoided the threat against the divine element in the sovereign's nature.

An even more serious event both for Alexis's reign—earning him the title of Antichrist—and for the future of Russia was the schism, the *raskol*. This was the result of the reform of the church carried out by the Patriarch Nikon. The symbiosis of church and state had reached its apogee with the crowning of the first Romanov: Tsar Michael's father had been patriarch; the number of canonized sovereigns had increased, underlining their religious function as protectors of the faith and, through their piety, saviors of the nation. This symbiosis was to suffer all the more seriously from the effects and consequences of the schism. It came about as a result of Nikon's desire to revise the liturgical texts and make some changes in the church rituals. The response to these reforms, in reality fairly insignificant, was a violent explosion that went much further than the official dispute.

For those who rejected the reforms—the Old Believers, as they were to be called—it was a matter of basic principle. Russia, the Third Rome, was being led astray, away from the true path that legitimized the edifice of the combined church and state. They believed that the Third Rome was rotten to the core and dominated by the Antichrist—Tsar Alexis or Patriarch Nikon, or a fusion of the two. It was not possible to fight against this serious deviation, because those who were protesting dwelled in another kingdom altogether, that of the Truth. The only solution was that of total separation, the rejection and negation of the existing order dominated by church and state. Their message of the reign of the Antichrist and the quest for the kingdom of Truth was eagerly seized upon, because it was yet another variation on the theme that, for three-quarters of a century, had troubled the popular consciousness—the necessary distinction between the true and the false. The age of the false tsars was now followed by that of the Antichrist tsar, who was thus doubly false. Popular Russian culture, encouraged by history—and at the end of the seventeenth century, by the schism itself—had always been imbued with the idea of a quest for the kingdom of Truth. For those who did not join the Old Believers, there remained the nagging doubts, while for the state, the awful realization that the church, its guarantor and alter ego— even if the state was increasingly dominating the church—was no longer able to assure it of the support of society as a whole.

The Russia that emerged from this period of transition after the short reign of Fyodor, Alexis's son, was full of contradictions. The first Romanovs had been able to deal, provisionally at least, with the major external problems, even managing to annex the Ukraine. Above all, they had established a lasting dynasty. Despite the ghost of the Tsarevich Alexis that haunted the supporters of Stenka Razin as they traveled up the Volga, and the appearance of the Antichrist tsar, neither the rebels nor the Old Believers who, if not physically, then at least mentally had deserted Russia, had been able to overturn the legitimacy of this dynasty. The church, which had also been rejected by the Old Believers and was rocked by schism, nevertheless continued to support the authority of the throne in its central role of protector of the kingdom and the Orthodox population. But though the state was able to withstand these upheavals and the schism, it had not developed in depth, nor was it provided with an administration capable of carrying out its will in the far-flung reaches of so great a country. Nor was the state able to find the sources of finance necessary for the development of such an administration. The traditional idea still prevailed of the state and the tsar as a single entity that could demand everything from a society that was its patrimony. The apparatus of state—or that of the sovereign, since the two were one and the same—was insufficient to confer on the state the means for its modernizing ambitions. An ever-widening gulf was opening up between this ossified state and the tsars' abiding interest in the West and its political system. Either crisis or radical reform seemed inevitable.

This was made all the more likely since there were many elements that sharpened the tensions between an unchanging social culture, echoed by an unmoving state, and the few but not insignificant areas of innovation. The first of these were the revolts, which were a sign both of social unrest and, given their location—they emerged almost always in outlying areas that were less well controlled—of the need to adapt the structure of the administration to the extended territories and to the ethnic and cultural diversity which this implied. It was no longer easy for the Russian state to extend indefinitely its authority over such diverse peoples as the Tartars, the Ukrainians, or the peoples of Siberia. The conditions and cost of the control of these newly occupied territories would have to be thought out anew. At the same time, Russia was being swept by influences from abroad. The sovereigns of Russia had always attempted to control the mobility and relations of their subjects outside the country. With the development of foreign trade, however, and the arrival in Moscow of foreigners—Germans in particular, who occupied a whole district in the city—and the integration of the elites of the newly incorporated territories (notably the Ukrainians, who had many contacts with the Latin and Greek worlds), exchanges and influences began to multiply, progressively influencing the culture of the Russian elite, if not that of the ordinary people. The schism, which opposed tradition and change, destroyed Russia's unity and threatened the old belief in an absolute truth guaranteed by the partnership of church and state. All these critical elements still lay beneath the surface when the third Romanov tsar died. But they were to emerge with the renewed political instability that occurred at the time of a succession within the new dynasty. The year 1682 was to see a repetition of the uncertainties and tensions that, from reign to reign, had shaken Russia and threatened the throne.

Russia between Past and Present

"Just as the tsars could marry without regard to birth, they could also (in those days at least) choose a successor without regard to primogeniture. It appears that the rank of the wife and the heir of the sovereign was based solely on merit. The usage of this empire was, in this, much superior to the customs of the most civilized States." Voltaire's comments on the way in which Peter the Great finally came to the throne ignore the attempts made by a long series of sovereigns to draw up stable rules for the succession. The political upheavals and repeated conflicts that Russia was to see at the end of the seventeenth century, before the succession of Peter the Great, bear witness to the fragility of the institutional system in this matter, so essential to Russian stability. The death of the third Romanov tsar, like that of Vasily III almost a century-and-a-half before, revived the same questions: Who was the legitimate successor? How could he be chosen?

Since Fyodor had no heir, it was necessary to look to his brothers to provide one. From the two marriages of Fyodor's father Alexis, there survived two sons: Ivan, like Fyodor the son of Maria Miloslavskaya, and Peter, son of Alexis's second wife, Natalia Narishkina. According to the implicitly accepted rules of primogeniture followed by the first Romanovs, Ivan should have succeeded the dead tsar. But against him was the fact that he was, as Voltaire discreetly puts it, "ill-favored by nature." More specifically, he was physically weak, limped, and was almost blind. He spoke with difficulty and was feeble-minded. Despite his young age—he was only nine years old at the time—his half-brother Peter was quite different, being remarkably bright and lively. Furthermore, Peter's mother was the widow of the sovereign and thus in a position to act as regent. The court was full of her relatives, who were able to constitute an effective pressure group on behalf of their young relative. The Miloslavskys, by contrast, had been removed from all positions of importance at the time of Alexis's remarriage. Thus on the one hand there was a political tradition that all previous sovereigns had attempted to enforce; on the other, political power and a suitable heir.

The resulting battle had important implications. Unlike past occasions, when Michael and Alexis had named their eldest sons as successor on their deathbeds, the sickly Fyodor had died without expressing any opinion on the matter. His silence was all the more regrettable since the absence of a direct heir pointed to trouble ahead. The choice made would determine a principle of succession—the right of the eldest son, or that of the best—the future of a family and its supporters, and lastly the choice of a regent. The latter was indispensable because of the weakness of one possible heir and the youth of the other. In the absence of any guidelines, the decision was referred to the Duma of the boyars and to the church. The choice made by Patriarch Joachim and the boyars would have to reconcile the actual situation and the right of succession that was beginning to be established. Insisting on Ivan's unfitness to exercise power personally in the future, they favored the young child and entrusted the regency to the widow of the dead tsar. This choice of Peter also benefited his mother's family, the Narishkins, who immediately took over all the important posts.

Given the strength of these two ambitious boyar families highly placed around the throne on account of their kinship with two tsarinas, it was inevitable that the Miloslavskys would refuse to accept defeat. They were strengthened by the exceptional figure of Sophia, Ivan's older sister, who had received an education unusual for a Russian woman of the time at the side of her brother Tsar Fyodor. Theologians from Kiev had taught her well; she spoke Latin and Polish fluently and was versed in the sciences and arts. A remarkably intelligent and ambitious girl, she had refused to enter a convent, the usual fate of tsars' daughters. She also objected to the stifling atmosphere of the women's quarters. The succession held up the possibility of a future more fitting to her personality. She immediately assumed the role of spokesperson for the family, protesting at a decision that had ignored the rights of the eldest son. Ignoring the usual custom, she attended the funeral of Fyodor, in order to assert the rights of the senior branch of the family against the Narishkin faction. She gathered round her a kind of court whose members, all closely allied to her family, began to spread among the people alarming rumors about the reality and the legality of the tsar's power. At the same time, she sought the support of the *streltsi* who, at this period of transition and uncertainty, were brooding over their grievances—wages, promotion, common problems in any body of this type—which the Miloslavskys were able easily to exploit. Suddenly, the rumors hardened: young Peter was nothing but a front for a scheming mother who, in order to rule, had had Ivan murdered. Once again the old but never forgotten stories reemerged—an assassinated tsarevich, a usuper. Their circulation was enough to spark off the explosion.

To the clanging of the bells of the four hundred churches of Moscow, the *streltsi* and the crowd rushed on the Kremlin. The appearance of the regent, Natalia, accompanied by the two half-brothers, the young tsar and the tsarevich who, it was said, had been assassinated, should have been enough to calm the crowd. But this would be to fail to reckon with the strange mixture of rumors of a plot and the people's memories. It was enough to suggest to the rebels that, if Ivan was alive, then it was Fyodor who had been poisoned. An indescribable carnage resulted. The Narishkin family and their allies were impaled on pikes brandished in the courtyard to receive their twitching bodies, slitting some from top to bottom. Natalia's father and brother were torn from her arms and hacked to pieces. An old boyar was dragged by the beard to the cathedral square in the Kremlin and then tossed onto a row of sharp halberds. This terrible butchery, showing how the people could be inflamed to such excessive cruelty, was, it should be remembered, witnessed by the young Peter. It was an insupportable sight for a child of ten, but it conformed with tradition. The young Ivan IV too had, in the past, had such scenes engraved on his memory. Little wonder then that Peter the Great, like Ivan morally scarred by the horrors witnessed as a child, would one day follow the instinct for cruelty so far as to turn his own son into a victim. This repetition of identical tragedies of so exceptional a nature is not the least of the peculiarities of Russia's misfortune.

A Shared Crown

The first effect of the events of May 1682 was to upset the dynastic order yet again. With the extermination of the Narishkins, the way was open for their rivals, and first of all for Sophia who became regent in the name of her two brothers, Ivan and Peter. Though there had been other innovations in Russian history, it was the first time that the idea of sharing the crown had been proposed. Biblical and Byzantine precedents were cited in its support—Pharaoh and Joseph, and Basil II and Constantine VIII.

The regency began badly. Sophia's behavior was thought shocking and she was nicknamed "the Scandalous" (*Pozornoe litso*). In addition, her ideas on religion were too modern, while the *streltsi,* who had ensured her success, were inclined to the old faith. An admirer of the West, this active woman was determined to govern over both internal and external affairs despite opposition. She had a remarkable adviser in the figure of Prince Golitsin, who favored ideas that challenged the entire existing order in Russia, starting with serfdom, which he dreamed of abolishing. He failed in this, just as he failed to "people the deserts and enrich the beggars." But his foreign policy, also conceived on a grand scale, was crowned with success when a peace treaty between Russia and Poland was signed in 1686. Less successful was his attempt to quell the Tartars of the Crimea where the Russian army was faced with numerous and well-disciplined troops receiving Turkish aid. This painful defeat put an end not only to Sophia's international ambitions, but also to her reign.

Sophia realized that the moment had come when she would either have to seize power once and for all or lose it. The two co-tsars had married and Peter was becoming increasingly interested in military affairs. The only way to realize her dream of becoming empress was to carry out a coup d'état. But whom could she count on for support? She did not entirely trust the *streltsi,* whom she had pushed to one side since 1682 when she had used them to help her get rid of the Narishkin family, fearful that they might one day become involved in some plot against her. Herein lay her weakness. The troops she needed had no reason to owe her any gratitude; and to assist a woman to absolute power against the rights of two legitimate heirs was not a tempting thought. They had little respect for women in general and were not inclined to bring the right of succession into disrepute. Sophia planned a coup, but it was ill-prepared and the boyars, the *streltsi* and the patriarch rushed instead in the name of legitimacy to support Peter, who had taken refuge in the fortified Trinity-Sergius Monastery at Zagorsk.

Sophia had lost, and Tsar Peter—technically still co-tsar—was wary of the conspirators. He was then only seventeen years old and little interested in public affairs. He had easily overcome his sister, and he does not, at that time, appear to have been tempted to take harsh measures to prevent future plots. The repressive measures of 1689, carried out to teach his enemies a lesson, had not been his idea, but his supporters were enthusiastic and encouraged by the patriarch.

Prince Golitsin, accused simply of having ignored the rights of the co-tsars during the regency—he took no notice of their opinions and gave Sophia's name equal rank to theirs in official documents—escaped with his life, but lost everything else: his rank of boyar, his possessions, and the right to live in Moscow. He was exiled with his family to a village deep in Arctic Russia where he dragged out the rest of his life in a quarter-century of poverty and loneliness. His was an enviable fate, however, if compared with that of Sophia's lover, Shakhlovity, accused of leading the conspiracy, who was tortured at length before being beheaded. Her counselor, the monk Sylvester Medvedev, accused of heresy, was beaten with the knout and later beheaded. The military ringleaders who had not died were punished rather less severely, with the knout and by having their tongues cut out. There remained Sophia, who was finally to meet the fate she had so much wanted to avoid—the cloister.

Why was such severity used against those who, having no support, were no threat? The reason is clear: Sophia's entourage was punished not so much for having conspired, but for having tried to upset the order of succession, ignoring rules formed with such difficulty after so many crises. In order to avoid a repetition of these intrigues, the return to order should teach a lesson rather than exact revenge. The irony of history is that, in this instructive revenge, Peter included the man whom he would have found the most useful to him later on. Because he had sided with the usurping regent,

Prince Golitsin, whose forward-looking political vision was so close to that which was to guide Peter, was forever removed from the enterprise that was to see the triumph of his ideas. Instead, the boyars and the *streltsi* who, in 1685, chose Peter and rejected Sophia, made it their first task to remove from power all those who looked toward the West and condemned the ritualistic and ossified world that Russia had inherited from two-and-a-half centuries of Tartar domination, cutting her off from the rest of Europe. They supported Peter in the name of the status quo. Little did they suspect that through this choice, they were opening the door to radical change, to the break they had so anxiously sought to avoid. Peter's supporters belonged to the world that had gone before. When his axe made its decisive blow they were left behind forever.

But this old world was not just characterized by a fear of change. It should be stressed that it had also been an extraordinary period when, for seven years, a woman, with next to no support, had been able to break the chains that, for centuries, had kept her fellow women enslaved in the Russian court. Although powerless to see her plan through to the end, as regent Sophia was to pave the way for a series of women who, after Peter, were to give the Russian throne such brilliance. Muscovy had never accepted the idea that a woman could be worthy of power. The Kiev tradition seemed to have been lost forever. The regency held by the mother of Ivan the Terrible had, in the eyes of contemporaries, been nothing but a pure usurpation. Because she was remarkably intelligent and educated, Sophia was for seven years a true sovereign. She was unable, perhaps, to carry out a profound political revolution, but her government was wise, scarcely ever taking a backward step. She was prudent, for two reasons: to have a woman in her place was sufficiently shocking without risking any excessive innovation that would have led immediately to accusations of heresy or witchcraft.

As a victim of her position as a woman at this time when she was the first to have broken the locks that enclosed her fellow women in their quarters, she had to be careful to proceed slowly. Installed as regent, thanks to an ambiguous compromise but without a secure legal basis, she knew her power was disputed and challenged. She would have either to accept it as it was, which was to say, accept that one day she would have to return to the world of female submission from which she had escaped, or make it her ultimate aim to seize total power. There was no other way to achieve permanent emancipation. It is hardly surprising if she had to subordinate other more general ambitions to this goal. Even though it was to be Peter who made the decisive break in the history of Russia, Sophia deserves recognition for her part in this process. After her, women were able to claim total power and achieve it . . . by the traditional means of murder.

Peter I's "Universities"

At seventeen, the age at which Ivan the Terrible had been crowned, Peter I was on the throne, his ambitious half-sister now safely out of the way. His half-brother was scarcely a hindrance. For five years, until 1694, he left the reins of government in the hands of his mother, Natalia, and her entourage, Patriarch Joachim and his uncle Lev Narishkin, a pleasant but weak-willed man who happily accepted little more than the trappings of power. These were five years of transition during which Peter asserted himself against an environment hostile to the Western world and very different from what he longed for. Those close to the throne wished to eradicate the memory of Sophia's regency in the name of a "Russian" order. The result was deplorable. Under the authority of a fiercely xenophobic and intolerant patriarch, the frontiers of the country were closed to foreigners, all missives from outside were submitted to strict police control, the Jesuits were expelled, and the inhabitants of the German suburb, known as *Nemtsi* (Germans), whatever their real place of origin, began to feel the discomfort of their position.

In 1690, when the patriarch died, this development became even more pronounced. Of the two rival candidates for the patriarchal throne, Metropolitan Marcellus of Pskov, a scholarly man, speaking several foreign languages and open to influences from western Europe which he had traveled from end to end, and the metropolitan of Kazan, a symbol of Russian conservatism and the rejection of the West, the court chose the latter. He had the remarkable advantage over his rival of possessing a beard untouched by the barber's scissors. In those conservative times, the length of the beard was of paramount importance, dividing those who called themselves Russians and good Christians from those suspected, from the shortness of their beards, of having connections with the Evil One. It was because of the backward-looking attitude, permeated with narrow-minded pettiness, of these early years, that Peter, ruling more in name than in practice, was unable to exercise any political will or make important decisions.

Although absent from the field of government, the young tsar stood up against anything that was done in his name with a view to some other design. The seventeen-year-old was following his instincts rather than a precise plan, but both these instincts and his whole person already had something about them to alarm those in power. Peter's "universities"—for these were indeed to be the first stage in the formation of his character—were disconcerting to say the least. A giant, well over six feet in an age when people were shorter than they are today, Peter inevitably dominated all those who surrounded him. In order to carry on a conversation with him when he took a walk, his interlocutor was forced to run along at his side, trying to keep up with the speed and length of his steps. Though his appearance still had the charm of youth—an angular body, and rounded face punctuated by a small mustache—the trait that was always to embarrass him was already apparent: a twitch on the left side of his face, a fleeting tic or a more prolonged convulsion, disconcerting to the onlooker and provoking in Peter an intense suppressed rage. The imbalance in his character was to feed on this anger.

Just as all those who met him were impressed by his gigantic physique, so also were they by his dazzling intelligence. Although he had received little education in his childhood—the tragic events that punctuated it were enough to explain why—Peter insatiably devoured any book that chanced to come into his hands and learned all he could from those who crossed his path. He had all the positive characteristics of the autodidact—a boundless thirst for knowledge, an amazing memory, and the ability to seize on and classify information in his methodical mind. Two lasting passions dating from this period were the sea and weapons, and hence the arts of war in general. In a land cut off from all access to the open sea, with only one port, Archangel, on the edge of the Arctic Circle and icebound for half the year, his constant obsession was to lead him to find an opening to the sea and the creation of a fleet. In the years 1689–94, when it appeared that Peter did nothing but indulge in feasting, drinking, and chasing girls (despite the marriage arranged for him by his mother), his mind was elsewhere, on the high seas, dreaming of ships.

This energetic giant was capable of accomplishing all things at once. He summoned shipwrights from Holland to build ships that were first tried out on Lake Pletchevo, eighty miles from Moscow, where his naval vocation had taken shape in his early youth. In 1693 he went even further, to Archangel, to discover what the real sea was like. It is hard to imagine what such a journey represented at that time, and that a young tsar who undertook it would cause such scandal. There his design began to take shape: despite its geographical limitations, his country would have to be a sea power, if it was not to be excluded from the circle of the great nations. He also stepped up the number of military exercises on land; from the age of eleven he had begun, in his war-games, to replace pretend armies with real ones, armed with real ammunition. Behind the games and the orgies, the strategist and visionary was beginning to emerge.

But the lake, the sea, and the field of maneuvers were not enough for his eager spirit. He was constantly drawn to his close foreign friends in the German suburb. Through them he heard ever more about the West that so fascinated him, so different from the rigid world around him. From this period, Peter became a stranger in his own home, and he saw that this static Russia embodied by the patriarch and his entourage would have to be shattered by force. The animated life of the German suburb offered him a remarkable example of the open world that lay beyond the seas; he was soon to embark on the task of fashioning Russia in this image.

Suddenly events began to move. Peter's mother died in 1694, leaving the reins of power in his hands. He demonstrated this right away with a dazzling success, the capture of Azov, Russia's opening to the Black Sea. As soon as he had come to power, he had become involved in his predecessors' eternal obsession: how to destroy the last bastion of the Turkish domination on the edges of his country and gain access to the sea. There were only two ways of achieving this: either to push toward the Baltic and confront the powerful Swedes; or to make for the Black Sea, controlled by the Turks. Everything inclined him toward this second solution. For a Christian sovereign, what could be more urgent than the defeat of the Turk who had long ago defeated the Byzantine Empire? To attack this enemy of the faith seemed like a true crusade. And in this enterprise Russia, which had known no crusades, found one of those causes with the power to unite a people with its leader in a great outpouring of fervor. At the start of a reign, it was also a sure way for the sovereign to win the hearts of his people and the approval of the church. And, should he be victorious, what a blow it would be against the Tartar khanate in the Crimea which enjoyed the support of the Sublime Porte!

Peter launched his entire land forces against the citadel of Azov, but he lacked the fleet that would have allowed him to surround completely the seaward side of the excellently defended fortress. After two unsuccessful assaults, he was forced to raise the siege. This was an intolerable defeat, for he had committed himself personally and totally to this campaign. He must not fail, for, to those who clung to tradition, defeat would signify the failure of his policy of modernization and his modern strategy. Far more was at stake than just the capture of the citadel. Peter could not capitulate. In a final effort, with the help of foreign advisers, he established a fleet and took Azov from the sea. The total victory canceled out the previous defeat: a victory over the Turks, against whom the young sovereign had struck a first decisive blow; a victory in the collective consciousness where Azov became one of the events symbolizing Russia's renaissance, the triumph of Christianity over Islam, revenge for two-and-a-half centuries of lost history. To the roll-call of names symbolizing the liberated nation, Kulikovo, Kazan, and Astrakhan, was added that of Azov.

It also was a victory over the past and over the geographical limitations of continental Russia. From this time on Russia was to be a naval power. Three thousand families set up in Azov, while the church and the whole of society—nobles, merchants, and officials—inspired by a sudden naval fervor, brought their material contributions to the construction of the fleet. Young men were sent abroad to study the naval arts, while foreign experts came to Russia. Peter himself did something hitherto unknown for a monarch: in 1697, he left for Europe under an assumed name—Peter Mikhailov—with 250 followers, to visit foreign countries, specialists in all disciplines, sovereigns, and ordinary townspeople, and to learn wherever he could and from whomever he met everything that the West had to impart. This "great embassy," which took him almost everywhere, nevertheless omitted one place: although his companions passed through France where Louis XIV was then at the peak of his power, Peter did not meet the Sun King.

This embassy, so revolutionary at a time when the slightest movement of a sovereign was accompanied with pomp and ceremony, also revolutionized Russia. Peter had from the start upset his subjects. His westernized tastes, visible even in his style of dressing—he dressed like the inhabitants of the German suburb—his disguise as a merchant during his travels, the foreign languages that he liked to use, and his choice of entourage where among his closest intimates figured an Irishman and a Swiss, all troubled the Russians. The great embassy was frowned upon: why did a Russian sovereign need to travel abroad? Why did he bring back foreigners—the embassy had brought some 850 home—when they had always been regarded with deep suspicion? To top it all, Peter returned from his pilgrimage quite overwhelmed. He had obtained everything he had hoped for from the distant countries of Europe, technical contact and good will, but he had also understood the extent of Russia's backwardness and the effort that would be needed to catch up with this fascinating continent. No indications of the extent of the gulf between the two universes had escaped his notice. The sentiment that he must have felt above all was humiliation. His immense country—men and things—horrified him in every aspect, appearing as a challenge to the civilized world from which he had just returned. His "education" concluded with a terrible realization: he had found his way, which led toward everything that the West had accomplished and away from everything that he had to abolish at home. In a prelude to reform a veritable fury of destruction of all the exterior signs of backwardness now possessed him.

"Death to the Beard!"

On his return to Moscow, Peter immediately knew what he must do. The boyars who had come to celebrate his return were suddenly subjected to an unexpected attack, more extraordinary and incongruous than any of the tsar's previous provocations—and they had been many. The story is well known. Taking a long razor from his sleeve, Peter quickly cut off the beards of all those who served him, sparing only the patriarch, one old man, and a close relative. In a country where the wearing of a beard was a sign of respect for the Creator—priests would refuse benediction to beardless men— the Russians were scandalized. Despite this shocking action, condemned by the church, Peter decreed that, with the exception of the priesthood and the peasants, all his subjects should be clean-shaven in the future. State officials would be empowered to take a razor to any bearded man they met. A tax would be levied on anyone who insisted on this ornament.

After the beard, he started on the Russian clothes. Instead of the traditional long robe with wide sleeves, Hungarian or German clothes should be worn. If Peter met someone who insisted on wearing the kaftan, he would hasten to cut the garment to a more fitting length and pull off the sleeves. He never went anywhere without his scissors and razor, the first weapons of the reformer. In addition, he authorized the sale of tobacco in his lands—the habit of taking snuff being another symbol of the West—and imposed a change on the calendar, bringing it into line with that of the West.[1] The confusion of his subjects can be imagined.

In the eyes of the majority of Peter's subjects, his constant innovations were not just disconcerting, they were the work of the devil. The old Russia, superstitious and conservative, haunted by the memory of the false sovereigns who had led it, so it was believed, into the paths of sin, and always ready to believe the most unlikely rumors, was suddenly and violently resurrected. Priests and Old Believers went about telling anyone who would listen that the

---

1. The Russian calendar started from the supposed creation of the world and the season when it took place. Thus, the year began on September 1 (the sacred moment of the harvest), and not on January 1; and 1698 was for the Russians 7206.

Antichrist was present among them. Had it not been foretold that he would be born of adultery, and was not Peter the son of the second marriage of his father, which amounted to the same thing? From this to calling him the Antichrist was no more than a step. For others, Peter's unlikely-sounding journey abroad was the source of the most fantastic rumors. According to these rumors, the disguised Peter had been kidnapped during his travels, shut up in a barrel, and thrown into the sea. Another version had him chained up in a dungeon, in the depths of Sweden, while a false tsar had returned to his place to Russia, indulging in such excesses that his people could no longer recognize him. Once again, a disconcerting tsar, who did not follow the usual path, was seen as a usurper. The idea of change was so unsettling that the idea of imposture was preferred. Furthermore, the myth of a false tsar or the theory of the Antichrist had the advantage, for those who harbored political ambitions, of opening the door to plots which, if the tsar was recognized as a usurper, would be perfectly legitimate.

From her convent, Sophia, the deposed regent, also tried to reestablish links with the malcontents. If Peter was a false tsar, who else was there to sit on the throne but Sophia herself? Foremost among the discontented figures of the new regime were the *streltsi*, who could play a decisive role in the plot that was taking shape. Since his accession, Peter had done nothing but humiliate them. In maneuvers, they had had to play the part of the "enemy" and thus of the losers. Peter's passion for education and ability had led him to encourage officers from distant parts of the country and ensure the promotion of foreigners in the army. To their fury at this threat to their interests was added the growing conviction that such an attack on tradition could only be the work of someone who was a stranger to Russia and the true faith. Seeing it as a sacred duty to hunt out the usurper, denounce the false tsar, and find the true one, the *streltsi* set off for the Kremlin. Their revolt was unleashed when Peter was still in Vienna. Rushing back, he found that the mutiny had been easily put down, punishment already decided on—150 hangings and hundreds of rebels thrown into prison—and that order had been reestablished. This time, however, he refused to show the clemency that he had exercised on a previous occasion. This passionate admirer of Western civilization was to react to a relatively unimportant rebellion with a demonstration of unbelievable barbarity. It seemed to mark the end of the lessons learned from his "universities."

Barbarity in the Cause of Progress

Voltaire, always indulgent when speaking of Peter I, rightly says "if the tsar had not needed to set a terrible example, he would have set some of those *streltsi* who were executed, and thus lost to him and to the state, to labor in public works. The life of men had to be counted dear, particularly in a country where the population demanded all the cares of a legislator. He believed he had to astonish and subjugate forever the spirit of the nation, through the nature and the number of punishments used." With these harsh words, Voltaire says it all. Peter had no need to take revenge. But he had understood Russia's recurring problem: power was not threatened so much by plots as by superstitions and obsessions that provided an excuse for action by anyone who aspired to power; the Russian people too often inclined to see the figure on the throne as an impostor and were ready to follow those who exploited this inclination for their own ends. The weakness of the throne lay precisely in this uncertainty among the ordinary people about the person of the sovereign. No sooner was the sovereign absent, or conflicts arose, or he showed signs of hesitancy, than the idea of imposture would begin to take hold. In order to establish definitively that the person on the throne was really the tsar and to eradicate from people's minds the attraction exercised by false tsars, it was necessary to show that the time of weakness had gone forever and to crush all those who might be tempted to revive them. It was a time for exemplary repression.

He stopped at nothing to deal with the *streltsi:* torture of every kind, hanging—the Kremlin square bristled with scaffolds—and decapitations. The total number of deaths is almost incredible: more than a thousand *streltsi* executed (two thousand, according to Voltaire), the priests who had comforted them condemned to death, two female companions of the ex-regent, Sophia, buried alive, the survivors and their families exiled to the most inhospitable regions of Russia. For five months, tortured bodies were exposed to the public gaze at their place of execution, and corpses were hung on all the Kremlin walls and in various squares in the town in order to keep alive the sense of repression. Peter took the opportunity at this time to repudiate his wife, Eudoxia, and shut her up in a convent. He had tired of her long before and had taken the young tsarevich away from her—to remove him, he said, from the influence of the tsarina's retrograde ideas. The same fate met his sister Sophia, and this time the convent regime was sufficiently harsh for him to feel confident that she would never reemerge.

Apart from acting as an example, the importance of this repression lay elsewhere—in the role the tsar himself played in it. He set himself up as executioner, and forced his boyars to share the task. Many sovereigns before him had amused themselves with the spectacle of torture, but none had hitherto dreamed of being involved personally or including the nobility. In a century when torture was a normal part of government, including in those European countries that Peter had taken as models, the separation between the role of the governor and that of the executioner was always strictly observed. For a moment, Peter was to abolish the dividing line between the two roles, evidence—since Peter was not unbalanced—of the peculiarity of a country where at the same time it was possible for progress to advance.

The "Civilized State"[2]

"We shall need Europe for a few decades, and then we can turn our back on her," Peter said to one of his collaborators. But having taken such a path, would it be possible to turn back? The surprising thing is that Peter had time for this "westernization," of which he dreamed constantly, even when his reign was a nonstop succession of conflicts. Only one year of his long reign passed without a war, yet he introduced countless innovations. Force was to play a decisive role.

The first problem he had to face—and the permanent state

---

2. This concept, developed by Marc Raeff in his excellent work *Comprendre l'Ancien Régime russe* (Paris: Seuil, 1982), which deals with this tragic period with great sensitivity, is perhaps the best key to approaching the reign of Peter the Great.

of war made it particularly urgent—was that of the army. The army that he had inherited was little suited to his broad vision for foreign and internal affairs: to ensure Russia's security, guarantee access to the sea, and have an army controlled by the state and not dependent on the good or bad will of his subjects. At the end of his thirty-six years of rule, his achievements were tangible: he had given his country a permanent army of more than 200,000 men, 100,000 auxiliaries, and 240,000 sailors. No other country in Europe could boast such military power. Peter stopped at nothing in his efforts to ensure that the state could rely on this army and escape at last from traditional ambitions and pressures: universal conscription,[3] the formation of elite regiments, modernization and standardization of equipment, and the development of an armaments industry. But a modern army required modernized financing. The old system of taxation of "hearths" (households), combining payment in money and in labor services, was excessively complex and was open to all kinds of evasions and disputes. It was replaced by a single poll tax. The immensity of the needs of the state was such that it had constantly to resort to expedients to raise money, suddenly imposing a reduction in the salaries of officials, doubling the tax paid by the Old Believers, or taxing baths, bees, and even coffins. . . .

The first to suffer from these changes were the peasants. The landowners, given the task of collecting the taxes, thereby increased their authority. As Peter had already abolished the difference between free sharecroppers—who, in exchange for part of their produce, farmed land belonging to the nobles—and the peasants already attached to the land, serfdom was now definitely established everywhere. The modernization of the country's institutions and the financial requirements necessary for this had the strange effect of bringing about the irrevocable subjugation of the peasant, whose status was now little more than that of a slave. One of Peter's edicts

---

3. Obligatory military service, which only became common in western Europe in the late eighteenth century, had long-lasting consequences for the relationship between the tsar and the peasantry. Although a peasant selected by lottery was thereby freed from serfdom, he nevertheless regarded military service as a death sentence. His beard was shaved off and he was torn forever from his family. For the peasant, who felt a terrible resentment, obligatory military service represented an intolerable act of violence.

is revealing: "Slaves should be sold by families, without separating husbands and wives, parents and children, and no longer like so many head of cattle, a usage no longer practiced anywhere. . . ."

Obsessed with the idea of progress, Peter imposed a strict educational system on society, so that those who came to serve in the army could meet the standards required for military efficiency. The schools that were opened for those who were to enter his service were, like the army, hedged about with restrictions. In 1714, a decree declared that priests could only issue certificates of marriage to individuals who could demonstrate their knowledge of arithmetic. . . .

Of all Peter's reforms—if one considers only those with an obvious influence on the future of the system and the solution to conflicts of power—two deserve a closer study, for they were to complete the effects of the changes to the fiscal system and the reforms in education. In 1700, Peter launched the first-ever newspaper in Russia, *Vedomosti,* to explain his policies. With this newspaper, he took a decisive step toward a new relationship with society. Until then, a rigorous secrecy had surrounded the throne, its actions, and its decisions. Suddenly society was being involved and the result was that the whole system altered. Another decision, no less important for later history, was the definition of "political crimes against the state" and the setting up of an authority to deal with such crimes. The code of 1648 had devoted a chapter to crimes against the tsar and their repression, but here it was only a question of the sovereign, and punishment was a matter for him alone. The discovery of such crimes had been by chance or from the habit of denunciation of one's neighbor; there had been no serious organization of "state security." Peter's great innovation was to bring crimes against the state to the foreground—and thus the idea of state security—and to institutionalize their prevention and punishment. A text of 1711 stated that anyone who denounced a noble failing in his obligations—now a crime against the state and no longer against the tsar—would be rewarded with all the noble's lands, even if he was himself only a serf. This repression of crimes against the state became increasingly professional. In 1702, a decree specified that attacks on the state would be dealt with henceforth by a special ministry—*Preobrazhenskii prikaz*—that had unlimited authority to make inquiries or suppress information, whatever the rank and status of the people or institutions involved. The actual date of the creation of this organ of state security is not known, but it is clear that this was the first known secret police, with its limitless powers and freedom of action that could not be called into question, and the ancestor of those notorious institutions that were to ravage Russia's history in the future. Under Peter the Great, the secret police tortured and murdered at will. No other authority had the right to interfere in its actions or the power to protect society from it.

Even a brief look at Peter the Great's policies reveals the great social and political changes they brought, but also their contradictions. All these reforms advanced the state, the sense of the state, and its primacy in relation to the sovereign. Peter the Great was the first Russian sovereign to refer to the notion of the public interest, and he did so constantly. He was also the first—and this derives from the very emergence of the state—to institute the concepts of political crime and state security.

Society too underwent an immense change. First of all the development of the idea of service to the state became apparent, with constantly increasing numbers. This was the case with the nobility, which more than doubled during Peter's reign, becoming more powerful politically. The Table of Ranks[4] gave it more independence, for it now no longer depended entirely on the whim of the sovereign. The rules of promotion that he drew up conferred an autonomy on the nobility that it was impossible to go back on. This freedom was further increased by Peter's promotion of education, which ensured a nobility that was intellectually more homogeneous and hence more conscious of itself as a class. Instead of the traditional dispersion of all those who served the sovereign, there grew up a feeling of belonging to a group of the same educational background, with the same rights and same duties and, gradually,

---

4. The Table of Ranks was set up in 1722. It replaced the old hierarchy of titles and ranks with a completely different system: in three areas of service to the state—the army, the civil service, and the court—the positions were fixed in fourteen ranks, in ascending order, the first being the highest. Each person had, according to his position on the scale, a rank or *chin*, which corresponded to the place that he occupied, while the whole scale represented the career of a state servant who went up through all the levels. Promotion depended not on birth but on merit.

with the same values. Thus a western-style elite began to emerge. With greater freedom vis-à-vis the sovereign—and the notion of service to the state assisted this—the nobility also acquired enormous and unprecedented power over the peasants. With serfdom fully established, the peasants were the ones to lose most in the reforms.

Thus beneath the surface of modernization in Russia lay many political and social contradictions. The first contradiction was the gulf between the theoretical and the actual functioning of the state. Peter had wanted to found a modern state, going beyond the person of the sovereign and giving society a role in the state through the continual promotion of new elites, through information, and through a meritocracy. But at the same time as he opened a door to social involvement in the sphere of politics, Peter the autocrat slammed it shut again by developing policies contrary to the wishes of a large portion of society—serfdom—or fearsome institutions from which society had no protection—the political police. This situation could not go on forever. A society that was given a glimpse of the possibility of influencing its own destiny but remained at the same time a prisoner of the whims of autocracy could not long remain blind to such a contradiction. The enlightened reforms of Peter the Great, grafted onto his ultra-authoritarian temperament and onto that part of it which he was to hand on to posterity, bore within them the seeds of serious conflict.

A second contradiction was that between the development, on the one hand, of the state as the supreme authority in political life and forum for the expression of society's interests and, on the other hand, of the power of the sovereign. The state came increasingly to be seen as a resort against the excesses of personal authority that the sovereign embodied, and was to contribute to the demystification of the figure of the tsar. The national interest and national consciousness that had developed around the "Little Father" came gradually to be identified with the state. The identification of Russia with the state and the tsar had seemed indestructible at the beginning of the Russian renaissance; now it began to be eroded.

To this contradiction embracing the whole of society was to be added another. The gulf between the sovereign and the nobles, the result of the reforms, was becoming increasingly apparent. Peter the Great had hoped to create a Western-style nobility, taking on the cultural values of eighteenth-century Europe, on which he could rely. Little by little, the nobles began to wish for not only Western values but also the kind of status enjoyed by the nobility in the West. For the Russian nobles, the obligations and structures of service built into Peter's vision were very far from the rights and freedoms of the nobles in the West. They were to seek to continue this process of westernization, thus challenging the state and questioning their obligations toward it. But, for all that, they did not realize that in wishing to free themselves from the state—and no longer only from the sovereign—they would have to take events to a logical conclusion and revise their own relationship to the peasantry. Serfdom, the nobles' reward for their service to the state, could have no justification once this service was challenged. But no one likes to lose privileges on acquiring new rights. Here again, between the lines of Peter's reform, lay a cause of major social and political conflict.

The "civilized state" desired, and in many ways and despite the wars, created by Peter, was to transform Russia radically. After 1722 the "old" Peter had disappeared. The reform similarly marked an irrevocable split in the social culture. At one extreme, at the top, was Western culture, secular and controlled by the state, which Peter wished to impose at all costs. At the other was the culture of a peasant society whose status was deteriorating. For the peasants the abstract idea of the state lacked the resonance of a tsar. They could no longer recognize the heir to the prince-saints and the Father of the People, the earthly image of the Eternal Father, in this beardless sovereign, who had himself painted in armor without any of the religious attributes of his predecessors. Instead of remaining "tsar" like the others, he had taken the foreign-sounding title of "emperor" as a result of his victory over the Swedes, and he had abolished the adjective *tikhaishii*, the "most gentle," from the prayers for the tsar. A divorce arose between the culture that Peter wished to impose on Russia, that of the "window onto Europe," and the traditional cultures of Russia. It was to be one of the most serious factors in the never-ending tragedy of Russia's history.

An Uncivilized Tsar

The enormous contradictions inherent in Peter's reforms were brutally evident in the contrast between his plans for modernization and his personal actions. Perhaps the origins of the excesses that were to give such a bloody aspect to these years of reform can be found in the very idea of the nature of the tsar. Political crime, legally defined for the first time during this period, was to be one of the most sinister aspects of Peter's reign, for he was also a murderer.

The supreme tragedy that, more than any other, was to stain this reign with blood was the murder by Peter, in 1718, of his son and heir Alexis. It epitomized the opposition between the two Russias and the two cultures. Peter had rejected the rigidity of the rules established by the church as they applied to his person and to the country. This brought him into conflict with his subjects' idea of the loyalty owed to him. He refused to observe the strict Orthodox rules about eating no meat and fasting during Lent. He sought foreign alliances through marriage and refused to make the princesses brought to Russia convert to the Orthodox Church. Unlike his predecessors, he paid very little attention to the demands of the church, particularly after 1722 when he abolished the patriarchate and replaced it with a bureaucratic authority, the Holy Synod, which had almost no power as against the state. But at the same time he was undermining the theocratic foundations of his own power. To the secularized image of authority he presented to his subjects, Peter added a more distant and less familiar personal image. His titles—*Gosudar' Imperator* (sovereign emperor) or *Otets otechestva* (father of the fatherland)—were not so easy for the Russian people to understand as the traditional "little father tsar." Since the tsar's title had been for centuries used and legitimized by the church in its prayers for the sovereign, the break with these old names seemed to reflect a break with the tradition of the church. Everything about Peter's new formalism seemed to suggest a world that was foreign to all that had gone before in Russian history and in the customs of the people.

Outraged by reforms that were imposed without warning— when the tsar had made up his mind, he applied his decisions without delay—and with consequences that were often tragic, for the peasants at least, the discontent in society was to assume many forms. Those who represented an organized dissident group, such as the Old Believers, attracted new support, but there were also sporadic explosions, sometimes organized by the *streltsi,* earlier victims of Peter's repression. And again rumors began to grow up around this strangely behaved sovereign.

The building of St. Petersburg put the final nail in the coffin of the traditional image of the tsar. It was through a series of decrees rather than an appeal to the people that the sovereign decided to establish his capital in the marshes, where no foundations could be laid without enormous ingenuity and where man's work was constantly threatened by flooding.[5] More than forty thousand men were involved in this project worthy of the pharaohs, and those pressed into labor died by the thousands. All the nobles and important men were obliged to build their new stone houses there, and in order to show symbolically that the capital of Russia had moved from its historic center to this imitation Italian city on the fringes of Europe, Peter sent for the relics of St. Alexander Nevsky. Thus Russia, having repelled the Tartars and begun to beat the Swedes, was moved in its entirety to this new center decreed by Peter. For many Russians this plan was highly provocative. Moscow, regarded as a holy city because it had sheltered the prince-saints and defended Christianity against the infidel invaders, was being abandoned. The fact that St. Petersburg—a German name—had been built by foreigners, Italian architects and workers not only from within Russia but from all over Europe, and that Protestant churches were being built there in large numbers because of the significant German population that Peter had attracted, were further causes of fury. Moscow, an essentially Russian town, lived according to Russian ways and confined its foreigners to a separate suburb, the German quarter *(sloboda).* St. Petersburg, the triumph of the West in Russia, was, on the contrary, opened up to foreigners who would, Peter hoped, import the example of their customs, habits, and material and spiritual culture. It was in St. Petersburg that Peter, inspired by

---

5. In 1705, the whole town was under water. In 1721, the only way to get about was by boat. Peter the Great barely escaped drowning on the Nevsky Prospect.

the Academy founded in France by Richelieu and of which he was a corresponding member, founded the first Russian Academy of Sciences in 1724. To bring new scientific life to the new capital—Russia did not yet have a university—he summoned Bernouilli and Delisle from France together with other foreigners.

A Clash of Two Cultures

Moscow symbolized the past, the Russian culture so furiously rejected by Peter; St. Petersburg was the window onto Europe, symbol of a new Russia wrenched from its past, from superstition, from intolerance, and from a history of misfortune and strange idiosyncrasies. In the rivalry between the deposed capital and Peter's new capital, two historic paths confronted one another. It was also a clash of two cultures: that of the elites created and elevated by Peter and that of a population to whom this plan was something foreign and strange. The old idea of the betrayal of the divine mission of the sovereign, of the plan conceived by God for Russia, now reemerged. By removing all the elements of his theocratic legitimacy and breaking physically and geographically with everything that represented it, Emperor Peter presented himself to his people in a new light, that of the pure autocrat. The legitimacy that he claimed was secular. He was emperor, heir of a dynasty that conferred on him the right to rule; but his person was now only that of an autocrat whose powers emanated from the existing political system and from his own personal authority.

Even if this decisive change in the ideas underlying the legitimacy of the holder of power in Russia escaped the Russian people—and perhaps even Peter himself—nevertheless, an insidious malaise began to spread. This strange Peter, so foreign to Russia, this tsar who had no respect for anything that his predecessors had respected, must obviously be an impious tsar. And yet the tsar was, by definition, pious, it being part of the divine essence of his nature to be so. The implicit accusation against him did not concern his faults as a man—his extreme violence and debauchery, for example—for they were a product of the human part of his nature and, as such, inevitable. It concerned rather that other side of his nature, and his defiance of the Law of God. The break with Moscow symbolized secularization and provided the focus for all the complaints against him. Since a tsar could not be bad, the theme of the false tsar made its reappearance.

In 1705, still smarting from the repression inflicted on them some years before, the *streltsi* became restless once more, and the rumor revived: the tsar was a usurper. The story ran that his mother had given birth to a girl and, for dynastic reasons, had substituted for her a boy who was now on the throne. Another version said that in the course of his jaunts in Europe—obviously an invention of the devil, for what did a tsar need to learn from Europe?—Peter had been assassinated and replaced by an impostor. The Old Believers, whose prestige had thrived on the martyrdom inflicted on them by the state, now went beyond a mere rejection of a power whose right to exist they challenged. Taking refuge in the distant forests, whole communities committed mass suicide[6] in order to bear witness to their struggle against the man they denounced as the Antichrist.

The growing anxiety about Peter's rejection of God's order was to take on essentially religious forms, showing that the conflict was centered around the decisive problem of the true tsar and his true nature. This explains why the revolt was not only secular, resulting from the agitation of discontented *streltsi* or Cossacks, but was also expressed in the proliferation of heterodox religious movements, the suicides of the schismatics, and the development of sects. One of these, originating in the previous century, was to see a great increase in its numbers, particularly after 1716 when its founder, Ivan Suslov, died. These People of God *(Bozhie liudi)*, more

---

6. Destruction by fire plays a considerable role among the Old Believers, thus creating a link between the two traditions of the pre-Christian god Perun and of Ilya Muromets, the best-known hero in Russian Christian folklore, who was supposed to have ascended to heaven in a chariot of fire like the prophet Elijah. After the condemnation of the Old Believers by the synod of 1667, many of them burned themselves and their families to death with the purifying fire in their wooden churches in the forests. Fire also recalls the "tongues of fire" sent by God to the apostles to purify and enlighten them. From that time, self-immolation by burning was a frequent ritual among the Old Believers, intended to underline the darkness that had descended on Russia.

often called the Flagellants *(Khlisti)*, were a secret society whose principal ritual was the mortification of the flesh by collective flagellation. Gathered around their spiritual leader—the "new Christ," Jesus being the "old Christ"—the People of God proclaimed, like the Old Believers, the necessity of living apart from the city that God had deserted. In both cases glorifying suffering and mortification as the paths to salvation, these religious groups were, at the beginning of the century, to attract many elements of a society confused by the secularization of power. The *streltsi*, in particular, frequently became fanatical followers of the schismatics or the Flagellants.

But such a divorce between the throne and society—society's tendency to retreat was to be characteristic of the Russian political system for a long time—obviously had long-lasting political repercussions. Whether he was seen as a false tsar or as the Antichrist,[7] Peter could not fail to provoke a reaction. No one was prepared to contemplate killing the man who was wrongfully occupying the throne: there was no actual proof that he was a usurper, and what was upsetting society more than anything else was the erosion of the social and religious order to which it was accustomed. The violence of the break with all that was Russian undertaken by Peter troubled people's minds to an extraordinary degree, and it was this loss of the old certainties that led to a double reaction: the revival of the myth of the dead tsar and the attempt to find the true tsar. The apocalyptic reactions of the Old Believers who cast themselves into the flames in order to present themselves purified before their Maker on the Day of Judgment—imminent now, because preceded by the reign of the Antichrist—or the self-inflicted sufferings of the Flagellants, were extreme manifestations of this quest for a truth that had been lost. Despite the many paths taken by a confused society, the Russians were unanimous in their desire to

---

7. The question was fiercely debated. For some, Peter could not be the Antichrist because the number 666 which symbolizes the latter could not be applied to anything concerning the tsar. For some of the Old Believers, on the other hand, Peter was definitely the Antichrist: having assumed the name of Father of the Fatherland, he had usurped a title belonging to the patriarch. This usurpation, followed by the dissolution of the patriarchate, was proof in their eyes of a diabolical plan, since in the last resort it was God that the usurper was claiming to replace.

return to the truth. Truth, on earth, apart from any apocalyptic vision, implied the necessity of uniting around a legitimate sovereign. And it was over this problem that the ultimate tragedy of Peter's reign arose: the murder of his son.

The Tsarevich Sacrificed

Born in 1690 of Peter's first marriage with Eudoxia Lopukhina, Alexis was early on torn between the two Russias now confronting one another. Brought up by a traditional and devout mother and surrounded by a family of similar views, Alexis was temperamentally inclined to succumb to such an influence. All the witnesses of the tragedy stressed how different in character the tsarevich was from his father. Gentle, passive, moderately intelligent, not very industrious, and, of course, pious, he was the true embodiment of the old Russia that Peter so detested. But he was the tsarevich. After the capture of Azov in 1696, Peter repudiated his wife, unable to tolerate any longer the old Russia that she represented, and shut her up in a convent before obtaining a divorce in order to marry Catherine, a servant-girl from Livonia, by whom he had several children. With the rejection of Eudoxia he was casting off not only a wife of whom he had tired, but above all the obscurantism and backward-looking influences from which he wished to snatch his son. In the eyes of the Russian people, however, he was rejecting the mother of the tsarevich and a legitimate wife; they shared only half-heartedly the church's indulgent attitude toward divorce. All their doubts about the strange behavior of the tsar were further confirmed by this introduction into the palace of a servant, and a foreigner at that. Could a true tsar marry a foreign servant-girl? Eudoxia, banished behind the high walls of a convent in Suzdal, was the symbol of the true dynasty. Her prestige and Alexis's nostalgia for his mother could only encourage the tsarevich to remain loyal to her views, particularly because these ideas directed the people's loyalty toward the two of them.

Peter the Great took the same line with his son as he had

taken with Russia, seeking to "reform" him and reshape him in western form. He surrounded him with carefully selected teachers, often foreigners, compelling him to learn foreign languages and geography, forcing him to join an elite regiment and brutalizing him—for kicks and abuse were more important than persuasion in Peter's theory of child rearing. Forced to marry a princess from Brunswick, Alexis accepted neither this union nor the plans his father had for him. Neglecting the duties required of him, he surrounded himself with monks and faith-healers who encouraged him to stand as a symbol of traditional Russia against the world that his father was attempting to impose.

To escape his father, the unfortunate tsarevich had to flee from Russia, seeking successive and temporary shelter in foreign courts. For Peter this was outright treason, for his son had not only left the country without permission, but also failed in his duties and run away from the reforms. Hunted down—the tradition of the pursuit of those who fled the country was firmly entrenched—the tsarevich was tortured before his father's eyes to make him confess to a supposed plot, for treason and plotting were one and the same. Finally he was made to sign an act of renunciation of his rights to the throne. Condemned to death, he died in prison as a result of further terrible torture before the sentence could be carried out. The rumors about this death were many and various: according to the official version he had died of a convulsive fit; he had died as a result of extreme torture; he had simply been imprisoned; finally, he had been beheaded by Peter the Great himself. It was this last version that Voltaire, one of Peter's admirers and no doubt horrified by the idea of such barbarity, undertook to refute, pleading that Peter had had unanimous approval of the death sentence[8] and thus did not need to resort to a criminal act. Furthermore, he states, the tsarevich's body was exposed for four days in the cathedral, "the head so well fitted to the body that it could not have been detached from it." Voltaire asks: "How could it have been possible for the tsar to cut off his son's head, when his son was given the extreme unction in the presence of the whole court? Was he headless when the oil was

---

8. The sentence "was signed by eight bishops, four archimandrites, and eight professors," specifies Voltaire.

applied to that head? When could the head have been sewn back onto its body?"

However unpleasant, these details bear witness to the deep anxiety provoked by the murder of the tsarevich. For Peter, there had been a plot, and he bore down cruelly on all those who had been involved even distantly, their names extracted by torture from his unfortunate son. First his mother, the tsarina Eudoxia, was accused, whipped, and then shut up again in a convent even more unpleasant than the first, where she was no longer treated as a sovereign. Her brother, Abraham Lopukhin, was beheaded after a long period of torture. Glebov, presumed to be the tsarina's lover, was impaled. As for the archbishop of Rostov, Dositheus, who had predicted Peter's imminent death—the supernatural still carried much weight—he was tortured on the wheel. More than thirty victims of torture surrounded the central figure of the drama, the tsarevich.

Two brilliant strokes set the seal on Peter's plan. In 1721, the Senate officially conferred on him the title of emperor together with the adjective "the Great." Thus he was able to abandon the theocratic legitimization for another type of legitimacy derived from personal greatness. With the title of emperor, foreign to Russian history, he emphasized the links of his regime with all previous empires, going back to that of ancient Rome. Peter the Great, first emperor of Russia, thus broke the link with the church that had legitimized his ancestors and inserted himself into a more ancient and global (or at least Western) tradition of power, linking emperor with empire, sovereign with state. The Russian mold, shaped in Kiev, was disappearing.

The result of this process of emancipation of the power of the emperor was the law of succession of February 6, 1722. In proclaiming that the choice of a successor was a matter for the sovereign and him alone, ignoring the principle of heredity that had been the essence of the monarchy until that time, Peter was breaking with all previous Russian history, even if he cited the example of Ivan the Terrible to justify his actions. For all that, he did not carry out his intentions and, in the three years that preceded his death (February 8, 1725), he was not to select a successor.

The citing of Ivan as a precedent recalls another similarity between the two sovereigns: the tragedy of the murder of a tsarevich by his own father. Superficially, there was everything in common between Peter and Ivan: they had both personally killed their heirs; and they had decided to break the unwritten rules of succession—in the absence of a proper law—that all sovereigns since Vladimir had struggled to establish. But the analogy stops there. The deaths of the two tsareviches, Ivan and Alexis, did not have the same meaning. Like Peter the Great, Ivan the Terrible did not recognize himself in his heir and was infuriated by their differences; but he killed involuntarily, in one of his fits of rage which had become increasingly frequent as his mind showed signs of sinking into madness. This murder crushed him permanently, turning him in a few hours from an aging man into an old man who was to suffer eternal remorse. We can never know if his death, in the humble habit of a monk, represented a reconciliation between his heart and his garb.

Things went very differently with Peter the Great. It was true that his son could not in any way satisfy Peter. This feeble character, although expressing a desire, against his father's wishes, to enter a monastery, was hardly a model of piety, being indolent and indulging in pathetic drinking sessions with a servant-girl, Evfrosina,[9] a pale copy of Peter's companion, the servant-girl from Livonia. It was neither an accident nor a fit of rage that led Peter, in the course of their dispute, when he was threatening to remove his son from the succession, to declare: "I would prefer a good stranger for heir to a worthless member of my own family." But it was not Alexis's character, nor his conduct, nor even his anxiety when Catherine, Peter's mistress whom he had married in 1707, gave birth to a son, that gave rise to the murder of the tsarevich. By killing him, Peter sought to kill the old Russia. "These long-beards could lead you into their ways," he wrote to his son when their disagreement was still only at the verbal stage. In his person and in the hopes placed on him, Alexis represented the past, that "barbaric" Russia that Peter intended to root out. He, on the other

---

9. Alexis's wife, Princess Charlotte, married in 1711, died in 1715, leaving him a son, the legitimate heir to the throne after him. Evfrosina, who followed him in his escape, returned afterwards as a chief witness against him, denouncing among his other crimes that of having desired the death of his father. It was only a step from this to the confession of parricidal intentions, and these were soon attributed to Alexis.

hand, was the future, Europe, reform; his son and heir embodied the past, Russia and tradition. By sacrificing him, Peter the Great was eradicating everything that still held Russia back. More than a punitive or vengeful murder, the assassination of the tsarevich was symbolic. It was necessary that the victim should be Peter's own son and that the blood of the dynasty should be shed. By thus spilling his own blood, Peter showed clearly that he was the man to make the break, that the choice of succession was not something preordained, but should be made in the light of the path that Russia had finally chosen. The shedding of this blood had quite another meaning from that of the prince-saints, the expiatory victims. Voltaire is right when he says that Peter was acting not as a father but as a king, sacrificing his son to what he believed to be the good of the nation and the state. In doing this, he was acting also as an absolute sovereign, with the power of life and death over all his subjects. With a single word he was able to dispose of the life of his son without having to account for his action to anyone—not even to God.

Murdered by his father, Alexis died as a guilty man who found peace in the pardon extended to him by his murderer: "The tsar came, tears flowed from the eyes of the father and those of the unfortunate son; the condemned man asked for pardon and the father publicly gave it." None of the witnesses mentions any signs in Peter of the anguish and remorse that had overwhelmed Ivan the Terrible after the fatal blow. In this upside-down scene, unity is reestablished by the father's forgiveness. The church played only a supportive role: it fell to it to administer the extreme unction and to exhibit the body of the tortured man to the people, but it did not have any say on the past or the present where the clash between father and son, between the tsar and his successor, had symbolized the clash between the contrary forces that were tearing Russia apart. Reconciliation and unity had been achieved through murder.

Sacrificed to history, the unfortunate tsarevich did not even have the same fate as those other princes murdered before him. In his lifetime he had been the focus for a Russia that did not want to die; when dead he was immediately forgotten. In fact—and this was his second death—he became a victim of the view that traditional society held of Peter the Great: Alexis was the son of the Antichrist or of the false tsar, he could not become the true tsar, the one whose death was to be denied and whose reappearance was eagerly waited for to save his country. Neither redeemer nor savior, like the other "sacrificed tsareviches," as Alain Besançon puts it, Alexis was to be as unloved by history as he had been by his father.

"Murder is the last resort of a coward," wrote Gibbon in his masterly work on the Roman Empire, and he is clearly talking about the political use of murder. Eighteenth-century Europe, of which Peter intended to make Russia a part, basically shared this view. After the terrible bloodshed of the wars of religion, the murder of Henry IV was to act in the long term as a revelation. The idea of killing for power—or through power—was now as shocking as it had been familiar before. The eighteenth century in Europe was a civilized century where political conflicts were dealt with in other ways than by bloodshed. Peter's Russia was a sinister exception to this tendency, and it is easy to imagine Voltaire's uneasiness when telling of the deeds of the emperor. But Peter had not only equipped himself with an institution specializing in political crime—unique in the Europe of the day—but also with a theoretician who was to devote himself to the justification not of Peter's use of murder, but of the absolute power he held, which authorized him to commit even the most horrible murders.

This theoretician, Feofan Prokopovich, provided him with a justification of his absolute power derived from Western ideas. He belonged to the circle of Ukrainian ecclesiastics steeped in Catholic and Western influences (the Ukraine had formerly been under Polish domination) that exercised a considerable amount of influence after 1667, when Kiev was reabsorbed by Russia. Peter had a marked preference for these educated clerics in the Jesuit mold over the Orthodox clergy, whom he classed without exception among the obscurantists. Prokopovich, well acquainted with the European *philosophes,* was fascinated by the ideas of state and sovereignty. In his writings, the themes of obedience, the city, the right of the sovereign, and the unity of the body politic in the person of the sovereign were clearly inspired by Hobbes and Grotius. In his most important work, *The Justice of the Will of the Monarch (Pravda voli monarchei),* as in his sermons which were subsequently published together, Prokopovich develops both the concept of the state and the power of the state and that of the nationalism of the people, to which he applies the previously little used term *rossianin*, forging a permanent link between the idea of Russia and that of empire. He proposes a secularized nationalism, a political system dominated by the interests of the state. He implicitly makes Christianity an instrument of state power, which is boundless because identified with the nation or society. In the final analysis, the relationship of the individual or of society to the throne is one of *obedience*, by the same natural law that requires children to obey their parents. Peter acted as a sovereign when he killed his son; implied in this murder was the relationship between him and his subjects. Like Alexis, they had no choice but to submit to him. Russia's conversion to the Europe of the Enlightenment, for all the reforms that it brought about, thus concluded with the theoretical and practical justification of a sovereign's absolute will that bowed to nothing and to no one.

7

Regicide in the Family

♦

Seventeenth-century Europe had been deeply shaken by the two great regicides that had darkened its history. Wars of religion and war in general had never spared men. But that two reigning sovereigns should be assassinated in a space of only thirty years shed a worrying light on the public perception of the sacred nature of the throne. While Ravaillac could be passed off as deranged[1] and the murder of the king, in this case, an accident, the public execution, after trial, of a reigning monarch accused of being an enemy of his people—Charles I of England, in 1649—was a challenge, rarely seen in the past, to the very principle of the monarchy. This double shock may explain why the attacks on tyranny in the eighteenth century were relatively moderate. Until the French Revolution, the sovereigns seemed to have recovered the position of inviolability that placed them out of reach of their subjects. Until this time, Russia, too, did not escape this rule. The sovereigns had assumed the power of life and death over others, but the figure on the throne remained sacred, even when his excesses passed the limits of toleration. The myth of the false tsar was a necessary substitute for any social reaction. Only a usurping tsar could defy divine law. If the Old Believers ran away, morally, from the Russian body-politic, it was because they knew that the sovereign, even if he was Antichrist, was protected by his throne. This explains why the fall of the Godunov dynasty was not possible until after the death of Boris, when Dmitri managed to convince society that he was the tsar and took Boris's place.

After the death of Peter the Great, another kind of "time of

---

1. Claiming that it was his mission to kill the king of France for apostasy, Ravaillac always denied having been the instrument of a conspiracy, affirming that he had obeyed God's orders. The research conducted by Roland Mousnier sheds much light on this point.

troubles" began. At first sight, the years that followed his death were peaceful. Nevertheless, the foundations of political order in Russia were profoundly shaken, and two regicides along with the murder of a tsarevich were evidence that, beneath the appearance of calm, the history of the country was about to take a strange turn. And these were to be unusual regicides, because the blows that were to strike down those legitimately installed on the throne came from that same throne.

The Whims of Succession

At the end of his life, Peter I had struck three blows, which were to prove decisive, against the principles of succession underlying the Russian monarchy. By murdering his heir, he had raised the problem of his own succession. The decision of 1722 giving the choice of successor to the reigning sovereign was the final nail in the coffin of the principle of inheritance, and it created a void around the subject of the rights of succession. Finally, the fate of Catherine, whom he married in 1712 and crowned empress in 1724, opened the way to a phenomenon that was still new in Russia—rule by a woman. Until that time, although some women had enjoyed a short-lived authority, they had only been regents, their authority challenged and kept within clearly defined limits by a council. As soon as they were suspected of wanting to change their status for that of tsarina, they were immediately removed. A single exception—even if it was to come to nothing—was the offer of the throne to Irina Godunova. But this plan was more the result of the disarray of the nobility at the moment of the disappearance of a dynasty than a political development. Irina Godunova was a childless widow, and could only have served as a shield—and this was the point of the plan—for the refound authority of the boyars.

By crowning Catherine, Peter the Great, who had just proclaimed his absolute right to choose his successor regardless of any rules, seemed to be suggesting that the empress could equally well be the sovereign. Whatever the case, for Russia as for anyone who was going to sit on the throne, Peter having chosen no successor, the legacy was daunting. There were two possible hypotheses, and both had their interested supporters, in other words, their families. From his first marriage, Peter the Great had a grandson, Peter, born in 1715, son of the unfortunate tsarevich whom he had himself murdered. If the law of succession followed up to 1722 had been retained, this ten-year-old heir would have quite naturally followed him. But in opposition to this child, whose rights had been abolished by the law of 1722, stood Catherine whose important services had been recognized by Peter, before he crowned her, in a manifesto of 1723. She had received the oaths of his subjects, had been associated with public affairs, and had learned from Peter what it was to rule.

It was a difficult choice. On one hand there was the heir of a legality denied by Peter and, furthermore, only a child, which implied the necessity for a regency and all the resulting intrigues and pressures. And, in any case, there was no suitable regent, for the child was quite without relatives. To these entirely logical arguments, which could be aired publicly, could be added others, which could not be confessed but were compelling nevertheless. Quite a few of those who had been called to participate in the decision— beginning with Bishop Feofan Prokopovich—had played a role in the condemnation of the assassinated tsarevich. To place his son on the throne would be to run the risk that the latter, when he reached adulthood, might decide to seek to avenge his father. For all those who had been involved in the death of the tsarevich, Catherine was the only possible choice. Nevertheless, there was an equal number of arguments against such a choice. First, there was the matter of her origins—a former servant-girl from Livonia, and a Protestant. Her conduct was equally unsuitable: she was rumored to have had a string of lovers before being taken up by Peter. Since then her conduct had been more cautious but equally shocking, almost resulting, in 1723, in her repudiation. This may explain why Peter, although he crowned her, remained silent on the matter of the succession. Furthermore, although endowed with great intelligence and judgment, often amazing Peter the Great, Catherine was practically illiterate. As for her appearance, the witnesses are many but contradictory. A German princess provides one description: "The tsarina was small and thickset. She had neither style nor grace, and her lowly birth was obvious at first sight. From her manner of dressing, one would have taken her for a German actress. Her clothes looked secondhand and were covered in silver and dirt. . . ." Lastly, no woman had ever succeeded to the throne of Russia; to put one there now would be to create a precedent with serious implications for the dynastic system.

Despite all these arguments against her, Catherine's faction won. The upholders of tradition showed themselves incapable of negotiating a compromise solution that would unite the two candidates to the throne and place Peter II under the guardianship of Catherine. It was easy for her supporters to plead that a regency would inevitably open the way to rivalry between the two camps, paralyzing the exercise of power and ending in mutual extermination. The argument was unanswerable, but it was no less true that the ghost of the murdered tsarevich hovered over the consultations, haunting those implicated in the murder.

Shocking as it might have seemed to the supporters of tradition and legitimacy, or even of simple propriety, the choice of Catherine was a good one. Though the Old Believers had to pay with their lives or a period of torture for their refusal to pay homage to a woman, Catherine rejected the claims of her lovers to substitute themselves for her in the affairs of government and continued Peter's work, maintaining a genuine internal peace.

The real revolution of Catherine's reign lay in the accession of women to the throne. Shortly before her death in 1727, she chose a successor, thereby following the law of 1722. But she chose her husband's grandson, Peter, who had been her rival two years before. Thus did this wise woman reconcile the rights of inheritance and the wishes of Peter the Great. It is true, though, that there were no heirs on her side, since her six sons were all dead. She did have, however, two daughters, closer to Peter the Great than his grandson. Having reigned herself, Catherine could have concluded that succession from woman to woman was now possible and that it would be better to retain the principle, making the inheritance follow the line of Peter's second marriage, rather than adopting an intermediate solution with the succession changing from one branch to the other. She opted for a compromise, uniting the two lines of descent from her dead husband: Peter would succeed her and the regency would be governed jointly by her two daughters, Anna and Elizabeth.

Like Catherine, Peter II was to have a peaceful reign. But like hers, it was to be a short one. In 1730, when he was only fifteen, the young sovereign was carried off by smallpox. With him died the last of Peter the Great's male successors to bear the family name. The importance of the opening of the throne to women could now be appreciated. The possible candidates, related to Peter the Great to a greater or lesser degree, were few and, for the most part, female. The two heirs closest to the throne in 1730 were the last surviving daughter of Peter the Great, Elizabeth, and the child born in 1728 to Peter's other daughter, Anna, Duchess of Holstein, who had just died. Otherwise, it would be necessary to change to another branch of the family, going back to the descendants of the first marriage of Alexis Romanov whose granddaughter, daughter of Ivan V, Anna, Duchess of Courland, was vegetating in Mitau. The newborn baby, Peter of Holstein, was out of the question: it would be too long before he would be able to exercise any kind of authority. That left the women.

The secret council[2] set up in 1726 by Empress Catherine and presided over during the reign of Peter II by the two regents, Anna and Elizabeth, became the authority entrusted with the task of organizing the succession. Following the law of 1722, it was to be submitted to a form of election. Russia was close, at this time, to following Poland in adopting a kind of constitutional charter that would have limited the powers of the autocracy. The lack of any obvious heir and the negotiations over the choice favored such a political development, since it was up to the secret council to decide on the right of succession. Peter the Great's reform, intended to consecrate a partially achieved autocratic power, resulted, ironically, in power being limited by an agreement that acted as a constitution.

The council's choice was Anna of Courland. She was a widow, weak in character and without children. It seemed conse-

---

2. The chancery or Supreme Secret Council, which consisted of six members in Catherine's time and eight under Peter, was, like the Senate created by Peter the Great, to be a body for the coordination of the administration. Neither of these bodies was successful, and the private council disappeared in the crisis of 1730.

quently as if she would be the person most inclined to accept this radical change in the Russian political system.[3] Elected under particularly restrictive conditions, Anna nevertheless showed at once, like Catherine before her, that women knew how to reign. She had no hesitation in ignoring all her promises, and with a sweep of the pen got rid of the council, governing with a smaller cabinet usually consisting of her favorites. Although such care had been taken before her accession to clip the wings of the sovereign to the benefit of the Russian nobility, Empress Anna removed the Russians from her entourage and from power, favoring instead Germans. Thus—another irony of history—her reign, which might have paved the way to a true constitutional monarchy, was marked by a new triumph of autocracy. Anna paid much less attention to the advice of the councils than any other sovereign since Peter, and her years of power, when the principle of *habeas corpus* was supposed to be introduced into Russia—it having been, as far as the nobles were concerned at least, part of the original bargain—were far more cruel and arbitrary than any since 1725.

Her reign was soon known by the name of *Bironovshchina*, from the name of her favorite from Courland, Biron. He took full revenge on the nobles for the restrictions they had tried to impose on the autocracy. Arrests, deportations, and executions multiplied.[4] The countryside was devastated by the systematic search for outstanding taxes overlooked by the administration. The methods employed, including the seizing of tools and animals, bore down harshly on the peasants. It is symptomatic that the name given by the Russians to this reign was modeled on the name once applied to the Tartar domination—*Tatarshchina*—and both were signs of popular hostility to what was seen as a foreign responsibility for the misfortunes of the times. But the people also found another expla-

---

3. When she came to the throne, Anna agreed to guarantee to the nobles the inviolability of their persons and their property. She was to consult the High Council on all matters. She could not declare war on her own, sign a peace treaty, decide on a tax, alienate an estate from the crown, or appoint anyone to a post or grade higher than that of colonel. Finally, she was not allowed to marry or designate a successor without first taking the advice of the council.

4. One of the chief victims of this arbitrary persecution was the Dolgoruky family, close to Peter II, accused of having forged a "false will" in which Peter designated them as heirs to the throne.

nation for their difficulties: female power. Everywhere people went about repeating that "cities governed by women have no future, and the walls that they build will not grow high." The peasants muttered that it could not be hoped that rule by a woman would favor the ripening of the corn. The Old Believers predicted a punishment from heaven. Needless to say, large numbers of the latter were victims to Biron's brutality. The general outrage might have led to an uprising if the empress had not very opportunely died in 1740, leaving the matter of the succession decided for once, though not very satisfactorily.

Anna came from that branch of the Romanov family descended from Ivan V, and she now decided to see this branch installed permanently on the throne, rather than the descendants of Peter the Great. Taking advantage of her right to choose a successor introduced by Peter in 1722, just before her death she named as her heir a baby of only a few months, Ivan VI, grandson of her elder sister. This child, born prince of Brunswick and from a family with little contact with Russia, would naturally require a regent. Anna resolved the problem by making Biron regent, thereby increasing the influence of the Germans in the country. This succession went completely against the aspirations of the Russians and they were unlikely to accept it. A sentiment of legitimism led them to regret that Peter's line had been pushed aside. Since women were now able to take the throne, they could not understand why the daughter of Peter the Great, Elizabeth, and a good Russian, had had to make way for the Germanized descendants of Ivan V. The hate inspired by German rule in general, and that of Biron in particular, lent extra strength to the longing for a Russian power. The first victim of this longing was to be the unfortunate Tsar Ivan VI. The time was ripe for action. There were two uprisings in less than two years: the first removed the hated regent; the second brought the reign of Ivan VI to an end, the crown passing to Elizabeth, the last surviving child of Peter the Great.

The coup d'état of 1741, which brought another woman to the throne, was important in several respects. First—and Empress Elizabeth was to make sure of this—it reestablished in practice, if not in the code of law, a hereditary succession that was to continue the line of Peter the Great until the end of the dynasty. As soon as she was crowned, Elizabeth, unmarried[5] and thus without a direct heir, sent for her nephew Peter of Holstein, whom she converted to the Orthodox religion and proclaimed her successor. Two years later she married him to a German princess, Sophia of Anhalt-Zerbst, who was to take the name Catherine on her conversion to the Orthodox Church. Peter and his wife were to reign in turn, as Peter III and Catherine II.

A second result of the coup d'état, and no less decisive, was the victory of Russia over the German faction, the victory of the Orthodox religion in its purest form over all the others. But, at the same time, Elizabeth's reign opened Russia to French influence. Peter the Great had learned from Holland, his successors had been inspired by Germany; with Elizabeth, France invaded court, culture, and manners, and Voltaire became the star of the court and the Academy of St. Petersburg.

At last, progress toward the civilized state seemed to have started once more. The two rebellions that reopened the path to the throne for those Romanovs descended from Peter were remarkable in that they avoided bloodshed. The cloister, the wheel, and various other punishments may well have marked the moment of the changeover of power for the supporters of the German faction and the descendants of Ivan V, but Elizabeth did not take the lives of her enemies. She was, in fact, fiercely opposed to the death sentence, even if the continued use of the knout as an instrument of justice often produced the same result. The fate of Ivan VI bears witness to these more gentle times. A dethroned sovereign, even if a babe in arms, represented a threat, serving as a rallying point for the discontented. Furthermore, the system for choosing a tsar in operation since 1722 opened the way to all kinds of adventures, since the legitimacy of the holder of the throne depended on one particular decision and not on a permanent rule. Many of Elizabeth's predecessors had got round a similar difficulty with the assassination of a possible rival. But, consistent with her ideas, the empress decided to spare the life of the deposed tsar, shutting him up in the fortress

---

5.   It is possible that Elizabeth secretly married Aleksei Razumovsky, a peasant of Ukrainian origin and church cantor, whose beautiful singing voice had seduced the empress. He was long to be in favor, but even if such a marriage had taken place, it would not have been publicly acknowledged.

of Schlusselburg. It was to be a tragic fate, reminiscent of the "Man in the Iron Mask." Tsar for a brief instant when he was too young to be aware of his rank, for twenty-two years—all his childhood and adolescence—Ivan VI was to be an anonymous prisoner, forgotten by all, and known to his guards only by the strange title of "Prisoner No. 1."

Down with the Emperor!

The peaceful return to the line descending from Peter, remarkable when compared with Russia's usual political habits, was to be no more than a parenthesis. The bloodless coups d'état of 1741–42 had suggested—and the influence of the French *philosophes* had a role in this—that a more balanced, less absolute style of rule was evolving in Russia, with rulers less sure of the basis of their legitimacy. However, from this context of instability new sovereigns were to emerge who were jealous of their immense imperial prerogatives— Peter III and Catherine II. The path they were to take in their reconquest of absolute power—regicide within the family—was something new in Russia.

All the indications, however, were of a period of peaceful and regular successions. Empress Elizabeth had not only named her heir, but she had also found him a wife; the several children from this marriage could, even if the existing system of succession did not give them the right, ensure the continuity of the line of Peter the Great. The heir to the throne was already partially involved in affairs of state and, when Elizabeth died on December 25, 1761, the coronation of Peter III was the logical conclusion of her decisions. But, on July 5, 1762, after only six months of rule, Peter III suddenly died. Forty-eight hours later, a manifesto announced to the people that he had died of a "hemorrhoidal colic aggravated by a stroke." But the man who died had already, before his death, lost the throne. On June 28, a coup d'état by members of the nobility close to the court had in effect deposed him without a blow being struck. His wife, now made empress, was acclaimed by the army.

They organized a ceremony of oath-taking, confirming her accession to the throne and making her eldest son, Paul, her successor.

Peter III had been arrested by the conspirators, and his death a few days later appeared to be the combined result of his poor health, which was well known, and the emotion aroused by the coup d'état deposing him. However, neither the medical explanation nor the public exhibition of Peter's body in full uniform fooled anyone. The rumor started up at once; he had been the victim of a murder. If opinions diverged on the perpetrators of the murder, some attributing it to the clergy, others to a plot of the nobles, the most widespread theory was the one that coincided with the historical truth: the real instigator of the murder had been the person who, as in a traditional detective story, derived the greatest profit from it—in other words, the new empress, Catherine, the victim's widow. Even Voltaire, who was her most consistent admirer, never denied this crime, which drew from him the delicious comment: "I know that she has been accused of some little misdemeanors à propos of her husband, but these are family matters that are none of my concern. Besides, it is no bad thing if one has a fault to amend. It causes one to make great efforts to win the public's esteem."

Murder, which so often features in the actions of the holders of power in Russia, had this time followed a path as yet unknown. Emperors who had repudiated their wives for personal convenience were legion in the history of Russia, and the convents were full of deposed queens. It is quite possible that it crossed the minds of some of them to get rid of a husband who was about to repudiate them. What is new here is that the wife of an emperor—the legal successor to the throne and crowned according to the law—had gone so far as to organize a plot to seize the crown for herself. In a Russia where, since the death of Peter the Great, people were anxious to find proofs of legitimacy for sovereigns chosen according to unstable rules, the claim of a minor German princess, whose only link with the dynasty was her husband whom she had just had murdered, seemed slight. Nevertheless, Catherine was to bring more glory to the name of Romanov than any of her predecessors since Peter the Great and than most of her successors. Her friend Voltaire, who called her the benefactress of mankind, said in homage to her virtues: "A day will come when all enlightenment will reach us from the North."

The story of the plot that brought Catherine to power is worth relating, because it sheds light on the ways of Russia at that time, and on those of the woman whom Voltaire believed to be "the best of European sovereigns." But the interest of this episode does not lie only in its anecdotal quality. It raises other questions: What exactly was this regicide committed by a wife? Was it a plot to gain the throne, a murder for mere personal ambition, or perhaps a true political conspiracy implying more complicated interests, from which a woman was able to profit? These are important questions because the implications for the future of this first regicide in Russia's history can be differently interpreted according to how we answer them. To understand the events of the days between June 28 and July 5, 1762, we need to return to the hero of this exceptional drama and to the political stage on which it was performed.

First, the victim: if Peter III was so easily dethroned and so quickly forgotten—his portraits disappeared everywhere and his name ceased to be mentioned—it was because he was personally unattractive and politically clumsy, capable only of causing ill-feeling in all circles. Even when he was the young heir to Elizabeth, the tsarevich attracted little sympathy. It was not that he was particularly ill-favored,[6] but he had a taciturn temperament and poor health, partly attributable to his harsh childhood at the court in Holstein where he had been beaten, half-starved, and more or less abandoned. Badly educated, brutal, and of only average intelligence, he was, furthermore, hostile to everything Russian. He was never able to lose his strong German accent and his adoption of the Orthodox faith was only half-hearted. He lacked discretion and Empress Elizabeth had to exclude him from many councils in case he broadcast to the world the matters discussed. As a result, his education as heir to the throne was no better nor any more complete than his education in general.

---

6. In 1744, chickenpox and smallpox, one immediately after the other, had badly scarred Peter's face, which remained coarse and pitted. Catherine wrote in her memoirs: "He had become hideous."

This complicated and clumsy boy was, at the age of sixteen, introduced to his future wife, Sophia, then a girl of fifteen. Tall and well-made, perhaps more attractive than pretty, her vivacity of appearance and wit were instantly seductive. Resourceful, determined, and eager to learn, she was equally eager to climb to greater heights than those offered her by the little principality of her birth. There was little in common between the adolescent boy interested only in music and military matters and this radiant girl who went through life with a list of philosophical works in her pocket to be read at the first opportunity. But a future emperor had a duty to take a wife in order to ensure his succession, while for Sophia—who was to receive the name Catherine on her rebaptism in the Orthodox Church—the throne of Russia represented a dazzling promotion.

The marriage, which took place on August 21, 1745, was a complete disaster. For years it was not consummated, as Catherine's memoirs attest, though not because of any incapacity on the part of the tsarevich who, over the years, had increasing numbers of affairs. However, on September 20, 1754, an heir, Paul, was born. An heir, certainly, but there was no knowing if he was Peter's son. This husband despised and ignored his wife. Furthermore, he appears not to have fathered any illegitimate children, despite his many liaisons, a fact that, given the customs and attitudes of the time, might suggest that he was sterile. According to contemporaries and some historians, Paul's real father was one of Peter's chamberlains, Sergei Saltykov, known as "handsome Sergei." To Elizabeth, it mattered little if the child was or was not her nephew's son: the succession was safe. She took charge of the child who, from that time onwards, saw little of his mother.

The private life of the heir and his wife is only one element in the file, but it is relevant. Peter can have had no more illusions about the paternity of the children his wife brought into the world than she did. Having nothing in common with her and sufficiently attached to one of his mistresses, Elisaveta Vorontsova, to think of making her his wife, Peter tried in 1758 to obtain Elizabeth's agreement to the repudiation of Catherine. From Peter's first indifference to his declared hostility, everything inclined Catherine, who now felt herself threatened, to wish to see her husband disappear as soon as Elizabeth died. For years her position had been almost untenable, and it is easy to imagine how her feelings toward Peter must have become more and more vindictive. Between her marriage and the death of Elizabeth, the deplorable state of Peter's health and his frequent serious illnesses led her to fear that his early death might result in the empress choosing another heir. With Peter alive and hostile, the other side of the threat was repudiation. Perhaps it was because of these private difficulties that the young Catherine became involved early on in foreign affairs, seeking support but at the same time risking a clash with the empress that might cost her the throne.

She intervened as intermediary between the Russian chancellor and the British ambassador at the time when Russia was hesitating between an alliance with England directed against Prussia—which Catherine and her friends favored—or a rapprochement with France and Austria against an Anglo-Prussian coalition, supported as a last resort by the empress. Whether Catherine, led on by friendship or love—this was the period of her liaison with the young Count Stanislaw Poniatowski who, on behalf of Poland, was agitating for the first proposal—confined herself merely to chatting, or whether she was able to pass on important information to her friends, we do not know. Whatever the case, her activities contributed to her difficulties in Elizabeth's lifetime, and even more so after her death, because she clashed with Peter's pro-Prussian sentiments. Thus to the difficulties in their marriage was added Peter's distrust of his wife's international contacts and meddlesome activities.

Catherine's situation became more serious when Peter succeeded to the throne. His short reign was marked by a contradictory mixture of liberal and conservative decisions that, with only a few exceptions, did nothing but make him enemies—a fact that was to facilitate his wife's path to the throne. His liberal measures included the abolition of the Secret Council—"this terrible tribunal . . ., worse than the Spanish Inquisition," reported one ambassador, and the ending of the persecution of the Old Believers who were allowed to leave their place of exile and return to their lands. Furthermore, in a manifesto of February 1762, he freed the nobility from its obligations of service, a measure that was to have considerable social and political consequences in the following century. He even considered for a moment the condition of the peasants, but took no action.

Otherwise, he did everything possible to make himself unpopular, and in this was remarkably successful. He upset the clergy by deciding—a long-standing plan of all sovereigns—to attach all church property to the royal estate. He doubly displeased the army: first, by reorganizing it along the lines of the Prussian army, taking Frederick II as his model; and second, by taking no account of the victories that it had achieved in the war against Prussia. For love of that country, far from wanting to turn his victories into definitive acquisitions, as Frederick expected, he made peace and handed over to his "old friend" all the Russian conquests in East Prussia and signing a defensive and offensive alliance. For Frederick this radical change of heart in Russian policy was truly miraculous; for the Russian army, it represented a sacrifice that was both useless and humiliating. Finally, Peter alienated the whole country, from the court to the humblest of his subjects—apart from the small Prussian faction—by the enthusiasm he employed to impose everywhere an imitation of everything Prussian, be it clothes, customs, cultural or social life. He constantly and loudly mocked "Russian barbarism" and the Orthodox Church, and in his most extreme moments he would shout to all in earshot: "Let's drink to the health of the king, our master [i.e., Frederick II]!"

Under this reign that was rapidly becoming a farce, the public outrage showed that an alternative solution was needed. A sovereign who could sign a peace treaty with Prussia, flying in the face of the national interest and condemned by the church, could not rely on his legitimacy for long. In the certainty that it was necessary to remove Peter III from the throne, a plot was soon hatched. The question was whom to replace him with. At first glance, there seemed to be only two possibilities, two Romanovs, one descended from Ivan V (the unfortunate "Prisoner No. 1"), and the other, Paul, great-grandson of Peter the Great, son of Catherine and, officially at least, of the reigning tsar. Ivan VI, perhaps because of his years of imprisonment, did not seem to have all his faculties. Through hatred of his wife and perhaps because of Paul's more than doubtful paternity, Peter III had, however, allowed it to be understood that he did not necessarily intend to name Paul as his successor. He had even summoned Ivan VI to the capital in order to assess his suitability as a possible successor. His dislike of his own son was revealed further in his refusal to give him the title of "heir."[7] Similarly, at the time when the nobility had sworn loyalty to him, he had included in the sacramental formula a promise to respect the heir "of his choice."

Threatened with repudiation, Catherine was well aware that her son also risked exclusion from the succession. Of course the wishes of a sovereign whom the conspirators wished to depose were not in any way binding, but Catherine had no wish to be a regent. Three women, since the death of Peter the Great, had established themselves on the throne as empress. Reign by a woman seemed to be an established fact and the position of empress was both more secure and more enviable than that of regent. Finally, if she managed to obtain the throne, Catherine knew that the choice of heir would rest with her. In any other solution, the interests of her son Paul might well be forgotten by those encouraged by a change at the top to pursue their own fortunes. Thus the attainment of the throne had, for Catherine, the triple advantage of ensuring her security, allowing her to achieve her ambition, and preserving her son's future. These advantages far outweighed the only advantage possessed by a sovereign hated by all, who despised his country and his subjects and who would one day inevitably fall victim to some other plot—his legitimacy.

The Plot

But Catherine was not the only one to plot. Around her, at the court, the plans for getting rid of Peter III were multiplying. Central to these was a man well respected by Catherine, who was to serve her for twenty years as minister of foreign affairs, Nikita Panin. He had for many years represented Russia in Denmark and Sweden, which gave him a sound knowledge of the internal political workings of these countries and of the international intrigues that each country could set up to protect its own interests. In 1760, Elizabeth had entrusted to him the education of the young Paul;

---

7. Paul was tsarevich, but did not have the title *naslednik* (heir).

he was thus inevitably involved in the future claim of this child to the throne, a child whom he had molded. As tutor to the young prince, Nikita Panin could hope for a central role in a possible regency under Catherine. He had gathered round him a number of supporters of this plan for the future. But Catherine herself had a strong pressure group supporting the more extreme solution of putting herself on the throne. The five Orlov brothers, most of whom had been at one time or another her favorites, undertook to win over the army.

Peter got wind of these plots, and even received a warning from the king of Prussia. But he answered that no one would dare attack the power—and far less the life, he thought—of the grandson of Peter the Great. At the same time he was for his part thinking—and he made no secret of the fact—of ways to get rid of his wife and child. It cannot have been easy to plan a conspiracy against the emperor in the very heart of the court, and the rumors that started to circulate and the contradictory plans as to what to do after the deposition of the sovereign must have hastened the plot inspired by Catherine. Thus it was that, on June 28, while Peter was at Oranienbaum inspecting troops on their way to fight in Denmark, against all logic or expectations the plot was put into action. The most urgent task for Catherine was to gain the throne; after that, anything was possible, particularly the deposing of Peter. To do things in the reverse order would be too dangerous: with Peter deposed, each faction would put forward its own candidate. Making the first move with the Orlov brothers, who had won over the elite regiments to her cause, Catherine arrived at dawn in St. Petersburg from the country. With Peter at Oranienbaum and all the authorities loyal to him out of the capital, she went immediately to the barracks where the famous Izmailovsky Guard was stationed, where she was acclaimed as empress. Meanwhile, a number of her supporters persuaded the other two elite guard regiments, the Preobrazhensky and Semyonovsky, to support the coup d'état. Thus acclaimed by the guards, Catherine then went immediately to make her peace with the church. At the Church of Our Lady of Kazan she took a vow to protect the rights of the church and of the Orthodox religion. After the disdain shown by Peter III, the church could hardly fail to support the empress. The same day, proclamations to the people and the army put the finishing touch to the transfer of power. These manifestos were essentially a list of accusations against the emperor, as yet unaware that he had been deposed, and a justification of Catherine's action. It was her duty, said the texts, to protect a neglected church, a humiliated army, and a foreign policy abandoned to the will of the Prussians by this reckless emperor.

Meanwhile, for twenty-four hours Peter had remained ignorant of the fact that he had been replaced on the throne by his wife. When he realized what was going on, it was too late to act. Catherine was advancing on Oranienbaum at the head of the troops. He was forced to abdicate unconditionally. His only request was to be allowed to live in a property close to Peterhof, in the company of Elisaveta Vorontsova.

Empress and Regicide

Thus, until this moment, everything had happened in a civilized, if not entirely legal, way. Although it was forced upon him, Peter's abdication did not threaten his life. Catherine's power seemed so undisputed that there was no suggestion of murder of the deposed tsar. And yet, less than a week later, he died, and despite the official explanation, it was clear he had been murdered. Contemporary accounts record a version that became generally accepted. It does little honor to the authors of the crime. In his enforced residence, Peter is supposed to have been joined by Aleksei Orlov, brother of Catherine's current favorite, and two accomplices who, in the course of a prearranged drunken party, are supposed to have poisoned or strangled him, or both.

What was the point of this murder, when all had been won already? What was Catherine's role in it? On this second question, a degree of agreement has emerged over the course of time, exempting her from the accusation of having ordered the murder. But she did not denounce any of the assassins and went along with the theory of a natural death. Furthermore, all those, murderers or not, who had helped bring her to the throne received pensions and posts at court and, where necessary, ennobled. The murder of Peter III was in fact vital for Catherine's security and for her retention of the throne. The situation created by the deposing of the tsar was, after all, a very unusual one. The women who had reigned before in Russia had all been of the Romanov family. Catherine's only link with that dynasty was by marriage to one of them who had just been removed by her from the throne. She was a princess, a foreigner, from an insignificant court, and only a convert to Orthodoxy; nothing justified her occupation of the throne. As mother of the tsarevich the most she could have aspired to was a regency. Her acclamation by the troops was quite unknown to any rule or practice for the succession hitherto used. Her actions were even more criminal than those of Boris Godunov, who was brought to a vacant throne by the *Zemskii sobor.* With Catherine, it was no more nor less than usurpation. In these circumstances it became dangerous to spare the life of a rival. Paul, her son, could not threaten her; his youth and probable illegitimacy were not in his favor. A living Peter, on the other hand, could quite well, in a period of discontent, attract to his person the sympathies and efforts of supporters in search of legitimacy. Alive, despite his abdication, he might once again be considered to be the "true" tsar, insofar as he was the grandson of Peter the Great. To this threat to Catherine's crown was added the fact that Peter was still her legitimate husband, preventing her from planning any other marriage. If she herself had not thought of such a thing, it is almost certain that Grigory Orlov did have a long-term ambition to become the husband of the empress.

The murder was also intended to remove another political possibility. Peter would never rise again in the heart of some popular movement. His death did not prevent, nevertheless, the appearance here and there of a series of impostors, each maintaining that he was the "true" Tsar Peter III, not really assassinated. This tsar was to feed the mythology of one of the most active sects of the time: a dissident branch of the Flagellants or *Khlisti,* called the *Skoptsi* (from *skopets,* a castrated man), a group that added to the already strict practices of the former the ritual of castration and regarded Peter III as their sovereign. The leader of the sect, one Selivanov, a former serf, claimed that he was Peter III—a castrated Peter III. The myth of the "true" tsar here became one with the myth of the "true" faith and the "true" nobility—which the *Skoptsi* contrasted with the "false" court of the "false" empress—and it attracted many followers from those who were excluded from the circles of power. Portraits of Peter III, whose supposed impotence, mentioned by Catherine in the manifesto of deposition, they linked with their own practice of castration, became the sect's icons. Catherine dealt with them harshly: they were beaten with the knout and deported to Siberia. No false Peter could be allowed to survive.

But the most serious eposide, involving a false Peter III, arose in 1772. Emelyan Pugachov, the man who had led the revolt of the Iaik Cossacks, proclaimed that he was Peter III: 'I am Emperor Peter Fyodorovich. It was I at Tsaritsyn. God and the good people saved me and, in my place, they beat a soldier of the escort. At Petersburg too, I was saved by a soldier." Strongly supported, Pugachov, who had sacked Kazan and won over to his side both Orenburg and Nizhni Novgorod, for a while represented a real threat to Catherine. Once again, a clash between a true and a false tsar had resulted from crimes committed around the throne. And Pugachov was all the more threatening in that Peter III had once been on the throne, and Pugachov was not a child and could at any moment claim to be reinstalled on "his" throne. It was not surprising that the worried Catherine took extreme measures to suppress the rebel. When he was defeated, Pugachov was exhibited in the streets of Moscow in an iron cage, so that the people could see for themselves that he could not possibly be the tsar, for who had ever seen a sovereign behind the bars of a cage? He was then beheaded, and the death sentence, now reinstated, was widely applied by the avenging regiments to "pacify" the villages that had believed in the resurrected Peter III. He now no longer existed. Nevertheless, between 1764 and the Pugachov episode, no less than seven false Peters had appeared in Russia.

But it was not only Peter who gave rise to reactions to an empress whose legitimacy was so suspect, despite her spectacular coronation on September 22, 1762. Tsar Ivan VI, for one, was still alive. And those who, at the time of the plot against Peter III, had supported the idea of a regency, resented the coup whereby Catherine had seized the throne. For a number of the conspirators of 1762, the feeling that they had been cheated by a woman who they believed had no right to the throne was too strong to be ignored. Since she had stirred up one coup d'état, they decided to reply with another. Everyone knew that Ivan VI was in no state to reign, but he was tsar and a descendant of the Romanovs. This would be quite sufficient to oppose the claims of an empress of modest origins, not of the Romanov family and, furthermore, a regicide or at the least an accomplice to regicide.

A first plot, ill-prepared and badly managed, intended to put Ivan VI back on the throne under the authority of a regency, failed in 1762. But two years later, in July 1764, a small group of conspirators led by a young Ukrainian, Mirovich, attacked the prison of Schlusselburg. He intended to free Ivan and have him acclaimed tsar by the soldiers of the garrison, to whom he would read a manifesto condemning the usurper and regicide on the throne. Thus he would have repeated in every detail the coup that had worked so well for Catherine two years earlier. It is easy to see what had inspired the plotters: the belief that in such troubled times, when anybody at all could get themselves installed on the throne of Russia, all that was necessary was a repetition of the first coup to achieve the same result. As far as legitimacy was concerned, Ivan VI had an unchallenged superiority over Catherine. Moreover, his weakened state made him a wonderful instrument for the manipulation of power for whoever managed to place him on the throne. The memory of the rewards distributed by Catherine to the conspirators of 1762 could not fail to awaken the envy of others. Who would not have wished to attain, by the same operation, similar rewards, particularly in the circles of the young and impoverished officers like Mirovich?

But just as history rarely repeats itself, so there are few examples of plots that repeat themselves or achieve the identical result. Catherine was too well aware of the precariousness of her position not to have taken an impressive number of precautions and made certain that Ivan VI would never leave his prison alive. The orders were clear: at any attempt at escape or rescue, the prisoner should immediately be put to death. Thus it was that when the conspirators rushed into Ivan's cell, they were confronted by his corpse. Mirovich was arrested and condemned to death. Since this was the first beheading to take place in Russia for twenty years, when the executioner presented the officer's head to the crowd, their emotion was so great that the Neva bridge, where they were gathered, almost collapsed.

Catherine was liberated from what was to be the last threat to her power, but she also found herself in a difficult position. It was a matter of urgency to put an end to the rumor suggesting that she herself had inspired Mirovich with the idea for this plot. Falling into the trap, he had thus got rid of Ivan VI for her. The orders given to the guards to kill Ivan at the least disturbance would also have to be hushed up, for if they were known they would give credence to the rumors accusing Catherine of being behind the whole thing. It can be imagined how this murder, following that of the sovereign, further damned the empress's already bad reputation. Two years earlier, a French diplomat had written in a dispatch: "What a scene! On the one hand the grandson of Peter I deposed and killed; on the other, the grandson of Ivan V languishing in chains, while a princess from Anhalt usurps the crown of their ancestors, starting off with regicide. . . ."

With her power now secured and possible rivals removed, Catherine could afford a tarnished reputation. As Voltaire says in his indulgent account of the facts, a fault might induce Catherine to make efforts to amend it and earn again the public's good esteem. Her reign, so long and so glorious, seems to vouch for Voltaire's theory. She managed to make her country and the rest of the world forget the circumstances of her accession to the throne and came to be known to future centuries as Catherine the Great.

The Political Consequences of the Regicide

There was, however, a postscript to the regicide at the time of Catherine's death, in a scene worthy of Greek tragedy. After Catherine died, Paul had his father's tomb opened and the bones disinterred. They were taken to the Alexander Nevsky Monastery in the Winter Palace to be exhibited alongside the embalmed body of Catherine II. Thus Paul reunited in death the deposed tsar and the woman who had usurped his throne and pehaps organized his murder. They were buried side by side and official mourning was observed for the imperial couple so lastingly separated by hate. This ironic reunion for eternity was accompanied by a posthumous homage and reparation made to Peter III, a striking revenge for Catherine's husband and a no less glaring snub to the empress, as well as a macabre settling of old scores with the authors of the murder. Not content with presenting Peter's remains—crowned, although he had never been crowned in his lifetime—to the public gaze, in a strange and sinister ceremony Paul forced the assassins, Aleksei Orlov and Prince Baratinsky, to stand in the front row of those taking part in the act of homage to their victim. Aleksei Orlov, the glorious victor of the battle of Chesme,[8] which had made Russia a leading naval power, was the star of the occasion. This giant of a man, covered with well-deserved honors, neither bent nor bowed by age, was made to walk in full dress uniform (his uniform of the time of the murder) alongside Peter's coffin, carrying his victim's crown on a cushion while his fellow conspirators acted as pallbearers. While the ceremony did not directly accuse Catherine, it reminded Russia of the original murder by bringing together for a moment, after so many years, the victim crowned with a glory he had never known, his assassins, and the woman accomplice who had benefited from their crime. It was an extraordinary revenge and a lesson for history, revealing both the powerful resentment and the tormented character of the new tsar.

Before moving on from this first Russian regicide, two aspects that were to be important in the political history of the country need to be emphasized. It completed the erosion of the myth of the tsar and yet, at the same time, it further contributed to it. In deposing and murdering the grandson of Peter the Great, the conspirators of 1762 had underlined the weakness of the sovereign and the continual change taking place in his image. Not only was the tsar now chosen instead of being imposed by right of birth but,

---

8.   The battle of Chesme, in June 1770, saw the destruction of the entire Turkish fleet by the Russian navy commanded by Aleksei Orlov. Eleven thousand Turkish sailors lost their lives. Like the battles of Lepanto and Trafalgar, Chesme represented an international event of the first order because of the new balances it created. It became an important name in the national mythology of Russia.

what was more, it had become apparent that the choice could be disputed. After Peter the Great, the accession to the throne of women descended from now one and then another branch of the Romanov family had had a disturbing effect. Furthermore, both Peter III and Catherine II had been foreigners, one in culture and ideas—for Peter was thoroughly German—and the other by birth. In this fluid situation where none of the traditional criteria seemed to apply any more, it was tempting, when a sovereign proved to be unsatisfactory, to depose him, or even to get rid of him altogether, as happened with Peter III. People were more shocked by the regicide than by the deposition, for it was no longer very clear by what right Peter had come to the throne in the first place. The old problem of the true and the false tsar took on a new dimension: what criteria could be used to decide whether or not a tsar was the product of a judicious choice? Now that sovereigns could be unconnected with the imperial family and were neither Russians nor good Orthodox Christians, what was left to legitimize their right to the throne? It was certainly not a part of the divine nature, since they had not come to the throne by right of birth. The accidents of decisions governing the various choices of successor since 1725 marked the end of any possibility of legitimizing imperial power.

In this respect the regicide—and no longer only the murder of a tsarevich—reinforced the doubt hanging over the legitimacy of the sovereign. The example of Peter III bore witness to this. As tsar he had received the oath of allegiance from his subjects. Pugachov, the false Peter III, was all the more able to demand the fidelity of those who came in contact with him because he did not claim to set himself up against the oath made subsequently to his successor, but invoked instead an allegiance that predated that made to the usurper, Catherine, whom he was denouncing. Since he had apparently once been the tsar, he did not have to prove his legitimacy. Those who swore loyalty to Pugachov after having done so to Catherine II were not committing perjury, since they were returning to their first allegiance, which had bound them to Peter III. It was to be the regicide and its consequences that made Pugachov–Peter III particularly threatening to Catherine II.

The regicide also confirmed a post-Petrine political development: the secularization of imperial rule. The emperor himself became the source of the power of the emperor. By setting up the plot to depose her husband, Catherine did not claim any other source of legitimacy than that of her desire to ascend the throne and her certainty of having exceptional qualifications for ruling—as she amply demonstrated. If power could thus be shaken and the holder of power supplanted and murdered, it was because it no longer had a divine source. The role of emperor brought with it its own justification, and thus its own deification, any other link with religion being only formal. The changes to the coronation ceremony of 1742 are evidence of this development. Until that time, the head of the Orthodox Church had placed the crown on the sovereign's head, symbolizing the bond between the church and the ruler of the state and the divine approval of the temporal power. Elizabeth and all her successors were to crown themselves in the Cathedral of the Dormition in the Kremlin while the head of the church had to be content with being a witness who merely passed the crown to the tsar at the right moment.

While the regicide of 1762 revealed the changes that had taken place in the ideological foundations of the function and the nature of the sovereign, it also underlined the ambiguity of Russian society's attitude to the nation. On the one hand, Peter III was unpopular because of his rejection of Russia and his obvious "Prussophilia." Catherine's task was made easier by the indignation of the nobles and the army at being compelled to go along with this "Germanization" of the state. Paradoxically, Catherine who incarnated at this time the interests and specificity of Russia was in fact herself German. It was no less paradoxical that Catherine—who, like the majority of sovereigns since Peter the Great, sought to westernize her country of adoption through reform—had begun by getting rid of the man who had railed so often against "Russian barbarism" and who had tried to impose a Prussian model and western habits on the country. But despite these contradictions, it is clear that the plot of 1762 was also a Russian reaction to the humiliation inflicted by Peter III on everything Russian.

But it was to be the most Russian elements of society, those attached to the extreme forms of Russian religious observance—the Old Believers—who were to swell the numbers of those who regretted the passing of Peter III and who rallied to Pugachov as a representative of the "true" faith of the Russian nation. Peter III had been accused by the nobles of behaving not like a tsar but like an emperor, which was true. For the people, for the Old Believers, only the "tsar" was legitimate; the "emperor" was the Antichrist. Nevertheless, Pugachov did not call himself tsar, but adopted the imperial style, as can be seen in his manifesto of September 17, 1773, which begins: "Decree of our great sovereign, Emperor and Autocrat, Peter Fedorovich of all the Russias. . . . As you, my friends, have served the previous tsars, even to the shedding of your blood, you, your ancestors and your brothers, so you will serve me for the Fatherland, me, your great sovereign, Emperor Peter Fedorovich. . . ." But the people knew what they wanted. One of the few songs to survive from this period runs:

> They were always looking for a tsar.
> Well, they found him, this tsar!

When the peasants followed Pugachov, it was not to oppose a state that oppressed them and denied them their rights, but to set up once more at its head a pious Orthodox tsar. They believed that the cause of all their misfortunes could be attributed to his disappearance and his replacement by a sovereign who was identified with a state that had gone so far astray. Despite his lack of education, Pugachov claimed to be the emperor; he claimed neither piety nor Orthodoxy, and identified himself with the state as it had evolved. In this rebellion, the old idea of the pious tsar and his state that were inseparable from the church coexisted with that of the imperial autocrat, the sovereign whose sacred character is intrinsic, with no link with God but bound to a state on the road to modernization, with secular foundations. It would appear at first sight that there was some confusion in the minds of the people. At a deeper level, it is indicative of the changes that were taking place in the collective consciousness. Believing that it was still attached to the idea of power as it had always known it, revering the false Paul III in the name of this idea, it was in fact moving imperceptibly toward another ideological system where the right to judge those in power, and to remove them, was no longer only the privilege of the upper levels of society. In this sense, the regicide of 1762, the condemnation of a tsar who rejected the Russianness of Russia, revealed that this nostalgia was becoming a thing of the past.

This regicide also had disquieting aspects. In Elizabeth's lifetime Catherine had been implicated in some dubious international dealings. She personified hostility to Peter's alliance with Prussia. Thus it would have been perfectly possible that foreign powers interested in a change in Russian policies might have had a part in this plot. It would have been equally logical if after 1762 Catherine had adopted a different foreign policy from that pursued by Peter, which she had condemned. In fact, everything seems to indicate that the coup was an entirely internal affair: apart from Frederick II's frequent warnings to Peter to be wary, no links with a foreign state can be found. The two factions certainly had different internal and foreign policies, but external influences seem not to have played a part in the events that overturned the throne of Russia at that time. As for Catherine's foreign policy, it departed less from that of Peter than might have been imagined, at least in the long term of a remarkable international activity. Following the advice of her minister for foreign affairs, Panin, on the necessity of an alliance with the north that could counterbalance the power of Austria, France, and Spain, she returned by this other route to certain of Peter's options, and first of all to his interest in Prussia. Her two principal successes were to quell Turkey,[9] an eternal problem for Russia, and to participate on three occasions along with Prussia and Austria in the partition of Poland—in line with Peter's views. After the French Revolution, and despite her long friendship with the French *philosophes,* Catherine II conceived a great hostility toward revolutionary France, breaking off all links after the execution of Louis XVI, which outraged her. Thus yesterday's Francophile suddenly adopted a Francophobia that was to stay with her for the rest of her life. The empress regicide could not forgive the revolution for having put an end to the life of their king.

9. The treaties of Kuchuk-Kainarji in 1774, at the end of the first Russo-Turkish war, and of Jassy in 1797, ending the second war between the two countries, gave Russia access to the Black Sea, the dream of all Catherine's predecessors.

The Empress against Her Son

On November 17, 1796, Paul I, eldest son of Peter III and Catherine II, ascended to the throne of Russia. The successor of two emperors and direct descendant of Peter the Great, the new sovereign seemed to embody a rediscovered dynastic order and a re-established stability. When Catherine had taken the throne thirty-four years earlier she had named her son as her heir. This succession, which reconciled the principle of inheritance with the law of succession determined by Peter the Great, seemed so natural but yet concealed profound contradictions. Paul's brief reign was to make them only too apparent.

The new Russian sovereign was now a man of forty-two, having spent long years waiting for power in the shadow of a mother who had no intention of giving it up. His was a complex and tormented character, oppressed by the weight of a double tragedy. First there had been the death of his father; the mystery surrounding this event continued to haunt him, as we can see from the staging of the funeral ceremony. Second, there was his difficult relationship with his mother. Paul had been a gifted child to whom Catherine, when she ascended to the throne, had given a very advanced education in every field: humanities, mathematics, sciences, foreign languages and all the accomplishments—nothing was lacking. A passionate devotee of French philosophy, she had even begged d'Alembert, in 1762, to come and take charge of the heir's education. He refused, revealing in a letter to Voltaire his reservations about Catherine: "I am too much subject to hemorrhoids, which are dangerous in that country," he wrote, alluding to the official cause of Peter III's death. Instead Nikita Panin became Paul's tutor. But from this time, the relations between mother and son became more distant. The latter was greatly influenced by his tutor, who supported the faction that had wanted to put Paul on the throne when Peter III died, making his mother regent. Since that time, Nikita Panin must inevitably have kept alive in the heart of his pupil a certain feeling of frustration and discomfort in relation to a mother whom he had scarcely known as a young child, having been snatched away from his parents by Elizabeth. Added to this confused bitterness was his growing indignation at Catherine's outrageous conduct. Her successive lovers lorded it about the court, treating the heir to the throne with condescension and, above all, offending his naturally puritanical character. As he grew older, Paul began to represent a dangerous rival to his mother and, in the eyes of the empress's lovers, a threat to their privileged position dependent on Catherine's presence on the throne. If Paul were to replace her, they could well imagine their fate. When Paul was eighteen years old, the problem became particularly acute. The only justification for her presence on the throne that Catherine had been able to put forward hitherto was the fact that her son was underage. How else would she have been able to make Russia accept the crowning of a German woman without links to Russia and half-suspected, furthermore, of having murdered her husband? Could her reign continue now that Paul was of age?

From then on, it was clear to Paul and Catherine that their views on all matters—whether in private life or political matters—were diametrically opposed. They knew also that in Russia there were many who wished to use the coming of age of the heir as an excuse to dethrone Catherine. The idea of power being shared, initially, between mother and son also had its supporters. While some tempted him with reminders of his rights to the throne, Paul was rightly worried by what his mother might dream up in order to delay the hour of their confrontation, or even to oust him altogether. He was not mistaken. In addition, he saw his mother squandering her wealth on ever greedier favorites. He opposed her openly on foreign policy. Finally Catherine did what Elizabeth had once done to her; she seized Paul's children and had them educated apart from and against their parents. She wanted to make everything hers, from the throne to her son's offspring. This long tension inevitably added to Paul's unbalanced nature, which dated back to his troubled childhood.

The crisis broke in the late 1780s. At one time amused by the Freemasonry then developing in Russia, Catherine had later become resolutely hostile to it, believing that the branch of the Rosicrucians, about which she received many reports, was revolutionary and perhaps even inclined to use Paul to further their aims. It had in fact been suggested that Paul was responsible for the Russian branch of the Rosicrucians; and while he always insisted that he had never been a member, it was clear from the inquiry set up by Catherine that he had many links with Freemasonry. Whatever the case, the moral views of the puritanical Freemasons, so different from Catherine's unrestrained behavior, made Paul the antithesis of his mother, and the possible architect of a reformed Russia.

For Catherine, these commonly held views were all proofs of her son's involvement in a plot against her. Making up her mind to oust him from the throne and returning to the tactic that she had used so successfully in 1762, she decided to anticipate events and change the order of succession. After all, she said, Peter I had given her the right to do so. She had the documents drawn up by Peter in 1722 carefully studied together with all the preceding texts concerning the succession. Her choice was Paul's eldest son, Alexander, then fifteen years old, whom she married to a young girl of his own age, Princess Louise of Baden. She pressed Alexander to join in her plan and tried to get Paul's wife to force her husband to agree to give up the throne. Furious at this questioning of his right to the throne, Paul became more obstinate, opposing his mother on every issue. But it was not his behavior that was to save him from Catherine's fury. If he escaped, it was first of all because his own son—influenced by his tutor, La Harpe—refused to deprive his father of the succession. It was also because Catherine, exhausted by age, excess, and the anxiety caused by this last struggle, conveniently died. Shortly before her death, it was rumored in the court that on St. Catherine's day (November 24) a new successor was to be announced. It was further said that she had left a will removing Paul from the succession in favor of Alexander. If the facts are true, this will must have been destroyed by agreement between the father and the son. Whatever the case, with Catherine dead, her son wasted no time in having a manifesto drawn up immediately announcing his accession to the throne.

This crisis, a sore trial for Catherine, had been no less alarming for Paul. Events of the past had taught him the extent of his mother's taste for power. Since he was a boy he had understood that for her he was first and foremost an enemy and a rival and only then a son. When his mother evoked the relations between Peter the Great and the Tsarevich Alexis in order to justify the distance at which she kept him, he could not but be fearful. For in fact, during the last years of Catherine's reign, the opposition between mother and son exactly reproduced the conflict between Peter and the tsarevich. Like Alexis, the champion of tradition against the reforms desired by his father, so now Paul stood up against his mother in the name of the moral rigor—which for him was more or less the same as religion—of the Russian tradition and of respect for the past. Once again, by opposing a parent, a son was threatening to destroy the vision of the future of the sovereign whom he was to succeed. Like Alexis, Paul was subjected to pressure from his parent to renounce the throne. He may well have asked himself whether he was eventually to suffer the same fate as the unfortunate tsarevich.

It is not hard to understand how his already unstable nature could have been further shaken and how a pathological suspiciousness combined with his disconcerting behavior betrayed his anxieties. On the other hand, when he ascended to the throne, he need have no fears about the behavior of his son and could be sure that his heir represented no threat. Alexander's loyalty to his father—unless it was simply a young boy's lack of interest in power—ought to have gone a long way toward soothing Paul's troubled mind. But after so many tragic or worrying events, it came too late to reassure Paul or restore his long-lost balance of mind.

Paul I: A Second Hamlet?

Paul's reign was short—less than five years on the throne after so long a wait. But the effects of this unhappy and eventful reign were to be felt by Paul's successor and for decades to come. This sovereign, whom contemparies sometimes likened to Hamlet, had nothing outwardly romantic about him. A sickly man, he seemed shrunken in on himself, presenting to the world a face with a snub nose and protruding eyes that were rarely lit up by a smile. Everything about the man indicated austerity and rigor, while his reputation for ugliness seems to have been fully deserved. Perhaps his physical unattractiveness further increased the gloominess of his character, in a court where his mother had loved to surround herself with men chosen for their good looks. But finally, from November 17, 1796, none of that was to be important. Paul was the emperor, determined to govern and very conscious of his authority. "Learn that there is no one of any importance in Russia except the man to whom I choose to speak, and he is that only for the time that I am speaking to him," he said once. Governing, for him, meant taking on every issue the opposite point of view of his mother.

His first important political decision, inspired by filial bitterness, was to have considerable implications for the future of the dynasty. On April 5, 1797, he abolished the decree of 1722 made by Peter the Great and, for the first time in history, clearly established a law of succession. Succession was to be based on primogeniture and excluded women from the throne.[10] This posthumous condemnation of the power given to Catherine had at least the advantage, for the future, of freeing Russian political life from the quarrels and doubts surrounding the choice of an heir. Paul's successor was immediately obvious and assured of a secure position. For all that, relations between Paul I and his son Alexander, who had refused to allow himself to be substituted for his father, were not made any simpler.

In the course of the first months of his reign, Paul adopted contradictory attitudes, partly as a result of his temperament but also from a desire to question all his mother's decisions. These had not always been very clear, particularly in relation to the French Revolution and the wave of liberal ideas that Catherine believed to be dangerous to the state. At the end of her reign, she had begun to manifest an extreme intolerance toward anyone who in her opinion questioned autocracy, be they freethinkers or merely Freemasons. During this period of "ideological reaction," the one-time friend of the Encyclopedists had thus thrown into prison two men whose intellectual influence among the nobility was increasing: Nikolai

---

10.   Even where, in the case of the lack of a male heir, the succession went to a woman, only a male could come to power. It should be noted that the act of April 5, 1797 was drawn up and signed by Paul, the "heir" (this is stated at the top of the act) and his wife on January 4, 1788, thus well before the death of Catherine II.

Novikov and Aleksandr Radishchev. The first, who had played a central role in the expansion of Freemasonry in Russia,[11] had sharply criticized Catherine for her Francophilia, which did not temper in any way her indulgent attitude toward social injustice. He appealed to the moral rigor of traditional Russia against the dissolute morals of the court. For Catherine this challenge was insupportable and smacked of treason. Another victim of her repression, Aleksandr Radishchev, the author of a violent polemic entitled *Journey from St. Petersburg to Moscow* which was privately published in 1790, attacked social conditions in Russia and Catherine's government of the country. Since the pamphlet had appeared without prior authorization shortly after the French Revolution that had so troubled Catherine, she was merciless toward its author. Radishchev, an aristocrat by origin and an intellectual by vocation, had done no more than expand on ideas that Catherine herself had formerly espoused; now he was accused of treason and condemned to be beheaded—a sentence then commuted to exile in the wastes of Siberia.

As soon as he came to power, Paul freed these two victims of Catherine's persecution, thus allowing the dissemination of ideas that he was, nevertheless, to oppose constantly. In the same way, he recalled to the court all those who had incurred the empress's disfavor. This clemency gave hope of a peaceful reign. But at the same time, he multiplied measures restricting freedom. More even than his mother, he had a deep-rooted hatred for the French Revolution, both because it was a crime against the established order and because it was French. Determined to prevent its spread into Russia, he was careful to protect Russian minds from the ideas of 1789, introducing a whole series of prohibitions. He attacked styles of dress, prohibiting anything—round hats, tail coats, waistcoats, large cravats—that smacked of Jacobinism. He did the same for the language, purging it of the words *société* (society) and *citoyen* (citizen) which had penetrated into Russia. He even forbade shopkeepers to use the word *magasin* (store) and sent in the police when necessary to

---

11. In 1776, Novikov founded a lodge in Moscow, based on the mystical and esoteric cult of the German Freemasons, as opposed to the more secular tradition of the English lodges. Its foundation in Moscow and not in St. Petersburg is significant: Novikov wanted to promote Freemasonry as a means of restoring Russia's culture and traditions.

force them to replace it with the Russian word *lavka*. Books, theater, and even music from Europe were harshly censored. Russians traveling abroad were called home, and the French had to show a passport signed in the name of the Bourbons when they wished to enter Russia. Censorship was so strict that the number of publications, reviews, and books fell dramatically.

Not content only to prohibit, Paul also imposed outdated usages. When he passed by, carriages had to stop and the people to kneel down, regardless of rain or snow. But what he wanted above all was to introduce Prussian order and Prussian manners. This once popular prince had represented the hope of a return to a greater respect for Russian traditions against an overly Francophile mother. Now he saw it as his first priority to impose another foreign influence, this time German. Everyone had to dress in the Prussian style, starting with the army. Instead of the Russian uniform, well-suited to the rigors of the climate, he introduced a German uniform with wigs, gaiters, and buckled shoes, which caused Aleksandr Suvorov, the future hero of the Napoleonic Wars, to say: "The wigmaker's powder is not gunpowder; buckles are not cannons; pigtails are not bayonets; we are not Germans, we are Russians." Paul put the same enthusiasm for detail into reorganizing drill and tactical formations according to the Prussian model so dear to his heart. The Russian army may well have been in need of reform in many respects, being old-fashioned in terms of technology and strategy. Paul, who adored military problems, was right to want to make these changes. But his petty and unstable character and his suspiciousness—he feared that the elite regiments that had formerly overthrown his father might want to continue their tradition of interfering in political life—meant that the necessary reform was reduced for the most part to the creation of new-style regiments and changes in the uniform. He immediately became unpopular, alienating the army as he was soon to alienate the nobility.

For all that, Paul's decisions were sound and their original inspiration was often a good one, but they were sooner or later compromised by his instability of character. Conscious of the frustrations of a society without direct access to the sovereign, he invented a sort of office of complaints and petitions that he installed on a staircase in the palace, where anyone could leave a petition for him to read without delay. Once his first interest in the needs of his subjects passed, he ignored these letters which started to pile up. Alarmed by their accumulation, which he took personally as a sign of hostility, he finally abandoned the whole thing.

In the same way, he undertook to bring order to the state finances, depleted by the constant wars of the previous reign. Catherine had kept the mint busy printing banknotes and Paul wisely suspended its use for a period. He had six million paper rubles burned publicly and brought their value into line with the ruble coin. In this way he hoped to raise the value of a currency that over the years had constantly depreciated. He was successful for a brief period, but it required other methods to save the ruble. He raised considerably the duties paid on imported goods and had the gold and silver plate of the various regional governments melted down. Illogically he then canceled the effect of these sacrifices by spending huge amounts on beautifying his palaces or building new ones. It began to be murmured—especially by the merchants, who were suffering from the customs duties, and by the provincial governors who had had to hand over their gold and silver—that Paul could not be quite sane if he could pursue such contradictory economic policies. He upset the nobles just as much—the fact was that he hated them for having formerly supported his mother—by taking over new measures to harass them, notably reintroducing corporal punishment from which they had long been exempt.

Paul's foreign policy was a similar mixture of perceptive understanding and inconsistency. It merits attention because his international policies were to be a factor in the plot that was to cost him his life. On his accession, he proclaimed his intention of pursuing a policy of peace: the size of the army was to be reduced (Catherine had decreed an exceptional recruitment figure of three men of every five hundred inhabitants, which Paul abandoned), while a circular letter to all the states of Europe informed them that, after forty years of uninterrupted war, Russia was to pursue a campaign of peace and would not take part in the anti-French coalition that Catherine had been thinking of joining. But forgetful of his proposals, Paul was shortly afterward to be the organizer of the second coalition against France, in which his armies, commanded by Suvorov, distinguished themselves. Subsequently, the tsar's enthusiasm for this coalition disappeared. Being of the opinion that his Austrian allies, and to a lesser degree the English, had not backed his military efforts in the campaign in the Low Countries in 1799, Paul turned his back on them and, with his usual excess of enthusiasm, became besotted with Napoleon. He admired both Napoleon's military success and his authority, which went well with his own principles. Conscious of the opportunity that such a reversal of alliances could offer, Napoleon for his part did all he could to seduce and win over the emperor of Russia. He returned the Russian prisoners captured by his armies, without conditions and dressed in new clothes, he offered to recognize Russian sovereignty over the island of Malta, denied by England—Paul like his ancestor Peter the Great was aware of the necessity of maritime bases—and flattered him in every way.

There were good reasons for the two to make common cause. Paul's envoys exhorted Napoleon to take the throne of France and proclaim the hereditary nature of the dynasty that he would establish. The future Napoleon I did not conceal the pleasure he found in these words. Thus a political alliance, opposed to the anti-French grouping, began to take shape. It reached a high point with Paul's "great plan" against England, now the common enemy and one that the two new friends decided to oust from India. Since the French were already occupying Egypt, Paul sent regiments of Cossacks to the Caucasus and central Asia to march on into India. The position of the English was becoming decidedly uncomfortable. To demonstrate his friendship for Bonaparte, in whom he saw the man who could bring the revolution to an end, Paul expelled Louis XVIII from Mitau where he had always been welcome in the past. Thus he managed to turn all sides against him: first the members of the coalition against France, and particularly England which could foresee, in Paul's confused policies, a threat to its economic, maritime, and colonial power; second, the legitimists and all the supporters of the restoration of the Bourbons in France, for whom the expulsion of Louis XVIII revealed Paul's support for another view of France's future. Even in his own country, Paul was hard put to justify his sudden Francophilia, following as it did so swiftly on the persecution of everything French.

Although prompted by sudden whims and bombastic declarations, Paul's foreign policy should not be dismissed out of hand. Behind the apparent disorder of contradictory actions, a precise plan and a certain continuity can be distinguished. In his *Histoire de la Révolution française,* Albert Sorel writes: "Russian policy emerged with a powerful simplicity from the nature of things and continued under the most diverse regimes and the most eccentric sovereigns." Paul I was no exception to this rule. Despite his hostility to the state emerging from the French Revolution in 1789, he had immediately attempted to reestablish relations with France, agreeing to forget the royal cause, so convinced was he that the interests of the two countries coincided. It was the Directory that refused to agree to his request that France no longer support the anti-Russian Polish émigrés, thus throwing Paul back into the arms of the coalition. France even, at this period, preferred to incite the Turkish sultan against Russia. If this was unsuccessful, it was because Bonaparte alarmed the Turks, who then sought Russia's assistance against his boundless ambition. Paul's difficulties with his allies in the coalition were to turn him back toward a France that Bonaparte was rapidly steering away from revolutionary extremism. But this and the excesses of his own character did not affect the essence of Russian foreign policy, with the exception of his claims to the island and the order of Malta which may perhaps seem rather incoherent. But here we have to look at the combination of traditional Russian interests in the Mediterranean and the factors that influenced Paul. That an Orthodox sovereign could make himself a Grand Master of the Knights of Malta and their protector might seem paradoxical, for what had he to do with a Catholic order of this kind? But the protection of the order implied that of the island, which was then occupied by French troops before being blockaded and occupied by the English. The island was an important stronghold in the Mediterranean; the struggle to control it, which had first made Paul and Bonaparte enemies, was to unite them as soon as the latter was evicted from it.

Another influence was that of Joseph de Maistre, who was able to bring Paul round to a greater sympathy with the Catholic Church. De Maistre belonged to that group of Frenchmen who had fled at the revolution and found refuge in St. Petersburg where, enjoying an independent position as ambassador from Sardinia, he had found a sure method of propagating his ideas. Convinced that the ideas of the Enlightenment were "a revolt against God" and the expression of a nihilism that he called *rienisme* (nothingism), responsible for the disastrous revolution, he hoped that traditionalist Russia would reawaken the counterrevolutionary current that would save Europe. He was horrified by the violence of the Russian methods of resolving disputes but, at the same time, he was fascinated by what he believed to be an "Asian remedy" that would at one stroke turn back the wheel of history. Everything about this strict Catholic, friend of the Jesuits, but equally a Freemason, attracted Paul. Joseph de Maistre's arrival in Russia had coincided with a certain political relaxation in relation to the Catholic Church—Paul had gotten the pope to agree to the return of the Jesuits to Russia and had authorized the setting up of places of worship—and the two men felt greater sympathy for one another as a result. The Frenchman's ideas about the destructive effects of the philosophy of the eighteenth century, his view of Russia, the home of antirationalist ideas, as the savior of Europe, and his assertion that violence, inseparable from Russian history, was an essential means of coercion encouraged Paul to pursue conservative policies, turning increasingly away from reform. When he had come to the throne, he had freed Radishchev, a man who had strongly condemned the social order in Russia and above all, serfdom. At the end of his reign, Paul found in Joseph de Maistre a justification for the increasing hardening of his position.

The evolution from a moment of hope to a time of despair, which made itself felt in all areas and levels of society, from the nobility to the serfs, was to lead to Paul's death. Even the church was to forsake him, unable to accept the welcome extended by Paul to the Jesuits and Catholicism. Abandoned by his countrymen and without allies abroad—Napoleon was unable to defend him against the growing condemnation from Europe of his irrational decisions, now increasingly seen as the result of an unbalanced mind—Paul I was nevertheless still the legitimate sovereign. He was, furthermore, the sovereign who had laid down the conditions for the choice of an heir. Could he be deposed? History took another course with a repetition of the events that, seven years earlier, had helped him to the throne. On the night of March 23, 1801, Paul was assassinated.

The Murder of Paul I: Parricide?

Paul's death, like that of his father which had so haunted him, was horrible. Trusting no one, he had got into the habit of locking himself in his bedchamber. As always, the palace was well guarded. That night, soldiers from the elite Semyonovsky Guards regiment were responsible for his safety. A handful of men succeeded, nevertheless, in bursting into his room around midnight, demanding his abdication. Paul tried to get away, throwing himself against the circle of murderers and defending himself fiercely. But he was alone and, in the confusion, the lamp that lit the scene was broken. He was then attacked from all sides. Finally he succumbed to their blows, strangled, his limbs broken and his head smashed with a snuffbox. Who it was that killed him is not known. The fury of his attackers, who dared not fail if they were to save their own lives, left a scene of indescribable chaos. Immediately, one of the conspirators, Count Pahlen, governor of St. Petersburg, went to the heir, Alexander, to announce to him that he was emperor. The country learned that Paul I had succumbed to an "attack," and hastened to salute the accession of a handsome young man who awoke, as ever, the dormant hopes of the people.

This regicide, the second in the space of two generations— first the father and then the son—was much more complex that that which had rid Catherine of her inconvenient husband, and more tragic. First, it threatened the position of the heir to the throne (the old system of the father killing his heir the tsarevich is reversed here), and raised the possibility of his involvement. Second, this was a truly political regicide, the only case of its kind in Russia. It was not a matter, as in 1762, of rescuing a candidate for the throne who was threatened. The heir to the throne was protected by the law of succession instituted by Paul I. Paul's assassins were not intriguers eager to bring to the throne a pretender who would protect them, but responsible men carrying out a political action.

The first question raised by this regicide is that of the role played by the heir. Was he an accomplice or merely the beneficiary of a murder that had horrified him? He was to spend the rest of his life attempting to prove his innocence. His relations with the conspirators shed some light on his position. They were, first of all,

Panin and Pahlen, the brains behind the plot. Then there were the men who carried out the plot and entered the emperor's bed-chamber. These men, who never denied their part in the deed, were General Levin August Bennigsen, the Zubov brothers, Yachvil, and other lesser associates. Count Nikita Panin was a respected vice-chancellor and as nephew of Catherine II's foreign minister, Nikita Panin[12] had earlier enjoyed the same favor at the court of Paul I as his father and uncle had known under Catherine. A few months before his death, however, Paul must have suspected that Panin—whose criticism of his foreign policy was becoming very strong—was plotting to remove him from the throne or limit his power, for he had Panin removed from his position of responsibility. This partly explains how it was that Pahlen came to be involved in the plot, later on but all the more active for that. Pahlen had impressed both the tsar and his heir with his great resolution and authority. Paul I had given him the prestigious post of governor of St. Petersburg, and counted on him to sniff out and defuse any plots against him.

Of those involved in the actual attack, the most important were the two Zubov brothers. One, Platon, had been a onetime favorite of Catherine II. The accession of Paul I had condemned him, along with his brothers, to vegetate far away from the capital (to which they had only recently returned), sharing in the disgrace hanging over all those who had been momentarily favored by the empress. In the weeks leading up to Paul's death, the Zubov brothers had taken advantage of an amnesty that the emperor hoped would win him new allies. But he was too late. The thoughts of the exiles of 1796 had dwelt too long on their resentment to prevent the plot. Another of their number was General Bennigsen, whose account of the murder, in which he in no way tries to conceal his involvement, sheds much light on the affair. Lastly, we should mention Prince Yachvil. Born of a great Georgian family, he had always hated Paul, as he wrote later to Alexander I: "From the day the unfortunate madman, your father, ascended to the throne, I

12.   Catherine II's minister was Nikita Ivanovich. His nephew, Nikita Petrovich, was the son of his brother Peter, a general, who had played an important part in putting down the Pugachov revolt.

resolved to sacrifice my life, if necessary, for the good of Russia which, since the time of Peter the Great, had become the plaything of favorites and eventually the victim of a madman. . . . Before the sovereign, I am the savior of the Fatherland. Before the son, I am the murderer of his father."

The conspirators, it is clear, were convinced that they were acting for the good of their country in removing from the throne a man who was losing his reason, or at least, because of his unstable temperament, was pursuing a dangerous path. There was a clear division of labor. At the time of the murder, Nikita Panin, who controlled most of the strings, was not in the palace. Pahlen did not directly take part in the murder.[13] By contrast, Bennigsen, Yachvil, and the Zubov brothers shared among them the task of putting an end to the emperor's life.

Alexander: Parricide?

And what did the heir know of all this? His character is worth examining, because it explains his behavior before and after the drama that brought him to the throne. His tutor, Protassov, left to posterity some harsh comments on the character of his pupil: intelligent, but lazy and happy-go-lucky; little inclined to reading, but fascinated by military exercises; incapable of concentrating, no sooner hearing a thing than forgetting it. In short, Paul's heir was charming, but from the time of his marriage—at sixteen—to the death of his father, he had not acquired any maturity. These defects in his character were particularly apparent at the time of the tragedy of 1801. Mixing constantly, during his father's reign, with the court and the officers, Alexander was well aware of the growing dissatisfaction with Paul. He could not fail to notice that constant reference was being made to Paul's mental state. In the act of April 5, 1797 dealing with the succession, the problem of mental derangement had been set down very precisely: "Legal incapacities forbidding rule

---

13. A story handed down by word of mouth has it that, while the emperor was being killed, Count Pahlen walked up and down the adjoining gallery admiring the pictures, complaining all the while of the din caused by the sovereign's cries.

or requiring a regency are: insanity, even if temporary . . . ." Alexander knew that his father was considered to be half-demented and getting worse; he knew equally that the law of succession meant that any solution would revolve around his own person.

In the year preceding the murder, the weaving of the threads of the plot and the links between the conspirators and Alexander can be clearly seen. Having rejected his grandmother's plan to place him on the throne in the place of his father in 1796, Alexander could feel that he had in advance proved his filial respect—insofar as Paul's mental state enabled him to be respected. But in the years that followed, the deterioration of the emperor's character was accompanied by a worsening of the relation between father and son, to the point where Alexander may have feared that his father was thinking of changing the order of succession. He was protected by the act of 1797, but the history of the dynasty had taught him that an autocratic sovereign could quite well change the law according to circumstances or whim.

Paul's reaction to the increasing general discontent was a growing suspiciousness and, as a result, a growing hostility toward his heir, whom he was beginning to see as a rival, for any plot directed against him would hasten the accession of his son. The two central figures of the plot, Panin and Pahlen, were to attempt to organize their plot with a concern for legality, in other words, by obtaining carte blanche from the heir. "Carte blanche" was indeed the expression used by Grand Duke Nicholas Mikhailovich, Alexander's great-grandnephew, in his research into Alexander's responsibility.

About a year before the plot, in the course of an interview with Alexander at the Russian baths—Paul was suspicious, and in the months leading up to the murder, the two leaders of the conspiracy tried to avoid any open meeting with the heir which might have aroused Paul's fears[14]—Nikita Panin referred to its possibility in barely disguised words. Later, Pahlen, who had great

---

14. Pahlen was to summarize the situation as follows: "The emperor's suspicions had been aroused regarding my links with Grand Duke Alexander. We were aware of this. I was not able to visit the young man and we did not dare speak together for more than a few minutes, despite our positions which brought us into frequent contact. Thus we communicated our thoughts and the necessary arrangements by means of letter. These notes were given to Count Panin and the grand duke answered with other notes that Panin carried back to me."

influence over Alexander, spoke more plainly and, in all probability, persuaded him to move from a clear approval of a plan limited to the deposition of the emperor to a tacit agreement to his possible elimination. Pahlen later related that, at first when "it seemed impossible to act without having the agreement and even the cooperation of Grand Duke Alexander . . ., I managed to overcome his filial piety and even to persuade him to devise with Panin and me ways to arrive at a solution, the urgency of which not even he could ignore. But I owe it to the truth to say that Grand Duke Alexander consented to nothing before extracting from me my most sacred word that no attempt would be made on the life of his father."

But if we look at another remark made by Pahlen, it is clear that, despite the heir's scruples, he was to go further in his support by removing from the emperor any possibility of being able to defend himself. The assault on Paul's apartments had been fixed for the night of March 9–10. When Pahlen informed Alexander of this, he made an objection that reveals the interest he took in the whole affair. He asked Pahlen to postpone the plot until the night of March 11–12, because then the watch would be taken by the Semyonovsky regiment, to which he was very close and which he thought he could win over to his side, whereas on March 9 the Preobrazhensky Guards, who were very loyal to the emperor, would be on duty. This delay, accepted only reluctantly by the leaders of the plot, so fearful were they that the sovereign's wavering sanity might lead him to some new extreme, was very nearly their undoing. On March 10, the emperor had Alexander and his brother Constantine arrested. It was time to remove him.

The reaction of the new emperor was ambiguous. All the witnesses of the first days of his reign have described him as being overwhelmed and almost prostrate. Grand Duke Nicholas, careful not to upset his family, and insisting on the innocence of the empress and of Constantine, accuses Alexander more of thoughtlessness or frivolousness, of an inability to think seriously about the possible consequences of a plot against his father, than of wholeheartedly supporting a criminal action. But this account does not totally exonerate Alexander, for, as Nicholas makes clear, he knew his father and he realized that his father would never agree to sign a deed of abdication. For the same reason he probably also knew, although perhaps was unwilling to admit it to himself, that the conspirators would have to use violence. With a sovereign who refused to abdicate, there would be little choice as to the type of violence.

Alexander's relative clemency with his father's assassins, so different from the deferred revenge of Paul I against those who had killed Peter III, would have been at the very least surprising if he had been merely a sorrowing son. La Harpe, to whom Alexander had revealed his dilemma, sent him a long letter on October 30, 1801, advising him on how to deal with the conspirators. Admitting that it had been necessary to remove Paul I from the throne and that Alexander had accepted this principle, he continues: "Your Majesty had to consent, after long resisting, to undertake to do, for the good of the country, what had been done legitimately and successfully elsewhere." But, since the instructions had subsequently been exceeded, La Harpe unhesitatingly recommended an exemplary punishment, stressing that "it is necessary to bring an end in Russia to the scandal of these regicides, who go constantly unpunished and are sometimes even rewarded, who prowl around the throne, even ready to renew their crimes."

Alexander may have punished them, but not severely. Panin and Pahlen were banished from St. Petersburg, never to return. Those who had struck the blow against the emperor retired voluntarily to their estates. As for General Bennigsen, he was only briefly eclipsed. After a period out of the capital, he once again took his place in the army, playing an important part in the Napoleonic Wars. It may be that he participated in Paul's murder because he had never been rewarded with a marshal's baton, despite his outstanding deeds in battle. But this is far from certain, for he was always close to the imperial family, who frequently called upon his services, as Alexander I was to do.

Whatever his degree of involvement, it is clear that Alexander I felt remorse for the rest of his life. However, unlike his grandmother, his support of the criminal plan was probably not prompted by personal interest. For Catherine, there was in 1762 no other way of attaining the destiny to which she aspired without removing her husband. Her personal ambition also led her to prevent her son from ascending to the throne in 1767, to refuse the regency, and later, to attempt to delay the moment of handing over power to her son by substituting her young grandson as heir. Alexander had only his father's unbalanced behavior to fear. He was only twenty-three when Paul was killed, and he had no burning desire to reign. An idealist in his youth, he often declared that he would have liked to have carried out a great reform in a short time and then left the throne to go and live in peace with his family. At the death of his father, he was unable to act and he had to be pushed to the throne.[15] This was probably due in part to his indolence. Alexander had been very strongly influenced by the two instigators of the murder, and as the plot began to take shape, he had shown himself to be incapable of expressing clearly his own desires. This may explain his devastation, certainly genuine, after the act. He appeared, witnesses said at the time, as if he were waking from a dream only to enter a nightmare.

The web of conspiracy that, to a certain degree, ensnared Alexander also was a complicated, even exceptional one in the history of Russia. Until then, only the internal situation had sparked such actions. But Panin was obsessed with foreign problems. Long sympathetic to Prussia, he had begun to be worried at the end of the century by the hostility toward England prompting Paul's actions, and its consequences.[16] We do not know how far this outward-looking man, whose foreign postings had brought him in contact with diplomats and important foreigners, acted as an intermediary for an English "faction." Although there is no evidence of such connivance with England, the theory was strongly suggested at the time of the murder and later. Supporting the English theory is the close friendship between Nikita Panin and the English ambassador at the Russian court, and the strong reservations expressed by the ex-vice-chancellor about the direction of Russian foreign policy. In the opinion of Nikita Panin, Paul's attitude toward England was

---

15. "You have been a child long enough; it is time to rule," Pahlen told him.

16. Besides the bizarre campaign for the conquest of India, Paul also put pressure on Prussia to declare war on England. The break with the latter country also had economic consequences, since it put a sudden end to the export of cereals and raw materials (hemp and flax) to England, which harmed the interests of the Russian landowners.

decidedly dangerous for Russia and should be opposed. Nikita Panin's overtures toward England are in this respect representative of a more general reaction among the Russian elite.

Whether there were foreign pressures or, more simply, whether those who were shocked or injured by Paul's excessive Prussianism welcomed a radical solution to the problem represented by Paul I, the significant thing about this murder is that for the first time in Russian history, a certain conjunction between the two political spheres, internal and external, is discernible in the violence that affected the throne.

Alexander I and His "Double"

Two regicides in less than forty years could not take place without leaving a mark on the legitimacy of the sovereign and on the social consciousness. As La Harpe had written in his letter to his former pupil: "The assassination of an emperor, within his own palace and in the bosom of his family, cannot go unpunished . . . without compromising imperial dignity." Every sovereign who held power during this violent period, including Paul I, needed to reinforce his legitimacy bearing in mind the shock to the throne represented by regicide. Catherine II rejected the suggestion made to her by Nikita Panin (the first of the two Nikitas) that the nobility should be given some power in the form of a Council of Empire that would have limited the authority of the sovereign, while she instead sought the basis for her legitimacy in the "enlightened" definition of absolute monarchy. In 1767 she had conferred on herself by a legislative commission[17] the titles of "Catherine the Great, the Wise, Mother of the Country," and issued the "instruction [*nakaz*] given to the Commission to prepare a new Code," which was in reality a statement of her own political doctrine. Russia was for Catherine a

---

17.   This commission consisted of 564 deputies (for eighteen million Russians at this time) representing all social groups except the serfs and the clergy, since only one ecclesiastic was included, representing the Holy Synod.

European nation whose legal system was a product of a rational order and no longer the traditional order (nor was it inspired by revealed religion), where the autocracy represented the interest of each man.

Unlike his mother, Paul I had not had to legitimize a usurpation of power, and thus was able to rely on the traditional order, all the more necessary in his opinion since the French Revolution and the spread of revolutionary ideas had made it necessary for absolute power to be based on solid justifications. Far from appealing to reason in order to do this, he looked to religion in its most extreme, mystical form and also to Freemasonry as another expression of a spiritual quest. At the time of his coronation, he took the title of "head of the Church," declaring himself the protector not only of the Orthodox Church but also of Catholics and Freemasons. Alexander I, who came to the throne in circumstances as dramatic as those attending his grandmother's accession, had only to make amends for the murder with which he was associated, but not to justify his own legitimacy. Now it was the principle of monarchy itself as it manifested itself in Russia in its absolute form that was questioned. The general hope was that the power of such a monarchy would be limited through reform.

On his accession to the throne, Alexander was guided by liberal advisers, foremost among whom was Mikhail Speransky, who believed that the moment for a transition to a constitutional monarchy had arrived, indeed was overdue. The tsar embarked on a policy of reform that appeared to justify these hopes. But after 1812 and the entry of Napoleon into Russia, the balance tipped violently back in the direction of absolute conservatism. It is true that by his very nature and even without the events of 1812, Alexander had always tried to keep his options open, maintaining preferential relations with advisers who supported the most differing points of view. Each man came away from an interview with the sovereign convinced of his profound agreement. Thus from one moment to the next, Alexander encouraged now the idea of a radical reform of the political system, and now that of a return to absolutism. His vague and indecisive temperament, which had accounted for his behavior at the time of the plot, was to influence the whole of his life.

In the period from Catherine to Alexander, beneath the crucial problem of restoring the legitimacy of the absolutist system lay another no less crucial problem, on which the entire future of Russia was to depend: how to reconcile the maintenance of absolute power and a strictly hierarchical social system with the reforms that were vital if Russia was to become a powerful European nation? None of the three sovereigns of this period found a satisfactory answer. But all three of them were to develop through their lives along the same road: reformers at the beginning of their reign, they were to come to rely increasingly on autocracy. Paul was a despot from the start, but even he nodded in the direction of selective reform.

If the sovereigns of this period were unable to find an answer to the dilemma in which they found themselves, the people reacted to their perpetually disappointed hopes with the traditional recourse to a false tsar. As we have seen, the memory of Peter III lingered, resulting in the mobilization around Pugachov of considerable numbers of malcontents who represented a real threat to the stability of the empire. It is curious that Paul I, the victim of assassination and a man who was haunted by the supernatural—he maintained that there were ghosts in his residence at Gachina—did not give rise to any false tsar claiming his name. He had only been tsar for a short time and it appears that society preferred to forget him.

By contrast, Alexander I was to have a strange posthumous existence that remains today, like that of the tsar of Uglich, one of history's unanswered questions. The remorse that racked him had before long led him to immerse himself in an extreme form of mysticism. This constant yearning toward the supernatural was particularly apparent at the end of his life. He may have taken the flood that had recently devastated his capital as a disturbing sign of divine anger. If so, it was a sentiment widely shared by the people. On November 19, 1825, when he was at Taganrog, he died of a fever known as "Crimean fever," which was probably typhoid. His death far away from the capital had unfortunate consequences for his body. Badly embalmed, it was transported in difficult conditions. That, combined with the autopsies performed and signed by various and too numerous people, resulted in the face of the sovereign being unrecognizable, while his physical appearance in general was notably altered. This may explain the speed with which the rumor of a false tsar was born. His body had not yet reached the capital when the word was already circulating that the tsar was not dead: he had "left," and his coffin contained the body of an ordinary soldier who bore no resemblance to him. At first the rumor was accompanied by an explanation that was later to be abandoned: Alexander I had fled in order to escape his enemies who wished to assassinate him. The myth was reinforced at the time by the memory of other recent regicides. But as time passed, the interpretation of the rumor changed and became a certainty: Alexander was wandering through the land, among his people, in order to share their fate and their suffering, expiating with them the sins of Russia. In 1830 the myth became more specific: in his new vocation, Alexander had a name and a face. He was Fyodor Kuzmich, a hermit living in Siberia until his death in 1864. For the people there was an end to uncertainty: Fyodor Kuzmich was the sovereign. In his desire to narrow the gap between himself and his people and to fulfill the proper mission of a tsar, he had come to live among his people to ensure their salvation. He was seen as a saint, the true vocation of a tsar.

The myth of Alexander-Kuzmich is important from the point of view of history and politics. History has never given a clear judgment as to the veracity of these popular beliefs. It is significant that, in the very heart of the imperial family, a seed of doubt was sown and the theory of the later death of Alexander I and his identification with Fyodor Kuzmich was never entirely denied. The theory is all the more interesting in that it is completely gratuitous. Unlike the case of Louis XVII, where the problem, beyond his own fate, was that of his heirs, Fyodor Kuzmich had no descendants and no one else came to claim to be Alexander I after his death. The problem of the real death of the sovereign thus remains.

But the importance of the myth of Fyodor Kuzmich is above all political. It is remarkable that in 1825, in contrast to what happened earlier with the false tsars, there was no multiplication of false resuscitated Alexanders, but a single identification and a single myth. The meaning was clear: Fyodor Kuzmich was not the "true" tsar opposed to the "false" Tsar Nicholas I who had succeeded Alexander, but the "tsar as incarnation of the true political agenda of Russia." It was no longer a matter of challenging the legitimacy of individuals but rather the political legitimacy of the concepts that were now the basis of the modern empire. The Tsar Fyodor

Kuzmich must be the tsar-saint whose duty it was to be among his people, with them, compassionate and suffering, in their image. For them, Alexander's abandonment of the throne and wanderings among his people symbolized the alienation of the state from the people. Conscious of this, they were led in turn to alienate themselves from the state. The two Russias, that of the throne and that of the people, were thus contained both in the myth and in the true history of the death of Alexander I. Whichever version one believes, there is only one conclusion to be drawn: the people were conscious of a shock to the system. The events of 1825 were to reveal its extent.

8

The Student Pugachovs

♦

The Decembrist Plot

On December 14, 1825, rioting broke out in St. Petersburg. The day was well chosen: with the death of Alexander I, the regiments were to take the oath of loyalty to the new emperor. The rebellious troops, convinced by their officers that the heir, Grand Duke Constantine, was about to be supplanted on the throne, rushed to the square outside the Senate shouting: "Long live Constantine!" and, in some cases, "Long live the constitution!" which a number of soldiers took to be a reference to the grand duke's wife. The government, supporting Constantine's younger brother, Nicholas, who claimed to be the true heir to the throne, sent out the city's troops, the majority of whom were still loyal, and put down the insurrection in the space of one night, without resorting to excessive violence. There was no wish to inaugurate the new reign with a bloodbath. The rebels, for their part, lacked resolute leaders who could lead their troops. With order reestablished, it seemed that the damage was slight: a few hundred rebels left dead on the square; a few hundred arrests; all the ringleaders brought before the courts. There had clearly been an attempt at a coup d'état, but its failure demonstrated the weakness of the movement, the absence of any popular support, and the ability of the regime to defend itself. But the affair was to have serious and long-lasting implications. The leaders of the insurrection were from noble families and, in some cases, the most important families in the land. Why had these sons of the privileged classes suddenly taken up arms against a regime that so greatly benefited them? Why, and in the name of what ideals, had they tried to bring it down?

The immediate cause—or, more precisely, the pretext—of the uprising was clear. As often in Russia, the question of the succession initiated a political crisis. Alexander I had no heir and his younger brother, Constantine, called on to succeed him, had renounced his rights to the throne in 1820 for private reasons.[1] The manifesto signed by Alexander I in 1823, transferring the succession to his second brother, Grand Duke Nicholas, had remained secret, as had the deed of renunciation. The death of Alexander I had, consequently, been followed by great turmoil, with each brother, out of respect for the law of succession of 1797, swearing loyalty to the other, Constantine in Warsaw and Nicholas in St. Petersburg. It was this initial confusion and the sudden publication of the manifesto of 1823 announcing the accession to the throne of Grand Duke Nicholas that had fostered suspicions of a plot among the regiments. The leaders of the coup d'état were able to take advantage of the situation, winning over to their side soldiers who were convinced that they were flying to the support of the true heir who was in danger of being ousted. The coup d'état was thus full of ambiguity: the leaders wished to shake the autocracy and impose a constitution; their followers believed it was necessary to defend the true tsar against a possible usurper, even if it were his brother. The eternal anxiety of mistaking the true tsar still troubled men's minds. Outside the capital the rumor spread that the true tsar, Constantine, had been removed from the throne by force.

But why did the nobility rise up and why did it reject the existing order in Russia? The effectiveness of the repression—the ringleaders were executed or deported to Siberia—was no substitute for an answer to these fundamental questions. There was a profound malaise among the nobility, who were beginning to realize that Russia's outmoded social order was by now unacceptable. This social order depended on serfdom, which the rest of Europe was horrified to see continuing in Russia even into the nineteenth century. The nobility could hardly fail to be aware of this incongruity, made all

---

1. Since Constantine had divorced and made a morganatic marriage in 1820, his children, according to the terms of the Manifesto of March 20, 1820 (article 361), could not succeed to the throne. He realized the necessity for him to renounce the throne himself and communicated this to the emperor in the act of January 14, 1822. The emperor's acceptance and the new order of succession were written into the manifesto of April 23, 1823. All these documents were secret.

the more apparent since it continued to benefit from serfdom when everything that might have justified its receiving these benefits had disappeared. One of the chief reforms carried out by Peter III—the decree of February 18, 1762, abolishing the nobles' obligation to serve the state in exchange for serfdom—freed the nobility,[2] but did nothing for the peasants. The latter continued to be in a servile condition, without their masters having the slightest justification for keeping them in that state. The social system in Russia after 1762 presented a paradox. On the one hand were the emancipated nobles, enjoying considerable rights and liberties (further confirmed and increased by Catherine II) whose lifestyle could rival that of their counterparts in the most advanced countries of Europe. On the other, there were the serfs, a class to this extent unknown in any other large European nation. The freedom of the nobles not only made them a privileged class, but insofar as it allowed them to do what they wished with the peasantry, it made them into parasites. The more enlightened members of this nobility could not fail to feel unhappy about this contradiction.

One of the first expressions of this malaise had been the publication, at the end of the eighteenth century, of Radishchev's *Journey from Petersburg to Moscow* which, as we have seen, earned the author Catherine's displeasure and banishment. But well before 1790 when he expressed those views about society that were to have such a devastating effect on people's ideas, the persistence of serfdom was provoking increasingly loud social criticism. It was clear that as long as serfdom remained, all Catherine II's reforms would come to nothing. Publications calling for its abolition had gradually begun to appear. But Radishchev did not mince his words: roundly condemning serfdom—calling it slavery pure and simple, an exaggeration but an effective one—he exposed the basic contradictions of enlightened despotism. In a burning attack he denounced both absolute power and its train of corruption, putting forward his proposals, both political (the setting up of a republic) and social (the abolition of serfdom). As for the "Enlightenment" that Catherine invoked to support her autocratic power, the author

---

2. This emancipation also included the right to travel freely abroad, which had been forbidden since the time of Ivan III.

demolishes it completely. Radishchev's work, together with the individualistic ideas and moral preoccupations of Freemasonry, then influencing the nobility, all contributed to make the nobles aware of the distance separating the talk of reform from the actual enacting of the most urgent reforms. Profoundly aware of the privileged nature of their situation, and of the price paid by the peasants for its perpetuation, the nobles—or at least that section of the nobility represented by men like Radishchev—concluded that it was their duty to further the social interest, since despotism prevented any hope that things might improve by themselves.

The Napoleonic Wars took these nobles to the very heart of France, and so to the center of revolutionary ideas. The voyages encouraged by the emancipating policies of Peter III and Catherine, putting the nobility in direct contact with Europe—a Europe that was astonished and intrigued by this Russia so riddled with contradictions—opened the nobles' eyes to the fact that, since those in power had been incapable of carrying out the emancipation of society, they would have to do it themselves. No longer required to serve the state, the nobles saw another function for their class: that of correcting the state and guiding it along the path of progress that it had so far failed to find. Secret societies multiplied at this time, where problems peculiar to Russia were discussed and solutions proposed. The first was the "Union for the Salvation of the Loyal Sons of the Fatherland," set up in 1817 by a group of guards officers returned from the French campaign, which concerned itself above all with discussion of the democratic reforms so urgently needed. Its primary objectives were a constitution and a parliament. But as well as the creation of representative institutions, the idea of a federal empire rapidly gained ground among the members of this society. (Too little representation and too much centralization—all the political problems of Russia in the early nineteenth century have a strangely contemporary ring about them.) Around this first group there grew up, between 1818 and 1825, many other secret societies. Alexander I became increasingly worried by this political ferment in which the privileged classes were deeply involved.

On the eve of their unsuccessful coup d'état, the political demands of those who were to become the Decembrists were quite moderate. They wanted a constitutional monarchy in which power would be organized on a federal basis, but, considering that a change in the political order was the precondition of any alteration of the relations within society, they said very little about social reform. The radicalism of one of these future Decembrists stands out, however, anticipating that of Lenin. Pavel Pestel was convinced that power was the essential element of any plan. It was first necessary to decide how to seize it. This could only be carried out by perfectly organized conspirators, who could keep their plans secret. Subsequently, power should not be diluted, for fear that it would become ineffective. Only a strong, centralized state (in other words, one that ignored any idea of a federation) could successfully carry out a political plan, whatever it might be. Pestel dreamed of transforming the Masonic organizations into revolutionary groups, since their tradition of secrecy struck him as that best adapted to the needs of a conspiracy, the only means of seizing power. Insisting on the importance of the character of the organizations involved in the conquest of power—in this he was a true innovator—Pestel adds another preoccupation, no less remarkable for a man of his time: the importance of assassination as a means of political struggle. Pestel was executed after the coup d'état, but his ideas survived after him.

The failure of the coup d'état was evidence of the isolation of the Decembrists. Society did not understand them or their theories. Their minds filled with the ideas of the European Enlightenment and the French Revolution, they offered society, at this decisive moment, a plan and a theory that were still foreign to it. How could the people understand what was meant by "constitutional monarchy" when they thought that "constitution" was a woman's name? The people believed that their misfortunes were the result of the disappearance of the "true" tsar and the activities of the "false" tsar. For them, a true tsar and a saint were still one and the same thing. They were deeply shocked that the Decembrists could threaten not a usurper but the very content of imperial power; the coup d'état ran counter to a divinely ordained order.

The ideas that inspired and mobilized the Decembrists—those of 1789, liberty, equality, and fraternity—were alien to Russia. The rallying cry that had more than once roused Russia was that of social justice, where each man is rewarded with his right place, according to the services rendered by him to the community. The individualism of the ideas of the French Revolution had little connection with the deep sense of community found in Russian history and in the social consciousness of the people. The conspirators of 1825, young idealists, were the bearers of a political program. In the depths of Russia, the people were waiting for another answer to the contradictions in its society. The failure of the coup d'état revealed a double alienation: that of the most progressive nobles in relation to the throne; and that of the masses in relation to these same nobles. The plan of 1825 had attempted to resolve the first. After the failure of the coup d'état, all those who followed the Decembrists and whom Joseph de Maistre aptly called the "student Pugachovs" were to understand the implications of the second.

Sin and Expiation

The two violent events that marked the first quarter of the nineteenth century in Russia—the murder of Paul I and the coup d'état against Nicholas I—do not, in fact, belong to the same historical period. The murder of the tsar was an eighteenth-century event, the last of an age when the entourage of a sovereign might get rid of him when their interests were threatened. Paul I in Russia, like Gustavus III of Sweden ten years earlier, was the victim of a decision made by the nobles, who felt obliged to remove him because of his increasing madness. No large political or social plan underlay these regicides: all that happened was that one man was substituted for another on the throne. In 1825, things were very different. Although unsuccessful, the Decembrist coup was inspired by a desire for political change. It was the first example of its kind in Russia, and it opened a new era, where the removal of a sovereign was thought to change the political and social destiny of the country. After this date, the concern of all uprisings was to be society, its fate, and its emancipation. The common feature of all ideas about the future of Russia after 1825 was the certainty that the privileged classes would have to pay for their privileges—a debt contracted with society—by giving them up and by giving the people their freedom. The Italian historian, Franco Venturi, author of a remarkable work on the intelligentsia and revolutionary ideas *(The Roots of Revolution)*, describes the difference between the Russian nobility of 1825 and the French nobility in 1789. On August 4, 1789, the revolution was already underway, and the French nobles had no option but to agree. In Russia, by contrast, there was no revolution and it was without any external pressure that the nobility chose to sacrifice its position of privilege. This unusual situation is well illustrated by a remark made by General Rostopshin, the man who set fire to Moscow in 1812 so that Napoleon would find nothing but ashes: "Until then, revolutions were made by cobblers who wanted to be lords; now it is the lords who want to be cobblers."

The reign of Nicholas I (1825–55) was, in Lamartine's apt words, that of *l'immobilité du monde* (the immobility of the world). It was during this reign, however, that the circumstances were produced that opened the way to the "student Pugachovs." Nothing about Nicholas would have led one to expect it. This huge and imposing man, full of the dignity of his office and passionately fond of anything military, always to be seen in uniform, was the very incarnation of autocracy. Violently hostile to the uprising in the capital at the time of his accession, he was determined to stop it in its tracks. Two measures taken in the early days of his reign were to perpetuate his reputation as a despot and exacerbate the relations between the throne and the emerging intelligentsia.

The first of these measures was the creation, in 1826, of the a political police force.[3] This was the Third Section of the Imperial Chancellery, officially there to ensure the protection of widows and orphans, but which rapidly became a true state secret police, designed to unmask conspiracies. It was made up of a specialized personnel and hordes of informers and *agents provocateurs*. The second innovation, in the same year, was the setting up of a system of censorship governed by a code of censorship under the authority of a committee whose job it was not only to prevent the publication of books or journals that were judged to be seditious or morally unac-

---

3. The *Preobrazhenskii prikaz*, created by Peter the Great, had been dismantled by Peter III and Catherine II. A short-lived ministry of police existed between 1811 and 1819, but its disappearance left the whole area of the surveillance of political movements unoccupied, at the very time that the secret societies were appearing.

ceptable, but also to encourage edifying publications. The collection of laws prepared by Speransky and published in 1832 included, in the volume devoted to the criminal code, a chapter on crimes against the state, bringing together and coordinating all the measures taken in the past. Notable among these are the sections making any attempt to limit the authority of the sovereign or change the style of government a criminal offense, punishable by death. Included in this definition of offenses were speeches, spoken or written, and any kind of publication with related aims. These could be punished by confiscation of property and exile.

These draconian measures did not, however, prevent the development of ideas critical of the existing government and social system. Between 1825 and the end of the 1840s, the debate chiefly revolved around the opposing historical views of the "Pro-Slavs" and the "Occidentalists." The romanticism that dominated European thought at this period also fueled ideas of Russianness and pro-Slav ideas. The quest for a history, cultural roots, and a national identity and the idealization of the past found a resonant echo in Russia. The pro-Slavs, although themselves receiving a westernized education, suddenly attributed all that was good about Russia to her past and her special identity. In the face of Western "materialism" they offered a religious and sometimes messianic vision of Russia's destiny, its tragic history, and the salvation that it could offer. Opposed to serfdom, they sought a solution that turned away from the West, in the ancient Russian peasant community, the *mir*. The Occidentalists, by contrast, totally rejected all that which was Russian, but, like their opponents, they too were steeped in religiosity and nationalism. In their view, Russia had always failed in the past, a failure that was all the more scandalous in view of its exceptional potential. For them, the West was a model of success, but one to be used in the service of Russia.

The intellectual and moral upheaval that led to the discussion of radical ideas and to a murderous radicalism lasted all through Nicholas I's reign, entering an acute phase around 1850. The revolutions of 1848 were a reminder to those who followed the new ideas that the era of revolutions was not over, emphasizing more strongly than ever the archaic character of Russian despotism. This was even more true since Nicholas, reacting against the spirit of

1848, was setting himself up as the guardian of the established order. And yet now within Russia itself profound changes were beginning to take place in the middle layers of society. The upper nobility, bearers of the constitutional ideal in 1825, had been closely involved in the debate on Russia's future. From 1840, however, the ranks of those discussing this problem swelled, and in so doing changed the very nature and scope of the debate. Ironically, it was largely as a result of Nicholas's policies, particularly in the field of education, that these new elites—the intelligentsia—had emerged. They were to be in the forefront of events from the 1850s, taking over from or including the nobility.

Russia in the mid–nineteenth century was a strange mixture: a country where serfdom still existed and yet one with a very advanced policy on education. Primary education was still undeveloped, because the regime had no wish to educate the peasantry for fear that schools might introduce the seeds of revolt into the enserfed countryside. Secondary education, by contrast, through the extensive network of state grammar schools, was free and open to all. Last, the universities, which enjoyed an almost independent status, were remarkable centers of intellectual life and education. The autocrat who intended at all costs to maintain the existing social order was also an intelligent man, conscious that the state needed servants capable of protecting his power, by means of which in turn he could preserve this anachronistic social order. He wanted, furthermore, to reduce the power of the nobility, whose critical attitude to the regime had been made clear by the coup d'état of December 1825. Through the network of schools he intended to promote an intermediate class, a sort of Third Estate or elite of state functionaries. The loyalty of these new elites was inevitably to be first and foremost to the state, which had ensured their very recent promotion and which they served. Allegiance to the sovereign did not feature prominently in their universe. From this time, everything inclined them to wonder about the best possible kind of state and the future of a society to which they were naturally so closely bound.

This development of the Russian elites in the first half of the century is incarnated in the figures of two contemporaries of Nicholas I, the writers Pushkin and Gogol. Pushkin, who died prematurely in 1837, was a member of that aristocratic Russia, obsessed with imperial glory, that he depicts in *The Bronze Horseman*. Gogol describes, in *Dead Souls* (published in 1842), a very different world, of the serfs and the poor, in his picture of provincial life and bureaucratic corruption. It is hard to reconcile these two pictures of Russia, viewed through the eyes of Pushkin looking down from the top of the statue of Peter the Great and those of Gogol looking up. Pushkin belongs to the world of the noblemen who carried out the coup d'état of 1825; Gogol is the forerunner of those who were to question the whole system and already incarnates the intelligentsia that, alongside the nobles, produced the new elites, formed of many different social ranks *(raznochintsi)*. Nicholas's despotism, more effective in theory than in practice, and his detailed but ultimately very lax controls had a double effect: they allowed the development of small groups and critical publications that gave nourishment to the ideas of the intelligentsia while at the same time irritating the intellectuals by the constraints they attempted to impose. The Crimean War of 1853–55 underlined Russia's weakness and had a decisive effect on this development. Military defeat taught the intelligentsia that their rulers were less powerful than they appeared, encouraging them to defy authority more than before. Just as the Napoleonic Wars had opened the way to the coup d'état of 1825, so, thirty years later, the Crimean War resulted in the radicalization of the intellectual movement.

It was now that the moral element, the distinguishing feature of the Russian intelligentsia, made its appearance. Since the existing system depended essentially on serfdom, a shocking reality that, by comparison, made all other social positions seem privileged, be it the nobility or the most recently formed elite, a profound feeling of guilt invaded the intelligentsia. Serfdom was Russia's original sin and since the time of Radishchev, it had haunted all Russians. When the intelligentsia raised the question of the future of the country and how to prepare for it, they did it through this feeling of guilt, or, in other words, in terms of expiation. It was the duty of any liberal mind to pay for these unearned privileges. This was the debt owed to the peasants, the victims of social oppression and fundamental injustice.

Thus in the minds of the intelligentsia an indestructible

joint image was formed: the victim and his executioner—or at least his exploiter—the peasantry and its subjugators. Until 1840, the nobles, masters of these peasants, thought that their sin could be wiped out overnight by an act of renunciation, such as the French nobles had performed in the National Assembly on August 4, 1789. By the early 1850s the intelligentsia had moved to a more complex position, since, for the most part, they did not feel guilty except insofar as they did not belong to the class of the victims. The intelligentsia would be, instead, the peasants' intercessors, the class that would fight for their emancipation. It might be said that this desire to emancipate others is not particularly original and can be found elsewhere in other forms. But in Russia, the political culture that developed through the centuries had its own unique characteristics: a diffuse religiosity, an apocalyptic vision of history, and a taste for extreme solutions. These elements colored the intelligentsia's view of its duty with the notions of sin, sanctification, even deification, of the victim—the idealized muzhik, later replaced by the "people" and then by the "proletariat"—and the certainty that there was no middle way. These "Pugachovs," products of Nicholas I's universities, were to become the Populists, who immersed themselves in campaigns to help the people and incite them to rebel.

The Nihilists, for their part, were to preach the negation of everything that gives life its meaning—history—or that makes it agreeable or more comfortable—spiritual riches, religion, art, and even science—in favor of a plan of immediate materialism. Nihilism, which through the influence of its greatest figures (Pisarev, Dobrolyubov, and Chernyshevsky) left its mark on all the intellectuals of the day, represented a major break with both the humanist and westernizing culture of the nobility and the traditional culture of the throne. In their passionate denunciations, the Nihilists demolished the Occidentalists' hopes of modernization and jeered at the idea of reform. Their watchword was not struggle but attack. Extremism had entered the arena of debate. In fact, it was with these men that what came to be known as the intelligentsia appeared in Russia. Dobrolyubov and Chernyshevsky were educated men from a religious background; their fathers were both clerics and they themselves educated at seminaries. They rejected this teaching, while making a new religion of the materialism that they were to defend so passionately. The heirs to the absolutism and dogmatism formerly promoted by the church were, paradoxically, to be those who, in the 1860s, denied all spiritual values. And they were to pass on this characteristic to the whole of the Russian intelligentsia.

The intelligentsia was in any case undergoing a change at this period. Increasing in number, embracing the sons of the lower classes, for whom education took the place of birth, this more democratic intelligentsia showed both less intellectual breadth and more moral strictness. To see this, one only has to look at the work that best represents Nihilism, Chernyshevsky's *What Is to Be Done?* The answer to the title's question is clear: follow the example of the hero, Rakhmetok, who strengthens himself and prepares for battle, which is to say for suffering and torture, by a constant asceticism. When a man sleeps on a bed of nails himself, he has the right to impose on others, for their own good, sufferings that he has borne himself. The morality of the Nihilists was demanding and also unmerciful. And even that aspect of this morality which seems most to benefit men—free love—is in fact part of an excessively demanding view of behavior. Free love was in no way intended to be pleasurable, nor to make life any easier; its justification was solely to bring back sincerity to human relations, and to end hypocritical constraints. The severity of the Nihilists, their quest for a genuine social justice, and not merely the appearance of justice, their asceticism, and their acceptance of suffering are in fact very close to the profound values of Christianity, even if they were inspired by an uncompromising materialism. Here the words have less importance than the content.

The 1860s were decisive years for Russia. The emerging intelligentsia[4] was beginning to become a true social class, and these intellectuals were becoming ever more certain that Russia, however disadvantaged and backward, had a central historic role to play both for itself and for Europe. Messianism, which in the 1840s

---

4. The word used to describe these men, who considered themselves to be a group critical of the rulers, is their own. Describing themselves as *intelligentnie*, or "thinking people," they thus consecrated the term *intelligentsia* which also appears in the title of Mikhailovsky's critical essay, *Letter from the Russian Intelligentsia*.

had characterized the pro-Slavs, was now more generally adopted, with two series of events striking a blow against the admiration felt formerly by the Russian intellectuals for western Europe: first, the failure of the revolutions of 1848, which suggested that Europe was no longer inclined to wild hopes and radical change; and second, in 1870–71, the defeat of France in the Franco-German War and the crushing of the Paris Commune seemed to mark the end, in a quieter France, of the chapter opened in 1789. Since Europe, and particularly the once-radical France, had been deserted by revolution, people would have to look elsewhere, to a country where an unhappy society seemed ready for change. Russia, with its teeming numbers of poverty-stricken muzhiks, finally liberated from serfdom in 1861 but nevertheless not free from poverty, seemed to be the ideal place to revive the hopes that had perished in the West. The intelligentsia, which since 1825 had been content to protest only, had at last found its course of action. This path, they believed, would reconcile them with that social class so peculiar to Russia, the peasantry. The Occidentalists had once dreamed of industrialization, of the rise of laboring masses who would bring about the great transformation; the intelligentsia now suddenly discovered the muzhik. The few attempts started in these years to stir up the workers in the capital had been unsuccessful.[5] Since Russia seemed so much more closely harnessed to what Bukharin later termed its "peasant cart," the intelligentsia turned toward the countryside.

The extraordinary summer of 1874 saw Populism devote all its human resources to a passionate movement, the like of which Europe had never seen. Suddenly, thousands of students, intellectuals, and nobles of all ages "went to the people, to the muzhik," to announce the coming of the new era. Dressed as peasants, the young intellectuals poured into the countryside to incite the muzhiks to take their destiny in their own hands, placing themselves at the peasants' service to aid them. Nobles gave away their land, or handed it over to the movement. All, whether young or old, male or female, took part, as if to expiate, by the division of property and their identification with the misfortunes of the peasants, their

---

5. In 1872–74, under the influence of Nikolai Chaikovsky, his followers tried to form groups to give a political education to the workers, who proved to be unreceptive.

original sin—the hated serfdom, only recently abolished—and that other ever-present sin, the exclusion of the peasants from cultural progress. This spontaneous movement, so admirable in its intentions and so typical of a Russia haunted by the religious notions of sin and expiation, was impeded by the harshness of the regime and, more seriously, by the incomprehension of the peasants themselves.

Alexander II, the reforming tsar, was terrified by what was happening. This spontaneous movement of the intelligentsia, uncontrolled and uncontrollable, which ignored the progress made by his abolition of serfdom and appealed to the primitive impulses of the peasants, must be crushed. The repression that followed was ruthless. As will be seen later, it marked Alexander's turn toward conservatism. The peasants completely failed to understand the generosity of the movement: they ignored it and they handed over to the police the young people who had come to harangue them. The gulf between the intelligentsia and the muzhik seemed unbridgeable. The intelligentsia concluded that it would have to pursue its own path and find some other way of rousing the people. What better way to attract attention, frighten the authorities, and waken the masses from their lethargy than that of violence?

The Terrorist Answer

The terrorist's weapon was the homemade bomb, and it was with this that the intelligentsia was now to arm itself. Since an uprising of the muzhiks seemed unthinkable in the short term, the attack on the social order would have to be led by the intellectuals. The coup d'état of 1825, when a sudden revolt by the army had been followed by the peaceful reestablishment of order, had shown the difficulty of changing the system. The absence of any alternative political structures seemed to leave no choice but violence. If assassination was to be involved, who should be killed—the despot, his entourage? The question of the use of murder to further a political plan had never before been raised in Russia, even in the abstract. In all the countries around it, by contrast, it was the only question discussed.

In western Europe, secret societies proliferated and the supporters of violence, like Buonarroti or Blanqui, were legion, even if they did not preach the assassination of isolated individuals, favoring rather armed insurrection and fighting at the barricades. Some secret societies, and notably the Carbonari, went beyond the generally still-moderate theories and did not hesitate to kill in order to clear the way to the realization of the ideas that they supported. But no one as yet dared to say explicitly that murder could be useful, and thus utilizable. The first, and deeply significant, breach in this discreet wall of silence came in a pamphlet entitled *Der Mord* (Murder) by Karl Heinzen, which appeared in 1849 in a journal published by German political émigrés living in Switzerland. "We must call a spade a spade. . . . Let us be frank and honest. . . . Murder is the chief agent of historic progress," writes Heinzen. He continues implacably:

> Revolutionaries must create a situation in which the barbarians will fear for their lives at every moment of the day and night. They must think that every glass of water, every mouthful of food, every bed, every drink . . . can kill. For them, as for us, fear must be the messenger and murder the executioner. Murder is their property—let it be their answer; they need murder— let it be their reward; murder is their means of expression—let it be the means of refuting them. . . . The barbarism that has developed in Europe leaves us no other choice but to devote ourselves to the study of murder and to bringing the art of assassination to its highest perfection.

Suddenly, at the end of the 1860s, the philosophy of political murder and its utility reached Russia. The first to discuss it was Bakunin, in letters to Herzen and Ogarev. Taking as his point of departure the exaltation of the Russian outlaw such as Stenka Razin and Pugachov—"he who expresses the people's despairing protest against an infamous social order, perfected on the western model and consolidated by the reforms of Peter and Alexander"—Bakunin asks the decisive question: "What, then, is our task?" His reply is unambiguous:

Even if we devote ourselves to no other cause than that of destruction, it should be realized that the forms available are infinite. Poison, dagger, slip-knot and all the rest. . . . Everything, in this struggle, is sanctified by the revolution. . . . The healthy spirit of youth must persuade itself that it is more human to stab and strangle dozens, or even hundreds, of hated beings, than to join with them to share in legal and systematic murder, through torture and the martyrdom of millions of peasants. This is the behavior of our officials [*chinovniki*], our priests, our shopkeepers. . . . The youth of our country must dedicate itself to the sacred cause, rooting out evil, purifying and cleansing Russia by fire and by sword, uniting with those who are doing the same thing in the rest of Europe.

Although he preaches violence, Bakunin's views differ from those of European anarchism. For him destruction is a work of creation, the creation of a new world in which he profoundly believes, which can accommodate Russia's unique character. He gives pride of place among the collective virtues to the spirit of anarchism, the spirit of revolt born of the peasants' despair. His heroes are those outlaws who, through the centuries, have called on the peasant masses to reject their fate: Razin and Pugachov. He is convinced that the Russian people, always ready to rise up, are now more inclined to do so than ever, because of their alienation from the idea of the state as source of power, which in his eyes amounts to barbarism. The reforming sovereigns had consolidated the state, introducing a system characteristic of the West and built according to the western model. They were to blame for the living hell that was the peasants' reality. Bakunin opposed organization, the established order, whether it was conservative or called itself revolutionary. This explains his deep hostility to Marx, the heir, in his opinion, of Prussian militarism. Bakunin's ideas are centered on the Russian peasantry, and he nostalgically recalls the great bands that followed Pugachov and the "good" bandits who helped the poor. Emotional and passionate, Bakunin pinned his hopes on one of these "young fanatics" whose role was vital to his plan for revolt.

The man in whom he placed his hopes was Nechayev.

Bakunin was quite infatuated with him until the moment he discovered the true face of his "magnificent fanatic" and took fright. Nechayev, turning his back on Bakunin's disorganized and generous version of terrorism, was to offer the Russian intelligentsia a veritable apology for and model of murder. In the *Revolutionary Catechism,*[6] he asserts the necessity of killing "anyone who gets in the way of the revolutionary organization. Sudden and violent death will frighten the rulers who, deprived of their most brilliant and energetic representatives, will thereby be weakened." Nechayev categorizes human beings according to their place in the framework of his revolutionary ideas and picks out one group of individuals who should be killed—the men in power—and various other categories that could be used in order to destroy the social order. Elsewhere he describes the ideal revolutionary; he should break with civilized life and social norms, abandoning feelings of friendship, love, gratitude, even honor, and above all pity—nor should he expect to receive these from others. The revolutionary has only one aim: to destroy. Only one science is of use to him: that which leads to destruction. Hence he should study "mechanics, physics, chemistry, and perhaps medicine." This fanatic—Peter Verkhovensky in Dostoyevsky's *The Possessed* was loosely based on him—believed that murder was the chief weapon of any revolutionary plan.

Even more specific in his writing, Nikolai Morozov was the true theoretician of terrorism. A member of *Narodnaia volia* (People's Will), and responsible for the assassination of Alexander II, Morozov published in Geneva in 1880 an article with the title *Terrorist Struggle.* In it he describes how the youth of Russia, with few but highly effective means, had been able to put pressure on the powerful and apparently invincible tsarist state. This was because they had used terrorist measures as preached by the secret organizations. He stresses that revolution, if it is to succeed, does not require large numbers of supporters or large means. It is enough, he writes, "to replace the mass movements, generally condemned to failure, with a series of individual political assassinations that always

---

6. Traditionally attributed to Bakunin, alone or in cooperation with Nechayev, but which Michel Confino has definitely proved to be the work only of Nechayev. Its ideas are certainly inspired by those of a group of revolutionaries, prominent among whom was, besides Nechayev, Pyotr Tkachev.

find their target." For Morozov, political assassination is not a last resort; quite the reverse, it is the surest way of effecting the desired change. As well as striking at the victims of its choice, it has the virtue of example. It shows the masses, always fearful in the face of authority, that they should not be afraid, since at any moment the most powerful sovereign or minister can be assassinated. And Morozov adds another compelling argument, for the combination of political murder and secret activities. Unlike open political action, secret actions bring the assurance of impunity. According to him, the weakness of revolutionary actions, whether collective or individual, has always lain in their reversability: sooner or later they open the way to revenge and reprisals, thus to the loss of those who carried out the revolution. By contrast, political murder prepared in secret by a murderer who immediately afterward vanishes guarantees the permanent impunity of its author, thus increasing his usefulness. The unavenged victim is doubly assassinated.

For the apostle of this form of struggle, murder is particularly useful in cases where the whole political system rests on the personal power of the tyrant; Morozov cites the examples of Napoleon and Bismarck. In such cases murder is the only effective and indispensable solution, regardless of the legitimacy of the holder of power, even if it is derived from the ballot box. Morozov suggests as a slogan for his compatriots the words of Saint-Juste: "All men have the right to kill a tyrant, and a nation cannot take this right away even from the least of its citizens."

Another member of People's Will was G. Tarnovsky, whose ideas were to undergo a marked change, for he was later to join the ranks of the extreme rightist and anti-Semitic terrorist organization, the Black Hundreds, becoming an important theoretician for the group. In his writings, he seeks to justify terrorism in moral terms. In his pamphlet *Terrorism and Routine,* published in Geneva in 1880, he writes that it is impossible to apply the norms of ordinary morality to a tyrant or a tyrannical system. It is tyranny that is contrary and foreign to moral norms; what should be judged in moral terms is the effectiveness of the revolutionary measures, in terms of the sparing of human lives (these lives, it goes without saying, being those of the innocent masses, not those of the ruling classes). Thus, nothing is better than "scientific" political murder, which strikes down its victim who is then unable to retaliate, which prevents a price being paid by innocent people.

Bakunin was concerned that the revolutionary should remain a human being and one guided by firm principles *(Printsipial'-nost')*. Despite his anarchism, he was horrified by the violence, the sectarianism, the amorality, and the lack of principles of Nechayev and his emulators. These characteristics must nevertheless be connected in part with the ideas of the man who was perhaps the most remarkable theoretician of the modern revolution, Pyotr Tkachev. Born of the provincial nobility and a product of the universities, he was a typical example of the Russian intelligentsia of the 1870s in his social background but, at the same time, very original in the views he was to develop. For Tkachev, the pure violence, imbued with hatred, of a Nechayev, who even preached the murder of one's own family, was only one of the means at the disposal of revolutionary radicalism. Tkachev was inspired not just by the desire to destroy, as in the case of Nechayev, but by a constructive program.

Tkachev was the first Russian (with the exception of Pestel) to put the accent on the conquest of power with the intention of exercising it. He was also the first to see that the most important instrument of this conquest and exercise of power was a rigorously organized professional revolutionary elite. He saw revolution as taking place in the name of the masses, but prepared and executed from above, through this elite organization. Tkachev counters Bakunin's anarchism with this program, and with it he completes and extends Nechayev's purely negative ideas. He presents the intelligentsia with a political program. In his theories, the only important thing is power, which must be destroyed in its present form in order to be rebuilt. He passionately defends the idea that an elite minority, organized and centralized, is both the best and the most just instrument for such a plan. This elite will be capable of undergoing this trial without being corrupted by power, and without becoming tyrannical in its turn. "What are you afraid of?" he wrote to his critics. "What gives you the right to think that this minority, entirely devoted to the interests of the people, partly through its social position, partly through its ideas, would be brutally transformed into a tyrant when it took power. . . .? Robespierre, a member of the Convention, master of the destiny of

France, and Robespierre, provincial lawyer, are but one and the same. Power has not changed by one hair his moral character, not his ideals, not his tendencies. . . ."

Given such a plan, all means were good, including the most extreme, murder, centermost in Nechayev's thoughts. But while repelled by Nechayev's cynicism—with what Vera Zasulich described as his dominant characteristic, "intense hatred" and the impatience engendered by this hate—the intelligentsia was profoundly influenced by the articulate nature of Tkachev's arguments. Lenin was to owe a great deal to his ideas.

The transition in the ideas of the intelligentsia from a Dionysian anarchism and a social concept of change to a conspiratorial vision of a group that is organized, centralized, and essentially political was striking in its suddenness. From Bakunin to Nechayev and Tkachev there ran a common thread: the need to strike a fatal blow at the existing order—a blow that, everyone admitted, would involve murder. But that aside, there was an enormous difference between these extremes. Some, like Bakunin, did not want to cut themselves off from the people and, like Razin or Pugachov, believed they could lead them. The others felt sure that their perfectly organized act of violence would make up for the people's inability to rise up to put an end, once and for all, to an order that both sides believed had had its day. The new Pugachovs of the nineteenth-century universities started from feelings of intense compassion for the people, and a wish to share their suffering. They came to feel that they represented the "will of the people," claiming the power to exercise it in the name of the people and to kill, in their name, the holders and servants of the power that it was everyone's duty to hate. Their feelings of guilt toward the people thus developed into a theory of the duty to kill on the people's behalf.

9

"The Fish Begins to Stink at the Head"

♦

The "student Pugachovs" were united in the belief that it was the duty of the people and their leaders to deliver Russia from oppression. No one believed the government could of its own accord carry out a revolution that would emancipate the country socially and politically. This contradictory concept of change and politics was characteristic of the nineteenth century: while the intelligentsia passionately took up the cause of the people, suffering with them and identifying with them, at the same time they believed that everything depended on the "head" of the body that was society and not on the body as a whole. The head was power, and particularly its supreme holder, the sovereign. It was he who was accused of perpetuating a system of iniquitous social relations and an unacceptable system of power, and it was his figure that attracted the attacks, the hate, and finally murder. And yet it was this same man, the holder of power, who was to carry out reforms that completely transformed the social reality and, to some extent, political relations in Russia. Alexander II, the reforming tsar, was to receive no credit for what he was and what he accomplished, paying with his life for the fact that he was the incarnation of the system. This change in the relations between the intelligentsia and the holder of power, against a background of far-reaching reforms, opens a tragic new phase in Russian history. The all-powerful sovereign of a throne still stained with recently spilled blood was successful in introducing a more peaceful regime, excluding violence. He did so perhaps to retain his authority, but in so doing he himself was to become the target for assassins outside the sphere of power who sought change. Thus we see a twofold development: violence and murder no longer emanate from the throne but are used against it. This violence was to illustrate a principle expressed by Mao Zedong a century later when he quoted the proverb: "The fish begins to stink at the head." In other words, one must strike at the head in order to bring down the whole body.

Reform or Revolution?

When Alexander II came to the throne, Russia was in deep disarray. The Crimean War had cruelly revealed that the country lacked the moral, military, and economic strengths needed to bring the war to a successful conclusion. With financial affairs in a bad state and the army weakened from within, at a moment when it had been believed to be the regime's most faithful and firm support, the time had come for hard questions. Why had Russia lost all its strength and cohesion? The reply was immediate: because of serfdom. The countryside was in a constant state of near-revolt. The peasants refused to carry out their duties toward their lords, burning estates, killing the stewards who tried to reason with them, and finally running away at the first opportunity. It was clear that the official social order was no more than a crumbling facade. Although no Pugachov appeared to rally the peasants to a general uprising, nevertheless the number and extent of local revolts grew throughout the latter years of Nicholas I's reign and the situation was on the point of exploding by the end of the Crimean War.[1] The repercussions of Russia's defeat and conditions in the countryside precipitated an economic crisis and a worsening of the situation of landowners. Serfdom had become unpopular with all sections of society.

---

1. One of the causes was that the tsar, driven into a corner by military defeats, had called in January 1855 for the recruitment of peasants into popular militias that were supposed to reinforce the weakened troops. The peasants assumed that the recruits would be freed; discovering that this was an illusion, they rebelled. Troops had to be withdrawn from the front to go and quell the growing unrest, so that the creation of these militias, far from reinforcing the military forces engaged in the war, in fact weakened them.

The peasants passionately desired to be freed from it, the landowners were increasingly frightened of their serfs and realized that the situation was doing little to increase their wealth, and meanwhile the intelligentsia was agitating. Thus, by the end of the Crimean War, it was clear that the time for serious reforms had come. Alexander II, whose two predecessors had been conservative rulers, quickly grasped the extent of the crisis rocking Russian society and immediately announced, in the manifesto announcing the end of the war, that the latter would be accompanied by a far-reaching reconstruction of social relations and of the political system.

It is important to examine as a whole the intellectual and political climate in Russia at this time. We have seen how a section of the intelligentsia had criticized the system and attempted to unite with the common people. But at this decisive moment in Russian history there was another side to political expression, that of the elite groups closer to the center of power. Alexander's promises opened up an extraordinary and unprecedented period of hope, and these elites participated in the plans for reform. Perhaps the only period to resemble the sudden excitement to be found in the journals, salons, and circles of the empire is that of the late 1980s with its overflowing of ideas and suggestions resulting from the policies of Gorbachev.

Alexander II announced to the nobles, in a famous speech of March 30, 1856: "It is better to abolish serfdom from above than to see it abolish itself from below." The nobility immediately involved themselves in the movement and began to prepare plans for reform. Not all had equally liberal ideas. While many believed that the rethinking of the status of the peasant was a matter of prime urgency, which if delayed would turn Russia into a dangerous powder keg, others, though only a few, tried to show that there was no hurry. However, for the most part, the work prepared by the nobility contained both general directions and concrete proposals adapted to the situations in the different regions. For once, then, a certain consensus united the views of the Russian sovereign and his nobles, on the one hand, and the peasant masses whose fate was under consideration, on the other. It was no small matter: the emancipation of the serfs obviously had a direct bearing on the landowners, but, above all, it affected a very large section of society, since the serfs represented nearly a quarter of the total population of the Empire.[2]

For a period of three years (1858–61) the reform of the condition of the peasants occupied the government, the nobility, and a whole body of specialists, while society waited with bated breath for the fruit of these efforts, not knowing whether the results would crown the hopes that had grown up, or whether, once again, the talk of reform would be followed by a few minor adjustments and a return to the status quo. The documents of February 19, 1861, were quite unambiguous. They abolished serfdom for all peasants attached to private estates (though not for those on the imperial estates, of whom there were only a tenth as many) and defined the conditions that would allow them to live, which is to say, to acquire land.

The importance of this far-reaching reform can never be sufficiently stressed. It enabled Russia to emerge in one leap from the "exoticism" and the legal and social backwardness that had characterized the country and join—in theory at least—the other nations of Europe. It gave all subjects equal status (the serfs on the imperial estates being emancipated two years later). It modified the economic relations of the greater part of society. What is more, all this was accomplished in time of peace, by those who would have to pay the price of the reform. This decision from the throne, with the concurrence of those who were to be deprived of their privileges— the fact that they were sometimes reluctant is of only secondary importance—was nothing more or less than a revolution. Whatever reservations were subsequently expressed about the manner of application of the reform, the fact remains that it allowed Russia at last to enter Europe on an equal footing—a Europe on which, because of the continuation of serfdom, it had until then resolutely turned its back.

Anything was possible now, for the freedom of movement permitted in future to the entire population would bring about great changes in the conditions for development in Russia, allow-

2. According to the census of 1858, the population of the empire was 74,556,000 people, of whom 59,415,000 lived within the borders of Russia proper. Out of this total population, 20,173,000 were serfs on private estates, of whom 9,803,000 were men.

ing, in particular, an expansion of industrialization. The Manifesto of Emancipation, read out on the church squares to the grave-faced serfs who heard the news of their freedom and equality alongside the other inhabitants of the empire, justly earned Alexander II the title of "the Tsar Liberator." But for all that, the problems did not go away. After the initial celebrations, when the newly freed peasants reassessed their position in relation to their one-time masters, new restrictions began to show themselves. While the new institutions of rural Russia were being set up, for a transitional period the peasant was not able to enjoy his new rights in their entirety, starting with the right to freedom of movement. The greatest problem, as with all revolutions of this type, was that of the reform that must follow: that which would give land to the peasants. An immense disillusionment was to result from this matter. The land was not given to them directly, but went to the rural commune (*mir*), the assembly of heads of households, that periodically redistributed the land among its members. The two-thirds majority needed to dissolve the commune was not easy to bring together. Finally, the land had to be purchased from the lords instead of being given,[3] so that peasant debts became an acute problem in years to come.

The difficulties inherent in all reforms of this type were well illustrated. The sovereign had embarked on this course less from personal conviction than because the problem, which had rumbled on for several generations, had reached an intolerable degree of urgency. He had to convince the nobility of the necessity of reform, but he could not allow them to be the only ones to suffer. The nobility considered that the conditions for the division of land robbed them of more land than was acceptable. The peasants could not accept that they would have to buy the land that they cultivated. Above all, they detested the commune. They wanted their own individual pieces of land, not subject to the rules of communal property within the *mir*. The resurrection of the old communal institution, which the Slavophiles and later the Populists had be-

---

3.   The principle of landownership was twofold; the land purchased from the lord was the communal property of all members of the *mir;* the arable land was redistributed periodically by the *mir,* while the peasant had sole ownership of the land around his house.

lieved best suited to the Russian soul and the peasants' interests, was nothing more than a creation of the intellectuals and did not correspond in any way to the desires of the peasants. If the sovereign had chosen this path, which was to turn out to be deeply unpopular, it was partly because he was influenced by the arguments of the intelligentsia, and partly also because this method of arranging peasant society allowed the extent of the reform to be limited. After the first period of enthusiasm in the countryside, when the moment of disillusionment arrived it provoked a wave of spontaneous violence among the peasants. The intelligentsia was to find in this same reform, so basic but so insufficient, a new arena for its activism against the sovereign. But even before becoming aware of the drawbacks, the intelligentsia was little inclined to give Alexander the credit for what had been achieved.

Alexander's reforms were not, however, confined to social relations; they aimed also to reduce the arbitrariness of the administration and the judiciary. His great ambition was to create in Russia a state based on law, and the legal reform of 1864,[4] inspired by texts and practices current in western Europe, was a key element in this plan. The measures he took to install a liberty still unknown in Russia were ones that were basic to all nations with a respect for liberty: independence of the judiciary; irremovability of the judges; equality of all citizens before the law; the right to a defense; public proceedings openly debated; competence of the official courts in all criminal cases, including crimes against the state; and replacement of police by judicial investigation. These reforms may not have been sufficient to make the authoritarian Russian state a liberal state, but they nevertheless set it on the right path to such a development. If we add to these measures the abolition of corporal punishment (except for peasants), a relaxation of censorship, and a far-reaching reform of the education system that was recruiting ever larger numbers of the intelligentsia, it is clear how far the early years of Alexander's reign took Russia down the road to political modernization.

The intelligentsia, which had urged the need for change, should have applauded and seconded this "revolution from above."

---

4. The report was to be published in its entirety in the official organ of the government, *Pravitel'stvennii vestnik (The Government Gazette).*

And yet, far from rallying to the reforming tsar, the intellectuals turned back to the peasants, whose grievances had revived, becoming still more radical, to the point where they saw the liberating tsar as nothing more than a tyrant. It was now that the idea of the need to remove him by assassination began to develop. The intelligentsia did not expect modernization to come from the head of society; it sought the road that would oppose this head. In order to do this, it would be necessary to get rid of him. The years that followed the reform were to be also the years when terror was directed at the creators of the reform. It was a tragic paradox, one that was to lead to the murder of Alexander II and a return to absolutism.

Terrorism versus Reform

Following the agrarian reform, Nikolai Chernyshevsky, a theoretician of Nihilism and also the true organizer of Populism, for which he drew up the program, expressed his views about the future fate of the peasants in no uncertain terms: the reform would make their situation worse. The abolition of serfdom, carried out in order to avoid a total reform of the political system and equally to guard against the threat of a social explosion, had resolved nothing. On the contrary, it would encourage a merciless struggle against the regime. Before Chernyshevsky had had time to announce the forms that this struggle would assume, the regime acted, focusing on the person of this remarkable man its determination to check the mounting opposition. Imprisoned from 1862 to 1864 in the Peter and Paul Fortress, then exiled to Siberia[5] after a "civil execution"—a strange ceremony intended to demonstrate how a "state criminal" (these words were written on a board hung round his neck) was excised from society—Chernyshevsky came to represent for the intelligentsia opposition to the system. The intelligentsia thus had

---

5.   He had originally been sentenced to fourteen years' hard labor—though in fact Katorga was a prison and no revolutionary ever worked there—and to life exile in Siberia. The first part of his sentence was subsequently reduced to seven years.

its martyr, and one of the first types of action that it undertook were plans to organize his escape. But the young intellectuals—the "fanatical youth" adulated by Bakunin—could not be satisfied merely with educating the people and making plans for a great man's escape. The question that he had posed: *What Is to Be Done?*[6] was raised ever more urgently at all their meetings, demanding a direct and violent answer.

At their daily work, in the countryside and in the factories, these young people could not fail to notice that they were failing to instill a spirit of insurrection in the peasants and workers. How were they to carry out a revolution when the masses were not ready and the political system hindered the setting up of a large revolutionary organization capable of impressing the crowds and carrying them along with it? The answer to this negative view was assassination. These impatient young intellectuals concluded that it was necessary to effect a shock that would radically change a situation that the sovereign had managed to contain by partial reform. The object of the attempt had to be the emperor, who embodied the state, who deceived the masses with illusory reforms, and whose removal would leave the state edifice momentarily leaderless, thus making any unified reaction impossible and depriving the masses of the only political reference point that they could understand. The idea and even the plan for killing the emperor were debated in a small group known as the *Organization,* which at first had seemed nothing more than a club for hotheaded young intellectuals.

But suddenly the feverish discussions were transformed into action. On April 4, 1866, when the tsar was walking in the garden of the Summer Palace, a young man rushed up to him and shot at him. The attempt failed; the would-be assassin, a student named Dmitri Karakozov, was either a bad shot or too nervous. But this attempt opened a new period in Russian history, that of tyrannicide. Until that time, no one in society had dared to raise his hand against the sovereign or against the servants of the state. This was a new period, too, in that this attempt was no isolated act, such as can

6. His book, *What Is to Be Done?*, written in prison in the years 1862–63, was to be the bible of the intelligentsia in the late nineteenth century.

be found in all societies from time to time, but the beginning of a style of struggle against the system that was to continue until the system was overcome.

The reaction to this attempt was violent and did not initially encourage its repetition. Karakozov was immediately arrested while the police relentlessly followed up all the leads to what they took to be a plot; more generally they neutralized all opposition groups. Karakozov was condemned to death and hanged; hundreds of people were arrested and more than thirty sent into exile. For the ruling classes, whether or not they had supported the reforms, the attempt marked a turning point: it was high time, they thought, to return to the firm hand. The policy of reform suffered a lasting blow. For all those who opposed the system, it was the signal for a radical turn in the opposite direction. The trial of Karakozov and his fellow accused was not, however, a parody of justice—far from it. They were protected by the legal system set up by the judicial reform that allowed the defense full exercise of its role. If the death sentence was pronounced, it was because this was incontestably a matter of an attempt to destabilize the state, and here the law was inflexible. Alexander II, who thought for a moment of exercising his prerogative of pardon, decided finally that the safety of the state required an exemplary punishment, to nip the movement in the bud.

More important than this rupture between the throne and a still-developing intelligentsia—a rupture that was the result of the assassination attempt and the subsequent repression—and besides its negative political effect on the sovereign, who was alarmed to find that his reforms had not disarmed the hostility of the intelligentsia, the most important factor in this event was the reaction of the people. For it was they who would guide the intelligentsia in its future decisions. This first attempt on the life of the sovereign could not fail to shock. In the eyes of the peasants, the Tsar Liberator was sacred, and the insufficiency of the reform was entirely accounted for by the lack of cooperation, or even the sabotage, of the nobles and landowners.

The story spread rapidly that the nobles, furious at having had to make concessions, had tried to assassinate the tsar in order to abolish the reforms. This type of plot, murder planned within the restricted circle around the throne in the interests of the nobles, was much more comprehensible to the peasant masses than a murder carried out on their behalf by men who claimed to do it in their name. Even the factory workers of St. Petersburg and Moscow failed to see that the attempt might have been legitimate and in the interests of the people. This popular condemnation, apparent everywhere, showed the intelligentsia that it could not count on the people and that the latter were still essentially bound to the sovereign and the monarchy, unable to imagine a different political order. The intelligentsia found itself once again faced with Chernyshevsky's question. Its reply would have to take account of the gulf between its own impatience and the aspirations of the people.

It was this disarray of the intelligentsia in the face of this realization as much as the increased political repression that accounted for the few years of calm that the regime was now to enjoy. But this respite only half-concealed the undercurrent of ideas, and the setting up of organizations whose actions were to prove far more effective than the isolated attempt by Karakozov. Nechayev, in particular, concerned himself with the difficulty of forming a true revolutionary movement and the need for a substitute for the will of the people. His solution was to propose the creation of small groups of conspirators.

Strangely enough, the murder that followed the failed attempt on the tsar was of a very different kind. Intended to set the seal on the internal solidarity of the terrorist organization[7] and to test, in regard to its own members as much as to the enemy, the methods developed in *The Revolutionary Catechism,* this act, a "murder among murderers," merits closer attention, for it was to set a trend. Nechayev convinced his companions, perhaps to test their loyalty and bind them to him forever, that one of his supporters, a student named Ivanov, whom he may have found hard to control, or perhaps distrusted, was a traitor who was going to denounce them. He organized a group assassination. For the government, this murder provided the supporters of increased repression with further

---

7.   Returning to Russia in 1869 after some time with Bakunin in Switzerland, Nechayev had founded an organization called *Narodnaia razprava* or "Popular Justice," which aimed to stir up the peasants to seize power, not spontaneously, but by provoking and guiding a Jacquerie. Nechayev's organization was to be, according to Bakunin, a "Stenka Razin collective."

ammunition. After a detailed inquiry, numerous arrests were made from the ranks of the revolutionaries. But it was important above all for the light that it shed on the violence and sectarianism present in a section of the intelligentsia. Bakunin was horrified. But years later, learning that Nechayev was imprisoned in the Peter and Paul Fortress, Vera Figner, one of the great female figures in the terrorist movement, tried to find a way to help him escape. The glow of the martyr's halo made his companions forget his extreme fanaticism and asceticism—not stopping at murder—which deprived him of all human characteristics, his tendency to spy on everyone, including his own followers, and the constant lies told in the service of his own personal truth. The murder of the student Ivanov and a relationship within the group of conspirators in which Nechayev assumed the power of life and death over those who surrounded him, compromising them when necessary by involving them in the murder of one of their own group, smacks more of Russia's future history and the political system of the following century than of the nineteenth century, where terrorism still tried to remain within the bounds of morality. Although not directed against the system, the murder of Ivanov was nevertheless essentially political, though, at the time, the only one of its kind.

At the time, this settling of scores, like the failed attempt on the tsar's life, seemed to lead to an impasse. Without the people, no action could lead to the overthrow of the political order; as a result, the end of the decade and the first half of the 1870s were devoted to a desperate quest for the people. . . . Whether they went into the country disguised as peasants or organized clubs for the workers, the enthusiasts of the Movement to the People were soon disillusioned. It was difficult to open the eyes of the people as long as the government drew from their strength and cohesion a legitimacy that the masses could not question. Once again it became clear that as long as the head, representing the state, remained in place, no movement could start from below. Furthermore, the supporters of Populism had to count the victims being sacrificed to their illusions. Many of their number had been arrested, deported, or left to die in prison. The need to combine two requirements, the continuation of the education of the people and the safety of the young Populists, led to small organizations. Without this type of structure, it was difficult to convince or train the masses, and the unfortunate young intellectuals who tried were left quite without protection.

Thus was born, or reborn, in the mid-1870s, *Zemlia i volia* (Land and Liberty). It was a proper political party this time, rather than a vague grouping, where men could bring about the political revolution which, they had come to realize, was the one true condition that would attract popular support. But how could this popular revolution be arrived at if not through violence? As the debate extended, so, all over Russia, more and more groups appeared, inspired by this plan. *Zemlia i volia* and its leaders increasingly found support from the most marginalized elements of society: the Old Believers and members of sects of all sorts. And increasingly they returned to the central question: whether or not to turn to murder. The state was well armed to deal with these expanding clandestine activities; repression became more intense and arrests more numerous.

A fatal cycle began: sporadic revolts in the country, demonstrations in the towns, and more repression. In 1876 this reached a peak: a demonstration in St. Petersburg, in front of the Cathedral of the Virgin of Kazan, resulted in mass arrests and a spectacular trial, followed by several more. By the end of 1877, uprisings and trials had taken a heavy toll. By the hundreds, those who had attempted to propagate their subversive ideas were sent into exile. Clearly, the government had decided to eradicate the protest movement. Any action taken by the latter, from the Movement to the People to the propaganda and agitation of the last period, seemed doomed to failure. One conclusion emerged: salvation lay in an assault on the machine of state. An article appearing in a clandestine edition of the journal *Land and Liberty,* headed with the same title, makes no mystery about this conclusion to which events had led the organization: "Political assassination is an act of revenge, or reprisal. It is only thus, it is only when the conspirators answer the systematic destruction of their members with murder that the revolutionary party can exist. . . . Assassination must count among the chief political weapons of our times. . . ."

Terrorism against the State

But vengeance for the victims of repression was not the only function of murder. The program of Land and Liberty, in the 1878 version, is very clear on this point. Speaking of the general tasks of the movement, it specifies that it is necessary to "weaken, upset or, in other words, disorganize the strength of the state, without which no plan for insurrection, however ambitious and well conceived, will be successful." To attain this, the section on disorganization proposes the following program: "The systematic elimination of the most harmful or influential figures in the government; in the final moments, the total liquidation of the government, and, in general, of those on whom this hated regime relies or could rely, whoever they might be."

Thus the step from political activity to terrorism was taken. It had not been forgotten that the people had been unable to accept an attempt on the life of the sovereign himself: this disorganization was aimed at his entourage and at all those whose disappearance from important state positions would contribute to the creation of confusion in the workings of the state. Furthermore, terrorism aimed also to strike fear into those who remained in their places. This change of tactics opened the way to a series of murders where women, as we shall see, played a remarkable role.

The first of the series was the murder of General Trepov, the chief of police in St. Petersburg, who was well known for his inclination to settle political problems with violence. When visiting a prison holding the 193 prisoners accused in a trial due to open in three months' time, Trepov had been angered by a prisoner who had refused to take off his hat in his presence, and had had him whipped. This man was a political prisoner, and this violence to the person of one of their members, unable to defend himself, was for the Land and Liberty group the last and insupportable straw. It resulted in a decision to put into practice the terrorist principles decided on in their articles. At the end of the trial in which Trepov's victim was one of those in the dock, a young girl, Vera Zasulich, emerged from the crowd, came up to General Trepov and fired at him, seriously wounding him. Far from trying to escape, she allowed herself to be arrested and explained that she had wanted to avenge the man whom Trepov had had whipped in prison a few months before. The shot, though not entirely achieving its aim, had, nevertheless, long-lasting repercussions.

Public opinion, already disturbed by the trial that had preceded the shooting and moved by the courageous bearing of the accused, was passionately aroused by the action of Vera Zasulich who, having shot at an unpopular man, received more sympathy than indignation. After all, there had been no threat to the tsar and the punishment inflicted by Trepov on an unarmed prisoner deserved harsh condemnation. The Ministry of Justice assigned Vera Zasulich's trial to an ordinary court, rather than to the senatorial commission that was normally assembled to deal with political matters—an indication of the concern in the minds of those even in the highest positions of state. Everything combined to put General Trepov on trial and not the woman who had fired at him: the reasons for Vera Zasulich's action, the quality of the debate and the speeches for the defense. (The lawyers, in trials of this kind, were increasingly identifying with their clients, including in their defense explicit indictments of the political system.) Although the accused did not deny having committed a premeditated act, she was acquitted and freed as a national heroine, even if subsequently she had to flee. The myth of a new Charlotte Corday, turning her back on the comfort and security of a rich home to avenge the oppressed, had taken root. The significance of the verdict was inescapable. Since this had not been a special trial, the law was tending to side with those who opposed the government. It came as a terrible shock to the servants of the state to find that it was not after all a crime to shoot down an important official going about his duties. The authority of the state was diminished, for to admit that one of its servants deserved such a fate threw doubt on all the others. State officials realized that terrorism had become acceptable in the eyes of society and that they were to be the terrorists' prey.

It would not have been surprising if this attempt had opened the way to renewed assassination attempts by others. And yet, for a moment, the revolutionary movement wavered, beset by doubt in the face of the clemency shown by the court that had tried Vera Zasulich and particularly the reaction of public opinion in the capital. Had the clumsy shot fired at Trepov had a profound political effect? Or had it shown the sovereign that it was urgent—although still not too late—to plan and accept the great political reform that was so necessary: the adoption of a constitution? This peaceful hypothesis did not suit the extremist element in Land and Liberty. The same reasoning prevailed as in 1861: it was useless to expect anything from the sovereign; only violence could bring about radical change. And so, despite a lack of persecution from the indecisive authorities, the assassination attempts started again.

On August 4, 1878, General Mezentsov, head of the Third Section, was struck down in the center of the city by two terrorists, Kravchinsky and Baranikov, one using a dagger and the other a gun. It was a remarkable job compared to Vera Zasulich's amateurish attempt, and with the victim dead, the two murderers were able to vanish into thin air at their leisure without being caught. In a few months the art of political assassination had made considerable progress. The assassination was hailed as a masterpiece by the clandestine press, and Kravchinsky, who had wielded the dagger, himself published an article asserting that this was the beginning of a new era when Russia would at last be purged of those who were torturing the revolutionaries. But the two motives of murder as revenge and murder intended to disorganize the state were confused. They certainly overlapped, and this confusion indicates that Land and Liberty, having decided to act through murder, had not yet fully defined its strategy.

After only a few months, on February 9, 1879, it was to be the governor of Kharkov, General Kropotkin, cousin of the famous anarchist, who was shot down by David Goldenberg. On March 13, 1879, the new chief of the St. Petersburg police, Drenteln, was shot at by a terrorist of Polish origin, Leonid Mirsky. Drenteln was not killed, since the assassin was on horseback and his target in a carriage, making it hard to aim accurately.

Demonstrations in many parts of the country revealed that the situation was becoming increasingly serious. The government was obliged to take firm action. After the assassination of General Mezentsov, a provisional order stipulated that terrorists would be tried by court-martial and sentences carried out without appeal, as in time of war. On September 1, 1878, a whole series of measures were taken intended to prevent terrorist activity. The harshest of these allowed the police or the gendarmerie to exile without any kind of trial any person even suspected of a political crime. By making suspicion equivalent to proven commission of a crime and treating terrorism as an act of war, the emperor was turning his back utterly on his initial desire to develop a state bound by law. Finally, wide-ranging judicial and police powers were given to state officials. The general agitation and the murder of those responsible for the maintenance of law and order obviously required the public authorities to do something, but perhaps not to go so far as to place Russia, which had wished to become more liberal, under a state of emergency. As always, these excessive and inappropriate measures had the opposite effect from that expected. The terrorists did not slacken their pressure, but changed their tactics. No longer were their actions inspired by vengeance, the desire to punish chiefs of police who used too much violence or who were too indulgent to the violence used by their subordinates. Since the state had not been destabilized by their "hit" operations against its more dubious servants, since it had refused to understand the meaning of these attempts, then they would have to strike at the head and kill the sovereign himself. In 1879 a consistent strategy was set up: the sovereign would be the sole target to which all efforts would be devoted. This was the beginning of the long series of attempts on the life of Alexander II, which gave the terrorism of the last years of the Tsar Liberator's reign its particularly tragic and paradoxical character.

The Pursuit of the Tsar Liberator

On April 2, 1879, the tsar was taking his usual walk in the grounds of the Winter Palace when a young man approached him and fired at him. Like Karakozov's attempt thirteen years earlier, this failed. The tsar, turning away to avoid the bullets, stumbled and suffered from no more than a fall. The assailant was arrested after a struggle with the king's bodyguards in which he tried to poison himself. Saved from the poison, he was sentenced and hanged on May 28 before an immense crowd. Although in many ways similar to Karakozov's attempt, this act, in its nature and consequences, was in fact to open a new stage in the violent confrontation between the tsar and the terrorists.

The man who had shot at Alexander II this time, Aleksandr Soloviev, had, like Karakozov, decided to commit this act on his own authority. During his trial, he described to the judges the road that had led a student like himself to an act of individual terrorism. He retraced his activities as a young intellectual won over to the cause of the people, the workers and the peasants whom he had tried in vain to educate after briefly devoting himself to the education of their children. It had been the realization of the futility of these efforts, given the extent of the popular apathy and the repressiveness of the government, that had finally convinced him that there was only one way out of this impasse, which would remove the obstacle, the tsar, overturning at a blow the people's certainties.

Soloviev's reasoning was simple: all the ingredients for an uprising of the masses were there, for they knew suffering and anger. But centuries of submissiveness and respect for the sovereign still clouded their understanding. It was vital to hasten the evolution of this consciousness with an extreme action, creating a situation both new and irreversible. And who else would bring about this shock if not the intellectual, who understood the existing situation and the means of changing it? Soloviev had acted in the name of and for the people, prompted by an imperious sense of the role of the intellectual, representative of society, even if the latter was as yet unaware of having issued such a mandate.

It is at this point that the attempt of 1879 differs from that of 1866. When he carried out his action, Karakozov was still relatively isolated in the populist movement. But at the moment that Soloviev was about to strike, *Narodnaia volia,* informed of his intention, had debated the attitude to adopt with regard to the project. Despite fierce opposition, possibly of the majority, it had agreed that those of its members who wished could take part in the attempt. The organization still supported the idea that to kill the sovereign was no substitute for revolutionary action. The destabilization of the state through the assassination of its important officials had only led to an increase in repression. To raise their sights to the tsar instead of the officials might simply be to risk an increase in the severity of the repression and ultimately to endanger the entire revolutionary movement. But the fact that those who refused to conform to this overprudent line were allowed the freedom of individual action bears witness to the confusion and division within the organization and, above all, to the fascination that pure violence held for some of its members.

Those who, like Plekhanov, condemned the action were not mistaken when they predicted the immediate consequences. On April 5, 1879, new measures were introduced that considerably reinforced the state of emergency set up the year before on September 1. The system, already introduced in Moscow, Warsaw, and Kiev, where the government was entrusted to the military, was extended to other towns where trouble was starting. Those in charge, the "temporary governors-general," were ordered to take over all the surrounding areas. Thus the most active revolutionary centers in the empire, Moscow and St. Petersburg in the north and Kiev, Odessa, and Kharkov in the south, were—like Warsaw, but for other reasons—placed for a time under military rule. The governors could at any time hand over to court-martial and condemn to exile by a simple administrative decision not only suspects, whom the law of 1878 had already entrusted to them, but equally all those who might in the future threaten civil peace and order, which were both defined in extremely vague terms.

The new system was made more repressive by the transference to the six regions in question of the authority of central government in the matter of the maintenance of law and order. This delegation of power underlined the inability of the government to provide any coherent response to the problem posed by the tide of terrorism. At the same time it created a very arbitrary justice since each governor-general pursued his own path, with different ideas of authority in different regions. Thus it was that the south was to feel the effects of the increased repression. Here the Populist and terrorist movements had become extraordinarily strong thanks to the influence of the revolutionary ideas and nationalist aspirations of the Ukrainians—as in Poland, where nationalist sentiments reinforced and widened the struggle, though to a lesser degree. The governors-general of Odessa and Kiev were excessively diligent in putting down the revolutionary movement, increasing the numbers of arrests, trials, executions, and deportations.

The tsar, who after the attempted assassination of April 23 had left for the Crimea, had set up a special commission to analyze the causes of the expansion of this radical movement which had almost caused his death, and to propose some constructive solutions. The commission, lacking in imagination, had no proposals to make except to increase the authority of the police and to rely on the stable elements in society, particularly the landowners—hardly an acceptable solution to a peasantry dissatisfied with the incomplete reforms of 1861. On two points, however, the commission showed a degree of insight: they discussed what would be the most suitable policy for education to prevent the schools and universities from being breeding grounds of discontent; and they suggested that, by making concessions to the Poles, still resentful of the repression of 1863, the government would prevent Russia's enemies forming an alliance against it.

The government hesitated between a policy of out-and-out repression that would crush all centers of unrest and the search for ways of regaining the confidence of the people. By setting up the commission, the tsar showed at least that, despite the fear aroused by the wave of attempts on his life, he was still prepared to consider what could be done to halt the cycle of violence.

Unfortunately for Alexander II and for the future of the system, the fascination with violence, far from abating, merely increased. Frustrated by the repression and obsessed with the certainty that there was no gradual solution to Russia's problems, the Populist movement continued to gain acceptance for a plan for assassination. Odessa, where the repression was at its most severe under the governorship of Totleben, was the stage where the conditions for this change of heart leading to tyrannicide—by now the sole revolutionary plan—were set. This development can be explained both by the extraordinary concentration of revolutionaries in the south of Russia, and by the oppression that they suffered and which drove them for the most part to violence (for there is no other way of escaping repression except clandestine organization, which allows no open social agitation). Finally, the excesses committed by the guardians of the existing order had an effect on public opinion:

for the first time, those who advocated assassination had the impression that opinion would not condemn them.

At this point there appeared in the forefront of debates of the *Narodnaia volia* movement and its activities new figures who were to give the organization its definitive and most extreme character. First there was Zhelyabov, from Odessa, who brought to the discussions in the capital his experience of a southern Russia overwhelmed by repression, and a remarkable stubbornness. Then there was Nikolai Morozov, who was to set up a splinter group, Liberty or Death, where the element of social reform was completely abandoned in favor of the political plan of seizing power by means of assassination. Lastly, there was Nikolai Kibalchich, whose chief preoccupation was to provide his comrades with the technical means to carry out an assassination. In an improvised laboratory in St. Petersburg, he devoted himself to the manufacture of home made bombs, which would ensure that the assassin would succeed where the bullets of the first terrorists had failed. It was this technician of the revolution who was to enable the terrorists to progress from an improvised and generally unsuccessful activity to far more spectacular attempts that truly struck terror into men's hearts.

Two key dates in the history of the terrorist movement determined the adoption of the assassination of the tsar as the chief goal. In June 1879, the movement met in Lipetsk in the Kiev region in order to set up an efficient organization—this had become vitally necessary for its survival in view of the increased repression—and to seek a common position on general strategy. The results of this meeting, a program and rules, bear witness to the changes that had occurred in the attitudes of the men assembled there. The program concentrated on the liquidation of the tyrant and the system. The Populists did not ignore—and Mikhailov, one of their theoreticians, reminded them at this time—the fact that the tsar had the reforms of the early part of his reign to his credit. They opposed to this the increasingly harsh measures that had followed, and concluded that all hope of a change of mind should be abandoned and that Alexander II no longer had anything positive to offer his country.

It is possible to see how far the Populist movement had come when, on August 26, 1879, after the setting up of *Narodnaia volia,* its members voted for the death of Alexander II. Henceforward, the movement was sure of its direction and the entire future struggle was subordinated to what seemed to be its central condition: the assassination of the tsar. Kibalchich's work contributed to the setting up of assassination attempts that were doubly effective: technically, in that dynamite was substituted for shooting, which was too risky and which the victim often survived; and organizationally, in that these were no longer isolated attempts, conceived by one man lacking information and assistance. Instead, they were the result of a general mobilization of *Narodnaia volia,* allowing more rigorous planning and benefiting from a diversification of men and equipment.

From this rationalization of assassination two attempts were to emerge, both unsuccessful, but demonstrating the technical development in methods. The first took place on the railroad linking Livadia, where the tsar was at the time, and Moscow. Alexander had decided to return to the capital in the autumn of 1879 via Moscow and was to go by train. The conspirators decided that this journey would provide them with an excellent opportunity to put their vote of August 26 into practice. In theory, dynamiting a train meant that anyone on the train was unlikely to survive.

The first phase of the plan was prepared in Odessa itself by Kibalchich, Vera Figner, and a few others. It depended on the idea that the tsar would come by ship from Livadia to Odessa, continuing his journey to Moscow from there by train. They decided to dynamite the railroad track, but this part of the plan failed for two reasons: first because the tsar, on account of bad weather, took another route; second, and chiefly, because the movements of David Goldenberg, who was supposed to carry the dynamite, attracted the attention of the police. As we have seen, it was Goldenberg who had shot Governor Kropotkin in Kharkov at the beginning of the year, skillfully escaping the police. At the time of Soloviev's attempt on the tsar's life on April 2, 1879, Goldenberg had been eager to take part, but had been rejected by Soloviev. Now responsible for the dynamiting of the imperial train, this usually resolute man lost his nerve and was persuaded by the police to reveal what he knew of the revolutionary organization. The principal figure at the second possible site for the attempt was Zhelyabov, a young man of peasant origin from Odessa, who had earlier been expelled from his university for political agitation. As a result of his acts of terrorism in prisons, he had gained great influence over his companions in the struggle. He undertook to place the explosive on the railway line at Aleksandrovsk, but once again the plan failed, probably for technical reasons, the explosive failing to react to the passing train. It would appear that it was not the explosive that was faulty but the installation of the various parts of Zhelyabov's device.

Near Moscow, the last stage of the plan, the attempt almost succeeded. The conspirators had bought a small house near the railroad and dug a tunnel linking the house with the track, placing the dynamite beneath it. The failure was this time the result of inadequate planning. Two trains passed, one shortly after the other, at the time when the imperial train was due (between 10 and 11 o'clock at night). The conspirators, who knew the timetable only roughly, were aware that the tsar was traveling in one train and his entourage in another, but they did not know in what order the two trains would come. The member of their group whose duty it was to fire the charger igniting the explosive chose the wrong train, let the first pass, and blew up the second. The emperor was in the first.

Although a failure, the attempt provided vital lessons. The emperor was forced to realize that repression had in no way weakened the terrorist movement. The police failed either to anticipate the attempt or subsequently to arrest its authors. For the conspirators, the lesson was both bitter and encouraging. They still lacked practical experience, that was clear, not yet handling explosives with ease, and they did not have enough explosives. They lacked the necessary accomplices in high places to organize an attempt with absolute precision—the mistake over the order of the trains was evidence of that—and there were human weaknesses in the organization. Goldenberg's confession had led to an extensive round-up in which many of those involved were arrested. These members often lived under false identities in the homes of respectable citizens with no contact with the movement. Goldenberg revealed to the police their false names and hiding places, striking a severe blow to the movement. For all that, the failed assassination concluded on a very positive note, for it was greeted by Russian society with the greatest indifference. The days when the idea of trying to harm the tsar would have aroused the greatest indignation in all levels of society were long gone. Those terrorists who had escaped arrest were encouraged, sure now that they had chosen the right path. People were becoming used to the repeated attempts on the tsar's life; their indignation was dulled, and the resulting renewed repression increased the unpopularity of the regime. Even when answered with arrests and executions, the use of terror, depriving the tsar of his aura of invincibility and especially inviolability, was at last bearing fruit.

On February 5, 1880, a new attempt carried out in the Winter Palace itself was partially successful. The exploding dynamite in one of the palace rooms killed eleven people and wounded fifty-five but missed the tsar, who was on the floor above. It was now the fourth time that the sovereign had escaped, but lessons were learned. This action had been very carefully planned. As early as September 1879, just when the movement was recovering from its failure in Odessa, the organizer of this future attempt, Stepan Khalturin, had got into the Winter Palace disguised as a carpenter, to set things up. The dynamite was placed under the imperial dining room, but on the day the emperor was delayed and was late in entering. The quantity of explosive proved insufficient to blow up the floor where he was at that moment. Nevertheless, the explosion could not have been more spectacular, taking place as it did where the tsar lived, in his own palace. The attempt showed that the terrorists were capable of infiltrating anywhere, that the measures taken by the police were ineffective, and that internal disputes among the ranks of the police were aggravating the confusion and inefficiency around the sovereign. Furthermore, the perpetrator of the attempt, Khalturin, vanished into thin air just like his predecessors. The result of this confrontation between the powerful empire and the terrorists was entirely to the advantage of the latter. The security of the chief figure in the land was a pure myth, as it seemed that he was surrounded by terrorists on all sides, who appeared for a moment to carry out an attempt on his life, then immediately vanished again, only to plan another.

In 1880, *Narodnaia volia* found itself facing a difficult choice. The attempts on the tsar's life and the elusive authors of these attempts had given the movement a definite prestige, but if it continued to miss its target, it knew that it would end by appearing powerless. Then another myth would arise—the "hunted," "condemned" tsar would become the invincible one, protected by fate, and he would thereby regain his authority. This analysis indicated the urgent need to step up terrorist activities and bring them to a successful conclusion.

At the same time, this impatient enthusiasm revolving entirely around the murder of the tsar was beginning to come up against an "economist" tendency that was starting to develop within the movement and that could not be ignored. A number of members of the Liberty of the People group did not accept the idea that the assassination of the tsar should take precedence over all other action. For these more politically oriented revolutionaries, it was society that would play a role in the great changes to come. That being the case, it was necessary to devote time and effort to organizing the workers whose numbers were growing in the capitals and the towns of the south, and whose standard of living was deteriorating. In 1880, economic conditions were reaching a crisis: work was scarce, the workers' discontent increasing. There were many who said it was necessary to take advantage of this situation, to intensify activity in the towns and the countryside, and develop a terrorism that was directed at those who were seen as being directly responsible for the crisis—the industrialists and the landowners.

Two different views emerged: terrorism at the top versus terrorism at the bottom. These two ideas did not entirely contradict one another, but rather they expressed two different views of the revolution. For the supporters of the first, the death of the tsar would be enough to deprive society of its reference point and push it forward into a new world. For the second, the assassination of the tsar would bring about terrible repression, plunging society, as yet unorganized, into chaos.

Nevertheless, it was the first point of view that prevailed, and 1880 was marked by a proliferation of plans for assassination. In May, when the tsar was expected in Odessa, two terrorists rented a store, dug a tunnel under the road to the point where the tsar was supposed to pass, and packed it with dynamite. He arrived earlier than expected and the plan was abandoned, as was the dynamite in the underground tunnel. The same thing happened a few months later near the Winter Palace, where this time the dynamite was placed in the bottom of a canal, under a bridge that the tsar was to cross. Once again he escaped death, his schedule being very erratic. Now and then the police would discover these caches of dynamite, but were always unable to lay hands on those who had left them there. Nevertheless, with the help of informers, they were able to arrest some members of the group. A trial would be held and they would receive judgment, but nothing decisive emerged. Even if the attempts at assassination seemed doomed to failure, the movement seemed destined to survive.

On March 1 all that was to change. On his way to the Sunday review of the troops, the tsar was passing along a canal, alone in his sleigh, when a bomb was thrown at him. Once again he was unhurt, but all around him lay the wounded. Getting out of his sleigh, he was walking to the scene of the explosion when a second bomb went off. This time it hit its mark. The tsar was taken to the Winter Palace, but died an hour later. The assassination had left twenty wounded, three dying shortly afterwards. The long pursuit of the tsar had finally borne fruit. How had this been achieved, after so many failures? And what was to be the effect of this success that, though so long expected, nonetheless was a surprise?

The assassination tells us, first of all, something about the development of the terrorists' techniques. The previous attempts had failed because of confusions over timing and the limited nature of the action. Seeing no alternative solutions, this time the terrorists had taken great pains with their preparations, planning an action with multiple variants. Everything hinged on the fact that every Sunday the tsar went to the riding school. His routes—there were two—were closely studied and the attempt planned for the portion common to the two. Various devices were to be used: a mined tunnel that would explode as the tsar traveled along the common portion; four terrorists with bombs would stand beyond the mined area, in case the dynamite did not explode; to complete the arrangements, Zhelyabov, who had already excelled himself in earlier attempts, was to hold himself ready to intervene with dagger and gun, should the other devices fail. With dynamite, bombs, gun, and dagger, it seemed unlikely that the tsar could escape what was no longer a traditional attempt on his life but rather a commando operation with a single object.

There were several figures who played an outstanding role in this assassination. First, there was Zhelyabov, the true author of the plan, who held all the strings and was the link. But, on February 27, forty-eight hours before the fatal moment, he was arrested. Although his role as organizer and his place at the time of the attempt were filled by his companion, Sofia Perovskaya, some of his worries about the aftermath of the assassination disappeared with him. While he had been organizing it, he had not ceased to wonder what should be done, after the assassination, to encourage society to rise up, transforming the murder into revolution. He was aware that the terrorist movement was isolated and its ability to spark off an insurrection doubtful, but nevertheless, he attempted to prepare the workers. In the panic following his arrest, his comrades lost sight of this aim. The assassination had become the only objective. *Narodnaia volia* had come to the tragic conclusion of its intellectual path, where murder had ceased to be the means and had become the only true end.

Another key figure in the attempt was the remarkable technician, Kibalchich, who had prepared the bombs. Their construction was indicative of the passion of the terrorists and the spirit of self-sacrifice that inspired them. Kibalchich's bombs were remarkably precise and were sure to kill within a radius of one yard, but needed to be thrown from a very close range. The victim could not escape, but neither could the assassin. Thus victim and murderer would be united forever, while this double sacrifice meant, if the bomb was thrown at the right moment, that the number of victims would be reduced.

Four young men had volunteered to throw the bombs: Nikolai Rysakov, whose bomb was to cause the sovereign's death; Ignati Grinevitsky, a young man of noble family; Timofei Mikhailov; and Ivan Emelyanov. From an observation point, Sofia Perovskaya was to give the signal by waving a white handkerchief. The attempt of March 1 might well have failed like the others, despite the wealth of precautions taken. Zhelyabov's arrest made both the tsar and General Loris-Melikov, who had overall charge of security, wary. After so many attempts, even if unsuccessful, the sovereign, conscious of the threat hanging over him, had hesitated to take his Sunday drive. The terrorists too had felt fate hesitate.

Finally, Alexander had decided not to change his routine; the terrorists, for their part, had decided to assume that he would not. This double decision to change nothing was to alter the destiny of Russia.

The End of a Myth

In 1881, Alexander II too had drawn some conclusions from this manhunt in which he was the quarry. He had in the past relied in part on a policy of repression hoping that it would hold back the tide of violence. The series of attempts on his life in 1879 and 1880 had made him take a closer look at the abilities of the famous Third Section, so manifestly incapable of doing its job. The balance sheet was astonishing: only seventy-two full-time employees and a tight budget, the greater part of which was spent on counteracting the propaganda of the revolutionaries. With such slender and badly organized forces, it seemed impossible to hope to control subversive activities in such a large country. It was true that the governors-general had considerable powers, but the Third Section was supposed to enjoy the direct protection of the tsar. Immediately after the failed attempt at the Winter Palace, General Loris-Melikov had been called on to reorganize the whole system and protect state security with greatly increased powers. In August he abolished the Third Section, replacing it with a central police force—the state police—attached to the Ministry of the Interior. This police force was given wide-ranging powers including the supervision of frontiers, foreigners, and everything that might be used for subversive purposes—from newspapers to the fire service's hoses!

Three divisions of gendarmes, with one each for Moscow and Leningrad, were directly answerable to the Interior Ministry. This reorganization effectively put an end to the idea of Russia as a law-based state, which Alexander II had dreamed of establishing. Russia now differed from the rest of Europe in two ways: first, through the dual nature of the police system, where the political police were separated from the ordinary police responsible for the protection of people and property; second, on account of the judicial powers of the state police, where, when the security of the state was threatened, the judiciary lost its powers and was replaced by a very specific system of police law. Needless to say, the exceptional status of this political police opened the way to the use of absolute and arbitrary power. This system posed a real threat to the terrorists, if they were going to continue their activities. Vera Figner accurately described the situation when she said that if the members of the terrorist movement had attempted for a moment to come out of hiding, even to organize a simple demonstration, it would have been an easy matter to disperse and arrest them without any need of the army, a few gendarmes being sufficient. In the face of repression of this type, *Narodnaia volia* had no choice but to choose terrorism.

But the tsar was not content to stop at repression alone. The need to carry out reforms, which he had so clearly understood at the beginning of his reign, began to obsess him again. He saw clearly that the reform of 1861 and the improvement in the education system both contributed to swell the ranks of those who aspired to increased rights and more change. Far from putting an end to these frustrations, reform ever and again opened the way to new demands, the legitimacy of which were undeniable, even if they could not easily be carried out immediately. In the early 1880s, it was clear that a new wave of reforms was necessary, both to satisfy the aspirations of the growing number of educated people and to cut the ground from under the terrorists and isolate them. The central problem preoccupying the tsar and his entourage was that of the gradual integration of society into the political sphere. In other words, political, and not only social, reform was necessary.

There was no lack of suggestions: the opening of the State Council to elected deputies; the setting up of elected consultative bodies; the reform of local administration; and particularly, the increasing of the powers of the provincial assemblies or *zemstvos*. Though the tsar welcomed these proposals, which fitted in with his own inclinations, he came up against a bureaucracy that was part of the established order and which deeply resented any interference with its prerogatives. Alexander II's son and heir, Alexander, had immediately sided with the most conservative points of view. The whole debate was not made any easier by the series of assassination attempts. The tsar could see that to do nothing was no solution, but the supporters of the status quo argued that it was a mistake to introduce reforms from a position of weakness, saying that first it was necessary to restore order, eradicate the opposition movements, and only then condescend to make changes.

In a general way, the conservatives were afraid that political reform, however limited, might set Russia irrevocably on the road to a constitutional monarchy. They objected that such a development would lead to revolution instead of preventing it. They maintained that Russia had a territory and a population that were too large and diverse for it to be possible to dispense with a highly centralized system. To emphasize differences and to give a voice to representatives of groups so different from one another in culture and standard of living would be to accelerate the centrifugal tendencies of society and lead to an explosion. Only an administration with great authority, the decisive instrument of centralization and cohesion, could prevent Russia from falling apart. Thus the administration ought not to be paralyzed by quibbles over the law, excessive legalism, nor, *a fortiori*, by powers emanating from bodies representing the people, which would only create confusion.

This vigorous defense of the bureaucracy and of centralism may have delayed Alexander II's desire for change, but it did not halt it altogether. Ironically, he was assassinated on the very day he was to attach his signature to the proposals drawn up by Loris-Melikov, who was well aware of the dangers of being trapped in a circle of repression. The proposals were not, of course, a constitution, but were designed to give a human dimension to an authority that had become more than a little dictatorial. The document Alexander had been about to approve proposed the setting up of a consultative assembly formed from two committees elected by the *zemstvos* and the towns. This assembly would prepare proposals for administrative, financial, economic, and social reforms, particularly in the area of agricultural policy. For Alexander II, these measures represented so many steps along the irrevocable path that would one day lead to the adoption of a constitution.

The murder of the reforming sovereign, intended by its perpetrators to hasten political progress in Russia, had precisely the opposite effect: it brought about a brutal regression. The bureaucracy saw a golden opportunity to crush a plan that had been its permanent nightmare. Alexander's ultimate aim of involving society's participation in political decision making was condemned to remain in the realms of fantasy. His son and heir, Alexander III, opted at once for a clear political position, entirely centered on the consolidation of the power of the state. The state, the sovereign, and his entourage were, by natural right, the only holders of power. Their sphere of action was politics, from which the people, no less naturally, had to be excluded.

At the same time, on the advice of his mentor Konstantin Pobedonostsev, Alexander III had to respond to the terrorists. The assassination of his father, so different in all ways from the previous attempts, was this time met with many arrests. The terrorists were forced to recognize that, politically, they had been completely unsuccessful. Horrified by the murder of the sovereign, the people sought for rational explanations, accusing in turn the nobles hostile to the planned reforms or the landowners still furious at having to give up their lands, but at no time did they think of rallying to the revolution. In their eyes, the tsar had fallen victim to those whose privileges he had sought to reduce in the defense of the interests of his people.

This revival of the figure of the "good tsar" pushed the terrorists' plans into the background. The last service they could render to their cause, in an attempt to revive its glory, was to occupy center stage in their trial. Zhelyabov, Sofia Perovskaya, and their companions pleaded passionately to the court—and in an open letter of March 10 addressed to the new emperor—that they had killed Alexander II in order to rescue Russia from a power that was inimical to the people. The murder was, they claimed, a necessity, the only means of ensuring Russia's salvation. To Alexander III they offered the choice between continuing along the path embarked on by his father—the terrorists continuing along their path also—or handing power over to the people—in which case terrorism, losing its justification, would cease. Neither their arguments nor their remarkable courage in the face of death—all the conspirators were hanged on April 3, 1881—had any effect. Not only Alexander III, but also the greater part of society, were quite indifferent to the world and the ideas of the terrorists. The distance separating them and the tsar was hardly surprising. The gulf between them and the rest of society, together with the abandonment of Alexander II's plans for reform, revealed that the terrorists had reached an impasse.

How did the assassination of Alexander II fit into the popular consciousness formed by such a long tradition of violence? In 1881—the end of an epoch—the figure of the tsar still basically conformed to the myth carried down through the centuries; he, like Christ, was leading his people to the realization of its destiny. Though weakened, this identification with Christ and with the people still survived. The repression of the 1870s had somewhat tarnished this image, but nevertheless the emancipation of the peasants, the judicial reform and other partial measures—particularly the *zemstvos*—confirmed the popular belief that the tsar embodied his people and their interests. The as yet incomplete idea of the state had not replaced the central role of the sovereign. Consequently, the murder of the tsar inevitably revived the old image of the tsar suffering the Passion as Christ had suffered before him. The martyrdom of Alexander II placed him in the ranks of the saint-princes. Thus his death, like that of Christ, was attributed to the betrayal of those close to him (the nobles, the new Judases) or those whose interests he had opposed in order to defend those of his people (the landowners).

The events of 1881 were to be the last time that this myth of the tsar as martyr for his people prevailed; other myths were to succeed in the people's imagination. In 1881 it was supported by the general climate of spirituality and identification with Christianity inherent in the social culture of Russia at this time. The debates, in which not only Dostoyevsky and Aksakov but also fervent Occidentalists like Turgenev took part, conceived of Russia in religious terms. The tsar and those who fight against him do so "in the name of Christ," or "in the name of the poor and humble," which comes to the same thing, and the words "martyrs" and "Golgotha" are applied equally to both sides. Underlying all the actions and all the discussions of the period that came to an end on March 1, 1881, lay passionate belief, ethical rigor, and the certainty that morality—and not economics or politics—directed history.

Thus we should not be surprised to find, even before the reaction of the authorities to the murder of Alexander II, that the voices of the most respected intellectuals—Leo Tolstoy and Vladimir Soloviev—were raised to ask the new tsar to act as a Christian should and pardon the murderers. Vladimir Soloviev stressed, for example, "that in this hour of darkness, the tsar of Russia has an unique opportunity to show the power of Christian clemency."

Thus the events were interpreted: prompted by a false idea of duty, Alexander's assassins had hurled themselves into the abyss; nevertheless, the motives inspiring them had been prompted by a profound moral sense and thus should not be ignored. By returning to the fundamental values of compassion, the tsar could reunite these contradictory tendencies of society, effecting a reconciliation with his wayward children, the assassins of Alexander II, and reviving the lost social harmony. Only a pious tsar could succeed in this.

Alexander III refused, opposing a pardon, and in so doing he rejected the role of pious tsar offered to him by Tolstoy and Soloviev, and dealt a death-blow to the myth itself. Henceforward the tsar would embody the power and the interests of the state. Repentance, forgiveness, and a humble death in a monk's habit were things of the past. Violence "from below" must be met with power and might "from above"—imperial authority. The "true" tsar had been succeeded by the real emperor.

What Is to Be Done?

After the tragedy at the Catherine Canal both sides were haunted by the question Lenin was to pose some twenty years later. What was to be done to ensure the permanent inviolability not only of an emperor who refused the role of suffering and passion but also of the state? What was to be done to replace terrorism, now appearing increasingly fruitless in the face of the many executions? Guided by the jurist Pobedonostsev, who had been promoted to the post of Procurator of the Holy Synod in 1880 and who was to be the ideologist of Alexander III's reign, the tsar was to opt for a policy dominated principally by the need for state security. The stage had to be protected from all outside—in other words, social—influences, this being the only way to guarantee the order and unity of society. This depended on the unfailing alliance of the autocracy and the church. In order to achieve it, Alexander III pursued a policy of counterreforms that canceled out all the earlier attempts at change. First there was the law of August 14, 1881, a temporary measure, but one that was to paralyze political life in Russia until 1905. Designed uniquely to counter revolution, this measure codified and tightened up all the previous regulations. Envisaging two types of situation, the "increased security of the state" (*usilenaia okhrana*) and the "extraordinary security of the state" (*chrezvychainaia okhrana*), the document defined all the emergency measures that could be applied, declaring what was essentially a state of siege.

As soon as they were proclaimed, these temporary arrangements[8] made it possible to apply "increased" measures to ten regions, including Moscow and St. Petersburg, without delay. As time passed more and more regions were involved, while a few were put under the "extraordinary" measures. The liberal economist Peter Struve described this latter regime in Russia as one where "an all-powerful police became one with the monarchy"; should the first collapse, then the whole monarchy would collapse. The police were given the task of issuing the certificates of loyalty (*blagonadezhnost'*) which every Russian had to produce in order to enter a university or apply for a job in the administration; it was the police that decreed who should be declared suspect and thus placed under permanent surveillance. These harsh measures were reinforced by the Code of 1885.

And yet a look at the figures indicates that these measures were neither appropriate nor effective. In 1880, when Alexander II was still in power, the police had registered some 1,000 cases of crimes against the state; 1,200 people at that time were given sentences of exile, with hard labor for only 60 of them. In 1890, the numbers were certainly higher, with 30,000 exiles in Siberia, but the majority of these were not there for political crimes. During these ten years we find only 17 executions for political crimes. This was too many, of course, but it should be stressed that Russia was at the time in the grip of terrorism, that these 17 executions were

---

8. They were supposed to run for three years, but after that were renewed annually.

connected with attempted or successful assassinations, and that at the time the population already numbered nearly 100 million. Compared to the size of the population and the powers of legal and police repression that the regime had at its disposal, the repression seems disproportionate, and all the more so since the state had other means at its disposal.

One of the most significant from this point of view was the reform of the education system. Those in power had realized that the schools and universities were breeding grounds for new elites who would not be satisfied with the existing order. The primary schools were placed under the moral authority of the Holy Synod. Entry to the secondary schools was made more difficult for the children of the underprivileged classes, in order to avoid creating discontent, and the number of pupils was generally reduced by raising the fees. The curriculum was purged of subjects thought to be too progressive in favor of traditional ones like classical languages, grammar, and religion. Finally, the universities lost their autonomy, and higher education for women was drastically reduced.

It is easy to understand why this last highly discriminatory measure was taken: the terrorist movement had been notable for the participation of a large number of women.[9] Often daughters of the petty nobility, or even of members of the upper administration, these women, far from playing a minor role, had carried out assassination attempts themselves, and sometimes also organized them. Vera Figner, Vera Zasulich, Sofia Perovskaya—the list of names that has come down to us is a long one. The wives of the Decembrists who had courageously supported their husbands and shared their exile still conformed to a traditional female role. The distance covered in the space of half a century between them and the Populists was remarkable. It was true that the empress had, in 1857, supported the creation of a grammar school for girls. From this school the girls had flocked to the university and, above all, to the Academy of Medicine, which was then under the responsibility of the War Ministry. When the authorities, unhappy with the

---

9. A document from the Ministry of the Interior calculated that the number of women taking part in revolutionary activities in the years 1878–87 was 166 out of a total of 1,083 known revolutionaries.

political activities of these women students, tried to close the doors of the universities to them, they chose exile, moving to Zürich to continue the studies they had abandoned in Russia. Educated, determined to play a role, frustrated in their desire for emancipation by the restrictive measures of Alexander II, from the mid-1860s these women found an outlet for their hopes and a compensation for their disappointments in revolutionary action. It is significant that the first woman to be executed for political reasons was one of these revolutionaries, Sofia Perovskaya. For the government—and it was not mistaken on this point—this female militance went far beyond the scandal represented by terrorism, and beyond these women gaming with death, so contrary to the classic notion of woman-liness. What was truly shocking was the motive that pushed these women to show that they could kill and die like men: beyond revolution, they were seeking total emancipation. The regime's response was to try to bar their way to knowledge and qualifications, in an attempt to force them back into their traditional roles.

But it would be unfair to reduce Alexander III's reign to nothing but repression, even if this was its main feature. He realized that economic modernization was vital if Russia was to occupy her true place in the community of nations. Through it the country might perhaps find the path to social harmony. In 1892, the appointment of Count Witte to the Ministry of Finance was to give a boost to this plan for modernization. From the early years of the new century it was apparent how quickly this policy bore fruit. This was a strange combination of repression—which included a worsening in the situation of the Jews and increased pressure on any group other than Orthodox and on the minority nationalities—and modernizing vision. Yet it managed, in the short term, to achieve the hoped-for effect: terrorism retreated before a state that had once again become strong.

The survivors of the repression of 1881 were forced to ask: what is to be done? Killing the tsar clearly served no purpose, failing utterly to rouse public opinion in such a way as to bring it over to the side of revolution. Furthermore, the new tsar, who derived his legitimacy solely from the doctrine of autocracy and the exercise of power, seemed less vulnerable to such a plan than his father, who had still embodied the religious beliefs of society. When

Alexander II was killed it did not occur to anyone to suppose that it might have been a false death, that he might reappear and point to another way to his people. The man who sat on the throne was the true tsar, precisely because he was there and because he held the temporal power. It was no longer a dream or a myth that needed to be rooted out; society had to be detached from a whole political system. Few terrorists now looked back to the old style of action; the majority of those who dreamed of change were once again to wrestle with the problem of how to involve society in the revolutionary struggle.

It seemed as if the time for assassination attempts had passed. Alexander III was never seriously threatened except once, on March 1, 1887, when a last handful of terrorists tried to reenact the murder of his father. This attempt, its failure, the trial that followed, and the executions that took place on May 5, 1887, are chiefly remembered for one fact: one of the five terrorists put to death that day was called Dmitri Ulyanov. Thirty years later, his younger brother, under the name of Lenin, was to complete the revolutionary plan that had obsessed his brother.

After 1881, those who wished to change Russia concerned themselves with analyzing the types of struggle used so far and the new perspectives opening up. With the development of his weapons of repression, Alexander III had exposed the terrorists' weakness. From the moment that the state ceased to hesitate before defending itself, the terrorists were forced onto the defensive, with the hunters becoming the hunted. Cut off from a society that did not yet accept the idea that the life of the sovereign could be attacked, and with no possibility of expanding their movement, the terrorists needed to rethink their response.

It was clear that Russia in the late 1880s had come a long way since the reign of Alexander II. Industrialization was bringing its economic, but also its social, fruits. Might there not be a possibility of creating from the rural and urban masses—uncertain of the future and, in an ever-changing present, unable to recognize the old political and social certainties—a people who were conscious that the existing political order had no answer to their disarray and their difficulties? Despite the lingering nostalgia of a few terrorists or their allies who continued to insist that regicide was a necessary precondition for social action and who glorified those who attempted it—such as Stepniak Kravchinsky[10] or the Ukrainian Dragomanov—there was a growing awareness of the impotence or uselessness of terrorism.

"The supporters of political assassination are only rarely aware of the fact that it is only the powerlessness of the revolution that gives terrorism its strength in Russia," wrote Lev Tikhomirov after his break with the movement. He added:

> Political assassinations have been able to upset the government as long as it thought that it was facing a threatening force. Having realized that this threat was nothing more than a handful of individuals who were playing at political murder with scarcely the strength to do anything really dangerous, the government, in my opinion, ceased to show the slightest sign of confusion. Though the private lives of the emperor and the various government figures attracting the terrorists' hostility may be poisoned by the ever-present possibility of an attempt to kill them . . . terrorism has little positive effect. By contrast, it has negative effects, at the bottom, on the revolutionaries themselves, and everywhere its influence is felt; terrorism teaches contempt for society, people and country. . . .

With Alexander III, the sovereign of counterreform, the state seemed to have recovered, saved from the constant fear of murder that had hung over those who governed it. Theoreticians of intransigent authority and an autocracy that was totally unyielding to popular aspirations, like Konstantin Pobedonostsev, were able to congratulate themselves on having won the battle waged by the terrorists against the tsar, ending a situation in which, in the words of Stepniak Kravchinsky, the terrorist had become a hero "as proud

---

10. "The terrorists could not overthrow the government, or influence it from outside Russia. But they could force it to neglect everything else in the struggle to deal with terrorism, thus making life for the government impossible," writes Sergei Stepniak Kravchinsky in *La Russie souterraine*.

as Satan when he rebelled against God . . . but a temporal god very different from the Jehovah of Moses! a trembling god who tried to hide himself from the courageous hands of the terrorists. . . ."

Like the statue of Peter the Great dominating St. Petersburg, the image of the triumphant tsar seemed to dominate the Russian people once again. Those who had hitherto seen terrorism as a way of throwing the state into confusion and bringing it down now anxiously asked themselves if the period of terrorism had been in vain. Might it not even have reinforced the bonds between the sovereign and his people, making them more conscious of their basic loyalty to God's representative on earth since he had been threatened? After the clashes of the previous decade, the "fish's head" had emerged practically intact. What was to be done? The theoreticans looked again at the masses and wondered how to persuade them once more to enter into a struggle that would, once and for all, rid them of a hated power. For a few years, Russia appeared to settle into immobility, a silent confrontation of power and those who dreamed of ending it.

For both sides, it was important to gain time. The regime needed time to recover from its internal wounds and reestablish its external power. Its enemies needed time to effect the in-depth education of the masses. It was a deceptive immobility and uneven in its effects. Russia's entry into the industrial era was alienating ever larger groups of society from the regime, whether because it gave them greater independence or because they were paying the price for it. Autocracy and industrialization cannot advance at the same speed, and police repression was finding it increasingly difficult to hold down the rumbling of discontent that was already announcing the coming century and its demands. The industrial age and a changing Russia could not make do with a few incomplete and unfinished reforms. A radical change in the government and its relations with society had become essential. The Russian state, at the end of the nineteenth century, was more of an oddity than ever. A European state, a police state, it had to go through the stages of its evolution. But how could this be accomplished, when the smallest concession threatened to revive the struggle and expose all the contradictions lying beneath the surface of national cohesion?

Realizing this difficulty, the government desperately buttressed up its rigid structures, ever widening the gulf separating it from a social reality in constant flux. The final crisis was to arrive very rapidly. Like all historic crises, it was to involve much bloodshed. Violence is never absent for long in Russian history.

10

The Death Throes
of Terrorism

♦

In 1887, three years after the attempted assassination of Alexander III, Lev Tikhomirov, the great theoretician of *Zemlia i volia,* made public his assessment of terrorist action. This assessment took the form of a break with the movement, but the content inevitably hastened the demoralization of the whole movement which, since 1881, had been forced to face up to its isolation and the pointlessness of its actions. Some sections of this indictment of the use of terrorism are worth studying:

> Terrorism as an instrument of political struggle is either impotent or superfluous. It is impotent if the revolutionaries do not have the means to overthrow the government; it is superfluous if they do have the means. From the point of view of political change, terrorism has little positive effect. It has negative effects, at bottom, on the revolutionaries themselves and everywhere its influence is felt. Terrorism teaches contempt for people, society, and country; it teaches the spirit of voluntarism, incompatible with any social regime. From the moral point of view, what power can be worse than the power of one man over another? . . . Oh, I well know that we shall hear:
>
> > And tear the crown from the despot
> > And give it to the people. . . .
>
> But the people do not want the crown; on the contrary, they demonstrate that they are always ready to crack the skulls of the "liberators." Only revolutionary romanticism allows the latter to treat the sovereign as if

he were a vulgar usurper. The Russian tsar did not steal his power, he received it from his ancestors, elected with due solemnity. . . . So who is the tyrant? The tsar or the men who, although perfectly aware that they represent a tiny minority, permit themselves to kill the representative of the people, the person whom the law recognizes as above the law, whom the church of this country, recognized by the majority of the population, consecrates with the title of secular head of the church?

The terrorists had already understood the central point of this evaluation. The people did not support the attempts on the life of their sovereign. Although perhaps not the sacred figure of former times—of the saint-prince or the "pious prince"—he was still legitimate, deriving his legitimacy from the existence of tsars through the centuries; he was the people's memory, the outcome of a regular succession, the living confirmation of the links with the church. Furthermore, although the tsar had been killed, nothing had changed in Russia, unless it was the increased dictatorial authority imposed by his successor, Alexander III. In the eyes of the people, everything confirmed the permanence of the tsar and his authority.

Despite this depressing realization, the debate that was renewed at the end of the nineteenth century on violence and murder differed from that of the preceding decades. Russia had changed profoundly, even if people's ideas had not yet caught up with altered conditions in the economy and way of life. In order to understand this debate, it is necessary to take a brief look at the state of the country at the transition from the nineteenth to the twentieth century.

A Changing Society

The contours of a new society were defined above all by economic change. The development of the railroads, which were to double in length between 1892 and 1904, corresponded to the expansion of the industrial areas and encouraged development in Siberia and the easternmost parts of the country. The state owned two-thirds of the 37,500 miles of track and encouraged the iron industry to supply it with the necessary materials. Industry, an obsession with the government, underwent a revolution. Industrial output doubled in the last ten years of the nineteenth century and made Russia into the fourth largest industrial country in the world. But there were negative aspects to this change, most importantly the massive influx of foreign capital on which Witte, the finance minister, had largely relied, while hoping that it would be only a temporary measure, for it would otherwise threaten the country's economic independence. Agriculture was another source of wealth, despite the bad harvests of the early 1880s and in 1891–93 (when the crisis was worldwide). Nevertheless, spectacular progress was made and agricultural exports—particularly cereals—guaranteed Russian foreign trade a continuous development and a surplus balance. This spectacular economic revolution had equally important social repercussions. The first indication was an increase in population and a change in the balance between town and country. In 1900, with the birthrate up by 45 percent, the population of the empire was 130 million. The towns grew: there were twenty with over 100,000 inhabitants and 13 percent of the population were town-dwellers. This change had a high social cost that was to affect all sectors of society.

In the country, the landowners and peasants were confused. Although agricultural production was increasing, the price of cereals in the world market was falling as a result of competition. The landowners saw their estates shrink and their incomes dwindle and had to sell out to the entrepreneurs—universally disliked upstarts who came to represent a new class of country landowner. Chekhov's *Cherry Orchard* gives a graphic picture of these changes. The condition of the ordinary peasant had considerably worsened. An average family had at most five acres of land, and lacked the most obvious necessities—draft horses and equipment. Their rent increased and so did their debts. The increase in the rural population made itself felt in the huge increase in the number of landless peasants who had only their labor to offer. These were the *batrak*. Traditional hand-crafted goods, made and sold by the peasant to supplement his income and occupy the long periods of inactivity imposed by the endless Russian winter, lost ground in the face of the competition from cheaper and more attractive industrial goods.

In 1891, this decline in the status of the peasants was exacerbated by the famine that caused thousands of deaths and exposed the precarious nature of Russian progress. The government attempted to stabilize the situation in the country areas. The Bank for the Nobility established in 1885, which made many loans at a low rate of interest, attempted to rescue the struggling landowners and preserve their lands intact. In fact, it was to be the speculators who made use of these loans. The Peasant Land Bank, created at about the same time, was intended to help the peasants enlarge their plots of land, but the high interest on the loans merely drove the peasants into further debt. On average, 80 percent of peasant income was absorbed in the repayment of debts arising out of the emancipation of 1861 or subsequent land purchases.

In the towns too there was a new and equally volatile situation. Thirty-one percent of the workforce was employed in 2 percent of the highly concentrated industrial enterprises. Giant factories often employing more than 10,000 workers were chiefly grouped in a few large centers. This double concentration, both geographical and functional, led to a rapid expansion of the pro-letariat. The situation of this new social class, newly arrived from the country, cut off from its roots, and not yet integrated into urban life, was anything but enviable. The primitive housing where the workers were crammed together, taking turns to sleep, anticipates the living conditions of immigrant workers in the late twentieth century. The adult working day was from twelve to fifteen hours; children between twelve and fifteen were legally supposed to work only eight hours, but this was often ignored, while many much younger children worked in the factories. The wages were miserable: a woman earned only two-thirds of a man's wage, which was already low; a child received only a third. Female and child labor, which cost next to nothing, was common in certain areas, particularly that of textiles. It is easy to imagine the human tragedy of industrializa-tion when we remember that these low wages were constantly being reduced by the fines handed out at the slightest excuse, while the employers frequently announced cuts in rates of pay.

In the country, the peasants erupted sporadically, murdering in forests landowners coming to claim what was owed them. In the towns, the workers' discontent was expressed in the waves of strikes, such as that of 1896 which paralyzed the entire textile industry for weeks. There were a few reforms: in 1886, it was forbidden to make women and children work at night, and a body of factory inspectors was established; in 1897, the working day was restricted to eleven-and-a-half hours. Witte was aware of the workers' growing discontent and tried desperately to halt it. But these reforms were insufficient in the face of the increasing frustration of the workers and the crisis at the beginning of the century when a number of factories were forced to close, leaving their workers unemployed.

The years 1900–1903 were ones of general agitation in Russia. The crisis hit both town and country, where new ideas were beginning to penetrate a society that had been profoundly changed by the speed of economic change and torn away from its age-old certainties. The situation of Russian society at this time was certainly not unusual and Russia was not the only country to undergo such a crisis, but in its case, two specific features appear. First, the lateness, brutality, and immensity of the changes: like everything in Russia, modernization was more excessive than elsewhere, both in its success—in the extent and duration of the upward curve—and in the suffering it inflicted on its people. Industrial development, always a painful process, was more than usually so in Russia. Second, these changes coincided with the great political debate and the disarray of the erstwhile terrorists.

It began to become apparent that perhaps, in a transformed Russia, with society in turmoil and confusion, this might be the moment to turn to the helpless masses and, with their help, change the political system, rather than attempting to provide a substitute for them and trying to resolve the problem with naked violence. A remarkable ferment among the intellectuals arose along with the social agitation. Both were reinforced by the discontent in a group that had hitherto lain outside this general fever—the administrative elites of the *zemstvos*.

These assemblies, the result of the administrative reforms carried out by Alexander II in 1864, existed on several levels.[1] Elected every three years by the various categories of voters, they dealt with all problems concerning local economic and social life,

---

1. The district *zemstvos* were elected by the landowners (45 percent of the seats) and the peasants (40 percent), the rest being divided between other categories. The provincial *zemstvos* were elected by the district assemblies.

under the control of government representatives. In spite of reduced means and increased controls, the *zemstvos* had the double merit of introducing society to a kind of democratic participation and offering it the means for local self-administration. The importance of this germ of political experience is obvious. Most important, the *zemstvos* employed a large number of people (47,000 in 1900), consisting of people of all callings, such as teachers, agronomists, doctors, statisticians, and midwives, who felt themselves to be in the service of the assemblies, and thus of the voters, rather than of the monarchy or the state. Thus a parallel service to that of the state was created, with parallel loyalties. Many liberals who wished to distance themselves from the state without, for all that, taking sides with the opposition found employment in this service. This "army of social progress" sought to modernize not only techniques but also attitudes, particularly in the countryside, and tried to reduce state intervention to a minimum. It represented an alternative method of serving the people to that of the Populists; the aim, however, was the same—to emancipate them.

As social tension increased, the *zemstvos* became highly suspect in the eyes of the government on account of the liberalism of those who used the asssemblies to exercise a social influence, because of their opposition to the bureaucracy which they tried to outflank in all areas, and because of the automatic criticism of autocracy implied by the electoral process and self-administration. For this reason a law was introduced in 1890 modifying the system set up by Alexander II, increasing the number of nobles participating in the *zemstvos* in relation to the other social categories (57 percent), and giving the governors greater authority over these assemblies.[2] To go back on reforms a quarter of a century after introducing them, when they had become a habitual part of social life, producing their own elites and a particular type of social relations, was completely unacceptable to those who had grown up within the framework of this system. The law of 1890 radicalized the local elites, leading them to the conclusion that the government was incapable of any

---

2. In 1892, the same rigor was applied to the municipal reform of the towns dating from 1870, eliminating two-thirds of the electors through changes to the electoral roll.

lasting reform, and that it was thus necessary to impose by force what reason had failed to make permanent. Despite a spectacular economic boom, the social situation was increasingly insecure. Everywhere could be heard again the eternal question, silenced or muffled for a moment by the failures of the terrorists between 1881 and 1900—what was to be done?

A Return to Terrorism

While the sovereign and his counselors, reassured by the increasingly rare assassination attempts and the apparent eclipse of the terrorists, were congratulating themselves on the success of their policy of increased severity, the debate on change and the role of violence was developing and taking on new dimensions.

This is not the place to reiterate the history of the revolutionary movement. Suffice it to remember the ideas that were to divide the more European Marxists, fiercely westernized, from those who wanted to follow a path more adapted to the situation in Russia. The former had encountered Marxism in their places of exile, particularly in Switzerland. Here Plekhanov, Axelrod, Vera Zasulich, who had moved away from terrorism, and Deutsch founded the Group for the Emancipation of Labor in 1883. They wanted to spread the ideas of Marx in Russia, against those of the Populists. They were certain of one thing: Russia was not a special case, and a special Russian path was not acceptable. Russia was part of the West, its development would follow the same route and, in the industrial era, it would be the working class that would play the leading role in history. The most significant figure in this movement, Plekhanov, violently condemned Tkachev's ideas, his organization, and his authoritarian and violent methods. In Russia, no doubt, those who were in contact with social reality—the condition of the peasants, the weakness of the working class, and the power of the autocracy—were inclined to seek a compromise between this intransigent Marxism and an adaptation to the reality of the situation. This was to be the work, above all, of Lenin. He rejected

Plekhanov's view that the revolution was solely the daughter of progress, which had to be patiently awaited, and attempted to bridge the gap between orthodox Marxism and the heritage of Russian revolt. Aware of the special Russian situation, and not prepared to wait for time to take its course, Lenin took from Tkachev the theory of the role of the organization, the substitute for a working class that was still too weak to act for itself, and the holder of its class consciousness. Above all, he believed that only a revolutionary elite would be capable of the necessary brutal action, and that the value of the means used in the seizing of power could only be judged in the light of their effectiveness. Lenin rejected two traits from Russia's past: the moral aspect, which tried to separate good from evil in the name of the ultimate aim (revolutionary power); and the idea of the spontaneous uprising of the people, so dear to Bakunin and the Populists, to which Lenin preferred an organization. A born organizer himself, fascinated by the model offered by Prussian organization, Lenin challenged anarchy, individual action, and the solitary use of violence. Anything that was not planned by the organization—the party—could not, in his opinion, be effective.

It was to be revolutionary socialism that took up the torch let fall in 1881. This movement was the heir to Populism. Like Populism, it looked to peasant Russia, though it was also aware that the country had changed and that the movement should also include the working class and a new layer of society created by the new elites of the towns and the *zemstvos*, a new middle class.

At the time of the creation of the movement, in the last years of the century, several centers of activity and powerful personalities stood out. First we should mention a legendary woman—women having played such an important role, as we have seen, in political assassination—Ekaterina Breshkovskaya, who came to be known as the "grandmother of the revolution." This extraordinary 56-year-old woman had dedicated her life to the revolution at the age of nineteen and would continue to do so until her death in 1934. An army officer's daughter, she began, like the other young people of her generation and class, by "going to the people." As a result she was deported to Siberia in 1878. For years she was to escape repeatedly and then, when recaptured, start planning new escapes. Freed in 1896, she traveled the length and breadth of Russia, reviving the terrorist movement. From 1900, based in Saratov, she participated in the setting up of the Socialist Revolutionary Party and its terrorist organization. She is remembered for her tireless activity as an agitator and the revival of terrorism, recruiting many of its brightest hopes. Around this extraordinary woman gathered other leaders who were to enrich the movement with ideas—particularly Viktor Chernov—and principles of organization—like Mark Natanson, formerly involved with Nechayev.

These men and women, united in the certainty that Russian history had to pass through another period of terrorism, were based in several centers. First and foremost, there was Saratov, the stronghold of the Socialist Revolutionary Party, where the large peasantry and the members of the *zemstvos,* particularly shocked by the ultra-conservative measures taken at this time, provided the revolutionaries with favorable conditions. Important too was Minsk, where in 1897 another woman, Lyuba Rodyonova, set up a branch of the Socialist Revolutionary Party, building on the work done in the previous months by the "grandmother of the revolution." The traditional centers of agitation in the south, Odessa, Kharkov, Voronezh, and, further away, Minsk, together with the capital, were shortly to see a reemergence of the debate on terrorism. The need to use assassination and strike, if not at the head of the system, then at least at those who served it in order to feed the latent popular discontent with a new period of terrorism were all themes believed forgotten, which were not always favorably received, but which the powerful personality of Ekaterina Breshkovskaya managed to revive and make succeed.

As this network began to spread rapidly through Russia, contact was established or revived with the conspirators of the 1870s who were now refugees abroad, chiefly in Zürich and Paris. It was yet another woman, Sofia Ginzburg, who acted as liaison. The violence that had marked the end of the reign of Alexander II, the epic tradition of assassination attempts, came to fuel the temptation to take direct action felt by the Socialist Revolutionaries. The refugees were bored and, encouraged by the revival of terrorism in Russia, devoted themselves in turn to a revival of the activities for which they felt so nostalgic. Thus, in a Parisian suburb, Pyotr

Lavrov almost killed himself in the explosion of a bomb that he had made in a rented house.

In 1902, to increase its efficiency, the Socialist Revolutionary Party created a "combat organization." Having accepted the principle of a return to terrorism, and with the setting up of the organization, it now remained to define a strategy of revolution and terrorist activity, and to decide which social group would underpin the historic movement.

The great strategic problem facing the Socialist Revolutionaries had in fact two aspects. While the Social Democrats, the Bolsheviks, and the Mensheviks agreed on the leading role of the working class, they had to decide if the revolution could emerge from the peasantry. Equally, they had to decide if the revolution could be associated with terrorism, or if the two aspects were unconnected. It was around their view of the peasants, elaborated in the early years of the century in long debates and taking account of the general Marxist view, that the Socialist Revolutionary plan was eventually to take shape.

At the end of the nineteenth century, the passivity of the rural population had discouraged those who dreamed of a great uprising with which to integrate their plans. Now, in the space of two or three years, their ideas underwent a radical change. Only those who refused to hear could now ignore the dull, but increasingly frequent, rumblings coming from the countryside. It was clear that the growing difficulties and resentment of the peasants were beginning to create the "spontaneity" (stikhiinost') that had formerly given rise to the great movements lead by Stenka Razin and Pugachov.

For the Socialist Revolutionaries, heirs of the Populists— and thus of the idea that in the organization of its countryside Russia concealed the germ of a kind of primitive communism—the reconciliation of past and present dreams took place instantly. They did not, however, make the same mistake as their predecessors, knowing that the peasants would follow their own instincts and not "preachers" from outside. Nor did they ignore the influence in the country of the new intelligentsia that was emerging from the people—and often from the peasantry—and was working for its progress. At the beginning of the twentieth century, there was a link between the Socialist Revolutionaries and the countryside that had been lacking for the Populists. It was now possible for the movement to draw the peasantry behind it in its new course and embark on an entirely new campaign of terrorist action, based this time on popular support and understanding. The efforts of Breshkovskaya, the revered "grandmother," and of those inspired by her beliefs sought first of all to establish close links with this intelligentsia of the people, already won over to the idea of revolution, and, through them, to set up small groups whose chief function was to educate the peasants. The government had believed after 1864 that it would transform and stabilize the peasantry by sending this army of modernizers into the countryside; though it had not yet realized the extent of its mistake, the Socialist Revolutionaries, on the other hand, were ready to take advantage of it.

Their theories began to take shape. The countryside and its future were central to the plan for revolution. Communal ownership, the *obshchina* of ancient tradition, represented Russia's chance; it was to enable the idea of socialism to take root. Thanks to this system of primitive communism, the peasantry was in the situation of the proletariat and could thus take its place. It was exploited by the landowners and especially by the state which derived from the peasants' labor, through the various taxes and income from exports, the means for the industrialization of which the state was the chief beneficiary. In practice, in order that the plan might be understood by the peasants, it was necessary to put forward the policy of the socialization of all land—in other words, the use of the land for those who cultivated it. It was essential for the Socialist Revolutionaries to avoid private ownership of land and the creation of a peasant bourgeoisie. But the plan was not only economic. The heirs of the Populists visualized the rural world, in this communal arrangement, taking its future in its own hands. The corollary of the socialization of the land was the democratic development of the peasant commune and of *zemstvos* at all levels. Collective self-management and the equal distribution of land would provide a program which, for the Socialist Revolutionaries, would allow Russia to exploit to the full the social heritage of its unique history considered for so long a misfortune. In these years of feverish theorizing, Russia's special characteristics came to seem in their eyes—as they had formerly to the Slavophiles—a real opportunity.

Nevertheless, the Socialist Revolutionaries did not ignore

the rest of society. They considered that it was necessary to involve in the movement around the peasantry all the mounting social forces: workers, students—between 1899 and 1904, the universities were to become centers of revolutionary ideas and activity—and even soldiers. The Socialist Revolutionaries' objective of forming small groups of activists in all these social categories shows the extent to which their ideas were not merely theoretical but intended to create effective strategies and tactics.

Another hotly debated subject was that of the introduction of terrorism into the rural areas. In the context of the early years of the century, this seems surprising, but it anticipates with remarkable accuracy the revolutionary history of agrarian societies in the second half of the twentieth century. Should the spontaneous indignation of the peasants—the assassination of landowners, the burning of their properties, and the theft of their possessions—be channeled into an organized movement? To use modern terms, should civil war—or rather, guerrilla war—be brought to the countryside? In the course of these heated discussions, the faction in favor of rural violence gained a good many supporters. But the leadership of the movement saw danger in such a strategy. Peasant spontaneity was undeniably a remarkable force, but one that was difficult to control. History had shown that the peasants could follow unexpected leaders, whether false tsar or false revolutionary. They could equally well break up into many different movements, all with different aims. The Russian peasant's inherent anarchism that Bakunin prized so much might be a threat to the existing state, but it could equally well rebound against those who wished to get rid of the state. Having thus decided to reject a policy of terrorism in the rural areas, the Socialist Revolutionaries were haunted by the fear that such a movement might develop outside their influence. They realized that their problem would be to reconcile their wise choice—the rejection of rural terrorism—with a careful vigilance so that if such a movement did occur they would not be isolated.

Thus the debates among the heirs of Populism had brought them a long way in a short time, and provided them with what seemed like an admirably clear program and a strategy. In reality, they suffered from two important weaknesses.

First, despite the quality of their members, they lacked a

proper organization and discipline. It was this that Lenin was later to bring to his party. In this sense, the Socialist Revolutionaries were the true heirs to the tradition of the "student Pugachovs." Although remarkable speakers, they lacked contact with reality, even if they understood it to some extent. The "organizers" from Tkachev to Lenin, though effective, represented something new in an already unique situation. They were not part of the tradition of the intelligentsia, or, at most, only a distant branch of it.

The second weakness of the Socialist Revolutionaries lay in the strategy itself, which led to a political impasse. They wished to combine their strategy with a blow against authority—political murder. Realizing the dangers of associating the rural population with this, and yet at the same time needing to continue their activities among them, they were attempting to square the circle. In fact, there was only one clear direction open to them: a return to assassination.

Power under Siege

In 1901, exactly twenty years after the murder of Alexander II, the truce came to an end, ushering in a period where violence took a decisive part in the formation of Russian politics, even if the assassins no longer aimed at the top of the system but at those who surrounded the sovereign.

A detailed catalogue of the attempts of this period would make tedious reading. To be convinced of the return to a strategy of murder, we need only look at a few figures and representative examples. From the beginning of the century to the assassination of Stolypin in 1911, the Socialist Revolutionary Party killed almost 150 people. This figure should be seen in the context of a rising tide of violence, especially in the countryside and on the borders of the country, where the assassination of agents of the state and wealthy landowners became increasingly common. Political murders, intended to destabilize the state and stimulate the activism of the terrorists, were much fewer in number, but of far greater significance:

1901

Nikolai Bogolyepov, the education minister, is assassinated by a student, Pyotr Karpovich.

Konstantin Pobedonostsev, procurator of the Holy Synod, is wounded in an assassination attempt.

1902

Three attempts are made on the life of Dmitri Trepov, chief of police in Moscow, who escapes unharmed.

Dmitri Sipyagin, the interior minister, is killed in St. Petersburg by a student, Sergei Balmashov.

The military governor of Vilnius is shot and wounded by a Lithuanian terrorist.

Prince Obolensky, governor of Kharkov, escapes unharmed from two attempts on his life in the space of two months.

1903

N. Bogdanovich, governor of Ufa, is killed in Kiev by a student, Igor Dulebov.

1904

N. Bobrikov, governor-general of Finland, is killed by a student.

G. Bogoslovsky, governor of the Caucasus, is killed.

Vyacheslav Plehve, the interior minister, is killed in a bomb explosion in the capital.

1905

Grand Duke Sergei, uncle of Nicholas II and governor-general of Moscow, is assassinated.

Count Pavel Shuvalov, chief of police in Moscow, is killed.

1906

Mikhail Gertenshtain, a member of the Duma, is killed by an anti-Semite.

Pyotr Stolypin, the prime minister, escapes a bomb that causes fifty deaths.

Stolypin is killed at the Kiev opera house in the presence of the tsar.

This list, far from exhaustive, suggests several conclusions about this final phase of the strategy of murder intended to undermine the foundations of the existing power structure. First of all, the chronology is significant. The most intense phase is that from 1901 to 1905, peaking in the period 1904–5. This was the moment when the Socialist Revolutionaries, the chief participants in this strategy, turned their backs on their doubts and debates, deciding that by a policy of spectacular and repeated blows against the state they would be able to provoke the necessary reaction in the rural areas. After 1905–6, when the government made some political concessions and initiated some constitutional reform, the movement went into decline, and the only sensational murder was that of Stolypin. The years of the highest number of political murders coincided with a period of another form of violence, half-political and half-criminal, that came to light as a result of the commissions of enquiry sent at that time to the borders of the empire (particularly the Pahlen Commission). While in the center of the empire the terrorists were attacking the leaders, in the more remote areas individuals or small and elusive groups attacked state officials and landowners in the name of the oppressed. These Robin Hoods appeared all over Russia; the population identified with them and protected them. The state, at which these attempts were aimed, rarely succeeded in capturing these popular heroes who defied it and then vanished—like "fish in water," another anticipation of modern revolutionary tactics. Something would have to be done.

It is important to realize, however, that the terrorism of this period stayed within precise limits. Despite the noticeable change in the mood of the peasants, the attacks were not concentrated on the tsar, but on those who represented his authority. Learning from past experience, the terrorists still feared that by attacking the person of the tsar, they might provoke a wave of popular loyalty. By contrast, attacking the representatives of public order and state authority made it clear that the target was autocracy itself. Their objective was twofold: to put the regime on the defensive, to lay siege to it, thus forcing it into repression and thereby increasing its unpopularity. By aiming at the minister for police and the governors-general, they were also able to show society that public order, in the person of those who had charge of it, was precarious, and that it would take only a small push to topple it. Finally, the series of assassination attempts—since it had been decided to spare the sovereign—had the immense advantage of accustoming society to murder, blunting its feelings and capacity for indignation. Little by little, the belief in the sacred nature of the system began to be replaced by the idea that it should be brought down by murder.

It should not be forgotten that terrorism, with its harassment of the government and its social education, had very few policies for social reform. At no time was any attempt made to support a political movement emerging at this same period—the constitutional movement—whose importance could have been decisive for Russia. The liberals, organized around the economist Pyotr Struve and the historian Milyukov, spoke and wrote constantly about the urgent need for a move toward constitutionalism that would bring the political state of Russia into line with the rapid economic modernization. For them, Russia had, in the space of a few years, gone through all the stages separating it from the rest of Europe; the political revolution would complete this evolution, the intellectual situation making it inadvisable to delay. From 1902, many social organizations—committees of teachers, doctors, a congress of *zemstvos* (1904) and, above all, a union that gathered together all these organizations—organized congresses and demanded reforms. These years punctuated with political murders were also years of an extraordinary "political spring" when a society that was just waking up to the need for democracy met in groups of all kinds to make its voice heard and its will known: a constitution and civil liberty. In theory the autocracy was intact. It even used repressive measures against these very varied movements, whose activities ranged from political murder to banditry to the holding of legal congresses. In practice, a new society was beginning to take form, a challenge to the autocracy and a denial of it. Like autocracy, terrorism ignored society's march toward democratization; political reform was of no interest to it, obsessed as it was with the destruction of the regime.

Thus it was that the revolution of 1905 and the political concessions that resulted—basic laws and the creation of the Duma—too timid for the radicalism of the Socialist Revolutionaries, had little effect on the development of their movement. In fact, they boycotted the elections—the electoral law in force at the election of the first Duma was moderately democratic[3]—showing how little interest they had in the attempts at political reform taking place at that time.

The Use of Terror

Thus we see that although the number of attempts at assassination declined after 1906, it was not the result of a link between political developments in Russia and the strategy of the terrorists. It was because the Socialist Revolutionary movement, and particularly its most active agents, were going through a profound crisis. The efforts of the Russian state to infiltrate the revolutionary groups had succeeded in deeply troubling their ranks. Once again, the terrorists wondered about the contradictions in their movement, its aims, and the difficult matter of who was manipulating whom. These problems were inherent in the revived strategy of terrorism. However, a closer look at some of the assassination attempts carried out at that time sheds some light on the new and characteristic features of the movement in the years preceding the revolution of 1917.

The first action worthy of note is the assassination in 1901 of the minister Bogolyepov, for it marked the return to the use of murder. The shots fired at point-blank range on the education minister on February 14 were, in a way, a repetition of the shots fired at Trepov by Vera Zasulich in 1878. Like her, Pyotr Karpovich was arrested, but far from emerging as the hero of the trial, the murderer was condemned to twenty years' hard labor (though he did not complete his sentence, managing to escape six years later). The personality of the assassin is not without significance. This Pyotr Karpovich was of petty bourgeois origin. There had been a noticeable move downward in the social scale in the intelligentsia over a

---

3.   Universal suffrage for men over twenty-five who were taxpaying landowners or tenants; indirect suffrage and representation of citizens divided into four categories: landowners, peasants, townspeople, and workers. The national minorities voted separately.

period of a quarter-century. Nevertheless, he was a true "student Pugachov," having been educated at the university in Moscow until he was expelled for subversive activities. When he shot at the minister responsible for the universities, like Vera Zasulich before him he wished to express condemnation of the excesses committed against the students.

Agitation in Russian universities since the turn of the century had resulted in a kind of "May 1968," but one that continued for several years, in a more tragic form against a background of political debate, and resulted in measures of a draconian repressiveness. The students who were expelled from the universities were sent to the army to be "disciplined"—a further proof of the blindness of the authorities. Far from calming their revolutionary ardor, these measures reinforced it, and they spent their time in the army sowing discontent. The Russo-Japanese War was to show that their efforts had not been in vain. Having taken refuge abroad after his expulsion from the university, Karpovich was so outraged by the measures imposed on the students that he decided to take revenge by assassinating the author of these measures. In 1901, the Socialist Revolutionary movement had not yet finalized its strategy; thus the shooting of Bogolyepov was an individual decision. The reemergence of terrorism depended on the isolated desire of certain individuals to use it, and on their certainty that there was no other way.

The case of Plehve, blown to pieces by a bomb in 1904, is quite different. The unpopularity of the interior minister was widespread, both among society in general and in the upper classes. To his natural harshness was added his responsibility, recognized by everyone, for the terrible massacre of the Jews of Kishinev in April 1903. This hated man, whose unabashed anti-Semitism shocked the entire intelligentsia, was the obvious choice for an assassination. From the autumn of 1903, he was "condemned to death," and plans to kill him multiplied. Among those who took an active part—this fact alone shows the importance of the target—was one of the most brilliant members of the Socialist Revolutionary movement, Boris Savinkov, who took charge of the operation. It was on his advice that it was decided to use a bomb, more reliable than the bullets of a gun. As much detailed preparation went into the months of planning for the attempt as had been devoted to the plan to assassinate

Alexander II in 1881, and equally many operatives were used. From Karpovich's isolated attempt to this assassination, so carefully and slowly prepared, there had been a development in the movement. Terrorism was now used with a collective understanding of the cause and a precise preparation.

Another complicated case was that of the assassination of Grand Duke Sergei in 1905. It took place at a time of exceptional terrorist activity, when the terrorists were occupied with preparations for the assassination of several potential victims: Trepov, the successor to Plehve, Muraviev, the minister for justice, the governor-general of Kiev and lastly, Grand Duke Vladimir Alexandrovich and Grand Duke Sergei. Nothing came of this frenzy of activity, however, for the plans were uncovered one by one by the police—helped by informers and double agents—and also because of the clumsiness of the conspirators. Only Savinkov, who led a strong group in Moscow—some like Dora Brilliant having proved themselves the previous year in the Plehve assasination—was able to complete his plan. On February 4, 1905, a bomb thrown at Grand Duke Sergei's carriage literally ripped it to pieces. The thrower of the bomb, Kaliayev, was arrested, condemned to death, and executed three months later, although he had previously received the forgiveness of the grand duke's widow—a scene immortalized by Albert Camus in his play *Les Justes* (The Just). This scene is revealing of the whole political history of Russia, where victim and murderer, murder and forgiveness are as one, where terrorism is bathed in a religious atmosphere, in a constant reference to the spiritual never abandoned since the earliest times.

But this assassination of the tsar's uncle—and also his chief adviser—signaled a change. Once again, the monarchy was no longer unassailable; the murder had happened very close to the person of the man who was protected by popular loyalty. A certain indifference in public opinion together with the forgiveness of the grand duchess revealed the extent of the decay of the imperial myth. Thus it was that the terrorists, meeting in 1907 to decide who should be their next target, opted first for the new prime minister, Stolypin. They prepared carefully for this attempt but then suspended the plan in favor of an attempted assassination of the tsar and Grand Duke Nicholas Nikolaievich. The bomb placed under the train in which the grand duke was traveling on February 13, 1907, was discovered just in time by a railroad worker. The attempt on the life of the tsar planned for the same time collapsed, thanks to the police whose agents had infiltrated into the heart of the plot. Police "entryism" into the revolutionary movement was then at its height.

In August 1907 a court-martial in St Petersburg tried twenty-eight terrorists. Three of them, accused of the attempted murder of the tsar and the grand duke, were condemned to death; hard labor and banishment were handed out to the rest. It seemed as if the movement had run out of steam.

There remained its last and constant target: Stolypin. A victim of some sort was needed, and Stolypin was the obvious choice because his plans for the transformation of rural life were cutting the ground from under the feet not only of the Socialist Revolutionary movement but of the entire revolutionary movement. His policy for the maintenance of law and order was harsh: eighty-two regions were put under a state of emergency; there was an increase in the number of courts-martial which operated without reference to common law;[4] a considerable number of newspapers were banned and their contributors arrested. These policies have contributed two expressions to the language that are still used today: "Stolypin carriages," which took prisoners into exile, and "Stolypin necktie" (the hangman's noose). Unquestionably, terrorism retreated—except from its pursuit of the prime minister himself, in which it was to triumph.

But there was another side to Stolypin. He had understood the aspirations of the country areas, had dismantled the rural commune (*mir*) so hated by the peasants, and had attempted to create a class of independent farmers whose individual efforts would ensure prosperity. He hoped to construct a stable basis for society on this private ownership—the dream of every peasant—and restore confidence in the political system. Aware that reforms need time to succeed, he had allowed himself two decades in which to accomplish all the necessary stages. Initially, between 1903 and 1909, progress was rapid, but soon the process began to slow down. Nevertheless,

---

4. Although only in force for two months, they had time to pronounce 1,000 death sentences.

it was enough to disturb socialists of all tendencies—and this is confirmed by Lenin—even if, at the end of the day, they were to rejoice at its consequences. Capitalism in the countryside brought about social diversification, with the proletarianization of a large section of the peasantry and the radicalization of those excluded from the reform. Stolypin's agrarian reform, based on an idea that was essentially fair, needed more time, and the lack of time meant that discontent increased, as is usual with all fundamental reforms. Stolypin had not, however, skimped on the provision for his reforms: loans from the Peasant Land Bank, inducements to encourage the colonization of Siberia, and above all an attempt to provide technical and academic training for the peasants. This complex man earned the hatred, for various reasons, of both the left and the right of the Duma as well as the minority national groups who offended his passionate nationalism. He had to go. He had managed until now to escape unharmed from the attempts on his life (in 1906, an explosion in his house had caused thirty-two deaths and a large number of wounded, including two of his children). Now his luck ran out: on September 14, 1911, a dubious character—half-terrorist and half-provocateur—named Bogrov finally succeeded in killing him in the middle of a performance at the Kiev Opera.

The Last Terrorists

By 1911, political murder was an outmoded form of action. Russia was entering a period of upheaval in which this type of operation had little place, and police infiltration in terrorist circles made their continuation impossible. Was this the moment for revolution to take over from assassination? Before attempting to answer this question, we should take a last look at the figures, from Vera Zasulich to Karpovich, who feature in this period of murder aimed at the tyrant or his servants.

It is not only terrorism that is hard to describe. It is equally difficult to understand these individuals who devoted their entire lives—often risking them without hesitation—to this policy of murder. This is partly because of the diversity of their characters, their fates, and their motives, and partly because of the evolution of the movement.

The part played in the terrorist movement by women has already been commented upon, a part that was to be one of its characteristics until the very eve of revolution. If it is mentioned again here, it is because the role played by women sheds light on the complexity of the ideas and aspirations dominating the whole enterprise. To a greater degree than elsewhere or at other times, the situation of women and their place in society were problems closely linked to hopes for revolution. Perhaps this was because in Russia the position of women was particularly difficult.

At various moments in its history, women had ruled Russia, and with great authority. From Olga in Kiev to Catherine II, their ability to govern alone—their lovers being no more than ornaments, rarely having any influence—was remarkable. But at the same time, these periods of female rule were set into a tradition where women were shut up in separate enclosures. Eventually the dynastic laws were to be successful in keeping them permanently away from the throne. This permanent contradiction explains why, when an emerging political consciousness focused on the emancipation of the peasants, educated women enlarged the concept to include female emancipation. Elisaveta Kovalskaya, who from 1871 was active in the Chaikovskist movement to educate the emerging working class, writes in her memoirs—a document of exceptional interest—of the difficulty in the relations between the two sexes in the movement and of the conclusions that her women companions drew from this. When she joined the movement with some other women including Sofia Perovskaya, they all noticed the men's reluctance to accept them, the current idea being that women should be in a separate group.

And yet this was just the time when women from the upper classes—Perovskaya was the daughter of a general—or from the families of small landowners or peasants who had come up in the world through trade and industrialization were wanting to be accepted as equals in society—first to learn and then to act. The list, gleaned from published or private memoirs, of their names is endless. Rebelling against their lives in the delightful but limited world of the family and artistic accomplishments, they devoted themselves passionately to the acquisition of the most practical and modern skills—medicine, science, and economics. Through these studies they were able to become part of the emerging intelligentsia. Elisaveta Kovalskaya became convinced that the cause of the emancipation of the serfs had an extra significance for her fellow women: while the condition of the peasants was certainly a reproach to the whole of society, why, when there were hopes of a radical change, should women not also be liberated from a more insidious but equally crushing servitude?

The women who invaded first the Populist movement and then the terrorist groups had strong and diverse personalities. There were the dazzling daughters of privileged society, who wanted for nothing, like Sofia Perovskaya, Vera Figner, and her sister Lydia, young and beautiful women, well educated, whose appearance indicated a life of ease. Then there was a figure like the "grandmother of the revolution," Ekaterina Breshkovskaya, the living symbol of the long struggle, on whom all depended as on a supreme judge. While the young women publicly slapped ministers' faces and unhesitatingly shot them, and two women—Vera Zasulich and Sofia Perovskaya—showed that women were prepared to dare all, the "grandmother" retained a moral authority over the long fight. It should not be forgotten that behind the romance of the assassin's bullet there lay the reality that followed: prison, hard labor, despair, and sometimes suicide—all accepted as the price of freedom. But history was to prove unkind. Although the revolution, in which women had so long played a role, was immediately to grant them equal rights, it gave such an unimportant place to this equality in political life that further thought should have been given to women's real emancipation and to the fruits of a struggle in which they had been in the forefront.

Pitiless to their victims, these men and women terrorists were equally pitiless with themselves. More important in their morality, however, than the courage to risk their own lives was the inevitable twin notion of sin and expiation. The terrorists were driven to take action by the idea of collective guilt, undeterred by the thought that, as the price of this guilt, and in order to bring a hated social order to an end, they would have to take the life of those condemned by the movement. For all that, they did not see themselves as innocent. Whatever the political justification for the murder they committed, it was for them still a murder, the inexcusable—if indispensable—crime of taking a human life. The crime implied expiation.

This essentially moral basis, common to all Russian terrorism—with the exception of Nechayev, needless to say—distinguishes the terrorists from those who, after the revolution, were to succeed them in the use of terror. For these young fanatics, the end did not justify the means or change a murder into an acceptable act; it called down punishment on its head. The judgment they brought to bear on their actions was harrowing and implacable. Spurred on by an internal necessity, they were nevertheless fully aware of the horror of their behavior, which brought them down to the same level as those whom they killed. To kill another, even if he be the greatest of criminals, is to identify with him. The terrorists had no doubts—their hand did not tremble at the moment for action—but they suffered before the act and willingly accepted their own deaths. Vera Zasulich, after shooting General Trepov, did not attempt to run—quite the opposite. She could not have known the unexpected turn that her trial was to take. Dora Brilliant, who took part in the attempt on the life of Plehve, said unambiguously: "We are murderers. I must die too." Perhaps the most telling illustration of this internal conflict and demanding moral code is provided by Kaliayev, whose bomb killed Grand Duke Sergei in 1905. He refused a pardon because he found in death both absolution for his murder and his life's fulfillment.

To stress these characteristics peculiar to Russian terrorism is not, of course, to glorify it. But it needs to be understood. The Russian terrorists of this period were not intellectuals steeped in abstract ideas. They bear witness to the strangeness of Russian history, its unique culture, and the spirituality that still pervaded the collective consciousness when faced with political and social problems. They were neither desperadoes nor irresponsible people, and they paid with their own lives for the lives they took. After them was to come a time of a more political and less moral attitude to change and the ways of achieving it. Terrorism was to take on a different meaning for those who would use it in future. In this respect the murder of Stolypin and the beginning of the period of the political revolution were moments that marked a decisive break with the past.

We come now to the most painful chapter in the history of terrorism, when it lost its bearings and confusion suddenly reigned in the movement. It was infiltrated by the police and it became increasingly difficult to tell the manipulator from the manipulated. Faced with the increase in terrorism, Alexander II's successors had realized that repression was of little use and that the best weapon against the terrorist was a police organization capable of infiltrating the groups with its agents.

It was Sergei Zubatov, the first modern policeman of Russia, who understood, well in advance of his time, the struggle against subversion. At the age of little more than thirty, this man had, at the end of the century, been made responsible for the special section of the Okhrana. He completely transformed this institution, introducing young men of a high caliber, weaving a police net that was to cover the whole empire. He was given the task of fighting subversion, and he brought to it new ideas and modern methods, including the fingerprinting and photographing of all suspects. His agents penetrated all parts of society, particularly those sections opposed to the system, in order to carry out this task. An admirer of Bismarck, Zubatov believed that the state could be the engineer of a kind of monarchical socialism, and that the state's leaders were in a position to take over and channel the people's aspirations into their policies. Zubatov's success in the training of the emerging working class was at least as great as his success in the complex task of infiltrating the terrorist movement with his *agents provocateurs*. The latter was a difficult business on account of the many ramifications of the movement, its clandestine nature, and the natural suspiciousness of its members. Nevertheless, from 1902, the police were able to penetrate the Socialist Revolutionaries' Combat Section. Since the 1880s the Okhrana had relied on the assistance of a number of repentant terrorists—the modern strategy of using such people has a long history—provocateurs, and above all the internal conflicts bred by the secrecy, constant danger, and suspicion within the movement. The most obvious example of this was the assassination of Ivanov, accused by Nechayev of treason. But until the end of the nineteenth century, the antisubversive activities of the state had been relatively amateurish, as yet unable to subvert the movement or throw it into confusion. With the beginning of the new century, by contrast, police activities gave way to a systematic manipulation, the effectiveness of which was to be increased by the conflicts inherent in the state—particularly during the much disputed reign of Nicholas II. The case of Yevno Azev illustrates this development, which culminated in the death throes of terrorism.

Despite the suspicions with which Azev was regarded, this strange, many-faceted figure managed at the same time to be seen as a hero, even by so wise and cautious a person as Ekaterina Breshkovskaya. He was able to deceive not only the terrorists, but also his employers in the Okhrana. The details of Azev's life are evidence of the possibilities for advancement provided by Russian education at this period. Born in 1869 of a very poor family, he appeared to lack none of the classic requirements for a member of the intelligentsia—secondary school, journalistic activities, and exile. But in 1893 he joined the Okhrana, while at the same time preserving his links with the revolutionary movement.

The task assigned to him by the Okhrana was to concentrate his energies on the group that appeared to be the most urgent and dangerous: the Socialist Revolutionary Party and its Combat Section that planned the assassinations. He skillfully managed to assert himself on both sides, and played a central role in the Combat Section, particularly after the attempt on the life of Governor Bogdanovich, when the many arrests made it necessary to form a new team. Rumors began to circulate about him—how was it that all around him, after meetings where he had been present and had spoken, increasing numbers of arrests were taking place, leaving him untouched? But he managed to explain them away and dissipate the antipathy aroused by his ideological cynicism—he declared that he had little belief in socialism—in those who were risking their lives for this ideal.

He was able to allay suspicion to some extent by becoming involved, in 1903, in the preparations for the assassination of the minister of the interior, Plehve. With the success of this plan, he acquired a reputation for being the perfect organizer, capable of rescuing a flagging terrorism from failure, everlasting debate, and constantly postponed plans. Azev was indeed constantly coming up with new proposals, organizing them from outside the country, and then returning to keep an eye on the execution of the arrangements. The indirect consequences were of course yet more arrests, the natural outcome of successful assassinations. It was not until 1912 that the Socialist Revolutionary Party finally accused him directly,[5] and even then he was able to plead that, by playing this double game, he had above all contributed to the success of terrorism by concealing his activities with false reports to the police.

Who had deceived whom? The terrorists were to look long and hard at this question as they contemplated the list of groups discovered and comrades arrested. Although it is difficult to know who suffered most from this manipulation, the state or its enemies, it should be borne in mind that Azev represented only the tip of an iceberg. His is only one example of the thousands of Okhrana agents who, between 1900 and 1914, infiltrated revolutionary parties and often participated in terrorist activities for motives unknown to the terrorists. It would appear that terrorism in twentieth-century Russia, already faltering because uncertain of the right path to pursue and unsure of its usefulness in a country undergoing such change, was to fall victim to this last distorting manipulation. The moral ideals that had for so long guided those who dealt out death and accepted it for themselves were becoming muddied in the ambiguous cohabitation between terrorists and provocateurs. It seemed at this point as if it would be the state, with its more subtle and diversified forms of action, that would emerge the victor from this twenty-year-old confrontation. But the state had not finished with murder. The neutralized or tamed terrorists—like Vera Zasulich who joined the Social Democratic Party and organized its political fight—were to make way for new categories of murderers.

---

5. A commission of inquiry including such diverse people as Prince Kropotkin and Vera Figner was held in Paris to investigate him.

II

The Blood of Rasputin

♦

The twentieth century will have had the sad privilege of seeing the development of murder on a world scale—and not just murder, but mass murder. Although assassination has always had a respectable place in the political history of human societies, it was suddenly to become one of the most favored and widely used political weapons.

And yet the century had, from this point of view, begun quite well in Russia. The assassination attempts of the first decade, the last gasp of a dying terrorist movement, were less important than the rational development of a political system. It is true, nevertheless, that on the edge of the tsar's empire a palace revolution in 1903 that stained the court of Serbia with blood[1] might, with hindsight, have been an indication of the events that, fifteen years later, were to put an end once and for all to hopes of reform.

The Fortunes and Misfortunes of Russia

The personality and policies of Nicholas II, who succeeded to the throne in 1894, are of interest, for with Nicholas was to begin the last phase of the monarchy. Although not going far enough, the

---

1. King Alexander I and Queen Draga were assassinated in the royal palace by a group of mutinous officers. It was a murder involving extreme violence, both in the number of victims—some twenty dead, including two ministers and the queen's brothers—and in the form it took, since the royal couple were first shot, then stabbed, and finally defenestrated. The result of the murder was to replace the Obrenovich dynasty with that of the Karageorgevich family and to reveal the international contradictions and the inherent conflicts in the policies of Serbia, a country that was becoming increasingly prominent on the European scene.

reforms of Alexander II had indubitably represented a radical break with the past, opening the way to both social and moral change. The conservative and frequently regressive policies of his successors, starting with Alexander III, may have tried to some extent to go back on Alexander II's reforms, but they at least had the merit of allowing Russia the time to assimilate these changes. Reforms that challenge centuries of social relations based on serfdom, on autocracy, on the exclusion of the majority of society from the political process, are too profound to be readily accepted by those who have to pay the price of the reform, even if they are seen to be indispensable. Reforms need time to develop in order to avoid an uncontrollable wave of social demands. It is this time that reformers have often lacked and it was to be the stumbling block for the great reforms of this century.

Alexander III's "iron hand" and his intransigent desire to preserve the autocracy had their merits in this respect. They reassured those who could not accept the reforms and kept the people's passions in check, allowing the tsar to embark upon his work of economic modernization. By absorbing the resentments of the former and the hopes of the latter, he hoped eventually that his reforms would turn Russia into a modern developed country. During this period of uneasy transformation, a few figures stand out, whose lucid political approach to the difficult problems of modernization and policy (general policies as much as isolated and dispersed measures) might have contributed to the realization of this aim. While history cannot be written in terms of "what if?" and its course cannot be reconstructed by hypotheses, it is interesting to list the directions that Russia might have taken and the different means that were put forward. Unless we opt for the comfortable certainty that events have only one possible course, it is important to assess the possibilities or chances of alternatives available.

Russia's chance lay—or might have lain—in the lucid vision of a few men. The first was Count Witte. Deeply interested in the railroads (in 1892 he was minister of transport), he was determined to unify the empire through the development of a rail network. He was equally determined to modernize his country, though anxious to control the speed of the "train" of modernity lest it rush off the tracks, putting the whole enterprise in jeopardy. Russia owed her industrial expansion to this man, whose greatest merit was to have seen clearly what was necessary and at what speed it should be brought about. We shall return later to the reasons that were to prevent Witte from completing this useful task during the reign of Alexander III and in the first years of the reign of Nicholas II.

A second chance came with Stolypin. He appeared to offer a different path, based on the modernization of the peasantry, but in reality his aims were similar, since he was concerned, like Witte, to have the reforms accepted into men's ideas. Because he was more concerned with the peasantry than the industrial world, he was generally accused of conservatism, ignorance, or underestimating the needs of the modern world. It should be remembered, however, that at the beginning of the twentieth century, Russia's population still consisted chiefly of peasants. To leave them out of any change or give them a less important place would be to condemn the change in its entirety. It was the failure to hear this message, nearly a century later, long after industrialization, that created the Soviet Union's economic problems. In order to save itself from decline, it has now had to listen to the proposals of a new reformer, Gorbachev, for what is essentially a return to the plan first put forward by Stolypin.

These men represented a chance for Russia. The other side of the coin revealed factors that would exacerbate its problems. First, in the period immediately preceding the revolution men of mediocre stature succeeded to power. Second, an enormous gulf separated Nicholas II from the needs of his time, but in this case this characteristic was so marked as to be deeply significant. It was a result not so much of the personality of the man himself as of the long development of the function of the monarchy to which he was the unfortunate heir.

Despite difficult beginnings, the country had developed relatively peacefully up to the end of the century. When Nicholas II came to the throne in 1894 he probably intended to follow the course set by his father and maintain the autocracy. But his conception of autocracy, like that of Alexander III and all the preceding Romanovs, served chiefly to define his relationship with society. The sovereign had total power over society which in his opinion should have nothing to do with the running of the country. The cooperation of throne and society that had forged the nation-state elsewhere was still lacking in Russia at the beginning of the twentieth century. The national independence conquered at the beginning of the sixteenth century had occurred too long ago in the collective memory to act as a cement for two such disparate elements. Society's loyalty to the sovereign had for centuries been assured by the support of the church and the familiar idea of the "father of the people" and his people.

Despite the court ceremonies that through the years had become increasingly elaborate, a tradition of contact between the sovereign and his people had been maintained for a long time, and handed down from father to son. The historian Marc Raeff has shown how this emotional link gradually weakened, until it disappeared altogether with Nicholas II. It was the sovereigns themselves who brought about this change, beginning with Nicholas I in the nineteenth century. This tsar, who, as we have seen, loved all things military, discontinued the public holidays and ceremonies that had periodically demonstrated the visible and almost physical link joining the sovereign with his people, in favor of what Raeff calls "paradomania"—a succession of military parades that effectively created a wall between the monarch and his subjects. To this first change was added another, which Nicholas II was to take to extremes: the encroachment of private life upon the image of the tsar. The "father of the people" was to become a mere paterfamilias, concerned for his family and withdrawn into his own private world.

The change in the function of the tsar had now been accomplished in all its aspects. The days of the "pious tsar," Christ's representative who held the fate of his people in his hand, were long past. Now the autocracy held the people in obedience. The last sovereign to have been seen, confusedly and to a limited degree, as suffering the Passion in His name was Alexander II, because he had been assassinated.[2] But apart from this exception, there was a completely new image of the tsar. "Secularized in the eighteenth century, privatized in the nineteenth," all that was now left was a

---

2. "This liberating tsar suffered like Christ at Golgotha for the sins of others. Pray God that his Passion, like that of Christ, may save his people," wrote the editor of *Russkoe slovo*, Evgeny Markov, in 1881.

man holding immense authority. Deprived of the dual protection of his divine nature and his role as father to a whole people, the tsar stood naked: he was a man like any other. Anything could now be imputed to him: disappointed hopes, failures and, later, military defeat—to him and to those who surrounded him.

To this divergence between the myth of the tsar and the person of Nicholas II can be added other aggravating circumstances: developments in the church and the quality of the liberal debate on the alternatives to autocracy.

Long subject to the state and guaranteed by it, the church too found itself in a state of change at the beginning of the century. The erosion of the imperial myth could not fail to affect it, since the church had acted as a prop to the sovereign. For several years, members of the Russian intelligentsia had been considering the whole question of "Holy Russia"; this accelerated the awareness of a crisis in the very heart of the church. From time immemorial, God and the tsar had been identified with one another and no one had hitherto challenged this identification. The intellectuals' debate that was to shake Russia in the last decades of the nineteenth century raised the question: is Holy Russia the Russia of the autocracy or that of the poor and the peasants? Could Christ, who had preached revolt and the greatness of the oppressed, perhaps have been a revolutionary? Certainly many terrorists had presented themselves as redeemers, sacrificing themselves for the salvation of the people. At the other extreme, Dostoyevsky, a nationalist and a conservative, nevertheless casts similar doubts on the identification of the tsar with Christ in Holy Russia. Without openly attacking the myth, Dostoyevsky seems to identify the Russian people, through their sufferings, with Christ, thus relegating the sovereign to a less clear role.

Although these discussions took place in intellectual circles, the church could not ignore the erosion that was beginning to take place. Its response in its defense was to seek something quite new in Russia—its emancipation. In March 1905, a group of clerics published a manifesto demanding freedom for the Orthodox Church and, particularly, what could be its most powerful weapon, the reestablishment of the patriarchate. The Holy Synod supported these developments and called for a council to elect a patriarch and provide the church with its own structure, independent of the state.

The matter was debated for almost two years, but got nowhere. Nicholas II, probably under the influence of Pobedonostsev, procurator of the Holy Synod, opposed the holding of the council, arguing that a period when Russia was going through such difficulties—the revolution of 1905—was not the moment for such a change. The tsar's authority was sufficient to prevent the church from pursuing this plan, which resurfaced only at the revolution. But it is indicative of the unrest long existing within the church that it chose to call a council a few months before the 1917 revolution, thus contributing to Russia's great upheaval, and elected a patriarch a few months later.

Although the tsar had apparently succeeded in blocking developments in the church, the consequences were nevertheless far-reaching. The crisis had proved that the church's guarantee of the monarchy was no longer total, thus further eroding the imperial myth. Realizing that from then on he would receive only qualified support from the church, the tsar now turned to the margins of the church to find an answer to his religious needs. Rasputin, only recently arrived in the capital and as yet unknown to the imperial family, was to find conditions ripe for his influence.

The ideas of the liberals and the alternative they offered also took on a new dimension in these difficult times. While Alexander III's "step backwards" had helped to give Russia time to assimilate the reforms without too great a shock, now the problem was what to do next. Alexander III had accidentally opened the way, and now economic progress demanded that society be involved in the development of the country to a greater extent and consulted on new enterprises. The necessity for an institutional system involving more participation was becoming increasingly clear. In addition, the existence—another consequence of the reforms—both of an educated and diversified urban society in a position to invest in progress, and of the elites working within rural society, underlined this need. A few years later, Lenin was to baptize this new section of society "the new democracy," an accurate term and one that demanded political change.

The inflexible regime set up by Alexander III and Nicholas II offered no outlet for these elites. They were often members of professional organizations and were to make up the greater part of the membership of the future Constitutional Democratic Party (known as the "Cadet" party, from its initials, KD). Looking to those countries with a strong democratic tradition—England, France, and particularly the United States—men like Milyukov and Maksim Kovalevsky discussed ways of replacing Russia's ossified and traditional system with a society based on law. What was needed, they said, was the end of autocracy, not through concessions and measures that might be reversed, but through a new legality, a constitutional democracy, of which Milyukov was to be the tireless champion. There was no question of interfering with the monarchy: the example of England showed that it could conform to the rule of law. The real obstacle preventing society from entering into the political sphere was autocratic arbitrariness. The struggle in Russia in 1905 to set up a new relationship between the tsar and society—directly inspired by the great nations of the West, with which the Russian liberals longed to catch up—was both premature, given the power of the autocracy, and too late since the times were already leading inexorably to revolution. Here too we cannot fail to be struck by the similarities between the early years of the century and our own time. The USSR today is struggling with the problem of how to preserve what exists and gain the involvement of society, of how to base this association on the rule of law. It is a moving echo of the efforts of yesterday's liberals.

The Reign of the Miracle Worker

This is not the place to relate yet again the story of Rasputin and his relations with the imperial family. But a few words have to be said about the two chief protagonists in the drama before coming to the murder that was to open the final phase of the empire and was unlike any other in its history.

When Rasputin arrived in the capital in 1904, the tsar had been on the throne for ten years. In spite of the serious student revolts of 1899 and the spread of discontent all over the country, and despite the assassination attempts directed not at him but at his ministers, Nicholas II had until this time enjoyed a relatively peaceful reign. His minister of the interior, Plehve, assured him that his intransigent authoritarianism was yielding results. In June 1904, after years of disappointment when they had produced only daughters, the royal couple gave the country an heir. No one knew then that he was seriously ill. The autocracy seemed to have been strengthened by this.

This calmness can be explained by the complex personality of the tsar, which lay concealed beneath an apparently simple exterior. Brought up by an authoritarian and self-assured father of powerful personality and imposing stature, Nicholas II was in many respects no more than a pale imitation. He had none of his father's strong will, stature, or authority. But Nicholas idolized his father and he adopted totally the autocratic point of view, for which Alexander III was so much better equipped. The father was an emperor, the son a sensitive, moderately gifted man, happy in the privacy of his home. In ordinary times, he would probably have made an excellent sovereign. But these were extraordinary times, a fact that Nicholas was never to grasp fully. It is striking to see the similarity between memoirs of an ordinary Parisian who lived through the French Revolution,[3] preoccupied with his health and his finances, noticing practically nothing of the cataclysm unfolding before his very eyes, and the reactions of Nicholas II to the revolutionary events noted down in his private diary. No more than did the Parisian did he see the seriousness of the events to which he was a witness, and more often than not it is his hunting exploits that take pride of place in his entries. The difference is that the first was an ordinary man who was witness to events over which he had no influence, whereas the second was the sovereign of a country whose whole political and social system was about to collapse. It was not the result of a lack of intelligence, but rather a character trait described by all the witnesses. An essentially private man, devout, and convinced that all things were a manifestation of divine providence, Nicholas met events with a profound fatalism. This quest for God's will was undoubtedly the most dominant aspect of his character. The tsarina's similarly fatalistic character merely reinforced his.

---

3. *Un bourgeois dans la Révolution*, Paris.

His constant inclination toward mysticism, coinciding with the void left by a church in search of a new freedom, was to lead him and the tsarina to seek solace on the fringes of religion—and eventually to Rasputin.

Before that, however, Nicholas had persuaded the church to canonize a saint for his reign. It is a significant episode because it reveals how, at the moment when the links between the church and the state were breaking down, the need to fix the role of sovereign firmly in a divine context was still strong. In the nineteenth century, a hermit living in Sarov, Serafim (1760–1833), had acquired a great reputation for saintliness and no less a reputation for seeing the future. For the reign at the beginning of the following century, he had prophesied great misfortunes before a period of peace. In his time, Serafim of Sarov had played an important role in the development of the hermit's life—he had renounced the monk's habit in favor of the simple clothes of the peasant—and after years of silence and meditation, had emerged to preach on the urgent need for a return to the Christian life. In a rationalist nineteenth century, the results of his preaching were a revival of the monastic life and an interest among many prominent intellectuals in places of pilgrimage and spiritual retreat, particularly Optina Pustyn. Here they sought refuge with an elder—*starets*—the bearer of the word of God. We find an example of one of these men in the figure of Father Zosima in Dostoyevsky's *Brothers Karamazov.* No doubt aware of this development and anxious to reestablish links with the saintliness that had deserted the dynasty, Nicholas got the Holy Synod to agree in 1903 to the canonization of the hermit of Sarov. It was an extraordinary ceremony for a secular age, with the tsar and tsarina, the court and the people gathered together around a unifying symbol of Holy Russia. But despite the symbolic gesture, the only effect of this attempt to reintroduce saintliness into the monarchy, though perhaps by a different route, was to give the people one more saint, St. Serafim, and some icons.

Thus began the reign of the *starets,* whose image, and particularly, whose role, is not yet fully agreed on by historians. Whatever the case, he appears in the entourage of the sovereign after a long series of miracle workers, whether genuine or false: Philip the Magus, Papus, and a good number of mystics, people of God and products of the people, introduced into the court by well-meaning souls to bear witness to a truth that was more reassuring than the political reality outside.

For Nicholas and the tsarina, the tragic events in the streets in 1905 were paralleled by a personal tragedy. The revolutionary upheavals that had forced the sovereign to issue the manifesto of October 17 were a blow to the principle of autocracy for which Nicholas felt responsible. It was the key to all his convictions, and he could not agree to hand it on diminished in any way. The other side of the tragedy was the discovery, in 1904, of his son's illness, hemophilia, inherited through the tsarina, and a permanent threat to the heir's life. The significance of the appearance in their lives of Rasputin can be explained by the double tragedy of Nicholas and his wife, parents agonized by the sometimes insupportable sufferings of their child and sovereigns clinging to a belief that they were the indispensable links in an eternal system. The tsar writes in his journal on November 1, 1905: "We have made the acquaintance of the man of God, Grigory." The influence that this man was to acquire over the imperial family derived above all from his acknowledged ability to stop the hemorrhages and relieve the sufferings of the young tsarevich. This man whom they took for a man of God could do what medicine was incapable of doing. And yet he was no more than a simple muzhik—though this too was not without significance for superstitious Russians: the onetime serf was also the redeemer. It should not be forgotten that even the birth of the tsarevich had been attributed to the intercession of St. Serafim of Sarov, a consecration of the sanctity later recognized by the sovereign. Thus, in the life of this tsarevich—the tragic tsarevich as victim appears again—Rasputin represented the other end of the spiritual chain that had brought him into the world and that now kept him alive.

It was also clear that this man of God would have no hesitation in interfering in political life, exercising a real influence over the tsar and tsarina and urging them to assert themselves. The tsar, once dominated by a father with whom he had tried to identify, may well have found in Rasputin another father who inspired him with the conviction that it was his duty to exercise authority. Rasputin also wielded a more usual kind of influence through his protégés. Every court or government has its coteries and intrigues. To overcome them would take the steely authority of a dictator or an Ivan the Terrible. Nicholas II was not cast in this mold and gave in to many a request for promotion or personal criticism from the "man of God." The problems were many. With a poisoned atmosphere at court, there was also the widespread unpopularity of the tsarina to contend with. Undeserved perhaps, this unpopularity was partly a result of the circumstances of her arrival in Russia,[4] as well as her nervous and timid character and the tragedy of the sickly child.

Many people were deeply worried by the sovereign's inability to face up to the difficulties of the times. There were constant disagreements over the best course to follow to deal with the most urgent questions—reform, repression, foreign policy. All these matters were exacerbated by the tensions of the period and the severity of the problems. Again, in normal times all this could have been reduced to a simple matter of a conflict of personalities. It was true that an almost illiterate muzhik, of highly dubious reputation, made a very bad impression in the hushed universe of the court, even if he was there to ease the sufferings of the tsarevich. But rumor, that most common of court diseases, made him both favorite and adviser of the imperial couple. Coming constantly to the tsar with one piece of advice after another, Rasputin alarmed the dignitaries of the church and set those in government against him. Stolypin, for example, was too much of a reformer for the tsar and for Rasputin, who thought he was undermining the autocracy. By attacking Rasputin, the various opposing figures were in fact defending their different political positions.

The real crisis broke after the death of Stolypin, in the very heart of the Duma, involving the president of the assembly, Rodzianko, and the prime minister of the day, Kokovtsev. The reason for the crisis was that the tsar had tried to make the minister of the interior clamp down on the press to prevent the frequent mention of the name of Rasputin, which was bringing the tsar into disrepute. It was to be a costly mistake. For the Duma of 1912,

---

4. She had arrived in Russia, as the tsarevich's betrothed, just at the moment that Alexander III was breathing his last, and for this reason, became for the Empress Mother and for the people the woman who had entered into the life of the country "behind the imperial coffin." It was an inauspicious sign in a superstitious country.

limited in its social recruitment and its authority since 1907,[5] this was a chance for a debate implicating the sovereign, his decisions, and ultimately absolutism itself. An out-and-out political scandal arose, with the "problem of Rasputin" plastered all over the press and in the Duma.

But though the immediate consequence was that Rasputin had to leave the capital for a period, all the elements of the final drama were already in place. Rasputin, closely involved in the private life of the tsar and tsarina and accused of using this position to influence the tsar's political decisions, was to prove doubly fatal to the tsar. Because the monarchy had tended to retreat more and more into its own private world, the doubts that hung over this private sphere were becoming very serious. As long as the sovereign was human only in part of his nature, the other part, lofty and divine, protected him from the gaze of his subjects. From the moment he became merely human, and thus unprotected, his slightest act or omission was exposed to the judgment of his subjects. The sovereign, a good man searching for spirituality, could see the legacy of absolutism, handed down to him so recently, crumbling before his eyes. That he could be so strongly influenced by Rasputin led people to doubt his ability to control the coming storm that, after 1912, everyone saw as a certainty. It was not only those involved in court intrigue who were worried by Rasputin—even when he was away for a few months. Members of the imperial family, and particularly the tsar's uncle, Grand Duke Nicholas, felt that the whole affair was bringing the moral authority of the dynasty, and the monarchy as a whole, into disrepute.

The war was to be a decisive turning point in this history where the irrational held so large a place at a time when rationality was more needed than ever. At the beginning, however, the war was greeted by a certain degree of national unity. The Duma rallied to the throne, voting through war credits without fuss; the national minorities declared their loyalty; and society, at all levels, demon-

---

5. Nicholas II had dissolved the Duma and changed the electoral law on June 16, 1907. Constituencies and electoral colleges were redrawn, resulting in glaring social inequalities. The Third Duma, lasting from 1907 to 1912, was in reality an "assembly of the rich." On November 15, 1912, the Fourth Duma was set up with an even more restricted membership.

strated its desire to participate in the common effort. A kind of national pact was established. It was not until the middle of 1915, almost a year after the beginning of hostilities, that a malaise took hold that was to lead to the final tragedy. The "fresh and joyous war" was going badly. The many defeats revealed the initial vagueness and lack of preparation. The sacred union of 1914 between the throne and society was splitting apart.

In the face of these reverses, the tsar demonstrated a growing authoritarianism to cover his inability to control the situation. This authoritarianism took different forms: in the government, where the prime minister was Goremykin, who had already given proof of his incompetence in 1906; in the army, of which the tsar took sole command, replacing his uncle, Grand Duke Nicholas, who was at least credited with doing the best he could in a worsening military situation. In the name of absolutism, the sovereign rejected the assistance that society—industrialists, local authorities, and the like—wished to offer to the war effort. The intransigence of this weak man resulted in a constant state of political instability—the ever-changing round of prime ministers and ministers between 1915 and 1916 is astonishing. Society accused two people for this lack of policy in the time of greatest need: the tsarina, whose influence over her husband was notorious, and, behind her, Rasputin, whose shadow hung over the whole of society. Seen hitherto as no more than an impressive charlatan, debauched and ambitious, Rasputin suddenly took on a more sinister aspect. He was the man who, in league with the "German woman"—just as Marie-Antoinette was called the "Austrian woman," so now, in time of war, Empress Alexandra, in fact devoted to Russia, was paying for her origins—was running Russia by manipulating his pathetic puppet, Nicholas.

There was some truth in this view of a throne surrounded by suspected treason and rumors of intrigue. There is no lack of documentation to prove that Rasputin tried hard to persuade the tsar that the war would bring down the throne and that he should seek a separate peace. It is equally true that from 1916 his influence increased in step with the opposition that it aroused and that the correspondence between the tsarina and her husband is filled with recommendations from "our friend," concerning both internal affairs and the running of the war. The situation in Russia was sufficiently worrying to justify the crisis that was about to break. The people, the Duma, and the existing social organizations, in their anguish over a badly led war, punctuated with defeats, begged the tsar to make changes that would halt this series of humiliations. The only response was another government reshuffle.

In 1915, after the first defeats, Goremykin, seen as relatively reliable, was replaced as prime minister by Stürmer, whose political and social program consisted chiefly of ignoring the urgent demands for a change in the political system. The three ministries dealing with the highly sensitive areas of war, the interior, and agriculture, whose responsibility it was to deal with the military situation and the most urgent social problems—unemployment, the reception of refugees fleeing before the advancing enemy, and the provision of food to the towns—saw a confusing succession of ministers and yet achieved nothing. The people were well aware that the responsibility for these decisions, invariably ineffective, could be attributed to the empress and Rasputin. Many contradictory demands were made of these men who appeared and disappeared like so many characters in a stage tragedy. The tsar still hoped to preserve the stability of the autocratic system and silence the Duma and the social organizations that were increasingly substituting themselves for a regime that was collapsing. At each change, these groups eagerly waited for a man who could understand that Russia's only hope depended on a sharing of responsibilities. The war and the government's inability to act now proved the necessity of those reforms forced out of Nicholas in 1905, which he had ever since tried to reduce. Everyone in Russia knew that the salvation and restoration of the country lay in this direction—everyone except the tsar, who was going in the opposite direction, and Rasputin, who saw a separate peace as the only way of healing Russia's wounds and restoring the authority of the monarchy.

While the rest of society saw a proper constitution as the only solution, Rasputin sought a change at the top. He had frequently been heard to say: "The empress is made for power. She is a second Catherine, whereas he is not an emperor, he is a child of God." Rasputin suggested to Feliks Yussupov, a reliable witness unlikely to alter the facts, that the best solution would be an abdication in favor of the tsarevich, under the regency of the empress.[6] Thus the stage was set for an assassination that, in the typology of Russian murder, is unique. In the doubly tragic atmosphere of a war that had caused more deaths than any previous war, and of an autocracy that was falling apart, the murder that was being planned was at one and the same time a political plan, a struggle for power, and a confused fight against "the forces of darkness." Those who were to carry out the murder believed that they were breaking up what they took to be a real conspiracy, in which Rasputin and the tsarina were plotting to reestablish a regency and, behind the regency, to place at the head of Russia an illiterate and debauched muzhik. More generally, it was the very fate of the monarchy, compromised by a quasi-supernatural being from another age, that was to force those around the throne to take action.

A "Shakespearean Murder"

The murder of Rasputin is sufficiently well known for the outlines to suffice here. Nevertheless, the events are of exceptional interest because an account of them was written by the principal instigator and author of the crime. Crimes are generally recounted by people other than their perpetrators; in those cases where the account is given by the authors of the crime, the details have often been altered in the course of time. Prince Feliks Yussupov's account was written shortly after the deed and without any departure from the truth. It was an act for which he felt no pride, but rather doubt and a crushing remorse.[7] It was an astonishing murder on many counts: the personality of the protagonists; the conditions in which it took

6. In justice, it should be said that the tsarina and Rasputin, for their part, believed that Grand Duke Nicholas intended to take advantage of his authority over the army to force the sovereign to abdicate in his favor.

7. In addition to the written sources, much of the following evidence is the result of the author's conversations with Prince Yussupov, his wife, and his brother-in-law Prince Fyodor Romanov.

place; the prophetic and supernatural atmosphere surrounding it; and finally, its consequences.

Let us look first at the actors in this drama. Rasputin was at the peak of his power as a result of his influence over the tsarina. The tsar on the other hand was by now rather tired of the problem posed by this man.[8] Rasputin, a mixture of self-indulgent debauchee and shrewd and sly peasant who combined pleasure and self-interest, was by now making his crude and demanding personality felt in ever wider circles outside the court. Opposing Rasputin were those who were to assassinate him.

The architect of the plot was Feliks Yussupov, "the most handsome man in the empire." He was a complex man, emotional, passionate, and deeply divided by the contradictory elements in his nature. Aggressively homosexual, he delighted to dress as a woman, enjoying the attentions of the guards officers in the cafés of the capital, who did not suspect their mistake. To make up for her grief over her lack of daughters, his mother had dressed the young boy as a girl. This was to affect him all his life, as he was later to admit. But at the same time, as a son of one of the greatest and richest families of the empire, he was every inch the nobleman. To his wife, Princess Irina Romanova, the emperor's niece and one of the most beautiful and renowned heiresses in Russia, he dedicated a devotion and a respect that lasted until his dying day. A restless, dual personality, fascinated by Oscar Wilde, the supernatural, death, and anything strange, Yussupov's life was a bizarre mixture. Around him the members of the imperial family, his relatives by marriage, debated constantly the best way of saving the situation—how to get Rasputin away from the tsar and tsarina, and how to get the tsar to agree to the limitation of his power implied by the adoption of a constitution. Yussupov became convinced that it was up to him to carry out the action that would save the regime. As long as Rasputin lived, it was impossible to remove him and impossible to persuade the sovereign to make the urgent concessions that were needed to

---

8. Isolated in Moghilev, from which he was directing military operations, the sovereign was less directly under the influence of the *starets,* which came to him via the tsarina's letters. From several of his remarks, one can detect his irritation and his desire to distance himself from Rasputin.

satisfy a disenchanted society. It became clear to Yussupov that the only solution was to kill Rasputin.

On December 2, 1916, Purichkevich, a member of the Duma, a talented orator whose politics lay to the extreme right and who was a fierce supporter of absolutism, spoke in the assembly for two hours, denouncing the "forces of darkness" that had descended on the dynasty and were destroying it. Fired with enthusiasm by this indictment which echoed all his own thoughts, Yussupov immediately summoned Purichkevich, revealing his plan to him and asking for his help. In a few days, these two very different men had gathered around them a group of conspirators. A physician was needed, and the army provided one in the figure of Dr. Lazovert. He was joined by a young officer, Sukhotin, and a friend from Yussupov's youth, Grand Duke Dmitri Pavlovich, first cousin to the tsar. The group was thus made up of the elite of society, even if, between the charming and superficial dilettantism of the members of the imperial family, the extremist fanaticism of Purichkevich, and the friendship of the other two conspirators, there was nothing in common other than their exalted belief in the need to smash the "force of evil" surrounding the throne.

The murder itself was no less bizarre. Flattered by the idea of finally meeting Princess Yussupov, Rasputin was lured to Yussupov's magnificent palace where his host had prepared a somewhat unusual banquet for him with poisoned cakes and glasses coated in poison. Dr. Lazovert guaranteed that there was enough poison to kill a whole regiment. Yussupov has given a vivid description of that night of surreal horror. Alone with Rasputin, while the others waited upstairs for the moment to carry away the body, Yussupov's amazement turned to terror as Rasputin took mouthful after mouthful of poison without turning a hair, begging Yussupov, who waited in vain for some sign of a death agony, to amuse him by singing to the guitar. Rasputin's superhuman ability to survive the effects of strong poison, and the feeling of being alone with his victim in the silence of the night, proved to be too much for Yussupov's nerves and his reason wavered. To save himself and it, in a last effort of will, he drew a gun and shot Rasputin who, far from dying, suggested that they go and finish off the evening in a gypsy cabaret. When death was eventually certified by Doctor

Lazovert and the body wrapped in bearskin, the conspirators were at last able to relax. Where the poison had inexplicably failed, the gun had succeeded. They had proved that Rasputin was only a man, perverse and threatening, but finally overcome. The shadows surrounding the monarchy seemed to recede.

Suddenly, in the midst of the joyful, uncontrollable, and almost hysterical excitement that inevitably follows a moment of such tension, the group of conspirators thought they were plunging back into madness and unreality: the dead man rose up and threw himself on his assassin, screaming and seizing him by the throat with a viselike grip. In an eerie nightmare it seemed as if Rasputin, poisoned, shot, and certified dead, had risen from the dead to strangle his killer who, though young, alive, and unharmed, could not tear his hands from his throat. When he finally succeeded, his victim fell groaning beneath his blows, only to rise again, leap to his feet, fight his way out of the room—though the door was locked—crawl up the stairs that led outside and run, staggering unsteadily, toward the outer door. Though pursued by five fit and healthy men, he almost managed to escape, shouting out as he ran: "Feliks, I'm going to tell the empress everything!" Purichkevich fired four more bullets, which all struck home, and then the five attacked the *starets,* beating him about the head with the butt of the gun and a club until he collapsed in the snow. Still not entirely satisfied that the body would not rise up again, they rolled the corpse in some curtains, tied it up, and threw it in the frozen Neva. Three days later, when the body was discovered, it was obvious that Rasputin had not died of the poison or the many bullets that had all penetrated the body, nor yet of the blows of all kinds that he had received. He had died from drowning and freezing, as if he had wished to prove that he was invulnerable to attacks by men and that only nature—that is, the will of God—could overcome the man who had for so long proclaimed himself to be "the man of God."

Many aspects of this extraordinary murder make it unusual. The whole affair was imbued with that mixture of religiosity and an inclination toward the more marginal forms of spirituality, sometimes authentic but sometimes a complete fabrication, so often found in Russian history. Who exactly was Rasputin? A real miracle worker, a simple debauchee, a man of God who, in the pilgrimages of his youth, had become one of the religious wanderers so revered in Russia? One thing is sure: he was a true product of Russia and her popular culture—a culture glorified by a guilt-stricken intelligentsia. He was first and foremost a peasant, in a country where the myth of the muzhik as victim and redeemer had held such a prominent place. Since the disappearance of the "pious princes," the common vision of what characterized Russia was centered on the peasant. Russia, Holy Russia, was that celebrated by the poet Blok, the motherland of legends, and the magic of the countryside. Rasputin was to bring all this with him from his birthplace in Siberia. Man of God or demon, in either case he was seen as a supernatural being and the expression of a distant world. As a man of God, he provided a substitute for a church that was moving away from the throne; as a demon, he took upon himself all the evil of the world, thus diverting it away from the tsar. He can be seen as representing both the role of the "good," "true" tsar and that of the "false" tsar. The old tension between good and evil, true and false, went together in this case with the Dionysian aspects of the *starets*'s religion, recalling the semipagan cults of many religious sects. He was also the product of a Russia where the feeling of an imminent political apocalypse, hanging over the country since the turn of the century, encouraged a belief in the supernatural. He was the prophet of an extraordinary age, and it is no accident that shortly before his assassination, Rasputin wrote to the tsar:

> I feel that I shall die before January 1. . . . If I am killed by ordinary assassins, and particularly by one of my brother peasants of Russia, you, tsar of Russia, will have nothing to fear for your throne and your power, nor for your children who will continue to reign for centuries. But if I am killed by boyars, by nobles, if they shed my blood, their hands will be stained with my blood that they will not be able to wash away for twenty-five years. They will have to leave Russia. Brother will kill brother, they will kill one another, and they will hate one another, and there will be no more nobles in the country. Tsar of the land of Russia, if you hear Grigory's death knell, know that if it is one of your family who caused my death, none of your family, none

of your children will live for more than two years more.
They will be killed by the Russian people.

This decidedly prophetic message was to add further to the mystery of Rasputin. Quite apart from the threatening content of the message—which must have affected the sovereign *a posteriori,* if only because it concluded with the definite statement: "I must be killed, I am no longer in the world of the living"—murder itself was unacceptable to the imperial couple. The morality of the terrorists—"a murder, whoever the victim, is still a murder"—was also that of these two passionate Christians, even if circumstances had led them to confuse the friendship of Rasputin with true mysticism. The idea that a murder could be committed by a member of their family—against a family friend, and furthermore a man of God— was quite unacceptable. Since the murder of Paul I, the only deaths that had occurred in the circles of the nobility were in duels of honor or through the law in defense of the state. For the emperor, often irritated by Rasputin's interference in military and state affairs—and who only "tolerated" them, according to Gilliard, tutor to the imperial children, because the empress thought her son's life depended on it—the very idea of murder was insupportable. "I am filled with shame to think that my family could stain its hands with the blood of a simple peasant," he was to say. His sister, Grand Duchess Olga, expressed the same sentiments: "That one of the grandchildren of the Tsar Liberator could assassinate a peasant proves to what depths we have sunk." The empress, for her part, placed in the coffin, next to an icon signed with all the names of the imperial family, a request for the prayers of the "blessed martyr" for all its members. She had no doubt about Rasputin's holiness, which went far beyond a mere ability to heal the sick. Her belief is evidence of the atmosphere of diffuse mysticism that surrounded the imperial family in these last years—a confused idea that divine protection, in these uncertain times, came less from the institutional church, which was itself wracked with uncertainties, than from a man of God such as had so often emerged from the depths of Russia, agents of a peasant wisdom and a semimystical link between earth and heaven.

In a remarkable work devoted to Dostoyevsky, the émigré

Russian philosopher Leon Zander has stressed this tendency to see the land, redemption, and Russia as a single entity. In the chaos of the war years when the secure world of the imperial family was suddenly shaken, who could better embody Holy Russia than this peasant *starets*—a man who was intelligent, adaptable, and careful never to reveal his debauched side to his sovereigns, showing himself always the humble peasant? To understand the blindness of the imperial couple, we should remember that they were also parents agonized over the illness of their son. But above all, we should understand the depth of the problem faced by the last Romanovs in reigning in an age so alien to their personalities and their idea of the role of the sovereign.

The human and intellectual qualities of the last emperor of Russia were indisputable and compared well with those of sovereigns reigning at the same period in England and the Central Powers. But he had been brought up in the belief that autocracy was the right path for his country and that a constitution would not be suitable for this vast empire. Although very much of the nineteenth century in his beliefs, he was at the same time, as a result of his civilized and gentle temperament and natural inclination toward a private family life, a man of the European twentieth century attempting to find a harmony between the authority of the state and a respect for the lives and choices of each man. He was doubly out of touch, both with the urgent need for change in his country and with the necessity, if he wanted to preserve autocracy, of showing himself authoritarian and brutal, another Nicholas I or Alexander III. His beliefs prevented him from following the example of Alexander II, his nature from imitating his father. This was his tragedy and explains why he could do nothing but place himself in the hands of God and chance. This also explains the rise of Rasputin. When a ruler is out of tune with difficult times, they give rise to irrational solutions and individuals. The murder of Rasputin is the other side of this strange and irrational Russia, indissolubly linked with that which preceded and gave rise to it.

Everything about this murder, its minute preparation, the extraordinary events at the scene, and the furious determination of the murderers, was unusual. It seems incomprehensible that these noblemen should undertake the deed instead of employing someone else to do it, until we remember, once again, the cultural dimension. To save the monarchy and to pay with one's own life instead of resorting to a hired assassin was, for the five conspirators of December 1916, the necessary sacrifice for the system that they were defending. But, although punished by the tsar and tsarina,[9] they never felt they had paid enough. The cause that they believed they had a duty to defend did not make them any the less murderers. For anyone who saw Feliks Yussupov relive, year after year until extreme old age, that tragic day, a penitent haunted by the memory of the murder, it is easier to understand what linked the bomb throwers of the late nineteenth century with the murderers of Rasputin. The only difference between Kaliayev and Yussupov lies in the fact that no one brought the latter forgiveness and the peace of a redemptive death.

The Extermination of the Dynasty

"To kill me is to condemn all your family and the dynasty," Rasputin had written to the sovereign. We can be fairly sure that those who were, by collective murder—the systematic elimination of a whole dynasty—to bring about Rasputin's prophecy had no idea that they were in a sense his avengers.

The violence inflicted in 1917 on the imperial family belongs to another category of murder, that which allows the triumph of the revolution through the shedding of the blood of the defeated. There was nothing new about that, but the form this violence took, even more than its extent, separates it in many ways from known models and prompts the question: was this really the product of revolution or rather a combination of classic revolutionary violence and a Russian tradition of violence?

Let us examine the facts. The revolution that put an end to the monarchy was accomplished with ease, without problems or

---

9.   Grand Duke Dmitri was sent to the army, to the troops fighting on the Persian frontier. It was this, when the revolution came, that saved his life. Yussupov, banished from the capital, went into foreign exile the following year. Only Purichkevich, protected by the Duma, was beyond the reach of the emperor's wrath.

opposition. Nikolai Sukhanov, a witness and, to some extent, an actor in the events, has shown vividly how the fall of the Romanovs in February 1917 was the result of a complete collapse of the system rather than of a clear and organized plan. Of course there had been many who, for nearly a century, had dreamed of a revolution, but the revolution when it arrived took all these dreamers and political parties by surprise. It was, one could say, an "accidental" revolution, the result of the exasperation of the people, exhausted by war, lack of food, and unemployment. The urban masses—initially those of St. Petersburg, rebaptized Petrograd during the war to sound less German, and Moscow—wandering in the streets in search of food, gathered together in spontaneous demonstrations. Despite the existence of measures to be taken against an uprising, formulated after the events of 1905, the disarray in the government meant that those responsible for the maintenance of law and order did practically nothing, allowing the reserve army, aware of the lack of leadership at the top, to side with the rebels. The public authorities simply vanished, abandoning the streets to the demonstrators, who were astonished at this bloodless victory. The provisional government set up on February 28 under Prince Lvov reflected the composition of the Duma and expressed the views of the Russian liberals. The latter did not even know themselves how far to push their demands: a constitutional monarchy, abdication of the emperor in favor of another member of his family, or the abolition of the monarchy? Chance and the spontaneous development of elements governing the uprising also determined the ensuing events: the monarchy was abolished.

Isolated in his headquarters, receiving news of the advancing revolution only by telegram, the tsar was unable to react. For him the autocracy was the only possible system, but he was totally incapable of defending it. For the liberals in power, the monarchy without the tsar could still provide a framework for a political compromise with the demands of the people. One solution presented itself: the abdication of the sovereign in favor of his son, under the regency of the tsar's brother, Grand Duke Michael, who still had considerable popularity. The archives concerning the abdication, now in the United States at Stanford, give powerful evidence of the efforts made by those in power to save the system of monarchy. They show also the role played by the personality of the sovereign, where private preoccupations merged into political theories, in the decisive days when anything was still possible. It was because this revolution had no plan and no leaders that events moved unchecked toward the point of no return. The tsar's hesitations over the abdication and then his agreement, on March 3, to the proposed solution—the first act of abdication made his son, according to the laws of succession, the new sovereign—kept the monarchy in line with legal form. It seemed that the revolution might stop here. But, a few hours later, the tsar went back on his decision, allowing private considerations to outweigh the interests of the state. He refused the inevitable separation from a sick child and renounced the throne on his son's behalf, deciding that the throne should go to his brother.

History sometimes repeats itself strangely. In three centuries of Romanov rule, there were only two tsars named Michael, although it was a common name in Russia: the founder of the dynasty and the man who brought it to a close. Grand Duke Michael was a worthy candidate to attempt to save the dynasty founded by his distant namesake. At the age of thirty-nine, he had given proof of his bravery in the army, had tried to influence the tsar when there was still time, and was now ready to take on the terrible responsibility of halting the course of the revolution by evaluating the necessary and possible concessions. But once again, the problem of dynastic legitimacy reared its head. The young tsarevich, legitimate heir to the throne, enjoyed at least the sympathy of the people on account of his youth, his sickness, and the very fact that he was the tsarevich. Grand Duke Michael, faced with this heir deprived of the throne simply by the desire of his father, could not legitimately be tsar. In the decisive hours when the fate of the monarchy was hanging by an ever thinner thread and the prospect of a republic loomed ever nearer, only the unassailable legitimacy of the tsarevich could still rally public support. Grand Duke Michael understood this, his eyes opened by those who supported the idea of the abolition of the monarchy, among whom the most passionate was Kerensky who exclaimed: "the revolution cannot come to terms with a change of line!"[10] Thus Michael, in his turn, abdicated. The monarchy was no more, having succumbed not to the unleashed mob but to the hesitations in the imperial family, to the prevarications that negated each solution at the very moment it was adopted, and to the determined declarations of a few supporters of a republic, like Kerensky and Rodzianko.

How was it that this peaceful revolution turned into a bloodbath? Why did the road to a republic, so easily embarked upon, lead to tyranny? How was it that this popular power emerging from the ruins of a discredited monarchy that had handed over power of its own accord was to give way to an organized coup d'état and the power of a single party? The chief reason was the fragility of Russia's experiment in democracy. But a second aspect of the answer, understood by Lenin early on, was the fact that real power can only be conquered and kept by means of a rigorous organization.

For a period of a few months, Russia tried to learn how to run a democracy. Given the cautious nature of the experiments in democracy before 1917, we can only marvel that such an unprepared society was able to assimilate so rapidly the ideas of political participation, civil liberties, self-administration through the soviets and, finally, the free election of a constituent assembly. Everything indicates that the Russian people and the minority national groups of the empire demonstrated at this time an exceptional political maturity. The historians of the revolution have over the years produced many different reasons to explain why this maturity was not able to build a lasting democratic system. Two of these reasons have a bearing on the subject of this work. First there was the indecisiveness of those installed in the various bodies of the provisional government. They had neither planned nor carried out the revolution, having merely taken over a power that no longer had a holder. This unusual situation partly explains their hesitations and their inability to make immediate decisions. Second, there was the problem of the legal standing of these men. Having taken over from an empire with legitimate rulers, they sought a legitimacy in institu-

---

10. In several conversations with the author in Stanford and Paris, Kerensky maintained that this problem of legitimacy was crucial, and the initial reason for the decisions made.

tions that did not yet exist, putting off all the most urgent decisions—particularly a response to the aspirations of the peasants—until the formation of a democratically elected assembly. But this came about too late. While those in charge debated the most appropriate electoral system for a perfect democracy, the people lost patience with this legalism and turned to those who offered immediate solutions—peace, land, and bread, as Lenin was to say—without quibbling over juridical details. Russia's chance of democracy was lost in this quest for the ideal system.

Obsessed all his life with the need to seize power and having forged the necessary tools for the job, Lenin emerged as the only man with an appropriate strategy, in a Russia where there was no one able to adapt to the times and the developments in society. Herein lies the paradox of the October Revolution: the ideology and the program were very different from the aspirations of the people, but the strategy was perfectly adapted to them. On October 25, 1917, Lenin and his companions took power. Unlike the majority of those who start revolutions, they were to retain this power, closing the door to change or a possible restoration of the monarchy.

The imperial family, since February 1917, and particularly since the tsar's abdication in March, was no longer involved in these revolutionary events, and hoped to be able to remain on the sidelines. After all, the collapse of other monarchies in the empires of Europe had not necessarily meant the physical removal of those who had been ousted, once they no longer had any influence on events. It was true that Charles I of England and Louis XVI had paid for their countries' revolutions with their lives, but they had both lived at a time when revolutions had marked an unusual interruption of existing political systems and when everything suggested that, with them alive, the interruption would be of short duration. They had been the symbols of the natural order and, as such, likely to be a focus for renewed loyalty. Charles I fought for his rights and turned toward Scotland. To bring him down and to break the legitimacy that he embodied, Cromwell appealed to another type of legitimacy: that of the court that condemned Charles for treason and tyranny and sentenced him to public execution This judgment was to break not so much the man as his legitimacy. It was the same in 1793 with Louis XVI, who had gathered round him an opposition convinced that revolutionary disorder (the opposite of the natural order) had no prospect of surviving long. The international climate of opinion was in agreement over this relationship between disorder and legitimacy. Louis XVI and Marie-Antoinette, like Charles I, were tried for crimes that destroyed their legitimacy, and their public executions were merely the visible translation of this delegitimization. The same reasoning can be applied, to a certain extent, to Maximilian, emperor of Mexico, who was shot in 1867.

The fate of the Russian imperial family in 1918 was very different. Monarchy was no longer the only norm in Europe and the advances made by republicanism legitimized other systems. All the great empires were collapsing. In Russia, the Romanovs were now merely ordinary citizens whose fate, in the extraordinary sequence of events of the years 1917–19, was of little concern to society. In the wake of the February Revolution, the provisional government had of course wondered how to resolve the "question of the imperial family." The first reaction was that there was no reason to execute the Romanovs, and Kerensky even tried to negotiate their exile. But this plan failed. Petrograd had become the center of the political struggle—since April 1917 when Lenin returned to Russia, he had been bringing all his weight to bear on the course of events—and the mood of the people in the revolutionary city was dangerously volatile. It appeared then that the crowds would be prepared to follow any leader in any wild plan. The provisional government decided that the imperial family should be removed from the capital for their own safety. For reasons of security concerning their journey—the railroads were in the hands of the Bolsheviks—and their accommodation, a small and peaceful Siberian town, Tobolsk, with no industrial working class of any size and far from the political upheavals, was chosen. For several months the imperial family lived there. Conditions were uncomfortable, but they were able to feel relatively secure, attentive to the rumors of civil strife reaching them and hoping that an escape plan organized from outside would rescue them from their situation. Now that they had become ordinary citizens, the Romanovs hoped for a time that they would escape.

When the Bolsheviks came to power, they were equally unsure what to do with the Romanovs, although there was little doubt that the classic revolutionary solution—execution—ought to be applied to them. Events were to take an unusual turn. In April 1918,[11] the imperial family was taken to Ekaterinburg in the Urals, firmly in the hands of the Bolshevik soviet. On July 16, in the middle of the night, the whole family was assembled in a room in the Ipatyev house, where they had been staying since the move, by a detachment of the Cheka commanded by a local Bolshevik, Yakov Yurovsky. Without any kind of trial, the entire family was killed, parents, children—the tsarevich, ill again, was in his father's arms and had to be finished off by savage kicks. The servants who had accompanied them were to meet the same fate. A few days earlier, Grand Duke Michael had also been killed, and in the same conditions, in Perm. On July 17, six other members of the family were killed in Alapayevsk in the Urals (Grand Duchess Elizabeth, sister of the emperor, Grand Duke Sergei Mikhailovich, the three children of Grand Duke Constantine and one of the children of Grand Duke Paul). Finally, in January 1919, it was the turn of the four surviving grand dukes in the Peter and Paul Fortress. One of them was Grand Duke Nicholas Mikhailovich, a well-known historian and a long-standing liberal. To those who argued that this Romanov, who had labored so long to transform the dynasty and persuade it of the need for far-reaching reforms, should be spared, Lenin retorted brutally: "The revolution has no need of historians." Those members of the Romanov family who escaped the massacre were few in number and owed their lives to circumstance, not to the will of their executioners. It was to be the same for those close to them, with a large number of ministers and generals being ruthlessly eliminated.

The summary execution of the sovereign and the systematic liquidation of the entire imperial family by a regime that thus proclaimed its legitimacy—though of a new type—were hitherto unknown events and raised serious questions. Why had these executions, which the Bolsheviks appear to have wanted at first to hush up, taken place? On July 20, a document signed by Sverdlov, in the name of the presidium of the Central Executive Committee, approved the decision of the Urals soviet to shoot Nicholas II. The pretext was the advancing Czechoslovak Legion, supposedly in

11. From February 1, 1918, the dates given here are those of the Gregorian calendar, adopted at this time by the Bolshevik government.

league with the dethroned sovereign. Implied in the document was the crime or the possible treason of the prisoner. On the other hand, the communiqué asserted that the imperial family had been taken unharmed to a place of safety. The fiction of the single murder of the sovereign was abandoned in 1919, when the authorities admitted that the whole family had met their deaths in Ipatyev's house.

We shall return to the justifications that were given for the deed. First, it is necessary to understand the motive for carrying out a summary execution, rather than following the classic procedure of a trial and public execution. We know from Trotsky that this question was asked and that he, supporting the idea of a large public trial, had hoped to be the prosecutor. He longed to see the whole reign—its rural and national policies, its lack of preparation for and the circumstances of entry into the war—put on trial. For Trotsky, the charge should be more than a mere accusation of treason. He believed that a public trial in the presence of the press and particularly of radio, which could be relayed to all those places where people assembled, would serve an educational purpose. It would teach a useful and ideological lesson since, by exposing what was evil, it would thereby legitimize those who wished to break with it and who embodied what was good. Such a trial would have a triple purpose. By blackening the sovereign, it would help to eradicate his image from men's consciousness. Society as a whole was not sufficiently aware of having lived under the reign of a bloody tyrant. By rejecting all the decisions and policies of the former regime, the trial would also be able to substitute a new system of values, the opposite of that embodied by the tsar. A sophisticated intellectual like Trotsky was well aware of the long duration of old values in the social consciousness.

Second, the Bolsheviks believed that it was essential to prevent any ideological syncretism from merely grafting the moral world of which they were the guardians onto the existing social culture. They sought to create a *tabula rasa,* and what better way of doing so than by this public exposure of the evils of the monarchy? Finally, the tsar, accused of all the ills of the country, would legitimize those who had deposed him. This legitimization by self-criticism was greatly preferable to legitimization by history—something not easily understood by the collective consciousness—or at the very least its necessary complement.

Trotsky's plan, which would have placed the deposition of the tsar firmly in the historical tradition of revolutions, was abandoned in favor of a summary and distinctly dubious execution. Trotsky was to write an account of these events and quotes a conversation with Sverdlov after the murders had been committed. It was from Sverdlov that he learned of the exterminations of the imperial family—officially spared—and the conditions in which this collective murder had been decided. To the question of who had made the decision—the official communiqué had suggested a decision by local leaders subsequently ratified by the central leadership—the answer was precise: "We decided it here; Ilyich (Lenin) was convinced that we ought not to leave the Whites a symbol to rally round."

Could the local situation have incited Lenin to make such a decision? It is undeniable that, in the summer of 1918, the Czechoslovak Legion—45,000 prisoners of war whom Kerensky had persuaded to turn against the Austro-Hungarian army in exchange for their freedom—was a possible pretext. After the Treaty of Brest-Litovsk, these men were caught between the demands of the leaders of the Central Powers, who viewed them as traitors and insisted that they be disarmed and handed over, and the Bolsheviks, who were trying to do precisely this. To escape being branded as traitors, the Czechoslovaks, organized in a well-equipped legion, had turned to the anti-Bolshevik officers who were quick to realize the part that this orderly military force could play in the confused situation of the summer of 1918. In July, the advances made by the Czechoslovaks in Siberia and the Urals were impressive, and Lenin may well have feared that they might attempt to free the tsar by force and use him as a symbol around which to rally the people. The newly achieved revolution could still be reversed.

Although these events should be borne in mind, it is nevertheless true that, between October 1917 and July 1918, Lenin never made any clear decision about a legal solution to the problem of the tsar. It seems odd that such a cautious man, who thought of everything, was apparently so negligent over a question that had to be resolved in one manner or another. It is all the more surprising since the Bolshevik authorities in Ekaterinburg, who longed to assassinate the tsar but dared not do it without authorization, were making ever more frequent representations to the capital to obtain the necessary agreement. It is clear that Lenin, despite his legal background, was not keen on a trial. Furthermore, the extermination of the entire imperial family seemed to him to carry more weight than Trotsky's argument. To eliminate the tsar and his heir was to eliminate their value as symbols. Yet since the laws of succession operating during the reigns of recent sovereigns had made it impossible for women to succeed to the throne, the young grand duchesses could not become a rallying point. Thus it seems fairly clear that Lenin wanted to get rid of all traces of the Romanovs. In contrast to Trotsky's idea of the educational value of a legal trial, Lenin was proposing education through destruction and terror. The assassination of the entire Romanov family would be a tangible symbol, not only for Russia but for the outside world, of the radical break with past, the *tabula rasa*, and above all, the irreversibility of the revolution.

In pursuing this course, instead of following in the footsteps of the English or French revolutions, Lenin was making a clear statement: the Russian Revolution was like no other, it was the beginning of a new world that had no links with either the past or the outside world. The trial of the tsar would have been a symbol of a link between the past and the present, making the Russian Revolution and its ideology part of a long tradition. Lenin was later to defend his actions of this period. Through this radical step—the systematic extermination of an entire family, including the young grand duchesses and even the sick child—and the horrific nature of such an extreme decision, he demonstrated his refusal to compromise with tradition, reason, or feelings of pity. There was to be no going back. He behaved in the same way, though the circumstances were less tragic, when he dissolved the legally elected Constituent Assembly, the existence of which he had promised to respect. But, once in power, and following his own personal logic, Lenin intended to show that for the first time in history, the newly emerging world would brook no obstacles or reversals. The ruthless, apocalyptic, and single-minded, not to say totalitarian, ideas of the "student

Pugachovs" were thus put into effect, in this symbolic immolation of everything that had represented the old Russia, the Russia before October 1917.

Terror and Counter-Terror

Kill the tyrant! This theme had been familiar in Russia long enough for it to provoke little reaction in the chaotic society of the immediate postrevolutionary period. But never before had there been such a rapid transformation of the "antityrant" into a tyrant. Although Robespierre was accused by the Girondins of aspiring to a personal dictatorship as early as 1792, it was not until 1794 that he was to pay for his extremism. Lenin's extremism was immediately to brand him as a tyrant in the eyes of those who had always proclaimed the right to remove the tyrant: the Socialist Revolutionaries. The true representatives of the aspirations of the peasants and the winners in the only general democratic elections in Russian history (receiving 58 percent of the votes, more than double those of the Bolsheviks), the Socialist Revolutionaries could not allow Lenin, in the minority, simply to abolish the Constituent Assembly unchallenged. Lenin's response to the people's rejection of the Bolshevik Revolution was that the revolution took precedence over the ballot box, which merely indicated how social consciousness lagged behind the true course of history. The Socialist Revolutionaries' conclusion was simple: Lenin's tyranny—a simple variant of classic tyranny—called for the traditional methods of struggle against a tyrant. "The gun and bomb," which had for so long threatened the monarchy, were from then on to be directed against Lenin and his work.

The new revolutionary terrorists, convinced that the revolution was flawed, found their first targets in some German officials. The Treaty of Brest-Litovsk, welcomed by Lenin and allowing the Central Powers to concentrate all their forces on the western front, had never been unanimously popular—far from it. This compromise with the Central Powers had certainly saved the Russian Revolution, but it had also held back other revolutions elsewhere and it was rejected by almost all of Lenin's companions. The relentless hostility of the Socialist Revolutionaries toward the Germans, now present in Russia after the signing of the peace, was indicative of their rejection of a revolution that they saw as already distorted by a new tyrant. Just as they had once directed their efforts at the tsar's ministers, so now they made these German officials their targets, as if they had been Lenin's accomplices. On July 6, 1918, Count von Mirbach, the Kaiser's representative in Moscow, was shot by a Socialist Revolutionary. On July 30, it was the turn of Marshal von Eichhorn, commander of the German troops in the Ukraine.

But the real targets lay elsewhere: following a tried and tested strategy, the first assassination attempts were intended to shake the authority of the Bolsheviks. August 30 was to be decisive; in Petrograd, a young student member of the Socialist Revolutionaries mortally wounded Uritsky, the head of the Petrograd Cheka; the same day, in Moscow, a young woman named Fanny Kaplan fired three shots at Lenin. He was hit twice, receiving wounds that took a toll of his strength for a long time to come, but he survived. Meanwhile, the Socialist Revolutionary Party had tried unsuccessfully to gain control of some centers of power.

The cost of this use of terror against terror, high in the short term, was to prove even greater in the long term. Fanny Kaplan, like her predecessors, loudly proclaiming her responsibility and reminding her captors that she had already known prison under the tsar, was executed without even the pretense of a trial on September 3. Lenin was more ruthless with terrorists than his imperial predecessors, who at least tried them according to due form and sometimes pardoned them. The execution of these terrorists was followed by repression—in the name of "education." Increasing numbers of Socialist Revolutionaries were arrested, and in order to discourage any further attempts by other groups, the repression was extended to what was termed at the time "the bourgeoisie and its agents." The head of the Moscow Cheka was to boast of having carried out six hundred executions designed to reestablish order.

The terrorism revived in 1918 against the Bolsheviks was once again a peculiarly Russian phenomenon. Reborn with a new regime that it had once longed for, its motivation was not the struggle for power. It was true that the Socialist Revolutionaries disagreed profoundly with Lenin and all his decisions—whether it was his conditions for peace, rural policy, or policy in general—and they bitterly resented the cynical suppression of the Constituent Assembly. But the important element of their behavior was the judgment they brought to bear on Lenin. They condemned and intended to murder the "false" revolutionary, who was in reality a tyrant, representative of the "false" revolution, a new tyranny. They assassinated in the name of the "true" revolution. Thus even the Russian Revolution had not escaped from the eternal opposition of true and false, and the eternal return of the usurper—though this time it was Lenin, who had usurped revolutionary power.

A horrifying number of murders were carried out in Russia in less than two years. Revolutions are, of course, rarely peaceful. But besides the immediate deaths that revolution brings in its wake, of the opposition, the conquered, and those who oppose the holders of power, there was another series of murders that were not fully incorporated into its history. First there was the murder of Rasputin, killed so that the monarchy might survive, when other methods would have been more appropriate. He was killed also in order to destroy a confused idea of evil identified with the rising tide of revolution. In the eyes of those who killed him, Rasputin was the devil and thus, by definition, the bringer of disorder, for is not the devil a revolt against the divine order? Revolution, the revolt of men against the order willed by God, is a repetition of Satan's rebellion. However absurd Rasputin's murder may have been as far as its intentions went, we can understand the intellectual reasoning of those who carried it out. Second, there was the murder of the entire imperial family, a murder in the full sense of the word, for the regime was never to boast of it. For a long time it was not admitted and then justifications were sought, varying over the years and justifying nothing. The scene of the murder, Ipatyev's house, was never elevated to the rank of a historic site—in fact, quite the opposite. Then there were the murders of the German representatives in Russia, who had nothing to do with the upheavals of revolution. Finally, there was the murder of one of the figures responsible for state security, and the attempted murder of the leader of the revolution.

This apparently unconnected series, embracing such different motives, hatreds, and victims, has just one unifying thread, one common factor: it bears witness to the fact that the time of violence had returned and that this time violence had become a favored political tool. But those who were witnesses to these murders were not yet aware that behind these single trees, the shadows of the forest were to cover the whole land, bringing a horror rivaled only by that brought by the invaders of earlier centuries who had been responsible for Russia's backwardness and for a never-ending series of tragedies.

12

Apocalypse

♦

Russia was always a land of extremes and contradictions, and never more so than in the period between Alexander II and Nicholas II. On the one hand there was the march toward modernity. The path was never smooth, advances being followed by retreats or stagnation. Nevertheless, modernity was eventually to triumph. It meant not only industrialization and urbanization, but also a change in men's attitudes, through education.[1] But hand in hand with change there developed a strongly apocalyptic mood. In this Russia was unique. At all levels of society, there was a confused awareness that the world men had known hitherto was about to be swallowed up and plunged into the unknown. All points of view had to be fitted into this extreme framework: Russia condemned like Sodom, Holy Russia in need of defense, a future through redemption, or a future of destruction. Russia was not alone in feeling that an uncertain future lay ahead; the whole of Europe was aware that the Belle Epoque might be coming to an end, but in these other countries, premonitions about a different time to come remained within the bounds of the rational.

In 1914, the whole of Europe was to see the disappearance of life as it had been known. The civilization of postwar Europe was unrecognizable, and was to produce many tragedies. But Russia, by contrast, had not come to the end of its individual path—quite the opposite. Having fought for so long to become integrated into Europe, it was once more, as in the terrible period of the Mongol domination, to cut itself off in order to set up a separate Europe. While terror tragically dominated the countries of Europe for a few

---

1. According to the census of 1897, 21 percent of the population could read and write; the figure was 28 percent in 1913. If one looks at the development by age groups the improvement is even more remarkable: in 1912, 68 percent of army recruits could read and write.

years, in Russia it was to last for several decades. That which elsewhere was to seem exceptional, monstrous, and transitory was to become the rule in Russia. The apocalyptic visions of the Russian writers of the Silver Age and the popular tendency to interpret everything as a sign announcing the end of the world—the appearance of Halley's Comet in 1910 or Rasputin's predictions, for example—were to find a startling justification in the course of the history of this strange country between 1917 and 1953.

A Promethean Utopia

Two countries were outlawed from Europe by the First World War, though for differing reasons: Germany and Russia. They were both countries that were trying to find their way out of the ruins of a past order buried by the war. In both, various forms of violence were unleashed in the early 1920s and were to offer the world the terrifying spectacle of the systematic destruction of society. What differentiates them is that the violence in Germany was intermittent while that in Russia was continuous. Furthermore, Russian violence was set within the framework of a Promethean plan.

The murders in Germany of Karl Liebknecht and Rosa Luxemburg in 1919 through to Walter Rathenau in 1922 were linked with the confusion of the shattered empire and the struggle between alternative solutions. Hitler's violence, whether against his companions, as in the Night of the Long Knives, or against entire catetories of people, defined by their ethnic origin or way of life, had little to do with the murders of the 1920s and was the result of a simple, if not simplistic, ideology and a totalitarian approach.

Events in Russia were quite different. It has long been normal, or even de rigueur, to dwell at length on Stalinism and the horrific events of that period, but the origins of Stalinism are still not fully understood. Solzhenitsyn, in 1973, made a breakthrough with the publication of *The Gulag Archipelago*, ignoring taboos speculating about the intellectual and concrete origins of Stalinism. In 1988, when the intellectuals' demands for truth began to make themselves heard in the USSR, it was clear that it was "truth" in the full meaning of the word—*pravda i istina* (truth and certainty)—that was to result from their heroic efforts. Not until it is possible to examine the archives—before too long, it is to be hoped—can a proper balance of the murders committed in the terrible Stalin years be drawn up. While a study of Stalinism itself is not appropriate to this work, the political function of murder, its forms, and its development during this period provide much food for thought.

Since Solzhenitsyn, no one now dares to deny that it is necessary to start by looking at Lenin's original program and its legacy. The man who led the Russian Revolution of 1917 and seized power at the age of forty-seven seemed the perfect incarnation of the Russian intelligentsia of the previous century. Nevertheless, he differed from it in many ways. First, his character was different. His predecessors, the "student Pugachovs," sought a future, and an explanation for a world that they rejected, along many different paths. These idealists, torn between a sense of guilt and the hope of a new Golden Age, gave a passionate dimension to their theories that made them more human. Although a cultivated man, Lenin had only one idea: power. All his reading, traces of which can be found in his writings, bears witness to the fact that his entire intellectual and private life were concerned uniquely with the question of how to conquer power. His obsession with power left no time for speculation about the past and the future. Only the present was important and the struggle for power. Lenin had an extraordinary ability to adapt his ideas and his behavior to immediate demands, first the struggle for power and then later the struggle to keep power. Call this what we will—opportunism or pragmatism—it was the logic of this approach that gave Lenin his unique place, unlike any other, in the ranks of the intelligentsia. For him, the only thing that mattered was what was useful to power. For him, truth became one with this utility.

Lenin believed that the only practical means for the conquest of and survival in power was through organization. Even if the traditions of the intelligentsia provided a number of isolated precedents—Pestel and Tkachev in particular—an obsession with organization and above all the ability to make it work are characteristics that can be particularly associated with Lenin. The distinguishing mark of the Russian intelligentsia—even when involved in action—was more often than not its naïve, chaotic, and spontaneous approach to action. The intellectuals' sense of organization left much to be desired, and we can see a reflection of this in Bakunin's dislike of Marx, in the First International, as well as in the disorganized schemes of the terrorists. Lenin's answer to this disorder was the party. It would have a restricted and professional membership and would be based on the idea of "democratic centralism," an ambiguous formula that meant that the centralization of authority always prevailed and in which loyalty was owed to "party-mindedness" (*partiinost'*). This "party-mindedness," the mental universe of its members, was to pose a serious problem when it came to their relations with the people. Lenin's organization was intended to lead the people, a people for whom the party was the avant-garde, but an avant-garde that had emerged from the people and was consubstantial with them, so that the gap between the intelligentsia and the people, always a fatal stumbling block for the revolutionary movement, would disappear. And yet, while insisting on this basic unity of the people and their avant-garde, Lenin at the same time contradicted it in his idea of *partiinost'*. He had sown the seeds of the rift that was to arise between the two.

In another proof of his essential originality, Lenin realized that this organization needed an all-encompassing ideological system that alone would be capable of providing an all-embracing response to the problems of a society that was asked to break with all that it had known before. Here, Lenin, like so many others, speaks in apocalyptic terms: the end of time and the beginning of the new world require an overall plan, transforming everything, from the possible to the impossible—the dream of Prometheus. Gone was the time when partial proposals, reforms, or reasonable adjustments to the existing order would suffice. Lenin's obsession not only fits in with a millenarian vision but even seems to point the way to it. Lenin's organization had, furthermore, the great merit for his contemporaries of reconciling the two extremes of the traditional debate over the path to change. While passionately pro-western—his ideas were full of references to German philosophy and the political systems of the Anglo-Saxon countries—Lenin simultaneously held out a hand to his pro-Slav opponents, to all those who believed in Russia's special destiny and historic mission. As an organizer, he forged a weapon—the party, something international Marxism regarded with suspicion and even disgust—and used it as a lever to raise up his country, to break this weak link in the imperialist chain and, in so doing, to precipitate world revolution. Thus original Marxism, the theory of the historic development of western Europe, was married to the Russian dream of a Third Rome now called on to play a central role in the revolutionary redemption of humanity.

Finally, Lenin was able to unite around his plan, because it had a single goal, all the social groups that had, at various moments in the history of the intelligentsia, been taken up separately by the intellectuals and thus become isolated from the other groups. Like all his predecessors, Lenin looked to the "people," the only effective group to legitimize radical change; but unlike them, he brought together the various elements that made up the people. Although an orthodox Marxist, he was not content to rely solely on the working class. The actors in the historic drama that was about to take place, who as a group were the "people"—rather than the proletariat— were the oppressed, the poor, and those passed over by history. It was Lenin who coined the phrase "the people emerging onto the stage of history." These people were as yet on its fringes but he intended to harness their energies and abilities for his work. Workers, muzhiks, the intelligentsia, and oppressed ethnic groups all came together on an equal footing in the enchanted circle of revolution. Events have shown that it was precisely this social ecumenicalism—very alien to orthodox Marxism, but inherent in Lenin's voluntarism—that ensured its success and enabled it to take over from the disorganization of the February Revolution, harnessing the Dionysian spontaneity of Russian society in those troubled months, imposing Lenin's rigid, centralized plan, which was to become the "dictatorship of the proletariat."

Influenced not only by Russian political traditions but also by those of some of his predecessors, Lenin nevertheless differed from them in that he was able—and perhaps this is the essential point—to impose, as a consequence of his obsession with organization, a concept of morality that was to mark a radical break with the past. Morality, the basis of human behavior, had generally been accepted by the Russian intelligentsia as an objective reality, except in a few cases, the most obvious of which was Nechayev. Whatever the undoubted cultural differences of the various political classes and the intelligentsia, the social consciousness of the whole of society had long agreed on an ethical view of behavior, on the nature of good and evil, and on the demands of conscience. (The fact that the practice and the theory of morality often diverged widely is another matter.) It was this moral law, absolute and independent of contingencies, that had welded all the elements of society together in a common belief and culture. Lenin's important innovation was to make the moral law relative, in order to make it subservient to the demands of history and, ultimately, to the party. Thus, on taking power, he not only initiated a period that was radically new but also broke with the entire cultural tradition of old Russia.

It has long been debated whether the USSR is not in fact the old Russia in new clothing—above all ideological—or whether it is radically different. The answer can be found in Lenin's break with the old morality. History has shown that no revolution can entirely wipe out the past, and the Soviet state was certainly to retain many characteristics and burdens from the old Russia. Nevertheless, despite the continuation of certain old traditions, there were decisive changes that tipped the scales in the direction of a new and different order. The decisive element in this was Lenin's conception of morality. Though in many ways the USSR is reminiscent of old Russia—we have only to read the letters of the Marquis de Custine in the 1820s to see this—the essential is missing. It was Lenin, with his very personal approach to the problem of change, who made the decisive break. If the USSR was, as he had so passionately desired, the leading country in the new world of the revolution, this was because he founded it and because he based his actions on a completely new concept of morality, the applications of which we shall now examine.

A Bright Dawn

In the course of their struggle for a new world, all revolutionaries have dreamed of the society that would emerge from their revolution. As a general rule, their ideas, however fertile, lacked precision. They imagined a universe where the absence of conflict in society would lead to an end to the problems of power and the power struggle. When Lenin wrote *State and Revolution* on the eve of seizing power, he too was little inclined to give a concrete picture of the future, confining himself to a rough outline. Following Marx's remarks on the Paris Commune, Lenin says that the revolution does not immediately suppress the state, but goes through a transitional stage of state control under the dictatorship of the proletariat, during which it overcomes the resistance of the opponents of the revolution. His concept of this transitional state is remarkably utopian: it anticipates the exercise of a simplified power by the social "majority" that will assume responsibility for defense and public order, as well as all administrative and social duties, by arming the people. The reign of the common man was about to begin. At the same time, Lenin's ideas follow a contrary direction: to this vision of the simplified state that would eventually wither away, he adds the party. This tension between a society governing the transitional state and the party, the avant-garde of the workers, implicitly underlies all Lenin's theories, even at the time of greatest optimism, when he visualized the imminent takeover of power in Russia and the beginning of world revolution. The future he describes holds out a vision of a pacified universe from which violence has disappeared.

The February Revolution had already given rise to such dreams, despite the difficulties that had instantly materialized. The leaders had begun by abolishing the death sentence, a decision always symbolic of the end of violence. On October 25, 1917, the Second Congress of the Soviets, marking the triumph of the Bolshevik Revolution, confirmed this abolition. Lenin, however, far from applauding, was indignant: "How can we carry out a revolution without shooting people?"

In the place of capital punishment, a machine for repression was immediately set up. Lenin justified it by the need to defend the revolution from its enemies. Truth to tell, these enemies were rather at a loss. Whom could they depend on when the slogans of the revolutionaries—peace, land, and national self-determination—had persuaded all social and ethnic groups to support Lenin? With the election of the Constituent Assembly in November 1917 came the problem of social unanimity. Faced with the existence of a public opinion, of a people who had chosen to vote according to their preferences instead of showing unanimous enthusiasm for this party, Lenin was forced to condemn this "talking shop" and abolish it. He had never disguised his disdain for parliamentarianism, but before 1917 his attacks had been aimed at "bourgeois parliamentarianism." Could the importance of Russia's first democratic elections with universal suffrage be simply ignored? Lenin's answer was clear: "We shall tell the people that their interests go beyond those of a democratic institution. We should not accept the traditional illusion that subordinates the interests of the people to a nominal democracy."

However, when Lenin offers his own view of the intentions of the people, of which he and his party would be the repository in the place of democracy and a multiparty system, the inherent contradictions are immediately apparent. Since he does not accept arbitration by the people, what other kind of arbitration can there be except that of the strongest? And how can this strength be expressed except through the use of force? Thus no sooner had it appeared than the utopian idea of the maintenance of law and order by society itself disappeared again. Since the people's expression of its desires must be opposed—for that is what the suppression of the Constituent Assembly amounted to—and society must be taught to distinguish the "real truth" from the truth as society itself perceives it, then the instruments of repression must be drawn from this same society. But these instruments of repression would then exist alongside, rather than within, society, with their sights concentrated on it.

Lenin was assisted in this work in the defense of the revolution by two men. First, there was Bonch-Bruyevich, an old friend, who worked at his side in the Sovnarkom (Soviet of People's Commissars, chaired by Lenin) and who organized the first repressive measures. It was also Bonch-Bruyevich who had organized the operation to crush the Constituent Assembly. For a few weeks, the "people's order" described in *State and Revolution*—the police of which Marx had proclaimed that when handed over to the people along with the army, it would define the existence of popular power—consisted of Bonch-Bruyevich's small group of police with its henchmen who dispensed summary justice, pillaging and killing without restraint. The official explanation of these events was that the last remnants of the old order were being hunted out.

But soon it became clear that this disorder and growing anarchy was bringing the Bolsheviks into disrepute, and criticism began to grow both from within their own ranks and from the other parties that had participated in the Constituent Assembly. "What Russia needs is another Fouquier-Tinville!" Lenin was to declare, and he found one in the person of Feliks Dzerzhinsky. He had at the vital moment loyally supported Lenin's decision to launch the insurrection, against the advice of Kamenev and Zinoviev who hesitated to act. Dzerzhinsky, an early convert to Marxism and son of a Polish family of the petty nobility, was an unusual figure. Ascetic and intransigent, resembling the pure revolutionary hero dreamed of by Nechayev, Dzerzhinsky was hated by the European socialists and compared to the ghost of Banquo at Macbeth's banquet. If we are to believe his diary, he had, like many executioners, a soft spot for children and was capable of real friendships. He was, however, obsessed with the idea that terror was indispensable to the revolution, which was why Lenin, in December 1917, entrusted him with the task of creating an efficient institution of repression on a scale that would match the size of the country.

The result was the Cheka (Extraordinary Commission for Combating Counter-Revolution and Speculation). It was placed under the direct authority of the government, thus of Lenin, and immediately assumed the powers of the police and the judiciary, spreading a network over the whole country. It pursued and prosecuted "saboteurs," a vague category that could be interpreted at will. Meanwhile, the death sentence, which the Cheka had been using shamelessly and on its own authority ever since its formation, was officially reinstated on February 21, 1918. The decree restoring capital punishment confirmed the extent of the powers conferred upon the Cheka, which was allowed to pronounce and carry out its sentences without delay. At the same time, trials were being carried out in courts where crimes were interpreted from the revolutionary point of view.

All the old ideas of law had disappeared; there were no codes, no system of precedent, just two prescriptive elements:

"revolutionary justice," or the interests of the revolution, and "the people's interest." Lenin had borrowed the idea of the "people," the depository and guarantor of the real demands of morality, from the Populists, but he used the word "people" to cover an unlimited area, foremost among which was that of institutions. The ministers had become "People's Commissars," while any opponent was termed an "enemy of the people." The judicial system and the new sources of revolutionary law were supposed to come from the "people." In fact, this new people's law came from the men of the Cheka, who understood, defined, and applied it. Thus a discrepancy arose between, on the one hand, a system of repression decided on by Lenin and those close to him, which was able to develop rapidly through a tight network of institutions to become all-powerful, beyond the reach of any kind of social control; and on the other, the assertion that this was the people's justice and the people's law. In this discrepancy we see a striking illustration of what was to become a constant in the USSR: the language of propaganda.

In addition to the Cheka, which exercised an "extrajudicial" justice (*nesudebnaia rasprava*), and the people's courts, the government created on September 5, 1918, an institution that was to be infamous in the twentieth century: the concentration camp. In fact, Lenin had not waited for the Sovnarkom to pass this resolution, having already institutionalized the system of sending those deemed to be dangerous to the system to these camps. Three months earlier, Trotsky, who seems to have been the first to use this term, was demanding that the bourgeoisie, officers, and Czechs be shut up in them. Two months later, Lenin proposed the same punishment for "rich peasants, priests, and White Guards." From this time on, the concentration camps and the death sentence became the indispensable components of a system of terror that was, for Lenin, inseparable from the dictatorship of the people.

One last element in the system needs to be mentioned. This too emerged in the summer of 1918, when the "dictatorship of the people" exercised by Lenin was to provoke the anger of the Socialist Revolutionaries and bring the peasants to the edge of revolt. Dzerzhinsky declared, 'We must take hostages," making it clear that included in this term were landowners, members of the abolished nobility, and those connected with them.

It is not easy to draw up a balance sheet for these first few years of dictatorship. Although we do not yet have access to the archives—and in any case archives are rarely precise when it comes to summary justice—we do have the document written by Latsis, one of Dzerzhinsky's earliest collaborators, where he describes the "the first two years" of the institution (in fact, the first year-and-a-half, since it deals with 1918 and the first half of 1919). The figures we can deduce from this do not, however, cover the whole country. If we also take into account the information that Latsis is able to provide from other sources together with a certain amount of cross-checking, it is clear that the statistics are in need of considerable reevaluation. Even so, they are overwhelming: 8,389 people shot by the Cheka—which does not include all those deaths decided on and carried out by the people's tribunals; 412 counterrevolutionary organizations uncovered, and 82,000 arrests. And this is no incomplete or partisan set of figures. What Latsis meant to show by these figures was the insufficiency of the vigilance of his collaborators, not their excesses.

Solzhenitsyn has compared these figures with those in Russia between 1826 and 1906. It should be remembered that they were not compiled by the imperial government, but by the leftist intellectuals who used them to indict the regime for its cruelty. They are probably no more complete than Latsis's figures, but the contrast is striking. Taking the highest possible figures for eighty years of imperial repression, we find 3,400 death sentences for the whole period, 1,310 of which were in 1906, marking the reaction to the revolution of 1905. This is not to glorify the empire, more inclined to deal with opponents by condemning them than to attempt to reform itself. Nevertheless, we cannot ignore the fact that in the space of eighteen months the Cheka alone—and the people's tribunals were kept equally busy at this time—killed two-and-a-half times more "opponents" than the empire had in eighty years!

Furthermore, the figures from the imperial period are figures for death sentences pronounced by courts, which, as we have seen, operated within the law; and, what is more, these were sentences, not executions. It is possible that pardons, of which there are specific examples, may have modified these statistics. In investigating the role of political murder in the long history of Russia, we have described the move in the nineteenth century toward a more civilized state: the imperial authorities still executed those who opposed them, but increasingly they tried to act in accordance with the law. The situation was very different after 1917: the development of an official form of terrorism and the abandonment of the old-established juridical norms opened the way to a systematic use of violence to defend and reinforce the new political system. Legality now referred only to the situation of the moment, to enemies denounced, uncovered, or suspected by the government. The combination of a secret police with unlimited powers, acting without reference to any legal norms, and courts that operated according to a new, relative legality fit in with Lenin's belief that the independence of the judiciary and the absolute nature of the law were inventions of bourgeois society that no longer had a place after the revolution.

It can be objected that this period of illegal terror corresponds to the early period of Lenin's power, when it seemed that the only way to defend a position threatened by social discontent, the opposition of the former servants of the empire, and foreign intervention was to kill political enemies. War Communism, the translation into practice of the transitional state that was to lead to communism, was, in the chiefly peasant Russia of 1918, a declaration of war on society itself. This strategy—a forced march toward communism against the existing social reality and the aspirations of the majority—implied violence and the physical elimination of all those who resisted or found themselves in the way of this plan for a total break with the past.

By the summer of 1918, the peasants—about 110 million out of a population of 130 million—had understood the antipeasant direction being taken by War Communism and were opposing it. Against them the state brought to bear all the means at its disposal—the forces of the Cheka, the political machine of the party and the soviets, and even the army. To put down what had become an armed struggle, the authorities used not only the traditional methods of war, but also new methods undreamed of by the empire. First, there was the taking of hostages. The number of people executed in these serial murders in the interests of a policy rejected by society has never been counted. Second, language was used in a particular way to designate the enemy, in the place of the old legal system. Since the revolution had come about through a close alliance with the peasants, it could not, needless to say, allow the peasants to turn against it. Instead, an enemy of the "peasant people" was found: the kulak, the rich peasant. To the general astonishment, the countryside, devastated by war and the exactions that followed, was found to contain vast numbers of these kulaks. To put down any troublesome peasant, it was enough to call him a kulak. This name was a sufficient indication of criminality to justify summary execution, individual deportation, or the deportation of whole families.

Toward a Legal Terror

In 1921, Lenin's USSR broke with War Communism and adopted the New Economic Policy (NEP), which in some ways was a new policy in general. There is still disagreement as to the nature of this change. Whether it was part of a gradual and moderate view of change temporarily interrupted by the violence of War Communism as a result of early difficulties, or whether it was a breathing space in which to assimilate and overcome difficulties before returning to the original radical vision, in either case the NEP was the recognition of a setback. Presented as a desire for social reconciliation—the entire peasantry had risen in 1920, while the proletariat was refusing "the dictatorship of the commissars"—the NEP was a recognition that terror could not on its own solve social problems, and particularly not economic ones. A political power can use violence to break men, but executions and violence have no hold over the economy which, it would appear, has laws of its own.

Nevertheless, the NEP did not imply a return to a democratic view of relations with society. The opposition press, banned during the years of War Communism, was still not permitted, and political parties were still forbidden, it not being possible for social representation to have multiple spokesmen. The soviets, progressively deprived of power and means of action since 1919, were now little more than hollow shells; their subordination to the party was about to become complete. Together with the economic concessions of the NEP[2] came an increased bureaucratization of the system, apparently to prevent economic liberalization from spilling over into the political sphere. The Tenth Party Congress of 1921 integrated the trade unions into the state apparatus and prohibited splinter groups, thus preventing debate, already impossible outside the party, from emerging within it. This seems clear evidence that the period of "retreat and economic reconciliation" was intended to reestablish a viable situation, and not to move the system toward greater participation or toward simple control by society of the expanding bureaucracy and of the dictatorship exercised by the party over society and its own forces.

In this new situation, the problem of violence takes on a new aspect. With the Civil War at an end, the country entered a period of stabilization. When world revolution failed to materialize it became clear that the Russian Revolution could not continue to live on the margins of the outside world. The need for coexistence with continuing capitalism required the institutionalization, albeit provisional, of the Soviet state, in line with the dominant international norms. Thus it was that those in power were now to try to reconcile terror and legality. The legalization of violence used against political enemies is characteristic of the last years of Lenin's life. This sudden quest for legality can only be understood in the light of the NEP. While giving nothing away on the political level, the aim was to isolate the political sphere from the economic sphere, take account of the isolation of the Soviet state, and allow a temporary compromise with a dangerous outside world.

In the 1920s, the jurists were given the difficult task of reconciling a normative law and a relative law. In 1922 it became urgent to provide the state with legal terms of reference, for this was the beginning of the period of "educational" terror, which, through the example of the first show trials, was to inculcate the ideological rudiments of the new system into society. Two particular trials give a good illustration of the way in which "ideological murder"—the

---

2. An end to requisitioning in the countryside, support for the cooperatives, business concessions to individuals, the restoration of small private trading, attraction of and guarantees for foreign capital, etc.

suppression, through the liquidation of human beings, of alternative ideologies—was given a legal appearance.

This progression toward the legalization of violence occurred against a background of the adaptation of institutions and the law. A significant change, in a system where language played such an important role, was that made in the police organization. On February 6, 1922, the Central Executive Committee abolished the Cheka, replacing it with the GPU (Chief Political Administration), under the authority of the People's Commissariat of the Interior.[3] Although the name had changed, the same people worked for it, making it clear that it was a continuation of the same. But the change of name was highly significant. The Cheka had been set up as an "extraordinary commission," suggesting the temporary character of the institution and the situation that justified it. The name GPU made it clear that the state ought to have at its disposal normal institutions of political control. At this same period the jurists were occupied in drawing up the essential lines of the state, combining relativity with stabilization. Behind the change in name of the police lay the perpetuation and legalization of terror as a way of controlling relations with the emerging society. It marked a final break with the Marxist intention that the instruments for the maintenance of law and order should be in the hands of the people. From 1922, the maintenance of political order was undertaken by the state alone.

It was clear that the legal system could no longer depend on a series of improvisations; Lenin instructed the jurists to draw up a criminal code. The first outlines submitted to him in May 1922 caused him to say: "In my opinion, it is necessary to extend the use of execution by shooting to all activities of Mensheviks, Socialist Revolutionaries, and the like; a formula must be found that will connect such activities with the international bourgeoisie." Forty-eight hours later, he was to add:

> Comrade Kursky, I would like supplement what we
> discussed earlier with these ideas for a paragraph for the

---

3. After the foundation of the USSR, the GPU became the OGPU, to include the federated republics.

Criminal Code. . . . The main point is clear, I think. It is necessary to state clearly—politically, and not merely in strictly juridical terms—the principles that constitute the basis and the justification of terror, its necessity, and its limits. The courts must not suppress terror—to say that would be to lie or to lie to oneself. Instead it must be established and its principles legalized, without deception or concealment of the truth. It must be formulated in the most open way possible, for only revolutionary consciousness and legal revolutionary consciousness can create the conditions for its application in practice. . . .

Finding the plan as presented to him insufficiently "open," Lenin added an impressive list of crimes punishable by the death sentence: "propaganda, agitation, participation in an organization, assisting an organization (propaganda and agitation) thereby helping the international bourgeoisie. . .".

With this very specific intervention in the drawing up of the criminal code, Lenin introduced some very ambiguous ideas into the new law, open to many interpretations and uses against those whom the state wished to suppress. In this vague, fluid legal system—the negation of law in its accepted sense—the death sentence could be applied in an almost unlimited way. On June 1, 1922, the penal code was finalized and came into force. Although too late for use at the trial of church dignitaries in April, it was now available for that of the Socialist Revolutionaries which was to follow.

It is worth taking a brief look at the religious trial, not only for its consequences but also for the contradictions in Soviet law that it revealed. Religion was a particular target of Lenin's action, on account of the place it had held for centuries in the Russian idea of the state and in the popular culture. The creation of a new social and political consciousness, based on the ideological system of the party, made it imperative to suppress the body seen by the party as the alternative to this system. The separation of church and state had been declared in 1918—a decision that the Orthodox synod meeting in the spring of 1917 had, for its part, already made—and religion was henceforward deemed to be a private matter. This postulate was, however, untenable, since the ideological basis of the Soviet state was the negation of religion. For the church and state to be separated and the freedom of individual conscience to be recognized, the state has to be neutral. Lenin's state was an ideological state, with the aim of forming a new social consciousness in which atheism was an important element. Thus, depite the myth of religious freedom and private individual choice, the party embarked on a path of confrontation that was inevitably violent, since it sought to eradicate deeply embedded beliefs, around which the nation had been built.

When the moment came to defend the political sphere in the courts, the battle was fought over the NEP. Since the separation of church and state in January 1918, the church had lost its legal rights and its property, apart from its sacred objects. Under violent attack from the state, it tried, under the leadership of the recently elected Patriarch Tikhon, to preserve its existence in a system that saw its mission as being to reduce the church to nothing. The patriarch managed to retain a certain authority by avoiding taking sides in the Civil War and by bringing relief to the suffering, the church making many donations to help the starving. Aware of this stabilization of the church, Lenin decided in 1922 to hasten the showdown.[4] He stressed that the moment had come to attack the institution and outlaw it. Given the people's level of consciousness, the break would have to be instructive, showing the incompatibility of the world of religion and the new era. The trial held in Moscow between April 26 and May 7, 1922, included seventeen laymen and clerics of all ranks, accused of having propagated the appeal—deemed to be anti-Soviet—issued by the patriarch to resist the confiscation of the church's sacred objects. It was nominally a public trial, but with a public vetted in advance by the GPU. Eleven of the accused were condemned to death, five of these sentences being carried out. The remaining six went to swell the numbers in the Gulag. Patriarch Tikhon, called to the witness stand, was arrested shortly afterwards. The outlawing of the church continued a few weeks later in Petrograd where the most important of the eighty

---

4.   The pretext was the seizing of the church's sacred objects. The resistance of the clergy led to clashes that were interpreted as open opposition.

accused was Metropolitan Benjamin, elected in 1917 and very close to the people, who had worked tirelessly for a church independent of the state. As in Moscow, the pretext for the trial was the church's resistance to handing over to the state its last remaining property, its sacred objects. But the explanation for this resistance was explained by the accusation itself: "The church is a counterrevolutionary organization." Here again, the sentences handed out achieved the physical liquidation of the chief figures in the church, starting with Metropolitan Benjamin.

The lesson of these widely publicized trials was that the church was the enemy of the people—and of the revolution, which was the same thing. The condemnation of its most important leaders was to legitimize both the sentence applied to the church and the battles that were to follow. The year 1922, which opened with these trials, was to see an exeptionally high number of murders: 8,100 priests, monks, and nuns were shot during this period, through the application of the judgments of the two big trials. There was no need to hold other trials, since the courts had established the general culpability of the church vis-à-vis the people and the revolution.

Thus, as a result of these two trials, we see the emergence of a new type of legal system that began to take the place of the pure negation of legality of the preceding years. The trial and execution of those people who best represented a particular category—as the patriarch and the metropolitan represented their church and the community of the faithful—were not intended to establish particular accusations. The lawyer defending Metropolitan Benjamin was to declare: "Here we have no proof of guilt, nor facts, nor even an accusation. . . . The basic principle, as you yourself have stressed, is 'what is useful' to the Soviet state." It was important to establish the relationship of the state to the church, which lay in the strength of the state. The law that emerged from this practice derived from a view of the relations of strength and the criterion of utility to the Communist plan. When the relations of strength, which placed the church in the role of the guilty party, were codified through the court's decisions, all those connected with the church came under the authority of the same law, making it unnecessary to go through even a pretense of a trial. Anyone who is guilty should be punished, and the general principle of the guilt of the religious world had been established—in terms of this new law—by the trials of 1922.

The trial of the Socialist Revolutionaries (June–July 1922) was to put the new criminal code, hastily finished for the occasion, to the test. The complex accusation took as its starting point the accused's responsibility for the Civil War, concluding with a proof of espionage on behalf of the Allies. This trial was important in two respects: since the Socialist Revolutionaries were found guilty, it established that it was the Bolsheviks alone who had led the revolution, thus justifying their subsequent exercise of exclusive power; second, it tested a method whereby the accusations were contained one within another, like Russian nesting dolls. Taking a definite fact as a starting point—for example, that the Socialist Revolutionaries had certainly opposed the absolutism of the Bolsheviks since 1918—it would emerge with the assistance of the principle enunciated by Lenin a few weeks earlier that all opposition to the Bolsheviks was ultimately equivalent to cooperating with the international bourgeoisie. This system of using a trial as a method of legitimizing a carefully constructed accusation of treason was to be perfected within a few years and used against those very men who had devised the system. By an irony of history, the trial of the Socialist Revolutionaries was presided over by Pyatakov, who was to be, in 1937, the most important of those accused in the trial of the "Trotskyist Anti-Soviet Center" when many of the charges (particularly of espionage) made by him against the Socialist Revolutionaries were turned against him and led to his execution.[5]

From this time, the legalization of terror and murder on a grand scale was in place. It should be said, however, that, even if the murders, legal or completely illegal, were countless, the terrorist system still had some critics. Lenin's policy of terrorism, which concealed the setting up of a real terror, was still on the defensive. Despite press censorship and the suppression of opposition parties, the Russian intelligentsia, which had fought so long for the revolu-

---

5. In 1918 a Communist on the left, Pyatakov had opposed the Treaty of Brest-Litovsk—which the Socialist Revolutionaries were to be accused, in the trial of 1922, of having "sabotaged"—and Lenin's ideas, in which he detected traces of "peasant populism."

tion, did not stay silent. Even in the ranks of the party and among its closest fellow travelers, critics denounced the ever-widening gap between the utopia and the reality. Even Gorky, the most faithful of the faithful, raised his voice in dissent. Outside the Soviet state, in the very heart of the socialist movement, the direction stamped on the system by Lenin—dictatorship of the proletariat identified with the dictatorship of the party, and suppression of democracy—was not unanimously accepted. Before her death, Rosa Luxemburg criticized this process, predicting the future with great accuracy. The Third International, founded by Lenin, had not yet given its backing to his view of the march toward communism.

Lenin's ideas on terrorism and then his utilitarian and relative definition of revolutionary justice had at least the merit of being frank. He did not pretend to return to the law, but to a particular law that would legitimize his policies. In so doing, as Leszek Kolakowski has so justly stressed, there is no doubt that he was sowing the seeds of a system that was totalitarian and not just despotic. It was his successor who was to exploit the process thus initiated to the full, getting rid of anyone he wished in the name of a law that was constantly being adapted to this end.

The Right to Murder

Since the time when Stalin was first accused of operating a system of terror, the problem has been to date the stages of this deviation from the original system and to evaluate the human cost. When did murder become the chief instrument of the party? How many murders did Stalin commit?

In answer to the first question, the views of Solzhenitsyn and Kolakowski mentioned above have begun to gain ground. The answer to the second, depending on access to archives, is still to come and for the moment remains speculative. However, it is not our concern here to provide a catalogue of Stalin's murders or to attempt to assess their number, but rather to examine their original characteristics and try to classify them according to functional typology.

The majority of judgments pronounced on Stalin and Stalinism, often extreme, stress the excessive and irrational elements. "Stalinism is the syphilis of the workers' movement," Trotsky was to write near the end of his life. For the poet Osip Mandelshtam, Stalin was a monster, a man-eater. Others described him as a madman. The historian Roy Medvedev calls him one of the greatest criminals in man's history.

We are immediately struck by Stalin's multidimensional use of murder, and by the legalism governing it. This is perhaps the great difference between Stalin and Lenin. Lenin, it is true, had set up a system of terror and used murder generously, but, though he had relied on murder to resolve complex problems, he certainly did not see it as an instrument of universal power. He had recourse to murder when circumstances required it—in accordance with his pragmatic approach—and he was quite open about this. His justification of terrorism is clear and, even when he tries to give it a legal dimension, he stresses the relative and utilitarian nature of this law whose only basis is to serve the revolution. Trotsky, too, shortly after 1917, made no bones about the necessity for and legitimacy of violence. For him, to reject terror was to condemn the chances of socialism. To achieve the end one must be prepared to accept any means. "The state, before disappearing, takes on the form of the dictatorship of the proletariat; that is to say, the most merciless state imaginable, the state that imperiously embraces the life of all its citizens."

Stalin replaced this openly admitted view of terror with a variant disguised beneath an appearance of democracy and law. Little inclined to brutal formulas, he instead associated an image of legality and humanity with the use of terror. With the help of the jurists in the 1930s and the Constitution of 1936, he created the appearance of a state ruled by law and total democracy. The dictatorship of the proletariat was to make way for the state of the soviets with the participation of the people and the definition of the rights and liberties of individuals and groups. For the first time since 1917 a perfect electoral system was created: universal, direct, and secret suffrage. Stalin thus managed to combine three elements: political terror, a jurisprudence of terror, and socialist legality. In 1936, when the terror was at its height, he was to say: "Henceforward, the stability of the law is vital to us," and in order to make this clear to society, he was to banish to the obscurity of the labor camps or deliver to the execution squad those jurists who had tried until then to give shape to the relative law emerging from the revolution.

It would not be an exaggeration to talk of a legal counter-revolution, and it is significant that Stalin's director of operations was Andrei Vyshynsky, the prosecutor in the great trials of 1936–38. The Leninist principle of the relativity of law was now deemed to be a nihilist idea and it disappeared in favor of the blatant rehabilitation of a stable legal formalism. Procedure, its legality, the setting up of a legal superstructure made up of institutions and laws are all traits characteristic of the Stalinist era. A reader from a future century, ignorant of the facts and furnished with Stalin's constitution, the federal and republican criminal codes, and all the juridical literature of the 1930s, would never guess that behind this flowering of democracy and social guarantees a violence without limits was being practiced against society.

The separation of law and common murder was complete but, at the same time, it concealed a law whose function was to legitimize murder. In such a system, if there is murder, there must be crime, and Stalinism made it its business to unite these two. In the same way, the "man-eater" devoted himself to setting up a new system of social values that was to result in the myth of himself as the fatherly protector. In "the Soviet state one breathes more easily and more freely than anywhere else," because the "Little Father of the peoples," "children's best friend" is watching over the law-based state.

It is significant that one of the decisive stages in the construction of this image of the protector, this myth of the loving father, is linked with a murder. Pavlik Morozov (1918–31) was a young pioneer famed for denouncing his father as "an enemy of the people" and a member of a plot organized by the kulaks. For decades Pavlik was held up as a model for Soviet youth. This sorry deed provided Stalin with a double myth. First there was the myth of Soviet society as a family, loyalty to which in the course of time becomes more important than to natural blood ties. It had been in the name of this loyalty that Pavlik had not only rejected but also denounced his natural father when he had apparently been disloyal. In doing this, the little informer showed what was the true family—society—and who its true father—Stalin. In 1931, before Soviet society was fully converted to such ideas, Pavlik Morozov was killed by his family. Thus he supplied, in addition to the myth of the "political family" and the "political father," the figure of a child martyr. Thus we see the old myths, though now with a different content, spreading widely through the newly developing society.

The Function of Murder

A corollary to this legal counterrevolution was the systematic use of murder. This can be grouped into several categories.

No one today, with the exception of a few who still hanker after Stalinism, denies that Stalin was a murderer. His murders are still impossible to count—but in any case, to count in millions, far from simplifying things, further complicates them. Nevertheless, it is obvious that the murders followed a rational plan.

A Return to Fratricide

A first category, and perhaps the most straightforward, is that of the murder of those who got in Stalin's way and blocked his accession to absolute power. These are murders commonly found in the course of struggles for power, and they are of interest here only because they represent just one of the various and imaginative routes carved by Stalin. One murder of which he has sometimes been accused he can definitely be acquitted of—that of Lenin. It is true that when he was dying Lenin tried to remove Stalin from the position entrusted to him—Lenin had nominated Stalin general secretary of the party in 1922—but it is clear that his death, though premature, was natural.

Among those whom Stalin believed to be his personal

enemies, the most passionately hated—a hatred that was entirely reciprocated—and the man he was to pursue tirelessly until the end of his days was Trotsky. Stalin dedicated much time and energy to his attempt to rid himself of this opponent, calling into play most of his array of techniques for murder. He organized the first "murder" of Trotsky very early on, in the month when Lenin, already ill, was out of action and when Trotsky was involved in a systematic struggle against Stalin's bureaucratization of the Communist machine. Exhausted by this struggle, in January 1924 Trotsky left for the Caucasus for a rest. In Tiflis he was informed of Lenin's death by telegram but was not able to attend the funeral. Stalin used the funeral to begin to create the "cult of Lenin" and carry out a reorganization of power. It was a murder without a corpse, but a murder for all that. In his reorganization of positions in the party, Stalin gathered together Lenin's "companions" *(soratniki),* those who had led the revolution with him. By arranging for Trotsky to be absent from the funeral, Stalin was able to exclude him visibly from Lenin's spiritual family. The assassination of a comrade in arms was thus accomplished. Political death by exclusion, before physical elimination, was to be one of the hallmarks of Stalin's methods.

Not satisfied with merely making Trotsky dead in the eyes of the magic circle of the newly created "Leninists," Stalin was to go on to assassinate him in the eyes of the party and eradicate him from the history of the Russian Revolution. The clash between the two in the years 1924–29 was to be sufficient. Forced into exile from the homeland of revolution and dispossessed by Stalin in the name of revolutionary law, Trotsky was to be hunted wherever he went. Stalin finally caught up with him in 1940, having already assassinated as many of Trotsky's supporters as the Kremlin murderers could lay hands on. Isaac Deutscher has given the volumes of his biography of Trotsky titles that provide an excellent resumé of Stalin's strategy in this duel to the death. The second volume is called *The Prophet Unarmed:* Stalin had "disarmed" him of his armor of Leninism and of the party. The third volume is *The Prophet Outcast.* Political assassination, before physical murder, has the advantage of avoiding the risk of creating a martyr within the party.

Stalin was to apply this strategy of bloodless murder, which successfully purged the party and Lenin's succession, to the greatest possible number of Lenin's heirs. During the struggle over the succession in the years 1924–30, Stalin was to repeat the Trotsky method with all his rivals. Taking the middle ground, he established himself as arbiter of party conflicts, thus setting Left against Right and Right against Left. He insidiously imposed a single path on all of them: they were forced into taking up extreme positions against rejected adversaries at the other extreme, only to be obliged, at the moment of their own defeat, to admit that they had been mistaken, that they had deceived the party. Thus they gradually excluded themselves from the "family."

To aid and abet these internal conflicts, Stalin set up two related myths derived from the carefully orchestrated cult of Lenin. Lenin, embalmed and placed in a mausoleum open to the public's devotion—an intangible Lenin, clothed by Stalin with "Leninism" and a star to guide the survivors along the path decreed by history—could either be betrayed or faithfully followed. Anyone who attempted to defend another interpretation of the correct path at any given moment and in particular circumstances—such as Zinoviev, Kamenev, Rakovsky, or Preobrazhensky—and who was later forced to admit his error and, more seriously, to admit having used the party to protect himself was doubly excluded from Leninism. The most flagrant example in this respect, and also the most tragic, was that of Bukharin, the "beloved child of the party." Not only was he forced, within the apparently peaceful context of a debate in the party, to admit his break with Lenin, but before that, in 1928, he was himself to condemn his own policy and propose the change of line that was to imply an admission of his error and his exclusion.

Thus, from Trotsky to Bukharin, a new myth began to develop, that of the "lost companions" of Lenin. The reverse side of this myth gave rise to another, that of the wise man, the infallible companion, who had always sought to maintain intact the heritage and the "family" of Lenin. Through their failure, the lost companions confirmed the legitimacy of the person who maintained the tradition. The power that had been anything but secure in 1924—Lenin had advised that Stalin be deprived of his position and had finally recommended a complete break with him—was now, as a result of this strategy, all his. By their admissions of a break with Lenin, his companions further increased the void, leaving the center to be dominated by Stalin. In 1934, at the time of the Seventeenth Congress, the "congress of the victors," Stalin was to gather together for the last time his adversaries, now suddenly absolved of their past errors, in a demonstration of generosity and fidelity to a Lenin obsessed by the need to maintain unity of the party. The new mythology was firmly in place. In the mausoleum lay the Father of the Revolution; in the forum his faithful companion attempted to mend the rifts in a broken family. But their welcome back into the fold was to be short-lived.

From this period, though murder may have been bloody, it was also subtle. Mikhail Frunze died on the operating table, forced to undergo surgery for an ulcer that was no threat to his life—against the advice of the doctors who were unanimous in their opinion that this operation, imposed by the Central Committee, which is to say by Stalin, would certainly kill him. It was a modern variant of the removal of the adversary by hidden poison. In 1925, it was still possible to express an opinion about such convenient deaths, and Boris Pilnyak wrote a striking short story on the subject: *The Tale of the Moon That Would Not Go Out*. The journal that published it was immediately seized and its author was later arrested. The death had contributed to the creation of an atmosphere of fear among Stalin's companions; but it was a fear that paralyzed, not one that incited men to rebel.

There were many suspicious deaths at this period. But in this category of fratricide, involving the destruction of the Leninist family, one of the most interesting is that of Kirov, assassinated on December 1, 1934. It marked the end of the period of political extermination, opening the way to the physical liquidation of rivals. Since the Twentieth Party Congress in 1956, the theory that the assassination of Kirov was organized by Stalin has been generally accepted.

One can detect a certain ambiguity in the homage paid to Stalin at the Seventeenth Congress of 1934. Was he being hailed for what he had done, as the representative of a past era, who could now be superseded? Or was he hailed as the permanent and future leader of the Soviet state? Both theories have been put forward but, until the archives are opened, it is not possible to decide between them. In the opinion of the old Menshevik Boris Nikolayevsky, as for

Khrushchev, Kirov supported the idea of a respite after the difficult years of the first five-year plan. By removing a rival, Stalin was also removing an adversary. It was a very strange assassination: the normal guards having mysteriously disappeared, a unknown young man was able to shoot Kirov unchallenged, at a time when it was usual for important party members and their workplaces to be heavily guarded. The second theory disputes the idea that there was any plan to get rid of Stalin in 1934, and stresses, on the contrary, the close similarity in the ideas of the two men. Neither of these two theories, however, explains the strange circumstances of this crime, implying complicity at the highest level and strongly suggesting that Stalin engineered the murder. Whether or not he was actually behind it is, in the last analysis, of secondary importance. The essential point lies elsewhere: this bizarre murder was the instrument that was to make it possible for Stalin to embark on another category of murders that, by transforming political corpses into real corpses, was to open the way to the Great Terror and the perfection of a new political culture.

Murder as Spectacle

Robert Conquest, the author of a remarkable study of what he was the first to call the Great Terror, calls the murder of Kirov "the murder of the century," because it acted as a catalyst and a pretext for a more widespread terror. The more sensational aspects of this terror have concealed one essential point: the rational way in which the mass extermination of Soviet citizens, whether or not Communist, was carried out. This period, from 1934 to 1939, is at first sight confusing, because of the interval separating the catalyst—the death of Kirov—from the explosion—the trials that began in 1936. But to look at the Great Terror in a purely chronological way is to ignore one of its essential features: the establishment of a legal system that made it possible to carry out a whole plan of physical destruction within the framework of the law.

The Criminal Code of the Russian Soviet Federated Socialist Republic (R.S.F.S.R.) of 1926 provided Stalin with a convenient instrument of repression in the shape of article 58. Its terms were sufficiently vague to embrace any kind of opposition to the system.

Solzhenitsyn has said on this point that "where there is a law, there can also be a crime." On the night of December 1–2, 1934, Stalin signed a number of documents known as the Kirov laws, intended in principle to ensure the preservation of law and order and which in fact represented a jurisprudence of terror. The competent authorities—the NKVD which in that same year replaced the OGPU—were instructed to speed up the preparations for the trials of anyone accused of plotting or carrying out acts of terrorism, while appeals were abolished and punishments were carried out immediately after judgment. Originally, the investigative powers of the NKVD had limited authority, depending on the seriousness of the crime and the sentence given, while military tribunals dealt with the most serious cases. Gradually, this separation became blurred. In 1935, further measures gave the final touch to the legalizing of terror. The decree of March 30, 1935, announced severe punishments for anyone possessing a firearm or knife. Where would the definition of "weapon" end? On April 8, the powers of the criminal authorities, which could invoke the death sentence, were extended to include young people from the age of twelve. Finally, on June 9, 1935, a decree was issued extending the death sentence not only to spies and parasites, but also to those "who might know of such activities or related plans." These decrees constituted a whole with enormous implications. They established the obligation to denounce not only a criminal act, but also a criminal intention. They instituted the principle of collective responsibility. The application of this repressive law to adolescents, psychologically so impressionable and dazzled by the "heroic" myth of Pavlik Morozov, sheds light on the meaning of these decisions. The choice offered to adolescents was that of becoming either heroes or else "children of enemies of the people," and thus accomplices of these enemies. This was also the choice for all, and particularly for families, who were suppose to know exactly what was going on within the family circle.

This was the beginning of a complex, and always "legal," process. The tip of the iceberg was the melodramatic spectacle of the great show trials in Moscow. These, between 1936 and 1938, were to decimate the leadership of the original Bolshevik Party. On a slightly lower level, in all the towns of the USSR, there were trials of the "accomplices" in the various plots brought to light by the central trials. Like a stone thrown into the water, each of the big show trials caused ripples that multiplied into infinity. Beneath the surface of the show trials there were innumerable secret trials and executions without trial. The enemy was everywhere, in the party, in all the state bodies, in the army, and even in the police whose leading members, only yesterday the accusers, were now brought before the courts, accused of the worst kinds of crime. These trials are well known from the many books on the subject. What concerns us here, in this attempt to understand the logic of Stalin's murders, is the reason for these sinister and basically useless show trials.

At first sight, the show trials served little purpose. The men who were brought before the court had long been dead politically. It was as if a series of corpses had been lined up to receive the organized fury of the people. The trials did little to further the process of legitimization; indeed, by this time Stalin's legitimacy was not in doubt. They represented the final humiliation of his adversaries, allowing him to get rid of them by inducing them to confess to crimes that they had not committed. But since they accused themselves, no one was going to question the genuineness of their crimes. The important point is that these trials opened the way to a general repression with important consequences for the functioning of the system and for the formation of the myths that operate on the social consciousness. Thanks to the policy of permanent purges, a novel method for the selection of elites and the promotion of cadres was created. By constantly changing the entire personnel of the various institutions, Stalin was able to control the bureaucratic machine all the more closely. Those in power at all levels followed him blindly for fear of being removed—and at this period, "removed" meant sentenced to death, or at the very least, to a labor camp. Those nearest to Stalin cooperated in the purges in the hope of one day taking over his position.

Thus an immense machine was managed entirely to the benefit of one man. Though hardly economical in terms of human lives, it had, for Stalin, the advantage of being effective. The situation in the USSR and the underlying problems—generally underestimated, since historians have tended to concentrate on the struggles at the top—indicate that Stalin's power was never entirely safe. In the mid-1930s, the USSR was unbalanced and exhausted by the efforts of the preceding years. The peasants were waking up to a new form of serfdom, while the workers were little better off than before. The progress of industrialization may have been spectacular in statistical terms, but it did not bring electricity to the countryside nor the satisfaction of the smallest of society's needs. There was a vast gulf between the supposed reality of the system, the "joyful life," and the reality as lived by the people, giving rise to tensions that were no less real for being invisible. It became necessary to find an explanation for this gap, and this was the "educational" motive behind the trials. A myth was found that, while not original, had never been used to such a degree.

The "plot," for which the trials were the visible evidence, divided Soviet society into two parts. On one side was the increasing number of those who had betrayed Lenin, communism, and the people. They were to be blamed for everything, starting with the daily misery of the people. There are countless examples of the absurdities of the show trials, such as the confession made by Zelensky, accused of economic sabotage at the trial of Bukharin, that he had made butter unusable by stuffing it with nails, and that he would have done the same with eggs except that their shells made this impracticable. From a distance, the ridiculous and surreal character of such episodes seems almost laughable. But at a time of penury and tragedy, it is not hard to imagine the feelings of a population lacking the basic necessities of life on learning that the "people's butter" had disappeared. On the other side in the "plot" were the "good" people.

Thus society gathered around the man who, like Lenin before him, was attempting to hold back the mounting tide of conspirators. The myth of the plot, the Manichean division between good and evil, between murderers (the saboteurs, traitors, and spies) and victims, together with the identification of the enemy with the devil, all combined to create a new world, a new society and a new political culture, in which effort and sacrifice would overcome evil in this last battle. A chain of events can be seen leading to a new model of society. First a murder was fabricated and/or exploited. Next the show trials were held to legitimize power and the pursuit of a policy and make the developing myths explicit. Finally widespread terror was used.

"Social" Murder

Khrushchev's report to the Twentieth Party Congress attempted to date Stalin's murders from 1934, from the time when the work of the transformation of the social structures—collectivization and industrialization—was already complete. By concentrating on the fate of Stalin's companions and on the state machine, Khrushchev was still attempting to salvage the social achievements of that period, while ignoring the price paid and the methods used, notably the murder of the peasants. (He was to be less timid at the Twenty-second Congress.)

Stalin's aim was to accomplish the almost impossible task of detaching his country from its peasant background. In 1929, despite increased urbanization, the Soviet population was still essentially a peasant one. Even where the peasants had moved into the towns, a peasant mentality prevailed. Some historians, such as E. H. Carr, have suggested that collectivization came about as a result of an urgent socioeconomic necessity: the mounting crisis of the 1920s, caused by the behavior of the peasants. It is true that the peasants were not particularly cooperative with the Soviet government, and their reluctance to accept its demands became more marked. But there were other ways to resolve these problems besides this class warfare—or simply war—waged in the countryside. Collectivization was carried out with unheard-of violence. It, too, relied on the myth of the "plot," of the implacable enemy who, in this case, appeared in the guise of the kulak. Since there were not enough kulaks to explain the power attributed to them, they were invented, according to a quota fixed in advance. These "enemies of the people," these "vampires," were condemned to "dekulakization" (which meant being destroyed) with their whole families. Their terrible fate resembles nothing so much as that met by the victims of another man of the same ilk, Hitler, a few years later.

Murder was here deferred so that before their death these men, condemned merely for being peasants, could be used. Deported and thrown into camps where they had to work beyond the limits of human endurance, the kulaks provided a labor force for industry and the major building programs that cost virtually nothing. The capital needed for the development of the USSR was first and foremost human capital. This genocide—for that is the only name for the extermination of these people whose only crime was to be peasants—took various forms. To the kulaks, condemned to die from being overworked in inhuman conditions, were soon added the nomadic peoples, who were so effectively "settled" that almost a quarter disappeared from the statistics. While it is true that the great famine of 1932–33, which wiped out some two to four million people, particularly in the Ukraine, was the result of a disastrous agrarian policy, it was caused equally by a policy of systematic destruction of the peasant population. While the rural population of the Ukraine was literally dying of hunger and children killed and ate old people in order to survive, the grain silos were full and the country was exporting cereals.

In addition to the peasants murdered by dekulakization and famine, the populations of the minority national groups "punished by deportation" between 1943 and 1945 were physically decimated as a result of the conditions of their transportation. Stalin held up to the peasants who survived in their miserable kolkhozes and sovkhozes, forced to stay in one place by a legal statute very similar to serfdom,[6] an image of the devil, that of the exploiters, of the kulaks. In so doing he hoped to suppress the old rural world. Fifteen years later, he was to hold up a model of the "positive" nation by partially exterminating the "negative," traitorous small national groups. The pretext in this case was that of collaboration with the enemy in time of war. The accusation included even old men and babies, in no state to collaborate with anyone. No one was spared in the deportations, which meant death for human beings as well as for the soul of the peoples of the national minorities.

Even if we wanted to, it would be pointless to try to establish the numbers involved in these collective murders that can only be called genocide. It is not yet possible. However, even the most cautious data would give the number of peasant deaths between 1929 and 1933 as between five and seven million. The logic behind these murders is that of the vast, Promethean social plan that Stalin was attempting to achieve. From a society of collectivized peasants, he hoped to build an undifferentiated and uniform

---

6.   Until the end of the 1970s, in order to prevent the peasants from leaving the countryside, they had no "internal passport," the identity card that allowed freedom of travel and *a fortiori* the permission to live in one place or another.

society, which for him meant a society without links with the secular social culture, be it Russian or that of the ethnic minorities, of the greater part of the population. A veritable "cultural revolution" was now to take place. Tragically, it was all too successful, for it still oppresses the USSR today. By murdering, directly or otherwise, a society, its reference points, its solidarities, and its way of life, Stalin succeeded in destroying the civilization of the rural world. He replaced it with a "world of work in the countryside," with structures despised by those who were compelled by force to stay within them. And yet he was unable to create a new rural world. Nothing appeared to replace the village and village culture. In China in the late 1980s, by contrast, Mao Zedong's successors were able to revive agriculture with the help of a peasantry once again rewarded by the authorities for its hard work. This was only possible because in China rural civilization had survived, and has once again today become the comprehensible framework for each man's work. Their contemporaries in the USSR, in trying to resolve the same problems, were forced to recognize the fact that the muzhik no longer exists, and that the countryside is no longer a center of social or cultural life.

Exported Murder

The fourth and last category of murders is that which, beyond the Soviet frontiers, was to pave the way for the revolutionary expansion that had failed to materialize under Lenin. Stalin was to be able to boast of this as his personal achievement. At the negotiations between Germany and the Soviet Union on the eve of the Second World War, leading to the pact of August 23, 1939, Stalin had not made any secret of his ambitions concerning the countries lying to the west of the USSR. These were not just territorial ambitions; he wanted to extend the revolution to those countries where circumstances were favorable, in line with his centralist theories and through the use of terror. The revolution, in those places where it could be imposed, would be a revolution "from above," like the social revolution that he had imposed on his own country. It would reproduce exactly the Soviet model. In order to impose this model without opposition, it was necessary to remove anyone who might bring an individual dimension to the social changes, related to the different national cultures. Stalin knew better than anyone the part played by nationalist sentiments and ideals in the revolutionary struggle, for he had fought against it long before 1917, and again later, when he had wiped out all the national elites in his country. In the same way, before 1943 he had exterminated the foreign cadres of the Comintern working in Moscow. Accused of being party to the plots exposed by Stalin's show trials, these foreign cadres, although completely subordinate to the leader of the movement, paid for being the representatives of the Communist parties of other nations.

It was the same desire to crush the national elites that gave rise to the murder of more than 15,000 Polish officers. The bodies of 5,000 of these men were found at Katyn in 1940; 10,000 still lie in unknown common graves. After fifty years of efforts by Stalin and his successors to attribute the responsibility for this terrible massacre to the German army, present on Russian territory in 1941, and of reticence on the part of the countries of western Europe, the era of glasnost has finally brought the truth into the open. The evidence collected by Polish historians and the Soviet acceptance of this evidence have finally removed any remaining doubt that these 15,000 Poles, taken prisoner by the Soviet army in the early part of the war, had met their ends well before the Germans entered the USSR. This mass extermination was to pave the way for future developments in a Poland deprived of its most patriotic elements.

After 1945, when the USSR had a military presence throughout eastern Europe, Stalin was to repeat the process of social transformation undergone by his own country by imposing the same methods: public trials, purges, and mass terror. The logic of this system was moral unification in the Socialist field through the elimination of national elites and the traditions belonging to each of the national groups. In Stalin's eyes, the same blast of revolution sweeping through society as a whole ought to produce the same type of society everywhere.

Plots and Conspiracies

A cultural revolution is never finished, especially if circumstances open up splits in the society undergoing such a trial. A breach of this kind came about as a result of World War II, which claimed a huge number of lives in the USSR. Stalin was forced to call a halt to the terror, reaching a temporary compromise with social forces. After the victorious end to the war in 1945, however, Stalin brushed this compromise aside and, like Sisyphus, started once more to pursue the process begun in the 1930s. There was one difference, however: with the achievement of social transformation, the goal of his murderous policies had become purely political.

We are confronted once again with the problem of personal authority. Since 1934 no one had dared challenge Stalin's absolute power; after the war, however, and particularly after 1948, this total authority became somewhat eroded. This is explained by two factors. First, since 1938 and the end of the purges, those in positions close to Stalin enjoyed a period of relative stability and hence a new sense of security. Stalin, on the other hand, was to be seventy years old in 1949; everything pointed to an imminent change in the leadership. In this hitherto unknown stability, rivalries and alliances began to grow up on the edges of Stalin's power structure. The second, and no less important, factor was that since 1948, Stalin's absolute power had been faced with a threat from outside in the shape of Marshal Tito. Tito refused to submit to Stalin's will, and also refused to allow himself to be removed physically, never responding to Stalin's invitations. Naturally, against this implacable opponent, Stalin immediately applied the methods used formerly against Trotsky. He killed Tito politically by ejecting him from the Communist world, denouncing his "links with capitalism." In the past the transformation of an adversary into a political corpse had marked an important stage on the path to physical murder. But by 1948 it was impossible merely to repeat the same procedures: history can never exactly repeat itself. Strong in the knowledge that his country was behind him, Tito was not so easily to be put on the defensive, proscribed, or forced to travel the world in fear of assassins. Far from taking flight or bending the knee, he defied Stalin personally, and, furthermore, in the field of ideology. To replace the fiction of the unanimity of all revolutionary societies, he held up the reality of "revolutionary nations," whose character had been formed by both their political culture and their history. This national character survived through the progress of social struggle. Thus beyond the apparent unanimity of the socialist movement, the old debate, dating from the nineteenth century, was revived: is history just class struggle, or should it also take account of the secular solidarities of different societies, or, in other words, of nations?

To the challenge from reawakening personal ambitions at home and the confrontation with Tito, the implications of which went much further than a mere clash of personalities, was added an underlying challenge from society itself. Although a real tragedy for the country, the war had had the effect of reintroducing into the uniform culture of terror elements that it had been believed had disappeared forever—the church, nationalist feelings, and a degree of personal initiative. Stalin had made these concessions in order to create an upsurge of patriotism in a shattered and apathetic society. Finally, the exterior world was beginning to make a timid reappearance in the distorted perception of the Soviet people. The workers deported to Germany during the years of occupation and the Soviet soldiers who had crossed Europe into the heart of Germany, even if this was a Europe in ruins, were able to see the vast difference between the picture of the exterior world as painted by the Soviet authorities since the 1930s and the reality. The operations of a "Big Brother" are only possible in a closed universe, where there are none to raise a dissident note. The gates of this world were shaken in 1948.

The most effective tool with which to rebuild the closed society of the prewar period was that of the conspiracy. With the aid of this device, Stalin hoped to start up the purges again.

Stalin carried out his plan to bolster up his authority with a series of purges justified by accusations of conspiracy. However, though the techniques used were the same as those of the 1930s, their sequence was very different. In 1948, Stalin started with the plot and moved on to the purges instead of uncovering, as formerly, the plot through the purges. The conspiracies now became involved with the conditions of the Cold War—almost anyone could be suspected of being an American spy—and the old anti-Semitism that underlay Stalin's attacks on the "collusion of Zionism with imperialism." The number of arrests had been increasing since 1946, but their integration into a coherent framework was still lacking. By the beginning of 1953, everything was in place for the machine of repression to start rolling again. It started on January

13, 1953. In 1934, the assassination of Kirov had been the trigger. Two decades later, the process was sparked not by a murder but by the discovery of the "doctors' plot," in which a group of mainly Jewish doctors were arrested on the absurd charge of having plotted the assassination of various Soviet leaders "by medical means." The plot was supposed to be part of an international Zionist conspiracy against the Soviet state. Since the class struggle was long since over, it was natural that an external enemy should replace the internal enemy of the 1930s. Apart from these details, it seemed that the events of twenty years earlier were about to be repeated: public trials based on the confessions of the accused, and purges intended to dismantle all the centers of conspiracy.

The USSR was saved from a repetition of that tragedy by the death of Stalin. It did not, however, remove the questions raised by the use of murder as a weapon in the apocalyptic period from the revolution of 1917 to 1953.

Opposition to Stalin

The major figures who were the companions of Lenin and then Stalin, and who were assassinated by the latter, knew of the dangers surrounding them. They were aware of the setting up, scarcely had the revolution happened, of the machine of murder. Few of them, however, had the courage to take their analysis to its logical conclusion and admit that they themselves had contributed to the creation of a system that was preparing their own assassination and would expand its power through the use of collective murder. Perhaps the most clear-sighted analysis was that of Karl Radek who, at the Tenth Congress in 1921 when the party decided to prohibit factions, voted for the decision but remarked that he realized that, in so doing, he was preparing the noose that would one day hang him.

Trotsky, the most remarkable of Stalin's critics, and Bukharin compared Stalin to the great murderers of history—Nero, Cesare Borgia, and Genghis Khan. In so doing, they attributed to Stalin, to his murderous madness or his perversity, the responsibility for a violence almost unparalleled in history. When describing the tragedy lived through by the USSR over a period of several decades, even if the comparison with those men and their inclination to deal with everything by violence is a fair one, this reasoning by assimilation with such monsters of history raises two problems.

First, it ignores the establishment of a system of murder intended to establish and consolidate power, that is to say, the relationship between power and murder, and instead sets up a myth of "Stalinism" as the exclusive creation of a monster called Stalin. The first creators of "blank spaces" in the historical analysis of events in Russia were certainly the founders of the concept of "Stalinist deviation." We need to seek the answer in the philosophy that inspired those who set up this system.

The second problem is that to take Stalin for a mere murderer, albeit an exceptional one—as is implied by a comparison with Nero, Caligula, or others of this type—or for a madman is to ignore the unquestionable logic that guided his murders. It was a utopian logic requiring the destruction of what is and the construction of what should be, according to the founders of this utopia. Stalin, and Lenin before him, started out from the logic of a complete break with the past. The world they had dreamed of, which the taking of power put within their grasp, had come up against the real world, that of men. Convinced of the theory that man is the product of economic and social conditions—a simplified version of Marx's more profound ideas—they regarded man as merely so much material to be worked on by the political and socioeconomic conditions they intended to create. The original sin that was to dominate and pervert the whole revolutionary enterprise is clearly to be found here. Despite a long tradition of submissiveness, men had shown that they had an autonomous nature in the face of "objective conditions." It became obvious that one or the other—men or the new world—would have to give way, or at least be amended. In the choice that was made, man was to be the victim; the opposite choice would have meant renouncing utopia and compromising with the real world. It was a choice that explains many of the characteristics of these decades of terror and violence. These characteristics were in appearance unconnected, but in fact formed part of a pattern: the need to preserve utopia, even if it involved using force on the citizens.

There was only one way of dealing with opposition and that was to destroy it. Murder was the solution. It removed the strongest of opponents, created terror through example, and an atmosphere of unpredictability in society as a whole. It is not necessary to kill everyone in society in order to ensure submission; it is enough for each man to know that his life might be threatened at any moment. In his novel *Nineteen Eighty-Four,* Orwell rightly took as a symbol of such a society the all-seeing eye of Big Brother. In concrete terms, it was death that hung over each member of society—not natural death, the conclusion of all individual lives, but murder, a product of the system.

Necessary for the abolition of individual human nature, this murder could not be carried out illegally or in the absence of legality, since it was being used in the service of a clearly expressed utopia and not of an individual plan where the only logic was the interests of the killer. Attila and Genghis Khan burned and killed everything and everyone in their path because their empires consisted of territorial conquest rather than human slaves. Conquest without the pretense of building a new world allows men to kill without needing to justify their murders. This was true also for men like Nero or Herod, the latter resorting to the murder of children in order to preserve his power. There is no need of laws for this type of murder.

But the Bolsheviks claimed to be creating a world in which man could develop to the full, where his long march toward happiness could finally, after thousands of years, find its fulfillment. In the context of a plan of this nature it was necessary to use legal murder. A system that sets itself up as the depository of human happiness cannot kill without reason; it can kill anyone who rises up against the accomplishment of such a plan. Thus it is that we need to consider the right to murder in relation to the overall plan. Lenin appears to have been more concerned to set up a system of repression without delay, rather than to codify this right to murder, which he defined as being relative. This was for two reasons. He hoped, at least until 1920, that the spread of the revolution would sweep away everything that still stood in the way. He hoped, too, that human nature would be unable to assert itself any longer in a world that had become unrecognizable. It was an entirely political point of view. The only thing that counted for him, as we have said, was power, and power is first and foremost the relationship of strength. The law that allows the imposition of power and does everything to protect it may be simplified and relative, because it merely translates the state of this relationship at any given moment.

Stalin was both more ambitious and more realistic, as well as murderous by instinct. His ambitions were certainly political—to increase his power and make it permanent—but it would have been enough to murder just his rivals to attain this goal. This he carried out with great skill. But he wished to go further, adding his own achievement to the political tasks of Lenin's revolution: he wished to change men, not just to silence them, and to transform society. Stalin, like Mao after him, was the chief architect of the Promethean plan that is one aspect of Marxism. He aimed to create a new species—*Homo sovieticus*—cut off from its traditional culture and social roots. There were two sides to such a plan: the destruction of existing man, and the formation of *Homo sovieticus* whose behavior would be the product of an entirely new political culture. The destruction was accomplished through murder or the threat of murder; the laws drawn up at that time were intended to make this murder acceptable to those threatened by it. A guilty person would attempt to have himself forgotten rather than foment a revolt. The whole of Stalin's legal system, juxtaposing the legal state and repressive laws, placed the individual in the position of the guilty party. The law of August 1, 1932, on sabotage in the countryside is a good example of this. The law proclaimed that any peasant who sabotaged communal work in the countryside, or threatened collectively owned property, which amounted to the same thing, was liable to the death penalty. Thus the threat of death was made to apply to each and all, for the starving man who picks up a fallen ear of corn and the man who fails to "fulfill the plan," unrealizable by definition, fall into the same category. The law made each man a potential offender, and thus ensured his obedience.

With the terror, Stalin forged a silent and oppressed society, deprived of its memory. The "enemies of the people" were not only liquidated, they were effaced from the minds of their families and contemporaries: this also was the law. All trace of those who were condemned was removed. Underground Soviet literature has recorded this extraordinary mental mutilation. Lidia Chukovskaya's book *The Deserted House* tells how, in a few moments, a human being can be snatched from his family and swallowed up in a legal universe—the offices of the NKVD or the state prosecutor—liquidated without trace, and obliterated from the memories of the survivors. In order to save themselves, the latter are forced to sever all links with the "people's enemy." With memory destroyed, leaving nothing but fear, little remains of the individual.

The Creation of Myths

With both human consciousness and the country itself now reduced to this "deserted house," it was time for the other part of the plan: the reconstruction of personality in order to forge the new man by means of a series of myths for which the terror itself was the essential vehicle. Lenin had not had time, nor was he perhaps sufficiently interested, to carry out such a plan. The myths of the new world were products of the Stalin years. This is not the place to resolve the difficult question of the relationship between myth and regime and their effect on one another. Did the myths underlying the utopia determine the system, or did the system, born of the utopia, create these myths? However that may be, Stalinist political culture was created from the association of the system with a series of myths, each initial myth producing a larger and complementary myth which, added to the first one, endowed the political system with its final legitimacy. It is possible to class these myths into three general groups: political, social, and eschatological.

The central political myth was that of the conspiracy. Its development was assisted by the entire legal system of which the trials were merely the visible and educative manifestation. The plot was uncovered and punished on the basis of the evidence. The reverse side of the plot was the need, in the face of this threat, for a savior. The pitiful confessions of the accused in the show trials—that they had sabotaged the work of the revolution, the people's daily life, had wanted to assassinate the founders of the new state, above all Lenin—left the way clear for those who had not failed. The cult of personality that made such a remarkable appearance after World War II, with giant statues of Stalin raised in every town, was the cult of the man who had never wavered and who, because of this, had ensured the future of the work begun in 1917. Many of the epithets applied to Stalin, such as "great leader," the "greatest man of all time," reinforce this idea of the savior. So it was no accident that in the 1930s and particularly in the war years, Stalin was to recreate a national history suppressed since 1917. The heroes recovered from history by the Soviet regime were those who had retained an image as saviors: Alexander Nevsky, Dmitri Donskoy, heroes of the fight for independence, and Suvorov and Kutuzov, heroes of the Napoleonic Wars. The savior, Stalin, omniscient and omnipotent, took the place of Christ the Ruler of All, whose image had dominated the Eastern Church for centuries.

But myths also define social behavior. The figures who featured in the great myths of the 1930s were Pavlik Morozov, Stakhanov, and heroes of science and physical achievements, explorers and aviators and the like. The contribution of these mythical figures was threefold. Firstly, they marked a break with traditional behavior, representing man's ability to go further than ever before, to be "ever better" (Pavlik Morozov), "ever more productive" (Stakhanov), to go "ever further," "faster," "higher." In each case, this ability to excel was shown to be possible only within the context of the global plan for society; anyone who accepts this new society will become capable of the impossible. Thus this myth provided a wonderful answer to the initial debate of human nature versus socioeconomic conditions. It showed how, in the new socioeconomic conditions, anyone could achieve greatness, be he a poorly educated child from a kulak family (Pavlik Morozov), a simple building worker of average strength (Stakhanov and so many like him) or a young delinquent who later revealed himself to be capable of a remarkable flying achievement (Baidakov, who flew over the Arctic in 1936). The new world turned these disparate figures, for whom life appeared to offer little out of the ordinary, into *bogatyri* (knights and heroes of legend).

This myth of the decline of human nature and its rebirth in a changed world gave rise to another myth, that of the "father" and the "family." Everyone belonged, after all, to a single collective universe, a new family with new qualities. But a family needs a father, the model of authority. Thus again the myth leads us back to Stalin. He was "the children's best friend," and "father of the people," taking the place of the natural father, the traitor, denounced by Pavlik Morozov. When Stakhanov explained the miracle that had enabled him to accomplish a certain feat of productivity, he attributed it directly to Stalin and the inspiration he had found in one of Stalin's speeches heard the day before (the authors of this myth did not even bother to check the dates—this speech was a pure invention). Stalin was equally a spiritual father for the heroes of science and sporting achievement, such as Lysenko or Chkalov. The hero of the flight over the Arctic referred, like Stakhanov, to Stalin's inspiration and the guidance that it provided for him. Whatever their age or situation, all these "sons" attributed the credit for their exploits, triumphs over the limitations of human nature, to the "father."

One of the characteristics of this family dominated by the father is that it is essentially masculine. In a country where women had played such an important social and political role, there was not one female myth. There is only one female figure that stands out, and that of only secondary importance: the young Zoya Kosmodemyanskaya, killed by the Germans during the war. Her sacrifice is of a different order, in that it honored the people's common efforts in time of war. Although a popular image of Stalin shows him with a little girl, this utopian "family" is that which unites the sons to the father.

There is a final aspect to this mythology: the unity of society. Since all the class enemies had by now been killed, the kulaks being the last of these, it was now a classless society and hence a society without conflicts. The legal removal of the people's enemies left room only for the "people," a concept that, by definition, is a single unity. With the destruction of the church and the suppression of political parties and factions, there was unity of a system of values, proclaimed by the single voice of society and embodying the power of a single party. This unity, accomplished through the destruction of all differences, produced the supreme myth, that of the Golden Age. The Soviet state, born of this dream, had brought it about. "Nowhere can men breathe so freely or so joyously!" The Constitution of 1936 states that the door leading to the Golden Age has been opened. The function of terror is to make this mythical age become a reality—in a country where each individual is surrounded by the threat of death and where memory and natural loyalties are abolished. This dream, built up between 1917 and 1953, was to have a long-lasting effect. The systematic extermination of the imperial family and of all those opponents who could have offered an alternative to the existing order, together with the amputation of memory through terror, created an irreversible situation, for there was no longer a past to return to. Instead, the existing situation—Stalin the father, the savior, the leader of the Golden Age, acquired the dimension of truth. Systematic murder, in this apocalyptic period, suppressed the debate between "true" and "false," between lies and truth. There was now only one truth, from which there was no return, that of the apocalypse. That this truth in no way resembled the actual world was unimportant.

13
Thou Shalt Not Kill

◆

On March 5, 1953, the unthinkable happened. It was a moment never to be forgotten by those who were there. The austere notes of Bach's music, being broadcast on all stations in place of the usual tedious propaganda, were suddenly interrupted by the voice of the most famous announcer of the time, Levitan: "Stalin has died." The unbelievable had happened: the Savior, the father, he who sat in majesty brandishing his thunderbolts and whose shadow fell over half a continent, was a mortal after all. The official period of mourning of four days, the extravagant grief displayed by a distraught society and the incredible void that suddenly opened up before it, led to a final tragedy. Rushing to the Kremlin to see and to find out what had happened, whether possibly their supreme leader had been assassinated, the people were met by troops instructed to protect Stalin's heirs and terrified of what the frantic crowd might do. This clash resulted, once again, in death: nearly five hundred people died, suffocated or crushed. As he left the stage of history, this bloodstained figure remained faithful to his past, once again causing blood to be shed.

The Survivors' Pact

Stalin died in his dacha at Kuntsevo. Around the deathbed a strange watch began, described in similar terms by two people who were there, the "supreme leader"'s own daughter, Svetlana, and Khrushchev. A small group of survivors from the purges, Beria, Malenkov, Khrushchev, and Bulganin, who had shared the task of sitting with the body for two days, watched it and each other with alarm. The immediate reaction to this expected yet unbelievable death was one of relief. It had seemed as if the purge unleashed by the doctors' plot, like the conspiracy of 1934, would extend right to the top of the regime, eventually removing them all. With the death of Stalin, they were safe. During the vigil over the terrifying corpse, Beria expressed what they all felt, openly exulting, and insulting the dead man. "He was putting out the flags in front of the corpse before the coffin was even shut," Khrushchev was to say in his colorful way. But initial feelings of relief began to be replaced by fear. Although Stalin's death had temporarily saved their lives, who was to fill the present void, how, and at what price? It seemed that there might be a repetition of the events surrounding Lenin's succession, when Stalin, whose future deeds no one suspected, came to power and unleashed his destructive fury on his rivals.

There were several figures who might lay claim to power, and Stalin, like Lenin before him, had been careful not to indicate a preference. Just as in 1924, there was nothing, no law or unwritten regulation, to advise on how to proceed. Faced with this silence of the law, and remembering a practice that had proved fatal for so many of their predecessors, the survivors opted for a compromise and an implicit pact ensuring their mutual survival.

First of all the compromise was adopted. It involved the sharing of power, as in 1924. In order to block the figure among them who seemed to represent the greatest threat—Beria, the chief of police and a Georgian like Stalin, a man of unequaled brutality and cynicism—equal powers were given to the most plausible of Stalin's heirs.[1] On March 14, 1953, a balance was created by the creation of an official triumvirate—in reality they were four—including on the one hand side the government team of Malenkov (chairman of the Council of Ministers), Beria (minister of internal affairs), and Molotov (foreign minister), and, on the other hand, Khrushchev, who took a firm hold on the party machine. Within a few days, from March 6 to 14, 1953, the potential heirs had come

---

1. This "balanced" solution was arrived at after an earlier emergency solution which, on March 6, 1953, handed the leadership of the government and direction of the party to Malenkov in order to exclude Beria.

to an explicit agreement: they would divide up the enormous powers held by Stalin and keep the most threatening of their number, Beria, as far from the two machines of Stalinist power as possible.

At the same time they came to an implicit agreement: to do all in their power to avoid a return to the exterminations of Stalin's time. Anyone who kills in order to gain power risks being killed in his turn. The lesson bequeathed to them by Stalin, in the place of clear political rules, was that the only choice was either to refuse to use murder or to live eternally in the shadow of its threat.

Thus, in the race for power, they implicitly agreed to stop short of murder. But such a pact had to be consolidated and given a content that would make it irreversible. This was the underlying meaning of a first condemnation of the use of terror by Stalin, made scarcely a month after his death. On April 4, 1953, the USSR was shaken by a second piece of news almost as astonishing as the realization that Stalin was only mortal. On the morning of this historic day, the press and radio announced to the Soviet people that the "doctors' plot" was pure invention and that the accused had only confessed to crimes under the pressure of "illegal methods of investigation." At a stroke, everything that had underpinned the system of legalized terror collapsed, and the suspicions and presentiments of a cowed population were confirmed: the confessions that had formed the basis of the trials and the conspiracies and resulted in the disappearance of so many Soviet citizens were meaningless.

The announcement was a clear indication of a break with the Stalinist period, and made it impossible to use the same methods of control in the future. The implicit pact of survival was beginning to take shape. The party was to assist this process by passing a resolution a few days later, denouncing "violations of the law," which seemed to suggest that the doctors' plot was just one example. On March 27, 1953, an amnesty—albeit limited and chiefly benefiting ordinary criminals—further contributed to the sense of uncertainty. The disillusionment and growing impatience of all those who had suffered repression were to become manifest a few months later in the form of increased unrest in the labor camps and the multiplication of petitions under review by the chief prosecutor of the USSR. The leaders and the state security police, who had so long dominated Soviet society, were dismayed, no longer sure of where they stood.

To call a halt to the killing was not an easy decision to carry out in a system built on murder, particularly since no concrete solutions to the problem of establishing a stable power had as yet been found. The March compromise on sharing power was a stop-gap measure that did nothing to quell the ambitions of such men as Beria.[2]

On July 10, 1953, the press, which after a long period of apathy the public had started to watch closely for the astonishing details that emerged month after month, announced the arrest of Beria. He was accused of having cooperated in the past with the tsarist police, the Okhrana, and of having been a foreign agent and a persecutor of the people. An event such as the fall of the head of the security police, and the themes of the spy and the enemy of the people, had a familiar ring about them. Less familiar was the context, which in this strange period raised more questions than it answered. In December 1953, it was learned that Beria had been tried, condemned to death, and executed. A few months later the same fate befell Ryumin, accused of having invented the "doctors' plot." Next was Abakumov, who was held responsible for the repression in Leningrad in 1948. Finally came Bagirov, who was found guilty of carrying out repression in the Caucasus on behalf of Beria. All these men were tried in the Stalinist way: a mixture of real accusations and unbelievable crimes such as collusion with the imperialist bourgeoisie or the Okhrana. The myth of the conspiracy was revived.

For a long time it was commonly believed that Beria's trial—held *in camera*—was a pure invention concealing his summary execution at the time of his arrest. Now that some of the blanks of

---

2.   As minister of the interior in 1953, Beria promoted himself as the man who would get rid of the excesses of the past. He was responsible for the communiqué of April 4, measures relaxing previous regulations, decentralization measures hailed by the national minorities, and finally, a modification of international policies in the direction of détente with the West and less pressure on the socialist countries. From March to July, Beria was constantly proposing new initiatives to the party, which explains the others' disquiet.

this story are beginning to be filled, it would seen that a trial was held, albeit in secret, and that legality and the judicial process prevailed at a time of political struggle when an attempt was being made to throw off the legacy of murder. With the thaw of the Gorbachev period, some light has been shed on these little-known years and it is possible to see how far Stalin's heirs had come and how difficult a process it was. Although they wanted to avoid the use of murder, they could not at the same time run the risk of Beria's succeeding in his plan to seize power. There was no doubt that he was a recognized criminal, and his accomplices, tried and executed with him, were equally guilty. But none of Stalin's successors were exempt from the guilt of bloodshed. In order to survive in power under Stalin, it had been necessary to accept murder and carry it out.

This partly explains the ambiguity surrounding Beria's trial. The respect for legality, with a proper trial, was imposed by tradition, but also because Stalin's successors were concerned to appear as judges, not as murderers. The absurd nature of the accusations was a recognition of the impossibility of basing the trial on nothing but the truth. To bring Beria and his fellow accused before the firing squad for having tortured, terrorized, and lied would be to execute them for deeds committed by all of Stalin's successors in one way or another. The break with the system of terror, starting with the pact for survival, would have to go further in order to establish a lasting policy. It implied the need to move from the traditional lies to the truth. To present Beria as a special criminal—a traitor and conspirator in everything, like the men liquidated earlier by Stalin—was to retain the possibility of a return to illegality. It was a dangerous method for all concerned, leaders and ordinary citizens, and almost untenable in a society where knowledge of the facts was beginning to spread.

It was to mark the beginning of a progressive "thaw," to take the term used as the title of Ilya Ehrenburg's book, but it was a thaw that was part and parcel of the jockeying for power. After the admission of illegality, the competitors now had to compete on different terms with a recognition of the need for social compromise. The leaders tried to introduce new practices, without for all that upsetting existing relations between the leadership and society, by which the former had total responsibility for the fate of the latter. Malenkov, the head of the government, was aware of the social deprivation that existed despite the frequent announcements of economic triumphs. If terror was no longer to be the dominant element in political relations, then a way would have to be found to come to an agreement with society. Since the people were reduced to extreme penury, this meant first of all satisfying their most pressing needs: food, clothes, and shelter. The obvious place to look to find food for the people was the countryside. Like all Russian reformers, Malenkov first tackled the question of the countryside, producing many measures intended to encourage the peasants.[3] The result was some progress, but also a new hope in society which, like a sick man coming out of a coma, was trying to relearn how to live. With the renewal of hope came new demands.

Although the amnesty of 1953 only benefited a few thousand of the millions in prisons and camps, in 1955 two large groups were released, including the huge number of those accused of collaboration during the war. These ghosts from another world helped to awaken an anesthetized social consciousness. For years the memory of those who had been removed had been deliberately canceled out. Their reappearance—as yet on a small scale—raised questions: who was guilty and who was not? Who was responsible for the ruin of these innocent lives? Unequivocal signs began to reveal this growing awareness. In the early morning the women street-sweepers would find the statues of Stalin covered in filth. Petitions and complaints began to pour into government departments. *Not by Bread Alone* was the title of a work of 1954 by the novelist Mikhail Dudintsev. The government did everything it could to provide bread; it would have to face up to these other social demands that emerged confusedly from the turmoil of the immediate post-Stalin period.

---

3.   The peasant benefited both from the reduction in taxation, from the replacement of taxes in kind, which could be extremely arbitrary, by payment in cash, and from the remission of tax arrears. He was called on to devote himself to his plot of land and breed a few animals for his own benefit. The towns benefited from a spectacular drop in prices.

The Murderer Murdered

Between 1953 and 1956 everything indicated that the USSR had turned its back on Stalin. There were partial reforms, and detainees were freed. A certain openness appeared in public pronouncements: "It is time to improve the daily life of the citizen, neglected for too long." There were innovations in foreign policy, notably the reconciliation with the "traitor" Tito in Belgrade in May 1955. This time it was Mohammed who went to the mountain. Stalin's name was removed from the pages of the newspapers. And yet his body still lay next to that of Lenin in the mausoleum where the crowds came to contemplate the two men preserved for all time. Where was the truth? In the changes that were slowly coming about, or in the hieratic face that proclaimed the continuity and legitimacy of the revolution?

The answer came on the night of February 24, 1956, when, in a never-ending flow of words, Nikita Khrushchev ripped aside the veil of silence and lies, sweeping away at the same time the surviving ambiguities and clumsy compromises. For four hours in a closed session of the Communist Party, the first secretary read out his secret speech. It was like another murder such as those favored by Stalin, a political murder without a corpse. The victim this time was, of course, already dead, but this second death was of quite a different type. It transformed the savior into a murderer. Coming at the end of a congress that had confirmed the broad outlines of the thaw, Khrushchev's revelations to his colleagues at this secret session were both revolutionary and cautious. Revolutionary, because he recalled that Lenin had shortly before his death condemned Stalin, thus destroying the latter's hopes of being the natural successor to the founder of the USSR. Revolutionary also in that Khrushchev showed that Stalin, far from having been the wise and moderate leader of his party, had diverted it from its true path, imposing criminal practices in order to rid himself of all those who stood in his way by means of murder. It was revolutionary because in the place of the war leader and engineer of victory Khrushchev substituted the image of the man who had exterminated the military theoreticians before the war and who, through his incompetent

authoritarianism and constant interventions, delivered up his unprepared country to the invader. Once victory was assured by the
military leaders, Stalin claimed for himself all their hard-won glory.
Stalin's passion for power and murderous obsessions emerged from
every page of the long report. He had spilled the blood of the party
and sacrified whole nations on the pretext, sometimes accurate,
sometimes less so, of collaboration with the enemy: "If he could
have, he would have deported the whole of the Ukraine, but there
were too many Ukrainians!"

Nevertheless, this denunciation was carefully controlled.
While Stalin, his work, and his companions were accused, the
system itself emerged intact. It was Stalin alone who had threatened
the security of both men and the system. Three pillars remained
particularly firmly in place. First there was Lenin, the founder of the
system, whose documents showing the break with Stalin were
conveniently exhumed, making it possible to cut the umbilical cord
joining Lenin and Stalin. Second, there was the party: Stalin was a
monster, carried away by the desire for power, to which he sacrificed
his companions. The victims of this long tragedy were to be found,
above all, in the party. In the background of this sinister picture it is
possible to glimpse a suffering people, and national minorities
"punished" as an example to others after the war. But the report
focuses entirely on the tragedy lived through by the party, decimated by one of its own members. Thus it was the duty of the party,
and it alone, to establish the sinister facts and repudiate the man
who had more or less wiped it out. The last pillar concerned the
dating of the period of the "cult of the personality." According to
the report, this had begun in 1934. Thus it had not affected the
earlier period, which emerged unscathed. The earlier period was of
course the period of social and cultural revolution, of forced collectivization and industrialization, accomplished at the expense of the
peasants and of society. This chronology clearly indicates that the
party did not wish to dissociate itself from its pre-1934 achievements. The martyrdom of peasant society was not mentioned. The
party mourned its dead, judged Stalin's actions in their name, and
rejected him.

The thing that emerges most clearly from this ambiguous
indictment is the rejection of Stalin by the party. A usurper—he had

suppressed part of Lenin's last words—and a forger—rewriting history itself—Stalin epitomized the impostor, the bad leader. With the imposture revealed and the veil torn away, the truth remained: the "true" Communist, Lenin; the "true" heirs, those who had ousted the impostor and reestablished their links with the founding father of the party.

The party was shattered by the speech, and the effect on society, when the details were revealed to small groups over the course of the next few weeks, was even greater. The ordinary members of society knew that, beneath the cautious silence on the subject, lay their own unspoken tragedy. Lidia Chukovskaya, present at one of these meetings at the Union of Writers, expressed in words what many of those present felt: "I do not like to think in terms of this tragedy only affecting Communists, as if the ordinary people had not died in their millions. . . . it is like hearing an office for the dead." Society rejoiced, knowing that, although secret, the report was symbolic of a break with the system of terror. But the people's realization that this was not the whole story immediately affected the ability of the party and of Khrushchev, who identified himself with the report, to finish the job. The fact that the camps had been emptied, after the congress, of all the "enemies of the people" now seeking rehabilitation, contributed to a feeling of optimism. A long tradition of fear inevitably made people cautious and circumspect, but the questions that were now being asked were rapidly relayed by an intelligentsia that had suddenly remembered that its mission was not to repeat the words of the government but to express the aspirations and doubts of society. This gradual maturing of thought was a hesitant and gradual process in the USSR. In those countries where Stalin's oppression had been felt for a shorter time and where there had been a freer political tradition before the freeze, the reaction was almost immediate. In Poland and Hungary there were uprisings before the year was out—if Stalin was an impostor, then so was everything else—uprisings that ended in blood. Was it possible to break with the most ruthless of tyrants while keeping the tyranny intact?

There were several answers to this question. In Hungary, they rejected the whole regime and demanded the right to a different system. Elsewhere there was a return to violence in order to maintain the system at any cost. And then there was the path of compromise. The Hungarian solution being unacceptable, the Soviet government looked to the two others. The Hungarian uprising was crushed by Soviet tanks, while the Polish revolt was subtly diverted onto the correct path. The greatest compromise was that between the denunciation of the impostor and those who wished to continue his work without using his murderous methods. This explains the party's dilemma over Stalin's embalmed body. As a murderer and impostor, he deserved only scorn and consignment to the rubbish heap of history. Yet his work and system needed to be preserved. The body of this murderer, whom the Soviet people were beginning to say was unparalleled in human history, remained lying in the mausoleum. But the mausoleum was closed for "repairs" (*remont* is one of the most commonly used terms in Soviet life), a temporary solution indicative of the indecision of Stalin's successors.

Memory Regained

The period 1956–61 was a strange one, in which the USSR, for so long speaking with a single voice, was to follow a variety of different paths.

The reemerging intelligentsia—though by no means all—tried to resume its traditional role and contribute to the work of exposing the truth embarked on in 1956. In this difficult period, a central role was played by the reproduced and circulated word. After isolated attempts by Ehrenburg, Dudintsev, and the young poet Yevgeny Yevtushenko, writers tried to become organized. The poet Aleksandr Tvardovsky, editor of *Novyi Mir* from 1958,[4] sought to make the review a focus for new ideas. Boris Pasternak, beneath the fiction of a novel, *Doctor Zhivago,* put forward an iconoclastic version of the world, opposed to the whole system of ideas since 1917. This book, read by the intelligentsia in small groups, paved the way for other works that sooner or later the authorities would have to publish.

---

4. He had edited it from 1950 to 1954 and then again between 1958 and 1970. But after 1968 his position was disputed.

Young people came together to publish banned authors or read them in secret, and to ask the questions that had not been answered at the time of the denunciation of Stalin: How could one man impose such horror on such a vast country? How could the country, and above all the intelligentsia, submit and stay silent? One of these "angry young men," Aleksandr Ginsberg, founder of the first illegal review, *Syntax,* summarized the whole debate when he said: "We hate Stalin less than our own silence."

The party as a whole was unhappy to see part, albeit a small part, of society being drawn into this debate and taking over a political role. Though it believed that everything had been said and that it had finished with the impostor and the imposture, nevertheless the leader of the party, Khrushchev, hesitated and hedged. With the party, he now tried to take over the direction of the political-intellectual scene and revive a tried and tested system in which the intelligentsia served as a chorus for the party, reflecting its ideas and policies. He rebuked the intelligentsia, and took part in the public execution—political, not physical, the time of killing being past—of Pasternak. Rejected by all, accused of having betrayed his fellow countrymen, victim of a public opinion manipulated as in the heyday of Stalinism, which demanded that the great poet receive an exemplary punishment, Pasternak was a expiatory victim, a symbol of the desperate struggle between a system based on lies and the truth that had appeared so briefly but decisively in 1956. Since the authorities no longer executed people—the pact of 1953 and the secret speech made that impossible—they had to be content with this symbolic and exemplary execution. Far from producing the hoped-for silence and return to order, the result was to speed up the maturation of ideas.

Khrushchev had, furthermore, to fight on two fronts at once. On the one hand, the freedom of ideas was trying to gain ground. On the other the party, aware of the undermining effect of the secret speech, was militating for a partial return to the past,[5] accusing Khrushchev of imprudence, and trying to remove him in favor of others who would be better able to control this social awakening. In July 1957 the debate in the party leadership burst into the open. It was a struggle for power, it goes without saying, but also an attempt to set the limits beyond which de-Stalinization might not go. Disowned and apparently defeated by those who called him the "wrecker of the system," Khrushchev was to emerge triumphant by going above the heads of his fellow members of the narrow Presidium (the old Politburo) to the full Central Committee, calling on them to support him and condemn those who were condemning him. Accused of "antipartyism" (under Stalin, a man would be an enemy of the people and executed for far less), Khrushchev's opponents were deprived of their posts but not expelled from the party. The times had certainly changed and it was becoming difficult, if not impossible, to get rid of rival party members, even peacefully.

Khrushchev was to learn this to his cost. Challenged, even if he succeeded in 1958 in taking both the state and the party under his own control as Stalin had done, he soon discovered that living opponents do not lie down. In 1959, he called an extraordinary congress—the Twenty-first Congress—to try both to reassert his power, neutralized by his rivals, and to get rid of them by reopening the file on Stalin. This power struggle, lasting for six years, was never fully resolved, despite appearances. Although Khrushchev controlled all the machines of state, his decisions were constantly being sabotaged from beneath, forcing him to speed up the process despite the risks. The question that he intended to put before the extraordinary congress was one of those that the whole country was asking itself: was it possible that one man, even a Nero or Caligula, could oppress a country so monstrously and for so long? His challenge failed: the party closed ranks and refused to allow the subject to be reopened. Everything that was to be said had been said in 1956. The dead should be left in peace and the party allowed to get on with its job. It seemed as if the body in the mausoleum had triumphed over time.

Nevertheless, everything started up again in October 1961 at the meeting of the Twenty-second Congress. In the gloom of the Moscow autumn, with the progress of de-Stalinization bogged

---

5. On July 6, 1956, *Pravda* published an article stating that so far as the system was concerned, "the party alone is the guarantor of its democratic character." On January 7, 1957, Khrushchev was forced to say, in the guise of a New Year's message: "We are all successors of Stalin, we are all Stalinists"—which was not here an admission of complicity, but homage to the "impostor."

down, little was expected to come out of the congress. Solzhenitsyn has given us a good description of the prevailing mood: "After the colorless Twenty-first Congress which had buried without a word the wonderful possibilities raised at the Twentieth Congress, it was impossible to anticipate the sudden, thundering, and furious attack that Khrushchev had reserved for the Twenty-second Congress. . . . I read and reread his speech, and the walls of my buried universe began to shake." This miraculous congress marked the second death of Stalin, and the moment when memory was restored to the Soviet people.

No party congress had ever had such a large audience: 4,799 delegates, as opposed to only 1,430 at the Twentieth Congress five years before.[6] The debate was to be on a grandiose plan: to move the USSR from socialism to communism over a twenty-year period, to the realization of the ultimate goal of the uprising organized by Lenin in 1917. The continuity of the system left intact by the secret speech underpinned the whole project, which was little more than a propaganda exercise. Suddenly, however, as in 1956, but this time openly and in public, the truth came out. It was to be not only the truth about the past but also about the present, which meant about the system of Stalinism itself—and not just about a man, and a dead one at that.

The debate developed in two different but equally important directions. The first was concerned with the part played by Khrushchev's associates, who protected their own power by upholding his. Stalin was only able to be a tyrant, they said, because he had accomplices. Men like him, with bloodstained hands, sat in the party and, by suppressing the truth, maintained the Stalinist imposture. These attacks did not only condemn individuals; they had a deeper meaning. A party made up of tyrants—and not just an individual tyrant—contains within itself elements favorable to tyranny. If the tyrant denounced in 1956 did not bring down all his accomplices with him as he fell, it was because a deep-rooted sickness gnawed at the heart of the party. There was nothing to

---

6. The numbers of the party had in fact grown considerably: 6,800,000 members at the death of Stalin; 7,173,000 in 1956; and 9,275,500 at the time of the Twenty-second Congress.

guarantee that the party, which despite the secret speech had managed to protect other murderers, would not return one day to the
fatal practices of the past. The lesson learned from this first phase of
the debate was that the tyranny could not have been the work of one
man alone.

The second part of this post-mortem on Stalin was introduced by Khrushchev and was to be the most decisive. He had
learned the lessons of the restrictions of the secret speech, and of
secrecy itself. He concluded that the time for the full truth had
come. What had formerly been discreetly referred to as "an excessive
cult of the personality" was henceforth to be given its proper name:
"crime." Stalin's crimes—the full catalogue of which was now
revealed, adding to those revealed in 1956—had not only decimated the party and the army, but society itself. It was these deaths
that shook the country. At last the wall of silence protecting the
party was falling. Stalin's statue was broken forever. Stalin was
guilty in everything, and de-Stalinization was not just the business
of the party but involved the whole of Soviet society, because society
had been his victim. From this moment, it was society that had the right
to investigate the terrible tally of lives accumulated under Stalin.

Two symbolic events were to mark these unforgettable confessions. First, Khrushchev proposed that a monument be raised to
the memory of the suffering of Stalin's anonymous victims. Dead
party dignitaries had already been remembered on commemorative
plaques frequently seen by 1961 on the buildings of Moscow, as well
as in grieving obituaries rehabilitating the dead men. These previously unacknowledged victims had been forgotten. The Soviet
Union is a country full of commemorative monuments—the
mausoleum in Red Square, memorials to the dead, and giant
statues. Saluted by the crowds, visited by schoolchildren, and
honored by newly married couples, these edifices are symbols of the
Homo sovieticus that the party had attempted to create on the ruins of
the past. In this context, the raising of the monument to the
unknown martyrs of Stalin's repression represented the acceptance of
the millions of dead and disappeared into the social consciousness
and into future history books. It symbolized the return to the Soviet
people of their memory; it symbolized their real renaissance. Solzhenitsyn was right to suggest that, in order to give the symbol its

full value, the only possible place to erect the monument was Red Square, opposite the mausoleum, thus confronting the sin with its expiation. It took more than a quarter of a century for this decision to be acted upon.

The second symbol, complementing the first, was the removal of Stalin from the memory and the history of the Soviet Union. Not only the memory of an unparalleled criminal, but also what remained of the myth of Stalin was eradicated. In order to impose this decision, which involved removing Stalin's body from the mausoleum and detaching it from everything it represented—the revolution, the years of comradeship with Lenin, the years of the construction of the USSR, all of which had been left intact by the Twentieth Congress—Khrushchev arranged an extraordinary pantomime. It was quite in keeping with his character, and involved a considerable element of buffoonery, which was also in line with a long tradition in Russia.

October 30, 1961, the day of the second death of Stalin, began normally enough, even if the subject under discussion, the fate of Stalin's body, was unacceptable to some. The most normal aspect of the debate was the procedure followed to reach a decision. Several party members called for action, justifying this by the "demands from the grass roots," the "petitions" that were circulating around the factories and in the countryside. For decades, such arguments had been used to show that the "people" demanded the death of the "traitors," as in the 1930s, just as they had "demanded" an exemplary punishment for Pasternak in 1958. It was neither surprising nor impressive that this time the "people," so often mobilized in this way, should rally to the support of de-Stalinization. Astonishing, on the other hand, were the events that followed. An old Bolshevik, Lazurkina, a survivor of Stalin's labor camps, suddenly got up, crossed the room, and after recounting to the astounded congress her long history as a militant and then her interminable years in the camps, concluded: "Yesterday, I spoke to Ilyich [Lenin] as if he was alive at my side. And he said to me: It is insufferable for me to lie alongside Stalin!"

The scene was unimaginable: the party, which had always preached the rule of reason, was suddenly listening to a voice from the other world—and obeyed! They immediately voted with a show of hands for the removal of Stalin's body, demanded by Lenin, dead for thirty-seven years. Nowhere but in Russia, where so often the temporal and the spiritual have become confused, could such a scene, worthy of *Macbeth,* have taken place. It was evidence that the *tabula rasa* had only been partially achieved. The events that followed were heavy with consequences for the future: that same night Stalin's body was removed from the mausoleum and quietly buried, far from the eyes of the public. The mausoleum could now be reopened; the creator of the system and the savior were now one and the same—Lenin. The party had once again found the security of a reference point that no one could dispute. This decision was immediate and also irreversible. Stalin, responsible for so many deaths, was now really dead in the consciousness and memory of his country.

In 1961, the truth made great strides forward. Not only did society's fate in the Stalinist era receive its due recognition, thus gaining the right to ask how it could protect itself in the future from the rise of another such tyrant, but also, and at the same time, the party lost what society had gained. The party was not the only victim, nor was it in charge of the process of de-Stalinization. Its complicity, or at least its blindness, in the face of Stalinism deprived it forever of its aura of infallibility. The sufferings of the party paled by contrast with the martyrdom of millions of human beings, becoming one with the sufferings of society. It was also deprived of its position as the all-knowing embodiment of the social consciousness by the second death of the man with whom it had identified itself. No doubt the party itself, conscious of all the implications of de-Stalinization—but not total, for there were still many untouched areas—did not see things like this. It was to attempt to restore, if not this infallibility, then at least an appearance of infallibility. But, in the meantime, it was society, through the mouths of its traditional representatives, the members of the intelligentsia, that was hastening the discovery of the truth.

In 1962, as a result of the Twenty-second Congress, Tvardovsky was able to extract from Khrushchev the right to publish Solzhenitsyn's masterpiece, *One Day in the Life of Ivan Denisovich,* the product of refound memory, recalling for each Soviet citizen the events he, or one of his relations, had lived through. At this same period, *Pravda,* although the organ of the party, opened its columns to Yevtushenko who, in *Stalin's Heirs,* said out loud what everyone was thinking silently: how could they ensure that Stalinism would not be reborn? From all sides, the manuscripts poured into the offices of reviews and publishing houses, each one contributing a building-block to the reconstruction of memory. The majority of these texts did not, however, see the light of day, because the party rapidly blocked this flow of memories and accusations. It was clear that it would have to do something to get rid of the thoughtless and dangerous leader who had unleashed this storm in which the party was losing ground while society was gaining it.

The conclusion was simple: he would have to go. But how could they eliminate an adversary when his life could not be touched and when he might find support within the party itself, as in 1957, and in society as a whole?

Killing without Death

The plot organized against Khrushchev to reunite what he had divided—ideas, dogma, and expressed truth—and to suppress the facts that contradicted the party's truth, its past and its present, was, for once, a genuine plot. It was a difficult plot to set up, since it required that the life of the condemned man be preserved. On this point, the party had not changed since 1953. It had no wish to resort to physical elimination and run the risk of unleashing a new era of terror. The rule conveyed through the centuries and the Scriptures, "thou shalt not kill," was by now part of the political patrimony of the Soviet Union. But the plot was also part of a new set of rules and, in the end, was successful.

On October 14, 1964, Nikita Khrushchev was dismissed by his fellows, who cited as reasons his age, his incompetence, and an uncontrollable temper that had led him to make unforgivable mistakes.

Dismissed but still living, he was still in the way. He had embodied too many hopes—even if they had been partly illusory— for him not to be dangerous, particularly for a party intending to take a partial step backwards by silently resuming the leading role threatened by de-Stalinization. It was necessary to deal with Khrushchev without making him a symbol or a martyr, and without taking his life.

Political death, where a person is dead in the eyes of the world and buried in silence and solitude, is simply the modern version of the monasteries where once the Russian emperors shut up their opponents without needing to take their lives. This was the fate of Khrushchev, condemned to end his days cut off from the world, but living the life of a peacefully retired man. When his real end came he received a hasty, secret burial. Eventually even entrance to the monastery of Novodyevichi, where he was buried, had to be forbidden so that the eternal oblivion to which he had been consigned could remain total. Thus the man who had eradicated the dead Stalin from men's minds was to know the same fate in his own lifetime. The intention of his successors was clear: it was time to bring the Khrushchev period to an end and restore the party's authority. In order to do this, it was necessary to keep silent not only about Khrushchev but also about Stalin, and to take back the truth from the people and return it to the party.

Stalin's successors were not bad men. They wished to improve the condition of their citizens, in the name of the party and through it. They were convinced, however, that it was their task to seal all the breaches made in the structure of the system by their unpredictable predecessor. Although at the beginning they made praiseworthy efforts to revive the economy with the reform of 1965, and to stabilize the previously capricious conduct of foreign affairs, their efforts reached a stalemate that was one day to be christened stagnation. This immobility came about in response to the continued unrest among the intellectuals. Both inside the Soviet Union and in eastern Europe, they tried to contain this by the cautious and limited use of a subtle form of terror that remained on this side of murder. Those who sought to uphold the "real truth" were marginalized: removed to mental asylums, camps or—a less harsh fate—exiled. The determination not to murder remained constant, but it implied a necessary degree of repression. The rule was transgressed in 1968 in Czechoslovakia, where the uprising in support of truth and democracy was crushed by military force.

Nevertheless, internal and external violence remained the exception; Lenin's successors aimed principally at silence. The Soviet Union seemed once more to be the country of dead souls.

The Second Thaw

In the mid-1980s the Soviet Union appeared like a ship stuck fast in the ice. At first sight everything seemed to be frozen solid. The political system and those who controlled it had abandoned any movement or initiative. The plans for reform had long since been abandoned and the government confined itself with the discussion of the Constitution of 1977, a document in itself indicative of stability. It described the USSR as the country of "developed socialism," and its society as "a historic community of a new type," while the socialist countries of Europe gathered together "a deeply united family of different peoples, marching toward the same goal." In other words, history was moving inexorably toward the predetermined utopia.

The government controlled a society that was indifferent to these ideas and stuck in a similar immobility, concealing some strange phenomena. Behind the silence of society and the apparent obedience to the official line, it was becoming increasingly apparent that *Homo sovieticus* had two faces. He was a double man, as a Russian writer was to say. On the surface he conformed to the official version and the Soviet models held up to him, working to advance socialism to the stage where it would wither away and he would taste the fruits of his labors. But beneath the surface, Soviet man vanished and left a very poor citizen. He was increasingly inclined to escape into private life and individual interests. This private life ran to remarkable extremes, from systematic drunkenness to a growing religiosity. There was a growing interest in a distant past and national histories, very far removed from the idea of revolution. Old churches were lovingly restored by amateurs and strange sects began to blossom, whose power of attraction grew ever greater. As private life became increasingly important, so behavior became more schizophrenic. In the eyes of the exterior world, each Soviet citizen seemed to be performing his social duty, working, participating as a member of a community united round the symbol of Lenin's mausoleum. In reality, all this was merely a façade; now it was every man for himself and permanent deceit. The communal exterior disguised the divorce between those who embodied the system and those who lived it on a day-to-day basis. The traditional "them" and "us" was more true than ever.

But, at the same time, things were not as simple as they had been in prerevolutionary times, for they were falsified by the language of propaganda. This affirmed a state of affairs that did not exist. And there was a conspiracy between those at the top who maintained the dogma and those who had to suffer it to pretend that they believed that the dogma and the reality were one and the same. This perhaps indicates that a "new man" really had come into being, or that a section of the collective consciousness had indeed been taken over by new beliefs. On both sides they must have been well aware of the truth, but the magic of the dogma seemed able to disguise it forever and perhaps even, in the end, destroy it.

In this lie accepted by all, there was another new trait. Those who had traditionally embodied the social consciousness and interceded for it—the intelligentsia, whom Stalin's successors, with a scorn that the imperial regime, respectful of learning, would never have used, called *intelligentiki* (little intellectuals)—seemed to have disappeared from the scene. The subtle witch-hunts of the 1970s did not kill people, but they seemed to have killed the critical spirit that always opposes those in power. Henceforward the intelligentsia, when not absenting itself altogether, participated in the fiction of unanimity and the reconciliation of truth and dogma. With the power struggle within the government over—it now seemed more like any board of directors of a big corporation—and a peaceful society apparently participating in the benefits brought by this wise council, some observers concluded that social peace had arrived.

And then, suddenly, the ice trapping the ship began to break up. In March 1985, to fill a vacancy, a man came to power who embodied a new generation. This generation had nothing to do with the tradition of murder. It had not taken part in Stalin's killings, nor had it come to power by stepping over dead bodies.

Nevertheless, this generation, the product of the lies of a schizophrenic society, did not raise many hopes except those of a greater energy and competence. And it is true that at first, as it cautiously took over the helm of the ship, there seemed to be little change of course. But this continuity was gradually to crumble away, making way for the unexpected—even if the unexpected sometimes had an air of déjà-vu. The ice had broken and the ship was sailing into the open water. The book of reform was reopened at the page abandoned two decades before; the time for questions had come.

The Quest for Truth

It is always dangerous to try to analyze a movement as it develops, particularly when it proclaims itself to be a change and a break with the past. The science of politics is, however, always condemned to walk such a precipice, trying to grasp the meaning of events as they unfold, at the risk of crashing down with them. The future will bring a history of Gorbachev's Soviet Union that will have the advantage of hindsight, but today it provides an unparalleled opportunity for observers to try to understand these unusual events and piece together their origins in the light of a long tradition.

In the space of three years and a few months, from his accession to power in March 1985 to the astonishing party conference of July 1988, Mikhail Gorbachev has moved fast and made many proposals. Probably the most important things to consider out of so many changes are the underlying philosophy and the eternal problem of reform.

In many ways there has been a break with the ideas of the past. Arriving in power, Gorbachev did what custom demanded. He drew up a balance sheet, couched in traditional terms; his predecessors were incompetent, they should be condemned and their policies rejected. There was nothing particularly new in this. No one, particularly not in the Soviet Union, sets himself up in power without disputing his inheritance, contrasting it with his own views of the policies and decisions of the past. However, it soon became clear that something had changed: there was a change of tempo and a change of style. Taking as its starting point a cautious though certainly negative balance sheet—the state of the Soviet Union in 1985 made anything else impossible—the debate suddenly took off, going well beyond tradition. Not only were the "years of stagnation," the corruption and the misdeeds of the preceding leadership, raised but, perhaps because the disaster facing the country was only too real, the leader of the party was suddenly speaking a new language. It broke the conspiracy of hypocritical silence observed by both rulers and ruled for several decades. This new language was that of glasnost, meaning the will to say publicly how things are, reveal the truth, and bring together the word and the deed.

It was a dangerous enterprise, bound to upset a system where words were used to deform the truth and thus to mold men's minds. Gorbachev, although a product of a system that had, for decades, based its existence on such practices, challenged this use of words and ideas to shape men's minds. When he says: "It is necessary to speak honestly and find the truth," he implies that words must only convey what is. As one of the leadership, he cannot be unaware of the dangers of his policy. Only history will be able to judge from hindsight whether it represents for him a means of dragging the country out of its destructive immobilism or whether it is rather an end in itself. As a man with an exceptional instinct for politics, he must also be well aware that he needs to pursue this quest for the truth with circumspection, controlling it and directing it toward efficacy. To denounce the rampant corruption, for example, allows him to set up a new ruling class according to his own taste; to denounce the laziness of the workers makes it possible to demand new efforts of them. He has, at times, been content with delayed truth (Chernobyl, for example) or one-sided truth. Nevertheless, one thing is clear: he has broken through a wall of silence and destroyed many taboos.

The first of these taboos was that which said that it was not the business of society to influence the debate or choose freely what was to be debated. This initiative was reserved exclusively for those who led society, the party. The Constitution of 1977 is unambiguous on this point. Gorbachev may not be either the first or the only leader to have called on society to participate in criticism. Khrushchev, who used this device to a considerable degree, was eventually overtaken and overthrown by this movement which he allowed to run out of control; Stalin himself used it many times. But previously social participation had been no more than a kind of Greek chorus supporting those who, at center stage, made the official decisions. By freeing the means of communication, Gorbachev has been able to open up to society its own means of expression. Thanks to his efforts, the single voice of the old chorus now seems, at times, like a deafening cacophony.

The second taboo to be lifted was the idea that only the immediate predecessors in government could be criticized, but not the long history of the Soviet Union. As general secretary of the party, Gorbachev cannot, without putting his own power in jeopardy, do more than judge effects, rather than the underlying causes of the disaster he has exposed. Others, however, have written and spoken—and who is not doing this in the USSR today?—at length about the origins of the sickness. One example among thousands illustrates the phenomenon that is rocking the country like an earthquake. Soviet television showed a film, *The Muzhik of Arkhangelsk,* in which a simple but remarkable peasant unemotionally condemns the ideological basis of the Soviet system, responsible in his eyes for the disaster—the disaster that is the presupposition underlying the whole of today's debate. Should the individual conform to the social mold and accept that the collective interest must prevail over individual interest, or is the desire for unlimited individual profit the prime motive for man's efforts? After this public trial, echoed all over the country thanks to modern means of communication, little is left of the original utopia.

A third taboo concerns the results of past efforts. Until Gorbachev's time, it was accepted that the country had developed through various different historical stages—whether well or badly was another matter. It was accepted, too, that these stages—the stages of socialism—represented an undeniable progress over the past. Similarly, it was agreed that an invisible frontier, like the one separating past and present, separated capitalism from communism. The two sides were seen in black and white: backward-looking history on one side, history progressing on the other. Although the details of this Manichean view of time and space may be debatable, the opposition of good and evil is an integral part of the utopia. By boldly proclaiming that the seventy years of the Soviet state had led to nothing but disaster, that Soviet man was almost indistinguishable in his behavior from the man living under capitalism, Gorbachev calls into question the whole concept of the new historical period embarked on in 1917. He has shattered both certainties and the traditional use of dogma. Henceforth, everyone will know that words can lie and that the truth must be sought outside this dogma, a truth as perceived by each individual. A common, guaranteed truth is being replaced by a truth for which each man is responsible.

There may be no more killing of the Stalinist type in the USSR, but Gorbachev too, following the tradition established in 1953, has made some political corpses. It is perhaps a sign of progress that his corpses—Brezhnev and his colleagues, blamed for the stagnation—are usually already dead. Through glasnost, it has also been possible to revive some of the dead, physically or politically murdered in previous periods. The speeded-up rehabilitation of Stalin's victims and the gradual reappearance of references to Nikita Khrushchev have the great advantage of showing just how arbitrary were the condemnations and murders. Thus the way is barred to their repetition, even in a lesser form. Now that each man is called on to make his own judgment about the past and his own selection between good dead men and bad ones, the right of the leadership to judge and condemn, and thus to kill, is now nothing more than the product of circumstance, and open to the risk of human error. Glasnost has, in all areas, overthrown the idea of the absolute, the basis of the entire Soviet ideological system, substituting the relative. A utopia is, by definition, absolute; the moment it becomes relative, it no longer exists. Only the real, the contingent, then guides man's destiny.

Starting out from a relatively modest assessment of the failures of his predecessors, Mikhail Gorbachev has unleashed an earthquake in which successive shocks have engulfed everything on which the consensus of Soviet society and the authority of its leaders were based. But he did not initiate these events on his own. Glasnost could not be the work of a single man, nor just of the party; the intelligentsia played a part also. One of the decisive results of the reforms undertaken in 1985 was to enable the intelligentsia to find itself and its vocation.

The chorus that had for so long chanted the official line did not deserve the name of intelligentsia. In becoming domesticated, it had betrayed its function. Glasnost highlighted the corruption of the Writers' Union and the total divorce between this category of "functionaries of the intellect" and the true creators. The Writers' Union excluded Pasternak and Solzhenitsyn from the kingdom that was rightfully theirs, and denounced them as "impostors of the art," as once people were called "enemies of the people." Such events strikingly demonstrated the deviation and split in the ranks of the intelligentsia, a completely new phenomenon in Russian history. In the past, many writers had been condemned and censored, but the censor had never treated them as "impostors" or false writers. Similarly, regardless of the many different points of view expressed, society only ever recognized a single category—the intellectuals. By depriving culture of its autonomy, by integrating it into utopia, by forcing it to mouth propaganda, the Soviet system was able to break the unity of creativity, having first obtained society's approval for what the party proclaimed to be "real" art (at one time this was socialist realism). But a stage was eventually reached when hypocrisy was added to lies, where the situation was totally inverted: the denounced writers, whose works were not published, who were killed (Mandelshtam), whose deaths as creative artists were systematically organized (Anna Akhmatova or Pasternak, forced to do translating work), suddenly became the true representatives of creative art for a growing section of society. People began feverishly to recopy these works, circulating them from one initiate to another, while the officially approved authors became for them "false" writers, bureaucrats in charge of culture. One of the aims of glasnost was to put an end to this split in the heart of the intelligentsia. No system can long feel comfortable when it is supported by artists rejected by the rest of society and challenged by those whom society holds to be true artists. The conflict between true and false, central in the contradiction between dogma and the real world, thus even invades the sphere of culture. With his call for the freedom of creativity, Gorbachev wished to span this gulf.

Glasnost

The newly acquired freedom of expression and right of individuals and the media to discuss all subjects, social, economic, political, and historical, had an immediate effect. Newspapers and periodicals took advantage of these rights to a greater or lesser degree, depending on how closely they adhered to the ideas of renewal, but all felt free to debate anything and to invite society as a whole to enter into these debates. Although glasnost's function was particularly to open the door to the future, the pages of the newspapers were suddenly filled with references to the past, attracting the passionate interest of the public. Instead of looking forward to a radiant future, people indulged instead in an avid examination of the mistakes, silences, and lacunae of the past in an attempt to trace their origins. After an initial phase of waiting and skepticism, there was a sudden race between a political class attempting to place limits on the quest for the truth, and throwing ever more taboos in the path of the seekers after truth, and the intelligentsia for whom these limits were unacceptable. It could now be said openly that all the faults formerly attributed to Western countries also existed in the USSR: alcoholism, drugs, prostitution, corruption, and even natural or accidental catastrophes. The times had certainly changed since the days when a writer could be sent to the Gulag for "plotting against the Soviet railroads," by mentioning in his novel that the hero was standing on the station platform waiting for a delayed train.

In this reassessment of the past, Gorbachev and his companions in arms had already sacrificed that which Khrushchev had formerly managed to save—the sum total of Stalin's deeds. No one, of course, said outright that collectivization should never have happened, which would be to cast doubt on the entirety of the existing order. But to make Bukharin not only the victim of arbitrary justice but also to reinstate him as a wise economist is also to rehabilitate his ideas. Month after month, problem after problem, Gorbachev has stripped the system of its infallibility in the choice of policies, for example, the change of direction in 1929; in judgment, as in its long tolerance of the crimes of Stalin; and in its fundamental options, such as the preeminence of the social interest. There is nothing left to sacrifice, unless it is the lonely body of the founder of the system in the mausoleum in Red Square. Still the object of the people's veneration, Lenin continues to represent the immanent truth. Though the plan may have gone somewhat awry, he is the guarantor of an absolute truth in its purest form. As long as the plan and the actions of the founder last as a touchstone for any ideas of reform, the ship that set sail in 1985 will be able to hold its course. But it is not clear whether this course exists anymore, outside its symbolic representation in the body lying in the mausoleum. If it should be challenged on any point, the whole edifice built up on this intangible reference point will collapse.

In the race to reach the truth about the past, we can already anticipate two possible outcomes. One possibility is that the party will manage to deflect the intelligentsia's attention away from what it finds so fascinating—origins and the absolute—to rally it to more contemporary concerns. In this case, as in 1964, the system will emerge from the challenge modified, weakened, but still essentially intact, having managed to avoid coming to an outright split. Alternatively, the movement propelling the intelligentsia in its assault on the past will succeed. In many ways, the intelligentsia is showing a determination—even if the debate on Stalinism is not yet over—to get to the bottom of things. To discuss the conditions of the Treaty of Brest-Litovsk, imposed on the country by Lenin, as the playwright Shatrov has done in a roundabout way in one of his works, is to pose a central question: did the revolution justify the use of any means whatsoever? What was once just a subject for philosophical debate has become a serious matter, bearing the weight of the lessons of the last seventy years. Revolution is no longer a dream to which all can bring their illusions; it is the history of three generations of Soviet citizens. It can be judged by what these people have lived through, and not by what should have been.

It is here that Gorbachev's openness is destructive. Nothing in man's history can be judged any longer in the light of intentions alone, and the plan can no longer be confused, through the bias of dogma, with reality. What is now being gauged and weighed up is the history of individuals, the suffering and the blood of each man who lived through these seven tragic decades in the Soviet Union. When, in the name of glasnost, *Dr. Zhivago* was published in an official Soviet magazine, *Novyi Mir,* when Pasternak was finally able to shake the hand of his staunch brother Solzhenitsyn, the effect was equally devastating, but in a different way, from that made by the book when it was circulated and read in secret. The publication, in the blue-grey cover so long associated with the greatest Soviet literature, of Pasternak's ideas, Zhivago's views on man's fate as the plaything of events forced upon him by the voluntarism of the "student Pugachovs," had a resonance made all the greater by the fact that they were guaranteed by the official nature of the publication. The building in which Lenin lies, the sanctuary of absolute truth and the intangible reference point, is being dismantled stone by stone—not by the solitary voice of the dissident Pasternak but by the voice of official culture.

To finish this extraordinary work, it will not be enough merely to reassess the dead. The historians are not investigating only the crimes of Lysenko, Beria, or the others now exposed to their purifying fire. When dealing with the fate of the peasants and the history of collectivization, they are looking not so much at the mistakes or the figures as at the men involved, the individuals whose fate was sacrificed to an ideal. The same thing is happening with those who are cautiously tackling one of the original myths, the Civil War that was supposed to be the uprising of a people united by the revolution against those who wished to destroy it. The historians can already foresee the questions awaiting them at the end of their search. How much truth is there in this original myth? Was the Civil War really a sacred union of the people, united to save their revolution? Or was it rather a war imposed on the people in order to bind them irrevocably to the revolution?

And then there is the revolution itself: who was right? Was it the man lying in the mausoleum, who maintained against almost all the others that the hour had come, that the success of his calculations was evidence of their historical correctness and that this authorized, even obliged him, to take firm hold of the tiller, to stand there on his own, ignoring the voices of the people and the other parties? Or did truth lie on the other side, with those who, like Zinoviev and Kamenev, and then the Socialist Revolutionaries and Rosa Luxemburg after her imprisonment, believed that history could not be forced by one man's will alone, that social consciousness has a place and that it should be respected? Or did the truth lie with those liberals and religious believers who asserted that man is the most important thing and that true freedom is that of the individual?

Challenging the values of the revolution and of a society marching toward a temporal view of progress, new systems of values are emerging, seeking a place on the ship of glasnost. They are well summarized in the concluding question of Abuladze's excellent work *Repentance* (the choice of title is significant, repentance having played such an important role in the long intellectual history of this tormented country): "Which road leads to the temple?" Until now there was no doubt about the answer: all roads led to the mausoleum in Red Square. That the question has been asked so loudly, and repeated frequently in so many articles in the Soviet Union since 1985, in an altered form—"Where is the road which leads to the temple?"—is evidence of the extent of the revolution of ideas. For if it is a temple of truth, then the mausoleum must be an imposture, and the embalmed body inside no more than the father of a dynasty of usurpers.

The peoples integrated into the Soviet system have attributed to Russia, the heart of the USSR, all the responsibility for what has happened. The Russian intelligentsia, or at least that section of it now appearing at the side of Gorbachev, as it did once with Khrushchev, has for years accepted the evocative image of a society and a social culture "buried beneath the rubble." Khrushchev had opened the way, making it possible to clear away the top floor constructed by Stalin. His successor has today called for the same effort, and the intellectuals (often the same ones) have begun again to dig out the truth. But this time they are determined to dig to the bottom, and go back to the time when a relative, utilitarian truth was created—right back to the man through whom this work was accomplished. Could it be that the "mole" that tunneled its way beneath the well-ordered surface of capitalism will now perform the same function for socialism, and demonstrate that the absolute in the laws of history does not exist? For the majority of the communist peoples, such an enterprise is unthinkable. Glasnost, in its headlong rush, has transformed the peaceful ship of the beginning of the decade. Let us hope this is really the end of the killing—so think these conservative elements. What is more, the body in the Kremlin should be left in peace, so that it may continue to guide and reassure the living.

Reforms to Save the System

When he came to power, and had assessed the bitter failures of his predecessors, Gorbachev rightly concluded that everything needed reforming, starting with that which according to Marxist theory conditions the human environment, behavior, and attitudes—the economy. Three years were enough to convince him of the correctness of Lenin's belief that the most important factor is politics. To attempt to reform the economy while preserving the political system unchanged or merely tinkering with it would be to condemn the reforms to failure. The gap between the great plans for economic reform, vital to the Soviet Union's revival, and what has actually happened is striking but in no way surprising. Like all reformers before him, from Alexander II to Kosygin, Gorbachev has come up against the same resistance and the same fight.

Resistance has come from those who do not want another revolution and from those who no longer believe in it. The task of convincing these groups is made all the more difficult by the long divorce between dogma and reality, which has deprived words of their ability to mobilize public opinion. Words can still unite society in a semblance of an agreement which each man in his heart of hearts knows to be hypocritical, but they cannot infuse society with the necessary energy. It will take a long time and much education to change this relationship between consciousness and words. But as all reformers know, although reforms take a long time to produce results, they have only a limited time in which to be activated and to succeed. If no one believes in them, the battle is lost in advance. Sometimes they arouse excessive hopes and demands that race ahead of what can be achieved at any one time.

In the face of this resistance, Gorbachev has understood that a reform of the economy is no substitute for a program of social renewal. He has passed through to the other side of the mirror. At the party conference, called specifically so that he could arm himself through a renewal of the party machine with the necessary means to defeat the resistance to reform, Gorbachev moved from his initial plan and from the sphere of economics to the decisive political sphere and to the changes that needed to be introduced. His proposals have been sufficiently analyzed elsewhere to make repetition here unnecessary. What concerns us is the spirit of the plan. It lies in two fundamental proposals: the establishment of a state based on law and the inclusion of ordinary society—through the intermediary of the soviets, finally given real powers—in political life. Naturally Gorbachev has not thrown overboard everything already existing, and he has tried, in his plan, to protect the role of his party, the ruling party and guide of the social consciousness, by allowing it to preside over the soviets. This contradictory plan conceals an essential point: it represents a mortal blow to the beliefs and practice of the idol whom the crowds still flock to see in Red Square. A law-based state implies an immanent law, independent of the contingencies and demands of the political plan. It implies the autonomy of law, which Lenin always denied. It implies that society expresses itself through representative bodies endowed with real powers, consisting of permanent representatives of the people and of professional politicians. This equally presupposes a separation of powers and the autonomy of the judiciary. This was a heresy, a sign of "cretinism," always rejected by Lenin. However, without this fundamental reform, the very word "democratization," which Gorbachev has made a condition for the voluntary involvement of society in the process of reform, loses all meaning.

Thus we see how all the elements of Gorbachev's plan are inextricably linked to one another. In order to save the USSR from a decline that would mean the inevitable end of the system founded by Lenin, reform is necessary. In order to reform, it is not enough merely to adjust details. What is needed is a radical change in the political system; to do this, the central elements of Leninism must be forgotten. We are probably not witnessing an irreversible march toward a pluralist democracy, but nevertheless the locks of the doors placed by Lenin in the way of any developments other than those determined by him have been sprung. It may well be objected that the pragmatic Lenin himself might have followed other paths, abandoning much of the dogma in order to avoid the problems facing his successors. But the system was able to live on after Lenin—and there are few if any other revolutions that can boast of having lasted so long, of such victories in space—because it inherited not his pragmatism but his absolutism, the certainty of its irreversibility, based on intangible truths and principles. Gorbachev's proposals are another way of attacking this integrity, the symbol in the mausoleum.

Lenin asked: *Kto kogo?*—"Who does what to whom?", or more bluntly, "Who will kill whom?" Will Gorbachev's daring enterprise strike the fatal blow at Lenin, killing not the active Lenin, always ready to adapt to reality, even if only to bend it—"one step backward and two steps forward"—but Lenin the symbol, dominating his country and the system from Red Square as once the statue of Perun dominated Kiev, the ultimate reference point, the absolute belief? Or will Gorbachev be killed by the system and by those clinging desperately to it, knowing that he has vowed to change it? It would not, of course, be a physical death—"Thou shalt not kill" is now an integral part of the Tables of the Law—but rather removal or neutralization leading to political death.

Once again it is a matter of convincing society that it is not in the hands of an impostor; that he who is calling on them is he who has the right to do so—in other words, the "true tsar."

Conclusion

♦

E leven centuries of a history notable for its murders make Russia unlike any other country. To put it so baldly is, however, to ignore the interruptions and changes that are perhaps more significant than the usual view of the connection between murder and power.

In recent centuries, this long tradition of political murder has twice yielded ground and changed in nature. The first occasion was in the mid–nineteenth century. Until then, with very few exceptions, the tsar had had the power of life and death over his subjects. The authority of the sovereign and his relationship with society excluded any expression of the social will. The idea of disputing the power of the occupant of the throne, a semidivine being, was unthinkable. For all that, not all sovereigns were murderers, but the use of murder for political ends, as an instrument for the maintenance of a system in which society as a whole was the state's property, was always a possibility. It was for many centuries an integral part of imperial absolutism.

The mid–nineteenth century brought a decisive challenge to the idea of absolutism and, therefore, to the use of murder. It was probably Alexander II who first understood, or in any case who embodied, the need for a new relationship between state and society. The emancipation of the serfs in 1861 and the political reforms of 1864 brought society, albeit in a small way, into the political arena, formerly the monopoly of the state and the sovereign. Despite the absolutist ideas revived by his successors, this impulse toward reform was unstoppable. One day it would come about that the relationship between power and society would unite in an agreement based on dialogue and cooperation, and no longer just on the will of an autocrat.

Such reforms, when they go against the political traditions

of the centuries, cannot be imposed in a hurry merely by enshrining them in the law. It takes time, and generally they are accompanied by violence. What characterizes the reforms of the mid–nineteenth century is that the violence—the result of a desire to bridge the gap between the hopes raised by the reforms and their realization—although still present, changed its sphere of action. Now it was an impatient society that turned violence against the power that had exercised it for so long. Attempts to reestablish order by force between 1881 and 1914 were now nothing but rearguard actions. Even those who, like Alexander III, dreamed of returning to the old order knew that it was dead and gone. The modernization of the economy and of social conditions inevitably involved progress in the political system. If political murder was frequently resorted to in Russia in the half-century preceding the revolution, it was no longer murder intended to conquer or retain power. It was rather a means used by society, or society's representatives, to achieve a modernization of the exercise of power, from which murder would eventually be excluded.

The second turning point after the return—with a vengeance this time—to violence was that which occurred around Stalin's deathbed. All his successors, despite their differences, were to honor their renunciation of violence. When history is looked at in this way, the tragic post-revolution years, whose worst excesses came to an end in 1953, appear to be a parenthesis in Russia's long march toward the creation of a consensus between state and society. If we exclude this parenthesis, it is clear that, for more than a century, the history of Russia reveals that strenuous efforts were made to throw off its special characteristic described variously as "Asiaticism" (*aziachina*), "barbarism," or, more romantically, the "Slav soul." According to this the Russian people's tendency to meek submission brings down violence on themselves.

Since no reform has as yet been able to reach its ultimate fulfillment, what characterizes the uneven development of the political history of Russia is that society has still not found its true place. Called on to appear in the *zemstvos,* in the elected assemblies, and eventually in the Constituent Assembly, coming together spontaneously in the various organizations providing aid during the war, and then after the revolution in the soviets, it is possible to see how society in the Russian Empire started out on a long voyage of discovery—finding, as it progressed through different stages of development, its own autonomy and serving its apprenticeship in democracy. To say that Russia has had no experience of democracy is to forget this development—often interrupted, certainly, but incontestable. The Russians, and their brothers in the empire, learned through these social bodies how to exercise responsibility and show their determination to take their place in the governing of the country. Modernization, an ambiguous word with various implications, nevertheless has a precise meaning on this point. It means the change in ways of thinking, the emergence of a responsible social consciousness not prepared to submit to the ruling power, and a belief that the interests of all and the future of the nation made dialogue between state and society imperative. Russia had embarked on such a course in the second half of the last century and its effects were already becoming apparent on the eve of the great battle that was to swallow up the entire social order of eastern Europe. The state—on the surface at least—remained in control, but the moment it wavered, in 1915–16, the speed with which society was able to take over the collapsing institutions of the state is evidence of its maturity.

Lenin's view of the revolution and the utopia that he sought to bring about, forcing the pace of history in order to create the Golden Age out of nothing, made it necessary to return to a political order that was on its way out. The state—or the party, depending on the period in question—the bringer of utopia, the guarantor of the Golden Age, once again came to subjugate society, putting it at the service of its plan, at its pace, according to its own vision. To keep a society at the service of the state which has always been in this position is already no easy task, especially when this society has just entered upon the path of modernization. It is far more difficult, however, to go back to such a system, and ignore the modernization in people's ways of thinking, to assert that the progress achieved had never happened and that the Golden Age does not come about as the result of gradual change, but as a result of a break with the past and the radical policies of a political party. Violence was unavoidable in the attempt to impose this change of direction on a society that had already started out on the road to autonomy. The Soviet leaders gave this violence a dimension that no one could have foreseen, even in science fiction. Anyone who lived through the Stalinist years will recognize aspects of that time in Orwell's work, but will say that he has failed to depict the unchained violence, impossible for the imagination to grasp or relate. The mechanics of the system are well described, but the daily horror is missing, as well as the invincible, almost supernatural, character—because it was more closely connected with a utopia than with men—of this horror.

It has only rarely been asked why it was that in Nazi Germany, where Hitler's obsessions gave rise to a reign of equal terror, men dared to respond with attempts at assassination, while in the Soviet Union, a country where there was no lack of physical courage and terrorism, no one attempted to kill Stalin. The excessive precautions with which Hitler surrounded himself were every bit as thorough as those of his Soviet counterpart. The difference may perhaps lie in the fact that Hitler's plan had not wiped out all the constituent elements of society, whereas Stalin was faced only by a society that he had completely crushed through the use of unpredictable murder on a grand scale. Hannah Arendt has emphasized that "the isolation of man" was at one and the same time the beginning of the terror, its most fertile ground, and its result.

Murder "from below" in Russian history was the characteristic of a brief period when the quest for modernization of the political system induced the government to abandon its traditional use of violence. The way was thus opened to social violence "from below," encouraged by what seemed to be a weakening of authority at the top—the target of Russian "tyrannicide" was always the weakened "tyrant." Political murder "from above," in its last period, was to reemerge in a very different guise. In order to disappear as a practice without at the same time appearing as a sign of weakness, as had been the case in the second half of the nineteenth century, political murder after 1953 took on new forms: murder without death, bloodless murder, symbolic murder. Since the state remained autonomous and society could not be its arbiter, conflicts could not be resolved peacefully. But the losers in these conflicts were lucky compared to those who preceded them. Khrushchev was a political corpse, but was not subsequently destined to become a dead body. Erased from history and from memory, dying in obscurity, he nevertheless had a peaceful retirement. However bitter this forced retirement must have been, no one can have known better than he, a witness to Stalin's crimes, the progress represented by his situation. Furthermore, as time passed, even the political corpse, expiatory victim of struggles at the top, or rejected or condemned policies, came to know improved conditions. Nikolai Podgorny, purged and "killed politically" by his rivals in the mid-1970s, was eventually authorized to make a timid reappearance at an official festivity: death with resurrection. More recently, Boris Yeltsin, an isolated proponent of perestroika, was condemned for his extremism, but merely relegated to tasks of secondary importance. Furthermore, he was allowed to plead his case publicly before the entire party and before the country. This in turn enabled Yeltsin the Communist "political corpse" to be reborn as the anticommunist rival of Gorbachev himself.

But the most obvious sign of this evolution is that, at the end of the 1980s, the condemnations and witch-hunts have been directed more at the dead than the living. The most symbolic "murder" of this period has been that of Leonid Brezhnev, who was not made a political corpse until after his natural death. This inversion of Stalin's method seems to reveal a double concern: while not wishing to do away entirely with murder—the symbol of error and its punishment, of the return to the true path—there is a desire to end the practice of real murder. In this sense continuous progress had undeniably been made in the political system. Just as there have been no wars in Europe in the last forty years, but the weapons of deterrence are retained in order to guarantee this lasting peace, so political murder has been practically abandoned by the Soviet regime in the last thirty-five years. The weapon of symbolic death is the equivalent of the deterrent in the international scene. The "civilized state," the dream of so many sovereigns, is a state that still dominates society, but one that is able to maintain peaceful and well-regulated relations with it. The following stage is that when the state is at the service of society. Once again, the debate has been reopened on this difficult transition. It may be necessary for the state to keep control during a long-drawn-out and sensitive transitional period, in order to prevent it from becoming bogged down or carried away by the impatience of the people.

This perspective leads us once more to the old questions: what is Russia; what is the USSR; are the two countries, the two systems, one and the same; is the government of the people the same though bearing a different name; or are they two quite different political worlds separated forever by the radical breaks of 1917?

Readers of the Marquis of Custine, and the many others like him, would favor the first hypothesis and maintain that nothing has changed in Russia and that, in the words of a famous grand duke and historian, it is still "a tyranny weighed down by assassination." But that would be to forget that Custine saw Russia in 1839, when Nicholas I, haunted by the coup d'état of 1825, was successfully trying to impose silence on society as a whole. In fact Russia began to move a few years later, when the intelligentsia began to see its role and when Nicholas's successor, for his part, began to enter into dialogue, embarking on the first reforms. If one must talk of continuity and breaks, then it is perhaps in this direction that one should look. There was indeed a continuation of authoritarian political methods. But there was also a break between a time when the system depended on an all-powerful state that excluded society from the political arena and the later period, after 1861, when the desire for modernization inspired both extremes of society, the rulers and their subjects. The slow but inevitable entrance of society into the political arena is one of the basic factors in the process of modernization. It made great strides in the periods 1860–64 and 1905–17 and was assisted to a notable degree by the economic modernization that had originally been conceived as a means of strengthening absolutism.

The evolution born of the new utopia was, by contrast, to restore the initial equation: a society in the service of the state. The fact that this was in the interests of a remarkable and historic plan did not in any way change the fact that the entire evolution of the relations between state and society was, until the 1960s, inverted. Since then, cautious and hesitant attempts have been made by the political leaders, the intellectuals—the eternal intercessors, like the saints of other centuries—and society—which, having recovered its memory, is slowly awakening from its terrified apathy—to pick up once again the broken threads of modernization, and to replace the utopian idea of a forced entrance into the Golden Age with the idea of the political advancement of society. The USSR is not a continuation of the old Russia as a system of despotism; it is a continuation in its quest for modernity, even if the tragic parenthesis of the Lenin-Stalin period destroyed for decades the whole edifice that was just emerging in 1913 and that was to alarm Lenin so much, for he feared that these reforms might block the way to revolution.

The true continuity of Russo-Soviet history can be found instead in the country's never-ending tragedy, symbolized by the systematic use of murder as a means of retaining power and as a reaction to that power. This tragedy sheds light on the uniqueness of the history of the country.

Until the thirteenth century, Russia was not outstanding among other similar countries either in backwardness or in brutality. On the contrary, its centers of civilization, Kiev, Novgorod, and the other princely towns, seemed to point to a bright future. If people were killed, it was no different in other places, during a period when laws and political spheres were not yet fully defined. It was only later that Russia's lasting tragedy was to bear down.

It cannot be emphasized too often that Russia was first and foremost an open space, without frontiers. The country was itself a frontier between an emerging Europe and Asia. From the start, the princes of Kiev had had to defend every inch of their territory against the invaders who threatened on every side. The flowering of Kiev, under such conditions, is little short of miraculous. Equally miraculous is the stubbornness of those who ruled there and their final choice of Christianity and Europe. In the fatal year 1237, the Mongol army descended on the country, crushed the principalities, and imposed its domination for two-and-a-half centuries. Russia, a state without frontiers, which held the Mongols on its territories, was the frontier separating the Mongols from Europe. During these two-and-a-half centuries, the West was able to develop, protected by a shattered Russia.

When it was finally freed, Russia emerged from the shadows of a domination which left behind it a legacy very different from that inherited by the rest of Europe. It was necessary to create a "nation," define its territory, decide on its frontier—in Europe or facing Europe?— and set up a state that could administer and defend such a vast area, the protection of which required that the frontier be constantly pushed back. Other countries knew the glories of the Renaissance; Russia struggled with the nascent nation. Russia was never in line with the rest of Europe: lagging behind until 1917; rushing ahead in the following utopia.

The consequences of this chronological discrepancy in relation to a Europe that Russia protected against Asia but never coincided with were twofold. There was the time lag in its social system, based on serfdom, in a period where elsewhere men were free, that made Russia an object of curiosity or horror for the rest of Europe, together with its inability to develop a common cause that could unite around it both those who held power and those who submitted to it. The building of the cathedrals, the Crusades, and all that bound together the nations of Christian Europe was missing in Russia. Later there was no time to make up for these things. The eternal Russian conflict emerged from this absence of a common plan around which the myths of nations and their coherence develop.

Russia developed by juxtaposing two different cultures. There was the culture of the ruling class and of the elite classes, for whom the desire to "catch up with Europe," to become part of it or, alternatively, to define Russia's specificity in relation to it, was a constant theme. Then there was the horizontal and static culture of the people, which felt the effects of the culture of the elites as so many blows at its own existence. A symbolic but important sign of this cultural discontinuity was the frequent moving of the country's capital: from Kiev to Suzdal, then to Moscow, St. Petersburg, and then finally back to Moscow. These names reflect the progress of a power in search of its identity and Russia's decisive historical moments: Kiev; the Mongol period; the Time of Troubles; Moscow; Peter the Great's scheme to westernize the country; St. Petersburg; finally, the revolution. There was little here to enable the people to find their definitive identity or unite them to the masters of the moment.

It is this tormented history that has made the Russians an

unhappy people, constantly in search of consoling myths. This goes a long way to explain the lasting and diverse influence of religion. The search of this anguished people for a cultural identity and culture may well have found in the myths of religion the response that was most suited to encouraging the work of national construction begun in Kiev and that of reconstruction that began again in the sixteenth century. In the extreme moral poverty of Russia, religion had the added function of making such poverty socially acceptable. The sanctity of the tsar disguised the savagery of his reign. His extreme despotism required legitimization by something equally extreme: submission to the divine will. If the people's constant suffering was accepted, it was because the eschatological vision that underlies all political mythology made this suffering seem like a stage in the steps of the Christ of the Passion.

This view of religion combined in an extraordinary Orthodox Christian syncretism the rigorism of the Old Believers, the heterodox beliefs of innumerable sects, and vestiges of old pagan ideas. It was to guide the apparently modern ideas produced by the intellectuals: the people, chosen by God and suffering through His will, sin and the necessary expiation.

In this respect, the revolution did not represent a break with the past, even if it attempted to substitute its own myths for the mythology developed through the ages. The idea of salvation remains at the heart of a system searching for unanimity. The revolution took note of the existence of the two cultures that history had failed to reconcile, and at the same time as offering a new eschatological vision it resolved the cultural divorce by the use of propaganda. Pasternak has expressed perfectly in *Dr. Zhivago* this cultural conflict, central to Russia's tragedy and transcending centuries and events, right up to the revolution. Zhivago, whose very name, as James Billington has pointed out, comes from the Easter liturgy, represents within himself the majority of Russia's myths. This unhappy hero, who accepts without outward protest an order that is alien to him and which eventually destroys him, represents the alternative to *Homo sovieticus* who pretends to support the regime, merges with the collective, and becomes corrupted by double language. The Passion that Zhivago, who lives through the torment of the revolution, has to endure is that of the Civil War with its physical privations and moral degradation. It is symbolic of the destiny of the people, of Russia's tragedy. The violence that marks the book, an inevitable violence and a redemptive violence, is that of the whole of Russia's history. Zhivago's problem also conceals another eternal Russian problem: the rejection of distorted or disguised truth, the desire to distinguish what is "true" from what is "false."

For more than a century, men of good will—once Alexander II, yesterday Khrushchev, and perhaps today Gorbachev—have attempted to pull the country out of its tragic past and anchor it firmly in the modern world. The difficulties experienced by these reformers are evidence of the size of the task. Although they made a point of outlawing the use of murder in politics, the first two lost their lives, physical or political, in the process. But, in this long march toward progress, they themselves also committed symbolic murders—the murder of an entire system of social relations, the simultaneous murder of the serf and the serf's master, in 1861; the murder of the man who had committed so many murders in Russia, in 1956 and 1961. What murder today could bring the work to its conclusion? What would eradicate the remaining elements that have caused Russia's tragedy, the serfdom and the bleeding idols, and close the door once and for all on Russia's unique problems?

There could be no better way to conclude this work than by retelling a short story that spread secretly throughout Moscow some fifteen years ago and caused a furor. It is the allegorical story of a man who manages to get into the mausoleum, cut off Lenin's embalmed head, and carry it off. As he wanders about the streets of Moscow, brandishing his grisly trophy, the unseeing eyes of the passersby, the soldiers guarding the mausoleum, and the visitors to the tomb of the idol lead him to conclude that the mausoleum has been empty for a long time and that this useless carcass, like some words, has no relationship whatsoever with reality. The truth is in this absence, seen but not spoken of.

Perhaps we are seeing a political murder taking place around the mausoleum. By authorizing society to notice that the head of the idol has disappeared, it will give it back its freedom and mastery over its own fate. That which is, at the start, mere individual perception, which collectively people pretend not to see, when it becomes the common property of all and part of the common language, will put an end to that human "isolation" and "desolation" described by Hannah Arendt. A political society will then emerge where murder and terror, as in other countries, will be nothing more than accidents of history.

Chronology of
Major Events

◆

KIEV

RUSSIA	WORLD AFFAIRS
882 Oleg conquers Kiev and unites Kiev and Novgorod	
	913–59 Constantin Porphyrogenitus emperor of Byzantium
987–1015 Reign of Vladimir I	**987** Hugh Capet king of France
988 Baptism of Vladimir and of Russia	
1015 Assassination of Boris and Gleb	
1019–54 Reign of Yaroslav the Wise	**1054** Excommunication of patriarch of Constantinople by papal legates
1097 Conference of Lyubich	
	1099 First Crusade

RUSSIA	WORLD AFFAIRS
1113–25 Yury Dolgoruky (grand prince of Kiev, 1155–57)	
1157–74 Andrei Bogolyubsky (prince of Suzdal)	
1169 Andrei captures Kiev	

THE MONGOL PERIOD

	1180–1223 Philip Augustus king of France
1206–27 Conquests of Genghis Khan	
1236 Batu, successor of Genghis Khan, reaches Russia	
1240 Fall of Kiev	
1252–63 Alexander Nevsky grand prince of Vladimir	
	1265 St. Thomas Aquinas writes the *Summa Theologica*
1299 Vladimir becomes the see of the metropolitan	
	1302 Dante starts the *Divine Comedy*

RUSSIA	WORLD AFFAIRS
	1337 Beginning of the Hundred Years' War
1380 Victory of Dmitri Donskoy at Kulikovo, Tartar retreat	
1382 Tartars sack Moscow	

THE RISE OF MOSCOW

RUSSIA	WORLD AFFAIRS
1389–1425 Basil I	
	1431 Death of Joan of Arc
	1430–50 Development of printing with movable type
	1453 Fall of Constantinople, end of Hundred Years' War
	1461–83 Louis XI king of France
1462–1505 Ivan III	
1472 Ivan III marries Sophia Palaeologa	
1477 Annexation of Novgorod by Moscow	

RUSSIA	WORLD AFFAIRS
1480 Ivan III proclaims the end of Tartar domination	
	1516 *The Prince,* Machiavelli
	1517 Luther's Ninety-five Theses
	1519 Charles V elected emperor of Germany
1533–38 Regency of Elena, mother of Ivan IV	
1533–84 Reign of Ivan the Terrible	**1543** Copernicus announces his discoveries
1549–56 "Ivan the Reformer"	
1552 Capture of Kazan, real end of Tartar rule	
1556 Fall of Astrakhan	**1556–98** Philip II rules in Spain
1564–72 Rule of the *oprichnina*	
1570 Ivan IV takes Novgorod and massacres its inhabitants	
1571 Devlet Giray's raid on Moscow	**1571** Battle of Lepanto

RUSSIA	WORLD AFFAIRS
	1572 St. Bartholomew Massacre in Paris
	1580 Montaigne's *Essays*
1582 Beginning of the conquest of Siberia	
1581–92 Setting up of the cadastral register	
1582 Ivan IV kills his son	
1589 Creation of the patriarchate of Russia	
1584–98 Reign of Fyodor I	
1591 Death of the tsarevich at Uglich	
1598 End of the dynasty of Rurik	**1598** Edict of Nantes, end of the Wars of Religion in France
1598–1605 Reign of Boris Godunov	
1605 End of the Godunov dynasty	**1605** Publication of Cervantes's *Don Quixote* and Shakespeare's *Macbeth*

THE TIME OF TROUBLES, 1598–1613

1605
Coronation of the "false Dmitri"

RUSSIA	WORLD AFFAIRS
1606 Death of the "false Dmitri"	
1606–10 Reign of Basil Shuisky	
1610 End of the Shuisky dynasty	
1610 Throne of Russia offered to a Polish prince	
1613 Election of Michael Romanov and his proclamation as tsar	

THE ROMANOV DYNASTY, 1613–1917

1619–33 Patriarch Filaret assists the tsar	
	1637 Descartes's *Discourse of Method*
1645–76 Reign of Alexis	**1643–1715** Louis XIV king of France
	1649 Execution of Charles I of England
1654 Union of Ukraine with Russia	
1654–66 Nikon's reforms; beginning of the schism with Old Believers	
1670–71 Rebellion of Stenka Razin	

RUSSIA	WORLD AFFAIRS
1676–82 Reign of Fyodor III	**1679** *Habeas corpus* established by English parliament
1682–89 Regency of Sophia	**1685** Revocation of the Edict of Nantes in France
1689–1725 Reign of Peter the Great	
1689–1696 Shared reign of Peter and Ivan	
1696 Capture of Azov	
1697 *Preobrazhenskii prikaz:* definition of political crime	
1697–98 Peter the Great's European tour	**1697–1718** Reign of Charles XII of Sweden
1698 Revolt of the *streltsi*	
1702 Peter decides to found St. Petersburg	
1703 Foundation of the first Russian newspaper, *Vedomosti*	
1712 St. Petersburg becomes capital of Russia	
	1715–74 Louis XV king of France

RUSSIA	WORLD AFFAIRS
1718 Trial and death of the tsarevich	
1721 Peter becomes emperor Abdication of the patriarchate, replaced by the Holy Synod	
1722 Creation of the Table of Ranks Change of the law of succession	
1725 Foundation of the Academy of Sciences	
1725–27 Reign of Catherine I	
1727–30 Reign of Peter II	
1730–40 Reign of Anna Ivanovna	
	1748 Montesquieu's *Esprit des Lois*
1741–61 Reign of Elizabeth I	
	1751–78 Diderot's *Encyclopdia*
1761–62 Reign of Peter III	
1762 (2/18) Emancipation of the nobility	**1762** Rousseau's *Social Contract*
1762 (6/28) Murder of Peter III	

RUSSIA	WORLD AFFAIRS
1762–96 Reign of Catherine II	
1767–68 Legislative commission	
1772 First partition of Poland	
	1774 Louis XVI king of France
	1776 Independence of the United States
	1789 French Revolution
	1792–97 First Coalition
1793 Second partition of Poland	1793 Execution of Louis XVI
1795 Third partition of Poland	
1796–1801 Reign of Paul I	
1797 Return to the order of succession abolished in 1722	
	1798–1802 Second Coalition
	1799 Coup d'état of 18 Brumaire
1801–25 Reign of Alexander I	
	1804–15 Napoleon emperor

RUSSIA	WORLD AFFAIRS
	1805 Third Coalition
	1806 Fourth Coalition
	1809 Fifth Coalition
1811 Creation of the Ministry of Police	
1812 Napoleon in Russia	
	1815 Congress of Vienna
	1821 Death of Napoleon
1825 (12/14) Failed coup d'état	
1825–55 Reign of Nicholas I	
1826 Creation of the Third Section (political police) Code of censorship	
	1830 July Revolution in France
1832 Law code	
	1837–1901 Reign of Victoria in England
	1848 Revolutions in Europe

RUSSIA	WORLD AFFAIRS
	1851 Coup d'état of Louis-Napoleon
1857–81 Reign of Alexander II	
1861 (2/19) Emancipation of the serfs	
1864 Judicial and institutional reforms	**1864** Strikes made legal in France
	1864–76 First International
	1865 Slavery abolished in United States
1870 Obligatory military service	
	1871 Paris Commune
	1875 French Third Republic
1877–78 Trials of terrorists	
1878 Vera Zasulich shoots the St. Petersburg chief of police; tried and aquitted	
1878 (8/4) Assassination of head of Third Section	
1878–80 Repressive laws and abolition of Third Section in favor of a Department of State Police	

RUSSIA	WORLD AFFAIRS
1881 (3/1) Assassination of Alexander II	
1881–94 Reign of Alexander III	
	1884 Trade unions legalized in France
1887 Failed attempt on life of Alexander III	
	1888–1918 William III German emperor
	1889 Second International
1894–1917 Reign of Nicholas II	**1894** Dreyfus Affair
1904 Campaign for a constitution	
1905 (Jan.) "Bloody Sunday"	
1905 (Oct.) Imperial manifesto proclaiming civil liberties and a representative body	
1905 First Duma	
1907 Second Duma	
1912 Third Duma	**1912–13** Balkan Wars

RUSSIA	WORLD AFFAIRS
	1914 (6/28) Assassination of Archduke Francis Ferdinand in Sarajevo
	1914 (7/19–24) Austria-Hungary and Germany declare war on Russia
1914 (Aug.) Military defeat in the Mazurian Lakes	
1916–17 Fourth Duma	**1916** Battle of Verdun
1917 (3/3) Abdication of Nicholas II	

COMMUNIST RUSSIA, 1917–

1917	
4/3 Lenin returns to Russia	**1917 (April)** United States enters war
10/25–27 Bolshevik Revolution	
1918	
1/5–6 Opening and suppression of the Constituent Assembly	
3/3 Treaty of Brest-Litovsk	
3/12 Moscow made capital	

RUSSIA	WORLD AFFAIRS
July Socialist Revolutionary plot against Lenin July Beginning of War Communism, beginning of Civil War	
	1918 (November) End of World War I
1919 (3/4) Setting up of Third International in Moscow	
	1919 (June) Treaty of Versailles
1920 August Defeat of Red Army in Warsaw, end of Lenin's hopes of revolution November End of Civil War 1921 (March) Peasant uprising in Tambov Kronstadt commune Tenth Party Congress NEP and end of War Communism 1922 Famine until summer Feb. Cheka becomes GPU	

RUSSIA	WORLD AFFAIRS
April Stalin elected general secretary of Central Committee	
	1922 (October) Mussolini in power
12/30 Establishment of the USSR	
	1923 Failure of Hitler's putsch in Munich
1924 (1/21) Death of Lenin Troika in power: Zinoviev, Kamenev, and Stalin	
1925	
Jan. Trotsky excluded from leadership	
Oct. Trotsky excluded from Politburo	
Death of patriarch, leaving his see vacant until 1943	
1927 "United opposition" to Stalin	
Nov. Trotsky and Zinoviev expelled from party	
1928 Grain crisis	
May Trotsky exiled to Alma Ata	

RUSSIA	WORLD AFFAIRS
1928 Sixth Congress of Comintern: "Turning to the left"	
1929	
Jan. Trotsky expelled from USSR	
April Sixteenth Party Congress approves first five-year plan	
	1929 (October) Wall Street crash; beginning of Depression
Autumn Beginning of collectivization	
Nov. Bukharin excluded from Politburo	
1930 (Aug.–Dec.) Public and closed trials of "saboteurs": death sentences	
1931 Trial of Mensheviks	
1932	
5/15 "Five-Year Antireligion Plan"	
8/7 Law on the Protection of State Enterprises and Property; use of death sentence extended	

RUSSIA	WORLD AFFAIRS
Dec. Reestablishment of internal passports; peasants given no passports until 1970	
1932–33 Great Famine	1933 (1/30) Hitler becomes chancellor of Germany
1934	
Jan. Seventeenth Congress of the victors	
July GPU becomes NKVD	
6/8 Law on "treason"	
9/18 USSR joins League of Nations	
12/1 Murder of Kirov	
1935 (Aug.) Stakhanovism	
1936	1936 Popular Front
August First Moscow trial	Beginning of Spanish Civil War
Dec. Constitution of USSR	Hitler occupies Rhineland
1937	
March Second Moscow trial	

RUSSIA	WORLD AFFAIRS
June Execution of army chiefs	
Dec. Elections to Supreme Soviet	
1938	1938 Anschluss
March Third Moscow trial	Munich agreement on Czechoslovakia
Dec. Beria becomes People's Commissar of the Interior	
Obligatory work pass for workers	
1939	1939
8/23 Soviet-German Pact	March Hitler occupies Czechoslovakia
Sept. Division of Poland	9/3 Beginning of World War II
1940	
March Peace with Finland	
April Katyn massacre	
June Annexation of Baltic states	1940 (6/22) Franco-German armistice
August Assassination of Trotsky in Mexico	France occupied

RUSSIA	WORLD AFFAIRS
1941 (6/22) Hitler invades USSR	
1943	1943 Suppression of Comintern
Jan. Victory of Stalingrad	
Sept. Restoration of patriarchate	
1945 (5/9) End of Soviet-German war	1945 (October) Creation of UN
1946–48 "Zhdanovism"	1947 Creation of Cominform
1948–53 Purges	1949 Creation of Comecon
1952	
10/5–14 Nineteenth Congress of CPSU	
1953	
1/13 "Discovery" of the "doctors' plot"	
3/5 Death of Stalin	
3/6 Malenkov succeeds Stalin	
3/14 Succession reorganized in favor of troika: Malenkov, Beria, and Molotov; Presidium reduced from 25 to 10 members	

RUSSIA	WORLD AFFAIRS
4/4 Document from MVD on the innocence of the "doctors" and the "illegal court procedures"	1953 (June) Strikes and riots in West Germany
7/10 Fall of Beria; his arrest is announced	7/27 Armistice in Korea
8/20 USSR tests an H-bomb	
9/3 Plenum of the Central Committee: Khrushchev becomes first secretary, debate on agricultural problems	
12/23 Execution of Beria announced	
1954	1954
2/22–3/2 Plenum of Central Committee, Khrushchev proposes plan to open up unexploited areas	Jan–Feb. Four-power meetings on Berlin
	July Geneva Conference on Indochina
	7/20 Armistice in Indochina
1955	1955
2/8 Malenkov forced to resign but remains in Presidium	4/17–24 Bandung Conference

RUSSIA	WORLD AFFAIRS
2/9 Bulganin head of state; Marshal Zhukov named as minister of defenxe	
	5/14 Signing of Warsaw Pact
	5/15 Signing of peace treaty with Austria
5/26-6/2 Khrushchev-Tito summit in Belgrade: Soviet-Yugoslav reconciliation	
7/4–12 Plenum of CC, Suslov enters Praesidium. Decision to hold Twentieth Congress	7/17–24 Meeting of four major world powers in Geneva
1956	1956
2/14–25 Twentieth Congress of CPSU; Khrushchev's secret speech	4/17 Dissolution of Cominform
4/25 Abrogation of the workers' laws of 1940	
6/30 Resolution of the CC on the "elimination of the cult of personality"	
Publication of Lenin's testament	
7/14–9/8 Social laws on pensions and minimum wages	

RUSSIA	WORLD AFFAIRS
	10/23–11/4 Hungarian uprising, crisis in Poland
	Nov. Suez crisis
Dec. Plenum of CC	
1957	
2/13–14 Plenum of CC, creation of *sovnarkhozy*	
6/22–29 Plenum of CC, condemnation of "antiparty group"; Malenkov, Kaganovich, and Molotov removed from Presidium and CC; Shepilov excluded from Secretariat and CC	
10/4 Launch of first *Sputnik*	
10/26 Plenum of CC, Marshal Zhukov removed from all posts and sent into retirement	
11/14–16 Conference in Moscow of heads of Communist parties in power	
12/17 Plenum of CC	

RUSSIA	WORLD AFFAIRS
1958 2/25–26 Plenum of CC, plan to liquidate the machine tractor stations and sell agricultural equipment to the collective farms is adopted 3/27 Plenum of CC, Bulganin excluded from CC for belonging to the "antiparty group" 10/22 Pasternak receives Nobel Prize 11/2 Plenum of CC, plan of reform of education adopted 12/15–19 Plenum of CC, agriculture debate **1959** 1/27–2/5 Twenty-first (extraordinary) Congress of CPSU; seven-year plan adopted June Crisis in Sino-Soviet relations becomes public 9/15–27 Khrushchev in United States; Camp David summit 9/30 Khrushchev in China	

RUSSIA	WORLD AFFAIRS
10/4 Khrushchev and Mao hold talks	
9/22–25 Plenum of CC, agriculture debate	
December Plenum of CC	1959 (December) Victory of Fidel Castro in Cuba
1960	
1/13 Reduction of armed forces in USSR; 1,200,000 soldiers released from army	
5/1 American U2 brought down over Sverdlovsk	
5/4 Plenum of CC; Kosygin named first vice president of Council of Ministers	
	1960
5/7 Working day in USSR to start at 7 A.M.	5/16 Failure of Paris summit because of U2
5/30 Death of Pasternak	
17/13–16 Plenum of CC, debate on industry	
April–7/17 USSR withdraws technicians from China	11/10–12/10 Conference of 81 Communist parties in Moscow

RUSSIA	WORLD AFFAIRS
	November Castro proclaims Cuba a socialist republic
1961	
1/1 Monetary reform	
1/10–18 Plenum of CC, debate on agriculture	
4/12 Launch of *Vostok,* first manned spacecraft	
June Khrushchev-Kennedy summit in Vienna	
10/17–31 Twenty-second Congress; adoption of 3rd program and new statutes of CPSU. Stalin removed from mausoleum, Voroshilov, added to antiparty group, performs self-criticism	1961 (August) Building of Berlin Wall
Break with Albania	
11/10 Stalingrad renamed Volgograd	
1962	
3/5–9 Plenum of CC, debate on agriculture	
6/1 Rise in agricultural prices	

RUSSIA	WORLD AFFAIRS
August Riots and repression in Novocherkassk	
Oct. *Pravda* publishes Yevtushenko's *Heirs of Stalin*	
11/19–23 Plenum of CC. Reform of party, divided into two branches, industrial and agricultural	1962 (10/22–28) Cuban crisis
Nov. The journal *Novyi Mir* publishes *One Day in the Life of Ivan Denisovich* by Alexander Solzhenitsyn	
12/1 Khrushchev criticizes abstract art	
12/17 Intellectuals are called to order: "Ideology must come first"	
1963	
6/18–20 Plenum of CC, debate on ideology	
7/14 Letter from the Chinese CP: the Sino-Soviet split is official 8/5 Moscow Treaty agreeing to end nuclear tests	

RUSSIA	WORLD AFFAIRS
12/9–13 Plenum of CC on the technical conditions of agriculture (fertilizers)	1963 22/11 Assassination of U.S. President John F. Kennedy
1964	
2/10–15 Plenum of CC, debate on agriculture	
4/17 Khrushchev's jubilee	
7/15 Brezhnev "dedicates" himself to the Secretariat of the party, ending up second in rank to Khrushchev	
10/14 Plenum of CC: Khrushchev removed from all his posts and retired, Brezhnev is first secretary of CPSU, Kosygin head of state	
11/16 Plenum of CC: reform of party abolished, CPSU reunited	
1965	
3/24–26 Plenum of CC: debate on agriculture	

RUSSIA	WORLD AFFAIRS
9/24–29 Plenum of CC: reform of industry and suppression of *sovnarkhozy* proposed by Kosygin **12/9** Podgorny becomes head of state **1964–85** Era of stagnation **1965** Kosygin's reform	
	1972 Nixon in Peking First SALT Agreements
1973 Publication outside USSR of *Gulag Archipelago* **1974** Solzhenitsyn expelled from USSR	
	1975 Helsinki Conference **1976** Death of Mao Zedong
1977 Adoption of Fourth Constitution of USSR	**1977** Deng Xiaoping in power in China **1979** Soviet intervention in Afghanistan
1980 Sakharov banished to Gorky	

RUSSIA	WORLD AFFAIRS
	1981 Martial law in Poland
1982 (November) Death of Brezhnev, replaced by Yuri Andropov as head of party and state	
1984 (Feb.) Death of Andropov, replaced in same posts by Konstantin Chernenko	
1985, 3/10 Death of Chernenko, Mikhail Gorbachev general secretary of CPSU, Andrei Gromyko head of state	1985 (Nov.) Gorbachev-Reagan summit in Geneva
1986 Twenty-seventh Congress of CPSU	1986 (Oct.) Gorbachev-Reagan summit in Reykjavik
4/25 Chernobyl	
Nov. Death of Molotov	
Dec. Riots in Alma Ata; end of Sakharov's exile	
1987 Plenums in January and June (proposals for reforms)	

RUSSIA	WORLD AFFAIRS
1988 6/28–7/2 Twenty-eighth Congress of CPSU (proposals for political reforms) 7/28–29 Plenum, proposals for agrarian reforms (beginning of decollectivization?)	

Movement of the Seats of Power in Russia

Frontiers shown are those of the early twentieth century

- – ⟶ **1** Successive capitals
- † Chief religious centers
- ▬▬▬ Frontier of Russian Empire
- ⋯⋯⋯ Frontier of European Russia

BARENTS SEA

SWEDEN

Solovki

St. Petersburg †

BALTIC

† Novgorod

SEA

Trinity-
† St. Sergius

GERMANY

3 ● Suzdal

Moscow   4   ●Vladimir   Kazan †

Optina ● †
Pustyna

Kiev

AUSTRIA-
HUNGARY

† Azov

ARAL
SEA

RUMANIA

Kheirson

CASPIAN

BULGARIA

BLACK SEA

SEA

Istanbul
(Constantinople)

TURKEY

PERSIA

435

GENEALOGY OF THE ROYAL FAMILIES BEFORE THE ROMANOVS

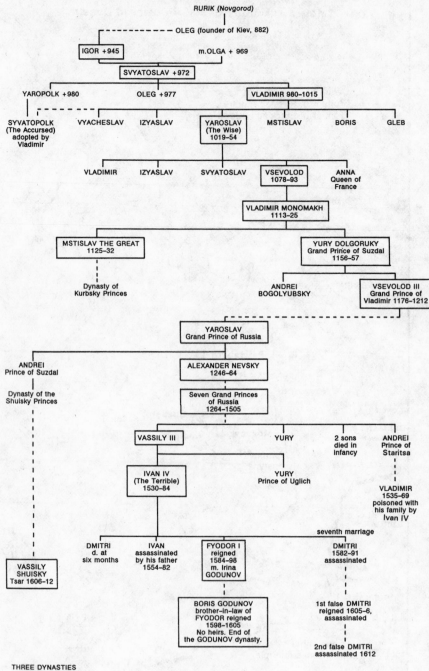

THREE DYNASTIES
1. Rurikids: dynasty ends
   in 1598 with Fyodor I
2. Godunovs: 1598–1605
3. Shuiskys: 1606–12

GENEALOGY OF THE ROMANOV DYNASTY (1613–1917)

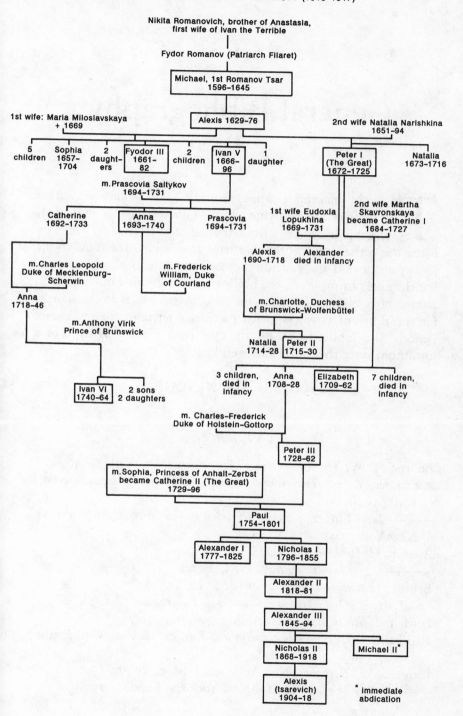

Nikita Romanovich, brother of Anastasia, first wife of Ivan the Terrible

Fydor Romanov (Patriarch Filaret)

Michael, 1st Romanov Tsar 1596–1645

Alexis 1629–76

1st wife: Maria Miloslavskaya + 1669

2nd wife Natalia Narishkina 1651–94

5 children

Sophia 1657–1704

2 daughters

Fyodor III 1661–82

2 children

Ivan V 1666–96

1 daughter

Peter I (The Great) 1672–1725

Natalia 1673–1716

m. Prascovia Saltykov 1694–1731

Catherine 1692–1733

Anna 1693–1740

Prascovia 1694–1731

1st wife Eudoxia Lopukhina 1669–1731

2nd wife Martha Skavronskaya became Catherine I 1684–1727

m. Charles Leopold Duke of Mecklenburg-Scherwin

m. Frederick William, Duke of Courland

Alexis 1690–1718

Alexander died in infancy

Anna 1718–46

m. Anthony Virik Prince of Brunswick

m. Charlotte, Duchess of Brunswick-Wolfenbüttel

Natalia 1714–28

Peter II 1715–30

Ivan VI 1740–64

2 sons 2 daughters

3 children, died in infancy

Anna 1708–28

Elizabeth 1709–62

7 children, died in infancy

m. Charles-Frederick Duke of Holstein-Gottorp

Peter III 1728–62

m. Sophia, Princess of Anhalt–Zerbst became Catherine II (The Great) 1729–96

Paul 1754–1801

Alexander I 1777–1825

Nicholas I 1796–1855

Alexander II 1818–81

Alexander III 1845–94

Nicholas II 1868–1918

Michael II*

Alexis (tsarevich) 1904–18

* immediate abdication

General Bibliography

◆

To avoid making a work covering such a long period of history—some thousand years—unnecessarily complicated, we have dispensed with extensive note references. Here are listed the authors and works that have contributed the most to the ideas put forward and provide the necessary historical background. For the sake of simplicity, the bibliography is divided into a general section of background reading followed by references to the sources for the different chapters, with particular reference to the earlier period. The bibliography for the twentieth century is kept to a minimum since the sources are well known.

General Background

Violence

Adorno, T. W. *The Authoritarian Personality.* New York, 1956.

Alexander, Y., ed. *Terrorism: National and Global Perspectives.* New York, 1976.

——, and Finger, S., eds. *Terrorism in Interdisciplinary Perspective.* New York, 1977.

Arendt, H. *On Violence.* New York, 1969.

——. *Le système totalitaire.* Paris, 1972.

Brutus, J. *Vindiciae contra tyrannos.* S. L., 1579.

Constant, B. *De l'esprit de conquête et de l'usurpation.* Paris, 1986.

Ford, F. *Political Murder.* Cambridge, Mass., 1985.

Kirkham, J. F., ed. *Assassination and Political Violence.* Washington, D.C., 1969.

Laqueur, W. *Terrorism.* New York and Boston, 1977.

——. *The Terrorism Reader.* New York and London, 1978.

————. *Fascism: A Reader's Guide*. London, 1976.

Lewis, B. *Les assassins*. Brussels, 1984.

Maffesoli, M., ed. *Violence et transgression*. Paris, 1979.

Wilkinson, *Political Terrorism*. London, 1974.

Revolution and Change

Almond, G., S. Flanagan, and R. Mundt. *Crisis, Choice, and Change: Historical Studies of Political Development*. Boston, 1973.

Apter, D. *The Politics of Modernization*. Chicago, 1966.

Arendt, H. *Essai sur la révolution*. Paris, 1967.

Aron, R. *Démocratie et totalitarisme*. Paris, 1965.

Baechler, J. *Les phénomènes révolutionnaires*. Paris, 1970.

Borkenau, F. "State and Revolution in the Paris Commune, the Russian Revolution, and the Spanish War." *Sociological Review* 29: 41–75.

Eckstein, H. "Theoretical Approaches to Explain Political Violence." In T. R. Gurr, ed., *Handbook of Political Conflict: Theory and Research* (New York, 1980), pp. 135–66.

Eisenstadt, S. N. *Revolution and the Transformation of Societies: A Comparative Study of Civilizations*. New York, 1978.

Faye, J.-P. *Langages totalitaires*. Paris, 1972.

Feierabend, Ivo. K. "The Comparative Study of Revolution and Violence." *Comparative Politics* 5 (1973): 393–424.

Friedrich, K., and Z. Brzezinski. *Totalitarian Dictatorship and Autocracy*. Cambridge, Mass., 1954.

Furet, F. *Penser la révolution française*. Paris, 1979.

Gershenkron, A. *Economic Backwardness in Historical Perspectives*. Cambridge, Mass., 1962.

Gurr, T. R. *Why Men Rebel*. Princeton, 1970.

————. "The Revolution, Social Change Nexus: Some Old Theories and New Hypotheses." *Comparative Politics* 5 (1973): 359–93.

Johnson, C. *Revolutionary Change*. Boston, 1966.

Kassof, A. "The Administered Society: Totalitarianism without Terror." *World Politics* 16 (June 1964).

Lasswell, H., and D. Lerner, eds. *World Revolutionary Elites: Studies in Coercive Ideological Movements*. Cambridge, Mass., 1966.

Mannheim, K. *Ideology and Utopia*. London, 1940 (2nd ed., 1956).

Moore, B. *Les origines sociales de la dictature et de la démocratie*. Paris, 1969.

Mousnier, R. *Fureurs paysannes: Les paysans dans les révoltes du XVIIᵉ siècle*. Paris, 1967.

Muller, E. "A Test of a Partial Theory of Potential for Political Violence." *American Political Science Review* 66 (1972): 928–59.

Nicolet, C. "La dictature à Rome." In Duverger, M., ed., *Dictatures et légitimité* (Paris, 1982), pp. 69–82.

Papaioannou, K. *L'idéologie froide*. Paris, 1967.

Poliakov, L. *La causalité diabolique*. Paris, 1986.

Rose, R. "Dynamic Tendencies in the Authority of Regimes." *World Politics,* July 1977, pp. 602–28.

Rouquie, A. "L'autoritarisme aujourd'hui: nouvelles formes, nouvelles approches." Introductory speech, Round Table of the Second Congress of the Association Française des Sciences Politiques, Grenoble, 1984.

Sartori, G. "Politics, Ideology, and Belief Systems." *American Political Science Review,* June 1969.

Skocpol, T. *States and Social Revolution*. Cambridge, 1979.

Witfogel, K. *Le despotisme oriental*. Paris, 1977 (particularly the preface by P. Vidal-Nacquet).

Zimmermann, E. *Political Violence: Crises and Revolution. Theories and Research*. Cambridge, Mass., 1983.

Russia

The following are some of the classic works that give a general history of Russia and the USSR.

Black, C. *Rewriting Russian History*. New York, 1962.

———. *The Modernization of Japan and Russia*. New York and London, 1975.

Durand-Cheynet, C. *Moscou contre la Russie*. Paris, 1988.

Karamzin, N. M. *Istoriia gosudarstva Rossii*. 12 vols., St. Petersburg, 1892.

Kliuchevskii, V. O. *Kurs russkoi istorii*. 5 vols.

Kovalevski, M. *Manuel d'histoire russe*. Paris, 1948.

Florinsky, M. T. *Russia: A History and an Interpretation*. 2 vols., New York, 1953.

Hingley, R. *The Tsars: Russian Autocrats 1533–1917*. London, 1968.

Leroy-Beaulieu, A. *L'Empire des tsars et les Russes*. 3 vols., Paris, 1881–98.

Malia, M. *Comprendre la révolution russe*. Paris, 1980.

Milioukov, G. Seignobos, and L. Eisenman. *Histoire de Russie*. 3 vols., Paris, 1933.

Nolde, B. *La formation de l'Empire russe*. 2 vols., Paris, 1952–53.

Pascal, P. *Histoire de la Russie des origines à 1917*. Paris, 1976.

Platonov, S. *Histoire de la Russie des origines à 1918*. Paris, 1929.

Portal, R. *Les Slaves, peuples et nations*. Paris, 1965; rev. ed. by F. Conte, 1986.

Pipes, R. *Russia under the Old Regime*. New York, 1974.

Raeff, M. *Comprendre l'Ancien Régime russe*. Paris, 1982.

Seton-Watson, H. *The Russian Empire 1800–1917*. Oxford, 1967.

Szamuely, T. *La tradition russe*. Paris, 1971.

Vernadsky, G., and M. Karpovich. *A History of Russia*, 5 parts, particularly Part 5, *Tsardom of Moscow*. 2 vols. New Haven, Conn., 1943–69.

Walsh, W. *Russia and the Soviet Union*. Ann Arbor, Mich., 1962.

Weidlé, W. *La Russie absente et présente*. Paris.

A large general history of Russia in Russian is:

Istoriia SSSR, s drevneishikh vremen do nashikh dnei. Moscow, 1966.

Leontovitch, V. *Histoire du libéralisme en Russie*. Paris, 1987.

Likhachev, D. *Kul'tura russkogo naroda X–XVII vekov*. Moscow and Leningrad, 1961.

Lossky, N. *Kharakter russkogo naroda*. Frankfurt, 1957.

Mchedlov, M. P. *Politika i religiia*. Moscow, 1987.

Pascal, P. *Avvakum et les débuts du Raskol, la crise religieuse au XVIIe siècle en Russie*. Paris and The Hague, 1963.

————, ed. and notes. *La vie de l'archiprêtre Avvakum écrite par lui-même*. Paris, 1960.

Schapiro, L. *Rationalism and Nationalism in Russian Nineteenth-Century Political Thought.* New Haven, Conn., 1967.

Soloviev, A. V. *Holy Russia: The History of a Religious Social Idea.* New York, 1959.

Soloviev, V. *Conscience de la Russie.* Paris, 1950.

Ulam, A. *In the Name of the People: Prophets and Conspirators in Pre-revolutionary Russia.* New York, 1977.

On Russian culture, see:

Arsen'ev, N. *Iz russkoi kul'turnoi i tvorcheskoi traditsii.* Frankfurt, 1959.

Berdiaev, N. *The Russian Idea.* Boston, 1962.

———. "Revoliutsiia i kul'tura." *Poliarnaia zvezda,* December 22, 1905.

———. *Les sources et le sens du communisme russe.* Paris, n.d.

Besançon, A. *Le tsarevitch immolé.* Paris, 1967.

Billington, J. *The Icon and the Axe: An Interpretative History of Russian Culture.* London, 1966.

Blum, J. *Lord and Peasant in Russia from the Ninth to the Nineteenth Century.* Princeton, N.J., 1961.

Boborykin. *Le culte du peuple dans la Russie contemporaine.* Paris, 1880.

Cherniavsky, M. *Tsar and People.* New Haven, Conn., and London, 1961.

———. "Holy Russia: A Study of the History of an Idea." *American Historical Review* (1958): 617–37.

Fedotov, G. P. *The Russian Religious Mind.* Cambridge, Mass., 1966.

Florovskii, G. *Puti russkogo bogosloviia.* Paris, 1937–81.

Friedlander, S. *Histoire et psychanalyse.* Paris, 1975.

Kartashev, A. V. *Ocherki po istorii russkoi tserkvi.* 2 vols., Paris, 1959.

Kologrifov. *Essai sur la sainteté en Russie.* Bruges, 1953.

Koyré, A. *Essai sur l'histoire de la pensée philosophique en Russie.* Paris, 1950.

Soloviev, S. *Istoriia Rossii s drevneishikh vremen.* 1st ed., 1851; 2nd ed., 15 vols., Moscow, 1959–64.

Spravochnik po istorii dorevoliutsionnoi Rossii v dnevnikakh i vospominaniiakh. 4 vols., Moscow, 1976–86. (Begins at the fifteenth century.)

Myths

Barthes, R. *Mythologies.* Paris, 1957.
Bastide, R. "Mythes et utopies." *Cahiers internationaux de sociologie,* no. 28 (1960).
Caillois, R. *Le mythe et l'homme.* Paris, 1938.
Cohn, N. *The Pursuit of the Millenium.* London, 1970.
Girard, R. *La violence et le sacré.* Paris, 1972.
Pareto, V. *Mythes et idéologies.* Geneva, 1966.
Rezsler, A. *Mythes politiques modernes.* Paris, 1981.

History of Ideas and Political History

Anderson, T. *Russian Political Thought.* Ithaca, N.Y., 1967.
Utechin, S. V. *Russian Political Thought.* New York and London, 1964.
Zenkovskii, V. V. *Istoriia russkoi filosofii.* 2 vols., Paris, 1950.
Zenkovsky, S. *Medieval Russia's Epic, Chronicle and Tales.* New York, 1963.
———. *Russian Thinkers and Europe.* Ann Arbor, Mich., 1953.

Russia through Foreign Eyes

There are many accounts by foreign travelers, but some works in particular have contributed, in France at least, to the formation of a particular image of Russia.

Cadot, M. *La Russie dans la vie intellectuelle française, 1839–1856.* Paris, 1967.
Custine, A. de. *La Russie en 1839* (published in 1855 in 4 vols. and a best-seller). Modern edition: *Lettres de Russie,* ed. Pierre Nora. Paris, 1975.
Kennan, G. *The Marquis de Custine and His Russia in 1839.* Princeton, N.J., 1971.
Vogüé, E. M. de. *Le roman russe* (with an introduction by Pierre Pascal). Paris, 1971.

For the Russian Revolution:

Ferro, M. *L'Occident devant la révolution russe.* Brussels, 1980.

Kupferman, F. *Au pays des Soviets: Le voyage français en Union soviétique.* Paris, 1979.

Marx, K. *La Russie et l'Europe.* Paris, 1954.

Sombart, W. *Russia and Western Man.* New York, 1950.

Bibliographies by Chapter

◆

Introduction

De Quincey, T. *Essays*. Edinburgh, 1862.

CHAPTER 1
The Age of Fratricide

Ahrweiler, H. *L'idéologie politique de l'Empire byzantin*. Paris, 1975.

Avenarius, V. P. *Kniga bylin*. St. Petersburg, 1903.

Baumgarten, N. de. "Saint Vladimir et la conversion de la Russie." *Orientalia Christiana* 37, no. 1 (1932).

Dvornik, F. *Les Slaves. Byzance et Rome au IXᵉ siècle*. Paris, 1926.

Fedotov. *Sviatye drevnei Rusi*. 2nd ed., Paris, 1985. (1st ed., 1931).

Fennel, J. *The Crisis of Medieval Russia 1200–1304*. London and New York, 1983.

Grekov, B. *Kevskaia Rus'*. Moscow, 1959.

Hrushevsky, M. *A History of the Ukraine*. New Haven, Conn., 1941.

Ingham, N. W. "The Sovereign as Martyr, East and West." *Slavic and East European Journal* 17, no. 2 (1973): 1–17.

Khorochev, A. *Politicheskaia istoriia russkoi kanonizatsii XI–XVI vekov*. Moscow, 1986.

Obolensky, D. *The Byzantine Commonwealth: Eastern Europe 500–1453*. London, 1971.

———. *Byzantium, Kiev and Moscow: A Study in Ecclesiastical Relations*. 1957.

Orlov, A. *Vladimir Monomakh*. Moscow and Leningrad, 1946.

Presniakov, A. *Kniazhnoe pravo v drevnei Rusi*. St. Petersburg, 1909.

Prisel'kov, M. D. *Ocherki po tserkovno-politicheskoi istorii kievskoi Rusi X–XII vekov*. St. Petersburg, 1913.

Tikhomirov, M. *Drevniaia Rus'*. Moscow, 1975.

Vlasto, A. *The Entry of the Slavs in Christendom: An Introduction to the Medieval History.* Cambridge, 1970.

Vodoff, V. *Naissance de la chrétienté russe.* Paris, 1988 (a work that brings together the most recent research).

Volkoff, V. *Vladimir, le soleil rouge.* Paris, 1981.

Zernov, N. "Vladimir and the Origin of the Russian Church." *Slavonic and East European Review* 28 (1949–50): 70–71.

To this should be added two collections of documents:

Povest' vremennykh let (the Russian Primary Chronicle), edited by D. S. Likhachev and B. A. Romanov. 2 vols., Moscow and Leningrad, 1950.

Pravda russkaia (Russian code of law), edited by B. Grekov. 3 vols., Moscow and Leningrad, 1940–63.

CHAPTER 2
The Renaissance of Russia

General:

Machiavelli, Niccolò. *The Prince.* Harmondsworth, 1968.
———. *The Discourses.* Harmondsworth, 1970.

and also:

Coville, A. *Jean Petit: la question du tyrannicide au commencement du XVᵉ siècle.* Paris, 1932.

Laski, H. *A Defense of Liberty against Tyrants.* New York, 1963.

Mallett, M. *The Borgias.* London, 1969.

Mousnier, R. *L'assassinat d'Henri IV.* Paris, 1964.

Skinner, Q. *Foundations of Modern Political Thought,* vol. 2. Cambridge, 1978.

Symonds, J. A. *The Age of Despots.* London, 1898.

The Renaissance in Russia

Fennel, J. *The Emergence of Moscow.* Berkeley, 1968.

Kovalevski, P. *Saint Serge et la spiritualité russe.* Paris, 1958.

Presniakov, A. *Obrazovanie velikorusskogo gosudarstva.* Petrograd, 1918.

Rouet de Journel, Fr. *Monachisme et monastères russes.* Paris, 1952.

Stremoukhoff, D. *The Third Rome.* 1950.

Tikhomirov, M. *Drevnerusskie goroda.* Moscow, 1945.

Wolff, R. "The Three Romes: The Migration of an Ideology and the Making of an Autocrat." *Daedalus,* Spring 1959.

Zernov, N. *Saint Sergius, Builder of Russia.* London, 1938.

Zimin, A. *O politicheskoi doktrine Iosifa Volotskogo.* Moscow, 1953.

CHAPTERS 3 AND 4

The Beginnings of Tyranny; Absolute Tyranny

Le Domostroi, ed. E. Duchesne. Paris, 1910.

Le Stoglav, ed. E. Duchesne. Paris, 1920.

Rasskazy russkikh letopisei, XV–XVII vv. Moscow, 1976.

Cherepnin, L. V. *Obrazovanie russkogo tsentralizovannogo gosudarstva v XIV–XV vekakh.*

Coquin, F.-X. *De la fonction monarchique en Russie au XVIᵉ siècle.* Paris, 1973.

Dmytryshyn, B., ed. *Medieval Russia: A Source Book 900–1700.* New York, 1967.

Eck, E. *Le Moyen Age russe.* Paris, 1933.

Fletcher. G. *La Russie au XVIᵉ siècle.* Paris and Leipzig, 1864.

Grey, I. *Ivan III and the Unification of Russia.* New York, 1964.

Herberstein, Baron. *La Moscovie du XVIᵉ siècle.* Paris, 1965.

Jenkinson, A. *Early Voyages and Travels to Russia and Persia.* London, 1886.

Kurbsky, A. M. *Prince A. M. Kurbsky's History of Ivan IV,* ed. J. Fennel. Cambridge, 1965.

Olearius. *Relation de voyage en Moscovie.* 1579.

Platonov, S. *Ivan Groznyi.* Petrograd, 1923.

Sadikov, P. *Ocherki po istorii oprichniny.* Moscow, 1951.

Skrynnikov, R. *Rossia posle oprichniny.* Moscow, 1978.

Smirnov, I. *Ocherki politicheskoi istorii russkogo gosudarstva 30–50 gg. XVI veka.* Moscow, 1958.

Tikhomirov, *Rossiiskoe gosudarstvo XV–XVII vekov.* Moscow, 1973.

Veselovsky, S. *Isledovaniia po istorii oprichniny.* Moscow, 1963.

Zimin, A. *I. S. Peresvetov i ego sovremenniki.* Moscow, 1958.

———. *Sostav boiarskoi dumy v XV–XVI vv.* Moscow, 1958.

———. *Reformy Ivana groznogo.* Moscow, 1960.

———. *Oprichnina Ivana groznogo.* Moscow, 1964.

———. *Krupnaia feodal'naia votchina: Volokolamskii monastyr'.* Moscow, 1977.

There are numerous biographies of Ivan the Terrible; suffice it to mention here the following:

Durand-Cheynet, C. *Ivan le Terrible.* Paris, 1981.

Payne, R., and N. Romanoff. *Ivan the Terrible.* New York, 1975.

Troyat, H. *Ivan le Terrible.* Paris, 1982.

CHAPTER 5

True and False Tsars

Besides the essential works by Cherniavsky and Besançon cited above (p. 438), consult

Polnoe sobranie russkikh letopisei. St. Petersburg, 1901.

Artsybyshev, N. S. "O konchine tsarevicha Dimitriia." *Russkii arkhiv* 3 (1986).

Belaev, I. S. *Uglicheskoe sledstvennoe delo ob ubiistve Dimitriia 15 maia 1591 g.* Moscow, 1907.

Bestuzhev-Riumin, K. "Obzor sobytii ot smerti Ivan Vasil'evicha do izbraniia na prestol M. F. Romanova." *Zhurnal ministerstva narodnogo prosveshcheniia,* no. 7–8 (1887).

Buganov, V. *Krest'ianskaia voina v nachale XVII veka.* Moscow, 1976.

Dragomanov, M. *Bor'ba za dukhovnuiu vlast' i svoboda sovesti v XVI–XVIII v.* St. Petersburg, 1887.

Dnevnik posol'stva litovskogo kantslera L'va Sapegi v. Moskovie v 1600 godu. St. Petersburg, 1858.

Ilovaiskii, D. I. Vol. 4 of his general history of Russia: *Smutnoe vremia.* Moscow, 1876–1905.

Kostomarov, N. *Kto byl pervyi lzhedimitrii?* St. Petersburg, 1864.

———. *Byl li lzhedimitrii Grisha Otrep' ev?* St. Petersburg, 1865.

———. *Smutnoe vremia moskovskogo gosudarstva v nachale XVII veka.* St. Petersburg, 1883.

Leopis' o mnogikh miatezhakh i o razorenii moskovskogo gosudarstva. St. Petersburg, 1771.

Litovskii kantsler Lev Sapieha o sobytiiakh smutnogo vremeni. Moscow, 1901.

Materialy po smutnomu vremeni na Rusi XVII veka. St. Petersburg, 1909.

Nechaev, V. *Smutnoe vremia v moskovskom gosudarstve.* Moscow, 1913.

Pavlov, N. "Pravda o lzhedimitrii." *Russkii arkhiv* 3 (1886).

Platonov, S. *Smutnoe vremia.* Prague, 1924.

Polosina, I. "Uglichnoe sledstvennoe delo 1591." In *Sotsial'no-politicheskaia istoriia Rossii XVI–nachala XVII veka.* Moscow, 1963.

Skazanie o smerti tsaria Fedora Ivanovicha i votsarenii Borisa Godunova. Moscow, 1957.

Tatishchev, I. "K voprosu o smerti tsarevicha Dimitriia." In *Sbornik statei posveschennyi S. F. Platonovu.* Petrograd, 1922.

Tikhomirov, M. *Istoriia Rossii v XV veke.* Moscow, 1962.

Vernadsky, G. "The Death of the Tsarevich Dimitri: A Reconsideration of the Case." *Oxford Slavonic Papers* (1954).

———. *The Tsardom of Moscow 1547–1582.* London, 1969.

Vremennik Ivana Timofeeva, (ed. Derzhavina and Adrianova-Perets). Moscow and Leningrad, 1951.

Zabelin, I. *Domashnii byt russkikh tsarei v XVI–XVII stoletii.* Moscow, 1869.

———. *Domashnii byt russkogo naroda.* Moscow, 1872.

Zimin, A. " 'Smert' tsarevicha Dimitriia i Boris Godunov." *Voprosy istorii* 9 (1978).

Biographies of Boris Godunov:

Durand-Cheynet, C. *Boris Godounov et le mystère Dimitri.* Paris, 1986.

Graham, S. *Boris Godounoff.* London, 1933.

Grunewald, C. *La véritable histoire de Boris Godounov.* Paris, 1961.

Platonov, S. *Boris Godunov.* Petrograd, 1921.

———. *Boris Godounov, tsar de Russie.* Paris, 1929.

Skrynnikov, R. *Boris Godunov.* Moscow, 1978.

Also useful are:

Margeret, J. *Un mousquetaire à Moscou.* Paris, 1893.

Mérimée, Prosper. *Un épisode de l'histoire de Russie, les faux Demetrius.* Paris, 1853.

Pierling, Paul. *Rome et Demetrius.* Paris, 1878.

CHAPTER 6

The Limits of the "Civilized State"

Listed are just some of the many studies of this period:

Absoliutizm v Rossii XVII–XVIII v, cf. article by N. Demidova. Moscow, 1964.

Bogoslovskii, M. *Byt i nravy russkogo dvorianstva v pervoi polovine XVIII veka.* Moscow, 1906.

Kotushikhin, G. *O Rossii v tsarstvovanie Alekseia Mikhailovicha, sochineniia Grigoriia Kotoshikhina.* St. Petersburg, 1906, 4 vols.

Panchenko. *Russkaia kul'tura v kanun petrovykh reform.* Leningrad, 1984.

Peter the Great. *Journal de Pierre le Grand depuis l'année 1698 jusqu' à la paix de Nystadt,* ed. Shcherbatov. 2 vols., London and Berlin, 1773.

———. *Pis'ma i bumagi Petra Velikogo.* 12 vols., St. Petersburg, 1887.

Andreev, ed. *Petr Velikii, sbornik statei.* Moscow and Leningrad, 1947.

Bogoslovskii, M. *Petr I. Materialy dlia biografii.* 5 vols., Moscow, 1940–48.

Bruckner, *Petr Velikii.* St. Petersburg, 1882.

Cracraft, J. *The Church Reform of Peter the Great.* London, 1971.

Dmytryshyn, B., ed. *The Modernization of Russia under Peter I and Catherine II.* New York, 1974.

Garrard, G. *The Eighteenth Century in Russia.* Oxford, 1973. (All the essays in this volume are excellent.)

Gasiorowska, X. *The Image of Peter the Great in Russian Fiction.* Madison, Wis., 1979.

Golikova, N. *Politicheskie protsessy pri Petre I.* Moscow, 1957.

Gordon, A. *History of Peter the Great.* 2 vols., Aberdeen, 1755.

Grunwald, C. de. *La Russie de Pierre le Grand.* Paris, 1933.

———. *Trois siècles de diplomatie russe.* Paris, 1945.

de Guichen. *Histoire d'Eudoxie Feodorovna, première épouse de Pierre le Grand.* Leipzig, 1861.

Herbert, J. *Le czar Pierre le Grand à Charleville.* Charleville, 1876.

Ikonnikov. *Russkaia zhenshchina nakanune i posle reform Petra velikogo.* Kiev, 1874.

Kapterev, N. *Patriarkh Nikon i tsar Aleksei Mikhailovich.* Sergeev-Posad, 1909.

Kliuchevskii, V. *Pierre le Grand et son œuvre.* Paris, 1853.

Korb, J. *Diary of an Austrian Secretary of Legation at the Court of Czar Peter the Great.* 1st ed., 1863; 2nd ed., London, 1968.

Lamartine, A. de. *Pierre le Grand.* Paris, 1865.

Lortholary, A. *Le mirage russe en France au XVIIIᵉ siècle.* Paris, 1951.

Lupov, S. P. *Istoriia stroitel'stva Peterburga v pervoi chetverti XVIII veka.* Moscow and Leningrad, 1957.

Massie, R. *Pierre le Grand.* Paris, 1980.

Melnikov (Pecherskii). *Polnoe sobranie sochinenii,* vol. 14. St. Petersburg and Moscow, 1898.

Miliukov, P. *Gosudarstvennoe stroenie reformy Petra velikogo.* St. Petersburg, 1905.

Muller, A. V. *The Spiritual Regulations of Peter the Great.* Seattle, Wash., 1972.

Moreau de Barzey, J. N. *Mémoires politiques d'un brigadier de sa majesté czarienne.* 3 vols., Paris, 1735.

Muliukin, A. S. *Priezd inostrantsev v moskovskoe gosudarstvo.* St. Petersburg, 1909.

de la Neuville. *Relation curieuse et nouvelle de la moscovie.* The Hague, 1699.

O'Brien and Bickford. *Russia under Two Tsars, 1682–89: The Regency of Sofia.* Berkeley, Calif., 1952.

Palmer, W. *The Patriarch and the Tsar: "The Replies of the Humble Nikon."* London, 1872.

Pascal, Pierre. *Avakkum et les débuts du Raskol.* Paris, 1938.

Patriarkhiia ili Nikonovskaia letopis'. Polnoe sobranie russkikh letopisei, vol. 12, St. Petersburg, 1901.

Pavlenko, Nikiforov, and Volkoff. *Rassiia v period reform Petra pervogo.* Moscow, 1973.

Poltava k stoletiu poltavskogo srazheniia—sbornik statei. Moscow, 1959.

Portal, R. *Pierre le Grand.* Paris, 1969.

Predtechenskii. Peterburg petrovskogo vremeni. Leningrad, 1948.

Raeff, M. *Peter the Great, Reformer or Revolutionary?* Boston, 1966.

Romanovich-Slavatinskii. *Dvorianstvo v Rossii.* Kiev, 1912.

Rumiantseva, V. S. "Tendentsii razvitiia obshchestvennogo soznaniia i prosveshcheniia v Rossii XVII veka." *Voprosy istorii* 2 (1988).

Sbornik imperatorskogo russkogo istoricheskogo obshchestva. St. Petersburg, 1867–1916, devoted to the trial of the tsarevich.

de Ségur. *Histoire de la Russie et de Pierre le Grand,* 2 vols., Paris, 1829.

Teil, J. du. *Le Csar à Dunkerque.* Dunkerque, 1902.

Tolstoi, A. *Pierre le Grand.* Paris, 1929.

Tregubov. *Religioznyi byt russkikh i sostoianie dukhovenstva v XVIII veke po memuaram innostrantsev.* Kiev, 1884.

Troyat, H. *Pierre le Grand.* Paris, 1979.

Ustrialov, M.G. *Istoriia tsarstvovania Petra Velikogo,* 6 vols., St. Petersburg, 1858–63.

Vallotton, H. *Pierre le Grand.* Paris, 1958.

Voltaire. *Histoire de l'Empire de Russie sous Pierre le Grand.* In *Œuvres complètes* (1784 edition), vol. 24.

———. *Lettres de l'Impératrice de Russie et de M. de Voltaire.* In Voltaire, *Œuvres complètes,* (1784 edition), vol. 67.

Waliszewski. *Pierre le Grand.* Paris, 1887.
———. *L'héritage de Pierre le Grand.* Paris, 1900.
Weber, F. W. *The Present State of Russia.* London, 1723.
Wittram, R. *Peter I: Tsar und Kaiser,* 2 vols., Göttingen, 1964.

CHAPTER 7

Regicide in the Family

For the reign of Catherine II, a very full bibliography can be found in I. de Madariaga, *Russia in the Age of Catherine the Great* (London, 1981). In addition to the classic works, for various subjects dealt with in this chapter:

Bilbasov, V. A. *Istoriia Ekateriny II.* 2 vols., Berlin, 1900.
Bolotov, A. T. *Zhizn' i prikliucheniia Andreia Bolotova.* Leningrad, 1931.
Catherine II. *Mémoires.* 1st ed., London, 1859.
———. *Sochineniia,* ed. A. N. Pypin. 12 vols., St. Petersburg, 1901 (especially vol. 12).
Dashbova, Princess. *Mémoires.* London, 1958; Paris, 1966.
Haxthausen, G. C. "Doneseniia datskogo poslannika o tsarstvovanii Petra III i perevorote 1762 g." *Russkaia starina,* nos. 158 and 160 (1914); nos. 161, 162, and 164 (1915).
Lebedev, P. S. *Grafy Nikita i Piotr Panin.* St. Petersburg, 1863.
Petrovich, M. B. "Catherine II and a Fake Peter III in Montenegro." *Slavic Review* 14, no. 2 (April 1955).
"Posobniki i storonniki Pugacheva." *Russkaia starina,* nos. 1 and 17 (1876).
Pushkin, A. S. "Istoriia Pugacheva." In *Polnoe sobranie sochinenii,* vol. 12. Moscow, 1949.
Pypin, A. N. *Russkoe massonstvo XVIII i pervogo chetverti XIX veka.* Petrograd, 1916.
Radishchev, A. N. *Journey from St Petersburg to Moscow,* ed. R. Page. Cambridge, Mass., 1958.
Ransel. "Nikita Panin's Imperial Project and the Struggle of Hierarchy Groups at the Court of Catherine II." *Canadian Slavic Studies* 4 (Fall 1970): 443–63.
Sbornik imperatorskogo russkogo istoricheskogo obshchestva 7.

Shchelbalski, P. *Politicheskaia sistema Petra III.* Moscow, 1870.
Solov'ev, S. M. *Istoriia Rossii s drevneishikh vremen.* 15 vols.,
Moscow, 1959–66 (vol. 3).

On the reforms:

Confino, M. *Domaines et seigneurs en Russie vers la fin du XVIIIe
siècle.* Paris, 1963.
Coquin, F.-X. *La grande commission législative 1767–1768. Les
cahiers de doléances urbaines.* Paris and Louvain, 1972.
Dvorianstvo i krepostnoi stroi v Rossii XVI–XVIII vekov. Sbornik.
Moscow, 1975.
Raeff, M. *Plans for Political Reform in Imperial Russia 1730–1905.*
Englewood Cliffs, N.J., 1966.
———. "The Domestic Policies of Peter III and His Overthrow."
American Historical Review 15, no. 5 (June 1970).
———. "The Well-Ordered Police-State and the Development of
Modernity." *American Political Science Review* 80, no. 15
(December 1975).
Safronov, N. M. "Konstitutsionnyi proekt N. I. Panina–D. I.
Fonvizina." *Vospomogatelnye istoricheskie distsipliny* 6 (1971).

On the Pugachov rebellion:

Dubrovin, N. *Pugachev i ego soobshchniki.* 3 vols., St. Petersburg,
1884.
Pascal, P. *La révolte de Pougatchev.* Paris, 1971.

Many general works have appeared in French on Catherine
and her successors, including:

Brian-Chaninov, N. *Catherine II, impératrice de Russie.* Paris, 1932.
Olivier, D. *Catherine la Grande.* Paris, 1966.
Tegny, E. *Catherine II et la princesse Dachkoff.* Paris, 1860.
Troyat, H. *Catherine la Grande.* Paris, 1977.
Waliszewski, K. *Le roman d'une impératrice.* Paris, 1893.
———. *Le fils de la Grande Catherine: Paul I.* Paris, 1912.

Grunwald, C. de. *L'assassinat de Paul Ier.* Paris, 1960.

Childer, N. K. *Imperator Pavel I.* St. Petersburg, 1901.

Kobeko, D. I. *Tsarevich Pavel Petrovich 1754–1796.* St. Petersburg, 1883.

Morane, *Paul Ier de Russie.* Paris, 1907.

Ragsdale, H. *Paul I: A Reassessment of His Life and Reign.* Pittsburgh, Pa., 1979.

Baratinski, Prince. *Le mystère d'Alexandre Ier, le tsar a-t-il survécu sous le nom de Fedor Kouzmitch?* Paris, 1929.

Childer, N. K. *Imperator Aleksandr pervyi.* 4 vols., St. Petersburg, 1897.

Czartoryski, Prince A. *Mémoires et correspondance avec l'Empereur Alexandre Ier.* 2 vols., Paris, 1887.

von Goerz. *Mémoire sur la Russie.* Wiesbaden, 1969.

La Harpe, G. de. *Mémoires.* Paris, 1864.

Liubimov, L. *Taina imperatora Aleksandra I.* Paris, 1938.

Maistre, J. de. *Mémoires politiques et correspondance dipolmatique.* Paris, 1859.

Nicolas Mikhailovitch, Grand Duke. *Légende sur la mort de l'Empereur Alexandre en Sibérie.* St. Petersburg, 1907.

———. *Le tsar Alexandre Ier.* Paris, 1931.

Sivkov, K. V. "Samozvanchestvo v Rossii v poslednei treti XVIII veka." *Istoricheskie zapiski,* no. 31 (1950).

Speransky, M. M. "Pis'ma Speranskogo k A.A. Stolypinu." *Russkii Arkhiv* 7, no. 9 (1869).

Tchoulkov. *Les derniers tsars autocrates.* Paris, 1928.

Vernadsky, G. *Russkoe massonstvo v tsartvovanie Ekateriny II.* Petrograd, 1917.

CHAPTERS 8, 9, 10

The Student Pugachovs; "The Fish Begins to Stink at the Head"; The Death Throes of Terrorism.

Many essential works have been published on the subjects of the intelligentsia and terrorism. The author owes them a considerable debt. The reader is referred to their bibliographies.

The Intelligentsia

Baynac, J. *Les socialistes révolutionnaires*. Paris, 1979.

Berdiaev, N. *Les sources et le sens du communisme russe*. Paris.

Billington, H. *Mikhailovski and Russian Populism*. Oxford, 1958.

Confino, M. *Daughter of a Revolutionary*. London, 1974.

Hingley, R. *Nihilists: Russian Radicals and Revolutionaries in the Reign of Alexander II, 1855–1881*. London, 1967.

Itenberg. *Dvizhenie revoliutsionnogo narodnichestva*. Moscow, 1965.

Leikina-Svirskaia, V. R. *Intelligentsiia v Rossii vo vtoroi polovine XIX veka*. Moscow, 1971.

Lunacharskii, A. V. *Intelligentsiia v ee proshlom, nastoiashchem, i budushchem*. Moscow, 1924.

Malia, M. *Hertzen and the Birth of Russian Socialism*. Cambridge, Mass., 1961.

Nahirnyi, V. *The Russian Intelligentsia from Torment to Silence*. New Brunswick, N.J., 1983.

Naimark, N. *Terrorists and Socialists: The Russian Revolutionary Movement under Alexander III*. Cambridge, Mass., 1983.

Pipes, R. *The Russian Intelligentsia*. New York, 1961.

———. *Struve: Liberal on the Left*. Cambridge, Mass., 1970.

———. *Struve: Liberal on the Right*. Cambridge, Mass., 1980.

Raeff, M. *The Decembrist Movement*. Englewood Cliffs, N.J., 1966.

Schapiro, L. *Turgenev: His Life and Times*. Oxford, 1978.

Tsimbaev, N. I. *Slavianofil'stvo: iz istorii russkoi obshchestvenno-politicheskoi mysli*. Moscow, 1976.

———. *Aksakov v obshchestvennoi zhizni po-reformnoi Rossii*. Moscow, 1978.

Ulam, A. *Ideologies and Illusions*. Harvard, 1976.

Venturi, F. *Roots of Revolution: A History of the Populist and Socialist Movements in Nineteenth-century Russia*. London, 1960 (essential).

Vucinych, A. *Social Thought in Tsarist Russia: The Quest for a General Science of Society, 1861–1917*. Chicago, 1976.

Walicky, A. *The Slavophile Controversy: History of a Conservative Utopia in 20th Century Russian Thought*. Oxford, 1975.

Education

Besançon, A. *Éducation et société en Russie dans le second tiers du XIXᵉ siècle*. Paris and The Hague, 1974.

Rozhdestvenskii, S. V. *Ocherki po istorii sistemy narodnogo prosveshcheniia v Rossii v XVIII–XIX vv*. St. Petersburg, 1912.

Shchetnina, G. I. *Studentchestvo i revoliutsionnoe dvizhenie v Rossii; posledniaia chetvert' XIX veka*. Moscow, 1987.

Studentchestvo v tsifrakh. St. Petersburg, 1909.

Uvarov, S. "Desiatiletie ministerstva narodnogo prosveshcheniia 1833–1844." In Gershenzon, ed., *Epokha Nikolaia I-go*. Moscow, 1911.

Reforms

Belonkovskii, I. *Zemskoe dvizhenie*. Moscow, 1914.

Briukhatov, L. D. *Znachenie "tret'ego elementa" v. zhizni zemstva, 1864–1914. Iubileinyi sbornik*. St. Petersburg, 1914.

Cherkassova, N. V. *Formirovanie i razvitie russkoi advokatury v Rossii 60–80 gg, XIX v*. Moscow, 1987.

Druzhinin. *Russkaia derevnia na perelome 1861–1881*. Moscow, 1978.

Gerassimenko, G. "Zemstva v oktiabriskie dni." *Voprosy istorii*, no. 11 (1987).

Korelin, A. P. *Dvorianstvo v poreformnoi Rossii*. Moscow, 1979.

Korotkikh, "Sudebnaia reforma 1864 g. v Rossii." *Voprosy istorii* no. 12 (1987).

Mitskevich, S. I. *Zapiski vracha-obshchestvennika 1888–1918*. Moscow, 1941.

Primurova, N. M. *Zemskaia intelligentsiia i ee rol' v obshchestvennoi bor'be do nachala XX veka*. Moscow, 1986.

Starr, S. *Decentralization and Self-Government in Russia 1830–1870.*
Princeton, 1972.
Le statut des paysans libérés du servage. Paris and The Hague, 1963.
Topukhin. *Nastoiaschchie i budushchie russkoi politiki.* Moscow, 1907.

Problems of State and Absolutism

Childers, M. *Imperator Nikolai pervoi.* 2 vols., St. Petersburg,
1903.
Eroshkin, N. *Istoriia gosudarstvennykh uchrezhdenii dorevoliutsionnoi
Rossii.* Moscow, 1968.
Konstitutsiia Loris-Melikova. London, 1893.
Korf, M. *Zhizn' grafa Speranskogo.* St. Petersburg, 1861.
Korkunov, N. *Russkoe gosudarstvennoe pravo.* 2 vols., St. Petersburg,
1899.
Lincoln, W. *Nicholas I: Emperor and Autocrat of All the Russias.*
Bloomington, Ind., 1978.
Meshcherskii, Prince. *Vospominaniia.* 2 vols., St. Petersburg,
1897–98.
Mosse, M. *Alexander II and the Modernization of Russia.* New York,
1958.
Pobedonostsev, K. P. *Reflections of a Russian Statesman.* London,
1898.
Speranskii. *Druzheskie pis'ma k Masal'skomu.* St. Petersburg, 1862.
Svod zakonov rossiiskoi imperii, vol. 1. St. Petersburg, 1892.
Zaionchkovskii, P. A. *Krizis samoderzhaviia na rubezhe 1870–1880-
kh godov.* Moscow, 1964.
——. *The Russian Autocracy under Alexander III.* Gulf Breeze,
1978.

The Early Twentieth Century

Chernenskii, E. D. *Burzhuaziia i tsarizm v pervoi russkoi revoliutsii.*
Moscow, 1970.
Ioffe, G. E. *Velikii Oktiabr' i epilog tsarizma.* Moscow, 1987.
Leikina-Svirskaia, V. R. *Russkaia intelligentsiia v 1900–1917.*
Moscow, 1981.
Mints, ed. *Neproletarskie partii Rusi.* Moscow, 1984.

Pakholenko, N. B. *Gosudarstvenno-pravovye vzgliady G. V. Plekhanova 1883–1903.* Moscow, 1987.

Petrunkevich. *Mémoires.* Berlin, 1934.

Politicheskaia ssylka v Sibiri XIX–nachalo XX vekov, istoriografiia i istochniki. Novosibirsk, 1987.

Savel'ev, S. N. *Ideino bankrotstvo bogoiskatel'stva v Rossii v nachale XX veka.* Leningrad, 1987.

Shatsilo. *Russkii liberalizm nakanune revoliutsii 1905–1907 gg.* Moscow, 1985.

Shepelev, L. E. *Tsarizm i burzhuaziia v 1904–1914 gg.* Leningrad, 1987.

Stolypine, A. P. *A. Stolypine.* Paris, 1927.

Ushakov, A. B. "Demokraticheskaia intelligentsiia Rossii na puti k sotsializmu." *Voprosy istorii,* no. 10 (1987).

Witte, Count de. *Souvenirs.* Berlin, 1922–23.

CHAPTER 11

The Blood of Rasputin

Rasputin

Amalrik, A. *Raspoutine.* Paris, 1982 (an excellent and subtle analysis, published posthumously).

Bienstock, J. *Raspoutine, la fin d'un règne.* Paris, 1917.

Enden, M. de. *Raspoutine ou la fascination.* Paris, 1976.

Gevakhov, Prince N. *La verità su Rasputin.* Bari, 1930.

Ioussupov, F. *La fine de Raspoutine.* Paris, 1927.

———. *Avant l'exil, 1887–1919.* Paris, 1952.

Murat, Princess L. *Raspoutine et l'aube sanglante.* Paris, 1918.

Nekliudoff, A. *Diplomatic Reminiscences before and during the World War 1911–1917.* London, 1920.

Pares, B. *The Fall of the Russian Monarchy.* London, 1939.

Pourichkevitch, V. *Comment j'ai tué Raspoutine.* Paris, 1923.

Radziwill, Princess C. *Rasputin and the Russian Revolution.* New York, 1918.

Rajevski, F. *Le ministre du mal. Mémoires de Fedor Rajevski, secrétaire privé de Raspoutine* (n.p., n.d.).

Rasputin, M. *Rasputin, the Man behind the Myth: A Personal Memoir.* Englewood Cliffs, N.J., 1977.

————. *My Father.* London, 1934.

Rodzianko, V. *Le règne de Raspoutine: mémoires du dernier président de la Douma d' empire 1900–1917.* Paris, 1927.

Simonovitch, A. *Raspoutine par son secrétaire.* Paris, 1930.

Spiridovitch, General. *Raspoutine 1863–1916, d'après les documents et archives privées de l'auteur.* Paris, 1935.

Trufanov, S. *The Mad Monk of Russia: Iliodor.* New York, 1918.

Wassiliev, A. *Mes souvenirs.* Paris, 1927.

Wilson, C. *Rasputin and the Fall of the Romanovs.* New York, 1964.

Wyrubova, A. *Memories of the Russian Court.* New York, 1923.

Yussupov, F. *Rasputin, his malignant influence and his assassination.* London, 1928.

The End of the Romanovs

Alexander, Grand Duke. *Quand j'étais grand-duc.* Paris, 1934.

Alexandra, Empress. *The Letters of the Tsaritsa to the Tsar 1914–1916.* London, 1923.

Andrei, Grand Duke. Extracts from his journal. *Krasnyi arkhiv* 27 (1928): 185–210.

Benckendorff, Count P. *The Last Days at Tsarkoe selo.* London, 1922.

Block, A. *Les derniers jours de l'Ancien Régime.* Paris, 1931.

Botkin, T. *Vospominaniia o tsarskoi sem'e.* Belgrade, 1921.

Buchanan, G. *My Mission to Russia.* 2 vols., London, 1923.

————. "The foulest crime in history." *Saturday Review,* 1935.

Bulygin, P., and A. Kerensky. *The Murder of the Romanovs.* London, 1935.

Buxhoeveden, Baroness S. *The Life and Tragedy of Alexandra Feodorovna.* London and New York, 1928.

————. *Left behind Fourteen Months in Siberia during the Revolution.* New York, 1929.

Gilliard, P. *Thirteen Years at the Russian Court.* New York, 1921.

Izvestiia, July 19, 1918 (information on the execution of the tsar).

Lloyd George, D. *War Memoirs 1916–1917.* Boston, 1934.

Nicholas II. *Journal intime.* Paris, 1925.

————. *The Letters of the Tsar to the Tsaritsa 1914–1917*. London, 1929.

————. *The Secret Letters of the Last Tsar.* New York, 1938.

Nicolai Mikhailovitch, Grand Duke. *La fin du tsarisme.* Paris, 1968.

Paléologue, M. *La Russie des tsars pendant la Grande Guerre.* 3 vols., Paris, 1921.

Trotsky, L. *Kak vooruzhalas' revoliutsiia.* Moscow, 1923.

————. *Diary in Exile.* Cambridge, Mass., 1958.

Wilton, R. *The Last Days of the Romanovs.* London, 1920.

Pares, B. *The Fall of the Russian Monarchy.* New York, 1961.

The Repression of 1918

Krasnaia kniga Ch-Ka, vol. 1. Moscow, 1920.

Latsis. *ChK v bor' be s kontr-revoliutsiei.* Moscow, 1921.

Mal' Kov. *Zapiski komendanta moskovskogo kremlia.* Moscow, 1962.

Peters. "Vospominania o rabote v ChK v pervye gody revoliutsii." *Byloe* 47 (1933).

Sobranie uzakonenii i rasporiazhenii rabochego i krest-ianskogo pravitel'stva. Petrograd, 1918.

CHAPTERS 12, 13

Apocalypse; Thou Shalt Not Kill

Besides the classic works on this period, cf. the bibliographies for the revolution in:

Ferro, M. *La Révolution russe.* 2 vols., Paris, 1967–77.

Gorodetskii. *Rozhdenie sovetskogo gosudarstva 1917–1918.* Moscow, 1987.

Ignatenko, T. A. *Kritika menshevitskoi kontseptsii istorii oktiabria v sovetskoi istoriografii.* Moscow, 1986.

Keep, J. *The Russian Revolution: A Study in Mass Mobilization.* New York, 1976.

Mints, I. *Istoriia velikogo oktiabria,* 3 vols., Moscow.

Pipes, R. *Revolutionary Russia.* Cambridge, Mass., 1968.

Savel'ev, P. M., P. Iroshnikov, and G. L. Sobolev. "Publikatsiia

dokumentov po istorii velikogo oktiabria i grazhdanskoi voiny."
Voprosy istorii, no. 10 (1987).
Walter, G. *Histoire de la révolution russe.* Paris, 1953.

For the early period, some of the more recent Soviet studies are:

Iroshnikov, M. "Documental 'naia letopis' geroicheskoi epokhi."
Kommunist, no. 15 (1986).
Izuchenie otechestvennoi istorii v SSSR mezhdu 25 i 26 s'ezdami KPSS.
Moscow, 1982.
Spirin, L., and A. Litvin. *Na zashchite revoliutsii. V. I. Lenin v gody grazhdanskoi voiny.* Leningrad, 1986.

For Stalinism, its origins and the present reassessment, we refer the reader to the proceedings of the Moscow trials of 1936, 1937, and 1938, the documents of the Twentieth and Twenty-second Congresses of the CPSU, and the classics and their bibliographies, including:

Brzezinski, Z. *La purge permanente dans le totalitarisme soviétique.*
Paris, 1958.
Conquest, R. *The Great Terror, Stalin's Purge of the Thirties* (revised ed.). New York, 1973.
———. *Kolyma.* London and New York, 1978.
Khrushchev, N. *Le Rapport secret de Krouchtchev ou XXe congrès,* ed.
B. Lazitch. Paris, 1976.
Medvedev, R. *Le stalinisme.* Paris, 1972.
Solzhenitsyn, A. *The Gulag Archipelago.* New York, 1973–78.
Souvarine. *Staline.* Paris, 1985.
Tucker, S. *Stalin as Revolutionary,* vol. 1. New York, 1973.
Werth, N. *Les procès de Moscou.* Brussels, 1987 (cf. its bibliography).

Among the memoirs of survivors of the camps are:

Alliluyeva, S. *Letters to a Friend.*
———. *Tol'ko odin god.* New York, 1969.

Chukovskaya, L. *La maison déserte.* Paris, 1975.
———. *Entretiens avec Anna Akhmatova.* Paris, 1980.
———. *Les chemins de l'exclusion.* Paris, 1980.
Ginzburg, E. *Within the Whirlwind.* New York, 1975.
———. *Le ciel de la Kolyma.* Paris, 1980.
Ivinskaya, O. *Captive of Time.* New York, 1978.
Mandelshtam, N. *Hope against Hope.* Harmondsworth, 1975.
Shalamov, V. *Kolyma Tales.* New York, 1980.
Solzhenitsyn, A. *One day in the life of Ivan Denisovich.* New York, 1970.
Vishnevskaya, G. *Galina: A Russian Story.* New York, 1984.

We have only indicated the most well-known works here. More complete bibliographies are to be found in others of this author's works: *Staline, la révolution et le pouvoir; Le pouvoir confisqué; La déstalinisation commence.* The present situation, where the whole of the official historiography of the USSR is in question and a flood of articles is appearing, inevitably makes drawing up a bibliography difficult. Some works that illustrate this reevaluation are:

Baldysh and Panizovska. *Nikolai Vavilov.* Leningrad, 1987.
"Chetyre vstrechi s Khrushchevevym." *Ogoniok,* no. 28 (1988).
Grossman, V. "Zhizn' i sud' ba." *Oktiabr',* Jan.–April, 1988.
 (Stalin is compared to Hitler in this work—a completely new political idea in the USSR about the nature of Stalinism.)
Kapustin, M. P. "Ot kakogo nasledstva my otkazyvaemsia?" *Oktiabr',* April 1988, pp. 176–93; May 1988, pp. 149–72.
Literaturnaia gazeta, February 24, 1988. Article by Burlatsky on the Beria affair.
Moskovskii Komsomolets, February 24, 1988. Article by Semenov on deaths in the Gulag under Stalin.
Nykin, A. "Idealy ili interesy." *Novyi Mir,* Jan. 1988, pp. 190–212.
Ogoniok, nos. 1 and 2 (1988). Articles on Lysenko.
———, no. 5 (1988). Article on the persecution of Tvardovsky.
———, no. 16 (1988). Article on the many faces of Lenin.
Pasternak, B. *Doktor Zhivago.* Reprinted in *Novyi Mir,* Jan.–April, 1988.

" 'Rossiia—krov'iu umytaia?' Artema Veselogo. Po materialam lichnogo arkhiva pisatel' ia." *Novyi Mir,* May 1988, pp. 135–62.

Seliunin, V. "Istoki." *Novyi Mir,* May 1988, pp. 162–90. (A discussion of Lenin's original decisions.)

Shmelev. "Novye trevogi." *Novyi Mir,* April 1988, pp. 160–76.

Tiutiukin, S. "Plekhanov i velichie uchenogo, tragedia revoliutsionnera." *Kommunist,* May 1988, pp. 90–100.

Voprosy istorii, no. 3 (1988). A round table on losses during the Stalinist period and articles by Iskanderov and Danilov on the Great Famine.

For the sources of the "founding fathers," see the complete works of Lenin, Stalin, and the works published by Khrushchev, as well as the various congresses of the CPSU mentioned in the classic works on the USSR listed above.

Index